CALIFORNIA
SCHOOL FACILITIES PLANNING

A Guide to Laws
and Procedures
for Funding,
Siting, Design,
and Construction

CALIFORNIA

SCHOOL FACILITIES PLANNING

Maureen F. Gorsen

Kevin Wilkeson

G. Christian Roux

Thomas M. Cavanagh

Dennis L. Dunston

CALIFORNIA

SCHOOL FACILITIES PLANNING

Maureen F. Gorsen, Kevin Wilkeson, G. Christian Roux,
Thomas M. Cavanagh, and Dennis L. Dunston

July 2006

Design by Julie and Pat Shell,
   Solano Press Books

Index by Paul Kish,
   Rohnert Park, California

ISBN 0-923956-89-1

 Solano Press Books
Post Office Box 773
Point Arena, California
95468

tel (800) 931-9373   email spbooks@solano.com
fax (707) 884-4109   internet www.solano.com

Disclaimer

Any opinions expressed in this book are solely
the personal views of the authors and do not
reflect the views of any governmental agency
or official, including, but not limited to, the
California Office of the Attorney General, the
California Attorney General, any of the Attorney
General's client agencies, or any other federal,
state, or local governmental agency. While the
authors have made every effort to avoid any
errors or omissions in this text, the authors
take sole responsibility for any mistakes of
commission or omission contained herein.

Publisher's Note

Before you rely on the information in this book, be sure you are aware that some changes in the statutes or case law may have gone into effect since the date of publication. The book, moreover, provides general information about the law. Readers should consult their own attorneys before relying on the representations found herein.

Chapters
at a Glance

Contents

chapter 1

History / 1

chapter 2

Funding / 11

Contents

Planning and Design / 73

Contents

Contents

Contents

Contents

chapter 5

Constructing / 185

Contents

Contents

Short Articles

Contents

Contents

Figures

Tables

Appendices

Preface

This book is written to provide a comprehensive overview of the laws and regulations governing the planning, funding, siting, design, and construction of public school facilities in California. It is written to be a tool for school facility planners and consultants who provide professional services for the planning and construction of public school facilities for grade levels kindergarten through twelfth grade.

From initial planning to final construction, a public school facility in California takes from five to ten years to build. During those years, school districts must employ the expertise of numerous specialized fields (*e.g.*, architecture, finance, toxicology, labor law, construction management, and, let's not forget, education) in order to build a school facility that meets the complex and ever-growing requirements and social goals of California's laws and regulations. Because at each phase the professionals involved will not be familiar with the other phases of the process, this book will assist in providing a base knowledge of all other areas from which all of the various specialized professionals may draw in order that the greatest efficiencies are achieved in the provision of school facilities.

The book is organized chronologically. Topics are addressed in the order they would be considered by a school district typically from the planning until the construction phase. Each chapter commences with an overview for the reader who merely wants a summary of its contents. Each chapter also contains a section describing the types of professionals and the qualifications needed for each phase of developing a school facility. Organized this way, the book is an easy-reference, single-source overview of the entire school siting and construction process, while also providing a more in-depth and detailed resource and guide at each phase of the planning and construction of the school facility.

Chapter 1, History, discusses the development of school facilities in our nation and in California to assist in a better understanding of the current complex of laws and goals that govern them.

Chapter 2, Funding, describes the many different sources of funds and methods for financing public school facilities in California.

Chapter 3, Planning and Design, guides school districts in both the district-wide planning for facilities and the planning and design for individual schools.

Chapter 4, Siting the Facility, guides school districts with respect to property acquisition and siting of school facilites and compliance with environmental and land use laws.

Chapter 5, Constructing the School Facility, guides school districts on the construction process from start to finish.

Throughout each of these phases or chapters, a school district must communicate and seek approvals from numerous state agencies. Due to the long period of time from initial funding stages to final construction, this book will provide an easy reference source to all district personnel, decisionmakers, and consultants who are involved in one or more of the stages of the five- to ten-year process. It will help ensure that steps taken early in the process are fully cognizant of requirements that develop later to prevent inefficiencies and duplication and loss of valuable time in the schedule. It will also help ensure that proper communication occurs at every stage with the relevant state regulatory agency and that transactions costs are reduced.

The California Department of Education (CDE) is responsible for approving proposed sites for schools as a condition of allocated state funds to districts for the acquisition of sites. CDE establishes standards and regulations governing school sites, particularly as they may materially relate to the educational program. For instance, site size standards relate to the policies such as lowering the class size in kindergarten through grade three, student safety, use of advanced technology, and fostering community involvement. The School Facilities Planning Division (SFPD) of CDE also reviews school sites. The review of SFPD often overlaps, and may even duplicate the review of the other state agencies. For instance, SFPD reviews for certain environmental hazards and also reviews construction plans, although the focus is mainly on the educational adequacy.

Disbursement and allocation of state funds is administered by the Office of Public School Construction (OPSC), which implements statutes and administrative policies of the State Allocation Board (SAB). OPSC establishes standards and regulations governing a school district's eligibility for state funds for acquisition, new construction, and modernization of existing schools, including local district matching requirements, financial hardship requirements, and a priority system for allocating funds among school districts.

The Division of the State Architect (DSA) reviews building design and construction, and provides design and construction oversight for K–12 schools and community colleges.

The Department of Toxic Substances Control (DTSC) is responsible for the assessment, investigation, and cleanup of proposed school sites to ensure that they are free of contamination or, if the properties were previously contaminated, that they have been cleaned up to a level that will be protective of the students and faculty occupants. All proposed school sites for which state funding is sought for acquisition and/or construction are required to undertake a rigorous environmental review and, if necessary, cleanup process under DTSC's oversight.

In addition to these state agency regulatory review processes, a school district must comply with the California Environmental Quality Act (CEQA), a further rigorous environmental review, which is a prerequisite or triggering point for the other state review processes. A school district may also have to comply with the adopted codes and regulations of local government land use authorities.

This book is a single-reference source for the laws and processes relevant to siting, funding, and constructing school facilities, but also provides guidance to school facility planners on how best to proceed and integrate the numerous processes with state regulatory agencies, local government, and district requirements to enhance efficiencies and avoid stumbling blocks.

This book primarily addresses the planning, funding, siting, and construction requirements for K–12 public education. However, much of the book is also relevant to community colleges. The DSA approval requirements for design and construction plans are nearly identical for K–12 and 12–14 grade levels at community colleges. Community colleges must go through similar siting, land use, and environmental review requirements as for K–12 public school districts, with some limited exceptions. Unlike K–12 school districts, however, community colleges do not have the ability to exempt themselves from local zoning requirements. Educ. Code § 31951. In addition, most colleges are not authorized to use design-build methods of project delivery. By special legislation in 2002, Los Angeles, San Jose-Evergreen, San Mateo, and eight other Community College Districts have been authorized to use design-build until 2007. AB 1000 (2002). Thus, with limited exceptions, the guidance in chapters 4 and 5 will be useful to community colleges, and the entire book may be useful for their siting and construction.

Since community colleges are not subject to the same educational specifications as K–12, and state funds are disbursed under different regulations and by a different state agency—the Chancellor's Office, California Community Colleges—chapters 2 and 3, which deal with funding and planning of school facilities, may be of limited use.

The book is the result of a collaboration of experienced professionals expert in each individual area of school siting and construction. In addition to describing what is required at each phase of the process, the co-authors, contributing authors, editors, and expert reviewers have infused the text with their hard-earned lessons and advice in their respective areas of expertise. The collection of authors, co-authors, contributing editors, and other reviewers, who have been involved at every level in the school planning, design, siting, and construction process, are specialists in their respective areas. Many have been keen observers of district, local government, and state government politics and policies over the past 20 years. This book contains the wisdom and observations from their collective experience and observation. The value-added from their contributions is immeasurable.

It has oftimes been said, half in jest, that in California it is easier to build a power plant than a school. By integrating the numerous regulatory, funding, and district-level review processes in a single comprehensive volume, in a manner that is understandable to school administrators, board members, support personnel, and their retained consultants not specially trained in each of the specialized fields involved (*e.g.*, architecture, finance, law), the intent and purpose of this book is to facilitate speedier and less costly school siting and construction in California.

> Maureen F. Gorsen
> June 2006

About the Authors

Maureen F. Gorsen, Esq.

In December 2005, Ms. Gorsen was appointed Director of California's Department of Toxic Substances Control by Governor Arnold Schwarzenegger. She also served as Deputy Secretary for Law Enforcement and General Counsel at the California Environmental Protection Agency, responsible for policies regarding implementation and enforcement of air, water, toxics, pesticides, and other environmental laws. Previously, Ms. Gorsen was a partner at Weston, Benshoof, Rochefort, Rubalcava & MacCuish, LLP, where she represented school districts, public agencies, and private developers with a focus on environmental compliance and land use counseling. Prior to that, Ms. Gorsen served as General Counsel for the California Resources Agency where, among other duties, she was responsible for reform and revisions of the California Environmental Quality Act (CEQA) Guidelines, issues relating to the California Endangered Species Act, the Williamson Act, and the Coastal Act.

Ms. Gorsen is a frequent speaker and author of articles on CEQA, environmental, and land use laws. Ms. Gorsen holds a B.A. from the University of Pennsylvania, an M.A. in international environmental policy from the Johns Hopkins University, and a J.D. from the Georgetown University Law Center.

Kevin Wilkeson, AIA

Kevin Wilkeson is an architect with more than 20 years' experience planning, designing, and constructing a wide variety of California education facilities. He is a Managing Principal and Board Chairman at HMC Architects, a full-service architecture practice that specializes in the planning and design of education facilities.

Kevin has been actively involved in all phases of the project delivery process for many school districts, colleges, and universities. Some of his projects include the California Academy of Math and Science in Carson, Martin Luther King High School in Riverside, John Burroughs High School in Burbank, and the Bronco Student Union at California State Polytechnic University, Pomona.

Mr. Wilkeson is a frequent speaker on topics such as avoiding construction claims, modernizing schools, building technology into learning environments, and the facilities impacts of education reform. Mr. Wilkeson attended U.C. Irvine and holds a Bachelor of Architecture from the California State University, Pomona.

Thomas Cavanagh

Mr. Cavanagh is the managing director of School Advisors, a subsidiary company to HMC Architects. For the past ten years he has assisted school districts throughout the State of California in the planning, justification, and financing of Capitol Development projects totaling over $2 billion in construction. Mr. Cavanagh is also very active in organizations dealing with school facilities, such as the Coalition for Adequate School Housing (CASH), the California Association of School Business Officials, and the Community Colleges Facility Coalition.

Tom is a frequent presenter at many CASH conferences and an instructor for the University of California, Riverside extension program on school facilities entitlements. He holds a B.A. degree in Accounting from California State University in Fullerton.

G. Christian Roux, Esq.

Mr. Roux is a Partner at Weston, Benshoof, Rochefort, Rubalcava & MacCuish, LLP and represents public owners, including school districts, in connection with substantial capital improvement projects. In particular, Mr. Roux is familiar with all applicable statutory requirements governing both new school construction and school renovation in California. He regularly provides construction counseling to clients on the myriad of issues that arise in connection with construction projects, including project planning and procurement, drafting and negotiating contracts, claims avoidance, and the resolution of legal issues that commonly arise on school construction projects. He has substantial experience both prosecuting and defending multi-million dollar public and private extra work, delay, and disruption claims in all forums, including state and federal courts, administrative hearings, and arbitrations. Mr. Roux also has considerable experience litigating construction defect claims.

Mr. Roux regularly speaks on public contracting issues such as bid protests, project start-up and close-out, claims, mitigation strategies and False Claims Act liability. He also recently completed a chapter on the subject of Construction Contract Pass-through Clauses which was published in the 1999 Edition of BLI's "Construction Contracts Desk book." Mr. Roux holds a BA Degree (with honors) from the University of California at Berkeley and a J.D. from the University of Virginia.

Dennis L. Dunston, AIA, REFP

Mr. Dunston is a California licensed architect and principal with HMC Architects. He has more than 22 years of experience in architecture, the last 18 of which have been dedicated to the design and construction of educational facilities in California. His experience ranges from the development of educational specifications for all types of school facilities to the design of new campuses. Mr. Dunston is also very active in organizations related to school facilities.

He is a member of the Board of Directors for the Coalition of Adequate School Housing (CASH) and serves on the Implementation Committee for the State Allocation Board. He is also a member of the advisory committee to the University of California Extension program in Educational Facility Planning; an instructor for the course "Site Selection, Educational Specifications, and Facility Design"; a former member of the California Department of Education's Task Force on the Facility Implications of the Restructured Curriculum resulting in the CDE document *The Form of Reform*; and active in the Council of Educational Facility Planners International (CEFPI), serving as president of the Southwest Region in 1996. Mr. Dunston earned a B.S. in Architecture and Masters of Architecture with a Minor in Energy Systems Engineering from Iowa State University.

Contributors, Editors, Acknowledgments

Contributing Authors

David J. Jensen, P.E., Camp Dresser & McKee, Inc.
Dwayne Mears, The Planning Center
Dr. Joel Kirschenstein, Sage Institute, Inc.
Mott Smith, Los Angeles Unified School District
Jeff B. Baize, Brookhurst Development Corp.
Stephen L. Hartsell, Esq., School and College Legal Services
Ernest Silva, Murdoch Walrath and Holmes
Janice Woody, Jacobs Engineering
Chris Taylor AIA and John Nichols AIA, HMC Architects
Marianne Tanzer, EIP Associates
Alexandra Parslow and Ariane Lehew, School Advisors
Greg Davis, Davis Demographics

Kevin Collins, Esq., Peter Nyquist, Esq., Raad Shawaf, Esq., John Zaimes, Esq., and Charles S. Yesnick, Weston Benshoof Rochefort Rubalcava and MacCuish LLP

Cartoonist

James Gilliam AIA, HMC Architects

Graphic Designer

Jon Richardson, Graphic Designer

Contributing Editors

Jim Bush, California Department of Education
Kenneth S. Levy, Esq., Miller Brown & Dannis
Maria-Elena Romero, Rosemead Unified School District
Charles Cohen and Jocelyn Thompson, Weston Benshoof Rochefort Rubalcava and MacCuish LLP

Other Editors and Persons Consulted

David Tanza, AIA, Strategic Construction Management
Brian Masterman, S&Y Capital Group LLC
Dr. Don Brann, Wiseburn School District
Edward De La Rosa
Susan Flakus, P.E., Tetra Tech, Inc.
Linda Sweaney, San Bernadino County Office of Education
Dr. Gwen Gross and Mike Clear, Beverly Hills USD
Jose L. Huizar, Esq., Board of Education, Los Angeles Unified School District
Trini M. Jimenez, Jr., Esq., Lennox School District
Dr. M. Magdalena ("Maggie") Carrillo Mejia, Montebello Unified School District
Dr. Bruce McDaniel, Lennox School District
Don Littlefield, Esq., Office of Public School Construction
Alexander Bowie, Esq., Bowie Ameson Wiles & Giannone
Jay Bell, Parsons Brinkerhoff Construction
Dr. Roland "Bud" Allen, Community College Services Group
Richard Conrad, California Department of General Services
Sean Corrigan, Conejo USD
Dave Doomey, San Juan Capistrano USD
Enrique Gasca, Office of Senator Tom Calderon
Richard Lyon, California Building Industry Association
Robert Manford, Los Angeles Community Redevelopment Agency
Michael O'Neill, California Department of Education
Hamid Saebfar, California Department of Toxic Substances Control
David Wald, Wald Realty Advisors
Michael Bradbury, Weston Benshoof Rochefort Rubalcava and MacCuish, LLP
Angelo Bellomo, Los Angeles Unified School District

Acknowledgments

Anthonie Fang
Keith Brush
Norma Henry
Sandra Acosta
Ceniza Reynoso
Julia North
Marlene Yokley
Michele Kearin
Pamela J. Privett, Esq.
Renee Guzman-Simon
Amanda Susskind, Esq.
Steven W. Weston, Esq.
Jessica Copen
Corinne Loskot

chapter 1

History

It is fascinating to examine the development of educational facilities over the centuries and how they relate to the educational practices of their time. How did the school building evolve from the one-room school house—a rudimentary space for learning and shelter for its occupants—into a complex and sophisticated educational tool designed to control and support the learning process?

This chapter provides a brief overview of the history of the design of school facilities in the United States and California. This background is useful to understand how we arrived at the current complex set of laws governing the siting, design, and construction of school facilities in California, and the educational, social, and fiscal goals they are designed to achieve.

National History

Early American Colonial Period (1600–1800)

Responsibility for the education of most colonial children rested with religious institutions. Early settlers believed that every child must learn to read the Bible in order to gain salvation. Consequently, church buildings served to accommodate educational activities as well as religious functions. For nearly two centuries, the church building—or one-room schoolhouse—equipped only with benches, a podium, and possibly a whipping post, was the school facility for most of America's school children.

American Schools in the Early 19th Century

The English Lancastrian school system arrived in this country around the turn of the 19th century. Joseph Lancaster (1778–1838) led a movement to establish schools in which more advanced students taught less advanced ones, enabling a small number of adult masters to educate large numbers of students in basic

For nearly two centuries, the church building—or one-room schoolhouse—equipped only with benches, a podium, and possibly a whipping post, was the school facility for most of America's school children.

and advanced skills at low cost. The school buildings that housed the Lancastrian system were designed to accommodate great numbers of students of every grade and achievement level.

School buildings were like most public buildings of the time—large, oversized buildings with wide corridors, imposing lobbies, and stately columns. The emphasis was on forms, shapes, and style, not on the functional needs for educating children. Lancastrian school rooms were often built for 500 students seated in a single 50' x 100' room; the use of benches rather than desks allowed the room to accommodate one student for each 10 square feet of space. This system relied on frugal economics. The students wrote on slate instead of paper because paper was expensive and slate was indestructible. One book per subject per class was used. Each page was separated and placed on a board suspended overhead—a group of 10 students at a time studied a page as a lesson, and then the groups rotated. Educators using the Lancastrian system claimed it cost $1 annually to educate a child. Thus, it made possible the education of all the children in a community through private philanthropic support. To communities not yet accustomed to taxation for police and fire protection, care of streets, or sanitary services, much less for education, the Lancastrian system was an essential factor in the evolution of schools for the masses.

The Lancastrian system survived in America for approximately 40 years. It influenced the development of our current educational system, establishing principles of group instruction and education for all children, and provided a basis for the tax-supported free public schooling we have today. However, very little consideration was given to how the school building should accommodate learning.

Establishment of the Public Schools

The Lancastrian system began to disappear during the 1830s, due in part to the ideas of Henry Bernard, Horace Mann, and several other celebrated educators of the day, who contended that educational facilities should be more than just shelters.

Horace Mann believed that schools should be the birthright of all children, whether rich or poor. Public schools could be the "great equalizer," eliminating poverty and lowering crime.

Horace Mann, born 1796 in Franklin, Massachusetts, was the first U.S. Secretary of Education. While Secretary of Education, Mann published a series of annual reports on the integral relationship between education, freedom, and the Republican form of government. He believed that schools should be the birthright of all children, whether they were rich or poor. Public schools could be the "great equalizer," eliminating poverty and lowering crime. According to Mann, there was no end to the social good which might be derived from the public school. Cremin, *The Republic and the School: Horace Mann on the Education of Free Men* (New York: Teachers College, 1957).

Between 1820 and 1850, the battle to create free public schools in the United States was fought and won. The first public common school was established in Lexington, Massachusetts in 1839. Mann reinvigorated an 1827 law establishing high schools, and built 50 high schools during his tenure as Secretary of Education. In 1839, the Massachusetts legislature mandated the nation's first six-month minimum school year.

Influence of the Transcendentalists

The Transcendentalists, of which Henry Bernard was the most prominent, believed that school buildings should enhance the process of education. Children were viewed as independent, rational persons who should be developing high ethical and rational standards (manners, morals, and mind) while attending school. Bernard believed that the appearance of the classroom and the way in which it was arranged had extensive influence on forming the characters of students.

The Transcendentalists called the school buildings of the early 1800s spiritually degrading environments. Henry Bernard painted a dismal picture of the condition of most pre-Civil War school houses:

> They are universally badly located, exposed to the noise, dust and danger of the highway, unattractive, if not positively repulsive in their external and internal appearance, and built at the least possible expense of material and labor.

McClintock and McClintock, p. 31, 1970

No other period in the history of American education has spawned greater changes in the nature and functionality of educational facilities. Arguments and debates among architects and educators over whether the spiritual growth of children was enhanced more by Roman, Greek, or Renaissance architectural styles gave way to practical ideas about comfort, efficiency, and the design of an effective school.

Efficiency was promoted as a positive cultural value in pre-Civil War America; consequently, instructional efficiency was the central predominant principle of the day. Self-education was the pedagogy during this period—people were expected to receive their education in the "school of life." Formal schooling received in a school setting was only necessary to provide basic skills essential for the real education that followed later in life. The sooner a child could complete his studies in the schoolhouse, the sooner he could get on with this more important learning experience.

Bernard realized that much time and effort was wasted because of inadequate schoolhouse design. He contended that with little expense, comfortable desks and seats could be built to replace the backless benches on which small children sat all day, their legs dangling above the floor. Bernard's and the Transcendentalists' ideas radically altered schoolhouse design in the United States, introducing or dramatically affecting decisions regarding location, size, construction methods, ventilation, heating, furniture (seats and desks), teacher arrangements, instructional materials, the library, school yard, and other external considerations.

The Late 19th Century: Progressivism

Towards the end of the 19th century, more "free schools" were established. These schools were the first efforts at dividing buildings into rooms for the separate grades. The principal of separation of grades dictated a different philosophy in the architectural design of the school buildings.

High Schools (or Secondary Schools)

The concept of high schools or secondary schools did not become generally accepted until the first decade of the 20th century. Given legal impetus by the famous *Kalamazoo* decision (*Stuart v. Stuart District No. 1 of the Village of Kalamazoo* (1874) 30 Mich. 69), the high school became an extension of the common school program and paved the way for all children, regardless of socio-economic background, to earn a high school diploma. ■

Bernard's and the Transcendentalists' ideas radically altered schoolhouse design: affecting location, size, construction methods, ventilation, heating, furniture, teacher arrangements, instructional materials, the library, school yard, and other considerations.

Progressivism was a leading philosophical movement at the turn of the century that advocated innovations and reforms in the political, economic, and social order, usually to alleviate the ills of society attributable to rapid industrialization and massive immigration. Progressivism advocated reforms to increase the role and responsibility of government for the social welfare of its citizens. Among its advocates, the learning theories of Heinrich Pestalozzi and John Dewey emphasized a curriculum and instruction that was child-centered, which optimized children's inquisitive, active learning style and the child as an individual. Dewey rejected the previous centuries' regimented methods of instruction, which he referred to as "sitting and listening" school.

As rote learning was replaced by the observation and investigation of experiential learning, the need for more accommodating instructional space became evident. Progress in methodology and the introduction of new subject matter required a variety of learning environments (*e.g.*, labs, art room, woodshop, kitchen). With this shift from mass learning to individual learning, average class size went from over 50 pupils down to a little more than 30 pupils.

The Quincy School, however, was the prototype for modern schoolhouse design that has, with modifications, been used throughout the 20th century. The school, since called the "Quincy Box," had four stories, a basement, and an attic. The four floors were divided into four separate classrooms of equal size. Each classroom was 31' x 26' (806 square feet) and housed 55 students. The major change was the provision for individual student desks, bolted to the floor in seven rows of eight. This provided much more comfort than did the boards that served as benches in the typical one-room schoolhouse. The instructional methodology of this time, which required pupils to sit and listen to the teacher, and occasionally stand beside their desks and recite, was well served by this arrangement.

The 20th Century

The First World War provided a stimulus for major changes in the construction of educational facilities. The great number of young Americans who were rejected by the armed services gave rise to increased emphasis on physical education in the public schools. Playing fields, swimming pools, gymnasiums, and playgrounds were built all across the country. Council of Educational Facility Planners International (CEFPI), "Historical Perspectives" (Jerry Lowe (1991)). It was also during the first two decades of the 20th century that communities began to consider schools partially responsible for the health of the child. As a result, schools began to include new space requirements for health clinics and nurses offices. EFO, 1960. By 1917, the federal government was supporting vocational and physical education programs at the secondary education level. The curriculum now also included science and commerce in addition to the normal courses for college preparation. More was required of school facilities to accommodate the growing curriculum structure as well as the increase in community use of school facilities.

In the early part of the 20th century, before the 1920s, school districts usually acquired very small sites for schools because there was little perceived need for outdoor play areas. The increased emphasis on outdoor physical education lead to the realization that larger sites were necessary. Before this interest in

CEFPI = Council of Educational
Facility Planners
International

physical education, many elementary schools with enrollments from 500 to 1,000 were built on one or two-acre sites, and high schools with enrollments of 2,000 to 3,000 seldom had sites of more than ten acres. These sites were so small that it was impossible to provide more than a modicum of playground space or outdoor facilities for physical education, and there was no space to expand the existing facilities. Most of the urban elementary school buildings were two or three-story block masonry buildings built above high basement spaces. The rooms were large to accommodate the very large class sizes, and were fire hazards because of the lack of properly designed evacuation areas. As a consequence, most of these buildings have been demolished.

"Finger" Plan

In the 1930s, the "finger" plan school was developed. This plan was characterized by constructing school buildings with wings—usually 30 to 40 feet apart that contain four or five classrooms in line with an open corridor on one side and an "outdoor classroom" on the other side. This architecture made possible the use of bilateral daylighting and cross-ventilation. These buildings are easily identifiable because of the louvers, baffles, and wide overhangs used for controlling daylight—many of them are graceful plants with sheltered but noninstitutional characteristics. Generally, the buildings are located on ten-acre sites and were built to accommodate about 650 students. Refinements in this "finger" plan concept of elementary schools continued through the 1950s.

A central element of this architectural model was large windows overlooking vistas, bringing natural light from the outside. However, this created problems of heat build-up and glare from sunlight. Energy losses and gains were high due to the large expanses of outside walls in the "finger" design. But with a plentiful supply of inexpensive energy, this design continued to be utilized through the 1960s.

Calexico Elementary School (c. 1950s) The Finger Plan included large windows and panoramic views.

Schools in California

Earthquake Safety

In 1933, the Long Beach earthquake resulted in the collapse of several schools in Southern California. This tragedy led to the enactment of the Field Act by the California Legislature in 1933. Educ. Code §§ 17280, 81130, *et seq.* The purpose of the Field Act is to protect children and staff from death and injury in public schools during and after earthquakes. It establishes more stringent building standards for public schools than for commercial or residential buildings.

Post-World War II: Larger School Sites and Expanding State Control

The end of World War II spawned a boom in schoolhouse construction, with a trend towards providing more space for student movement, activity, and individualism. Carpeting, air conditioning, moveable

Lowell High School, Long Beach (c. 1933) earthquake damage

Ontario High School (c. 1950s)
Larger school sites became the trend in the Post-World War II Era.

Hall v. City of Taft

Prior to 1956, who had jurisdiction over a school project was ambiguous. According to the Field Act of 1933, the state—now the Division of the State Architect (DSA)—was responsible for plan approval. This left local agencies in a quandary. They were accustomed to reviewing plans and having districts meet the local planning requirements. Some local agencies felt that state-funded schools were "deep pocket" projects: that is, the state would fund any requirement it could impose.

As state requirements increased, some local agencies began to require that school districts purchase new fire-fighting equipment (such as fire engines) as a condition of approval. This eventually led to the *Hall v. City of Taft* decision in 1956, holding that local agencies had only limited rights of review and approval over public schools. ∎

CDE = California Department of Education
DSA = Division of the State Architect
SAB = State Allocation Board

walls, and teaching pods were some of the innovations established during this period. Utilization of plastics, glass, fluorescent lighting, and concrete led to the single-story, flat-roofed structures of the 1950s. The single-story school, the expansion of programs to include health and food service facilities, specialized administrative quarters, auditoriums, and libraries, and physical education programs that often occupied 50 to 80 percent of the site resulted in the need for larger school sites.

In California, another post-WWII development was the role of the state as a funding source of local school facilities. In 1947, the State Allocation Board (SAB) was established by the California Legislature to allocate the newly created state loan program to poor school districts most severely affected by the enrollment boom following the war. In 1949, California voters approved the first statewide bond measure—for $350 million in bonds—to finance school facilities in poor districts.

Cluster Plan and Open Space Plan

During the 1960s and 1970s, educators and architects questioned the basic configuration of the school and the classroom as a self-contained teaching station. Various patterns of cluster plans were developed that offered greater interior flexibility within open space shells—team-teaching and large- and small-group instruction could be accommodated in a variety of patterns. New concepts for the classroom were experimented with, including open-space classrooms, individual heating systems for rooms, air conditioning, flex walls, pods, team teaching, and an emphasis on self-direction and individualization. With the value placed on open, colorful, comfortable, and flexible spaces, designs that were used in the 1940s and '50s no longer seemed adequate.

The open space plan, one of the most widely documented failures in educational facilities, did not win wide or lasting acceptance, and was soon modified to recapture the visual and sound separation provided by the self-contained classroom. The return to the self-contained classroom combines the flexibility of the cluster and open space plans with the relative isolation of the self-contained classroom. This arrangement is accomplished through use of movable walls, space-function adjacency design, scheduling innovations, and other design features.

Educational Program Goals as Key Determinant

In the mid-1960s, when the importance of educational specifications was recognized in the total facilities planning process, California's Department of Education (CDE) developed a functional approach for determining the size of a school site. Its approach was based on the area required to support the functions or activities of a proposed educational program. The approach assumes that, in order to determine a school site size, one must first study the following aspects:

- The ultimate predicted enrollment
- Grade levels to be served
- The type, number, size, function, special characteristics, and spatial relationships of instructional areas, administration, and service areas
- Building design (*e.g.*, compact campus style, multistory)
- Onsite parking and bus and auto loading/unloading requirements
- Physical education requirements, including outdoor space and gymnasiums
- Whether there are school-community joint-use programs (*e.g.*, parks, playing fields, and libraries)
- The necessity of child care facilities
- The use of temporary relocatable structures
- Special education needs

However, these considerations were limited by a maximum building area applicable to all school districts seeking state funds.

Montclair High School Library, Ontario, California

1970s and 1980s

Educational planners in the 1970s had to cope with a new range of complex issues and needs. In 1972, federal gender equity laws required that girls have equal access to physical education facilities. Educational Amendments of 1972, Title IX. Additionally, the energy crisis of 1974 required that school buildings be designed to conserve energy. California also faced increasing enrollments—there was a need for new spaces as well as for new uses for old spaces. New space also was required for career education, barrier-free facilities, and accommodations for special students.

In 1972, federal gender equity laws required that girls have equal access to physical education facilities.

The state's role as a funding source of local school facilities expanded. In 1976, the Leroy F. Greene State School Building Lease-Purchase Program (LPP) modified the state loan program to resemble a lease/purchase model. This legislative change, which allowed the state to maintain a lien on school facilities until a loan was repaid, was prompted to prevent school districts from using state resources to speculate on properties and potential school sites in anticipation of student growth. The SAB's role in regulating those funds also grew when it was authorized to implement the system to allocate funds according to need and priority established in the Greene Act.

LPP = Lease-Purchase Program

The Greene Act also had a significant impact on the design of school facilities. The LPP allowed districts to build a limited amount of building area and added incentives for the use of exterior corridors. The LPP also required the use of relocatable classrooms. These provisions led to a wide use of campus style planning with multiple buildings and exterior circulation on school sites. They also led to the widespread

Site-built relocatable classrooms

use of portable classrooms—not just as interim housing, but as permanent parts of school projects.

In 1978, the property tax revolution hit California. Prior to that, school facilities were primarily funded by local property taxes and local general bond monies. After the enactment of Proposition 13 in 1978, the ability of school districts to raise capital outlay funds through property taxes was severely limited.

As a result of Prop. 13 and the passage of the 1976 Greene Act, the state role in financing local school facilities changed again. The state moved from a loan program to a lease/purchase program. In the early 1980s, the California Legislature created new ways for local districts to raise funds (*e.g.*, the Mello-Roos Community Facility Districts). In 1986, Proposition 46 restored the school district's ability to finance schools with general obligation bonds based upon a two-thirds vote of residents.

Functional Approach

Just as federal gender equity laws increased the size of school facilities, equal access for low-income students and for the disabled required additional acreage at existing schools.

In 1997, the California Legislature provided funding incentives for districts achieving class size reduction to 20 students per classroom for grades K–3. The class size reduction program has had a direct impact on school design and land requirements. A school population of 600 with 20 students per classroom requires ten more classrooms and more land than the same population of 600 with 30 students per classroom. Yet, the state lease/purchase program did not allow for additional area.

The 21st Century

Arguably, no building type has undergone greater change in American history than the school building. In the 21st century, single-story buildings may give way to the multistory buildings of the previous century as land becomes more scarce, real estate more expensive, and the availability of public funds more limited.

As a dynamic reflection of the culture in which we live, the specific needs of the school facility must continually change to meet the demands of our educational and social goals and philosophies. Far from the mere shelter in which education is delivered, school facilities now have become a complex educational tool, capable of fulfilling our social goals and a wide variety of learning experiences for citizens of all ages, abilities, and needs. With taxes rising and significant taxpayer resistance to the construction of new school buildings increasing, the challenge of providing sufficient building capacity is formidable.

In the mid-1980s through the turn of the century, momentum has grown among educators for a new type of school design to support superior performance. It is quite different from the model of the mid-20th century: the long corridors lined with rows of rooms 30 feet by 30 feet, each the domain of a single teacher. Research suggests that schools would be more effective if subdivided into smaller elements of neighborhoods, or academies, and focused on accommodating a broader range of learning styles.

Educational researchers in the 21st century question the arrangement, the size, the uniformity of classrooms, and the role of the teacher. This is concomitant of public restlessness and discontent with large public schools in favor of charter schools, choice schools, school vouchers, and a more personal and individual learning-style.

In California, the necessity of retrofitting aging school facilities to provide superior learning environments will be particularly acute, given that the population is expected to increase by 20 million, and public demands for environmental protection from the effects of that new population will increase. Real estate prices will continue to rise as more land is set aside for conservation and open space, and demand outstrips supply.

The trend to smaller will continue, as it did from the 19th century Lancastrian classroom housing 500 students to the 20th century California classroom housing 20 to 30 students. Schools are expected to be designed in smaller functional modules and built to fit the learners and their learning styles. The challenge will be to redesign existing school buildings and to create spaces that optimize learning. In fact, California ust enacted new legislation (AB 1465 (2004)) to establish incentives for the design and construction of small high schools as a pilot that started in 2006. An even greater challenge is to develop methods of adequately funding these facilities. Perhaps the greatest challenge for the state is to develop a mechanism to fund school facilities when the need exists. The sporadic availability of state funding often forces school districts to bypass good planning procedures in the rush to get in line for funding.

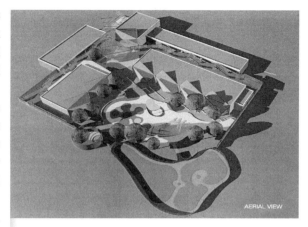

AERIAL VIEW

Eight-classroom Early Education Center prototype

The sporadic availability of state funding often forces school districts to bypass good planning procedures in the rush to get in line for funding.

chapter 2

Funding

Overview

Funding for school facilities in California is the most complex and frequently fluctuating aspect of the school siting and construction process. That complexity is exacerbated by the fact that funding sources do not match the need for funding. This sets up competition for the scarce resources among school districts, and encourages annual (if not more frequent) changes in laws, regulations, and government policies governing the funding in order to continually try to achieve a more fair and equitable allocation of those scarce resources.

In order to determine the feasibility of its Master Plan, and whether it can meet its educational program goals, a school district must first identify the sources of funding for which it is eligible, and then be compliant with the legal, regulatory, and policy requirements to secure that funding.

This chapter provides an overview of the most common funding sources for school districts, including the regulations and policies relating to their allocation. First, it will cover the history of state bond funding and its frequently-changing eligibility rules, including the most recent state bond measures (Propositions 47 and 55/Assembly Bill 16), from which funds became available in January 2003 and March 2004. It will discuss the school district's options for debt financing, including running a local bond program or establishing community facility districts and certificates of participation. The later part of the chapter will cover the rules governing a school district's ability to charge developer fees. Finally, other potential revenue sources for school facilities will be identified, including federal and state grants, surplus property disposition, and airport sound mitigation funds.

History of School Facility Funding In California

School facility funding in California has evolved over time. The passage of the Morrill Act in 1862 provided land grants for colleges and established a policy that schools should be built to last. In 1874, advocates for "free schools" won over the

To determine the feasibility of its Master Plan, and whether it can meet its educational program goals, a school district must first identify the sources of funding for which it is eligible.

Regarding Laws and Regulations

Due to frequent changes to the laws and regulations in this area, this book will identify the regulatory agency responsible for implementing and administrating funds or sources of funding and other information resources. It is imperative that school districts not rely solely on the information provided in this book and check with these sources before proceeding.

For example, Title 2 regulations governing distribution of the November 1998 state bond funds were revised 21 times between 1999 and the end of 2002. In 1999, the regulations were revised on October 8, October 13, and December 22. In 2000, the regulations were revised January 7, April 12, June 26, July 17, September 12, and December 27. In 2001, the regulations were revised on January 2, April 5, July 25, August 13, and December 21. In 2002, the regulations were revised on April 10, June 1, August 12, September 9, October 4, and November 4. Several proposed changes to regulations are pending as we go to press.

While regulations may change frequently, new statutes are enacted annually as education-related bills are popular among legislators. ■

public, and schools became a matter of local pride, with communities supporting and "paying" for construction with local taxes. The state's role was to establish standards and provide assistance through the Public School Building Loan Fund.

1952—School Building Aid Law Enacted

When the legislature passed the 1952 state School Building Aid Law, it created a new detailed and comprehensive school facility program that enabled California to provide new schools and purchase school sites, but did not provide funds for repairing older buildings. The program allocated approximately 15 percent of the funds spent for California educational facilities. To qualify for the state program, a district had to be bonded to capacity, and ask its voters to agree to increase their tax rate to repay the loan.

1966—New State Loan Program

In 1966, the legislature, recognizing that funding school facilities should also provide assistance in rehabilitating or replacing existing structurally unsafe school facilities, enacted a mechanism for repayable state loans to school districts (primarily those districts located in urban centers) for that purpose. In 1968, the law was amended to allow funding for "modernization" of existing school facilities. State loans were repaid by local school districts from the proceeds of local bonds, general funds, or other methods such as the sale of surplus property.

1972—New State Sources of Funding

Student enrollment began to decline in the 1970s, and other problems emerged. School buildings contained asbestos and inefficient energy systems, lacked access for the disabled, and were saddled with inadequate or failing mechanical systems. They required modernization to address growing health and safety concerns. In 1972 and in 1974, statewide bonds for the state School Building Aid and Earthquake Reconstruction and Replacement Bond Laws were placed on the ballot and passed. The bond monies were used for rehabilitation, reconstruction, or replacement of school facilities that were not in compliance with the Field Act, and for the repair of those facilities damaged by earthquake.

In 1972, SB 201 established a mechanism for school districts to charge fees to developers to help pay for school facilities needed to house new residents. Fees ranged from $200 to $7,000 per home.

In addition, the Landscape and Lighting Act provided an assessment that allows property owners to pay for landscape and lighting improvements based on the benefit their property receives. Although considered controversial, the Act provides various types of improvements including landscaping, public lighting facilities, and the installation of park and recreational improvements. Assessment procedures do not involve an election by a district's registered voters. Instead it involves the school board's adoption of a resolution of intention to levy assessment and the calling of a noticed public hearing to approve the levy. School districts may use this law, alone or in partnership with a recreation district or a city, to finance the construction, acquisition, maintenance, and servicing of recreational facilities for the community.

1976—A Watershed Year for State Role in Funding School Facilities: The Lease-Purchase Program Is Established

In 1976, the legislature enacted the Leroy F. Greene State School Building Lease-Purchase Law. The Lease-Purchase Program (LPP) changed the role of state funding from a loan program to a lease/purchase program. Under the LPP, school districts entered into a 40-year lease-purchase agreement with the state for payment of $1 per project. The level of payment by the district was determined by deductions of property sale proceeds or other revenue options. While the LPP seemed to work well initially, there was little demand on the new program due to a decline in student enrollment.

1978—Proposition 13 Revolution

Prior to 1978, schools were generally funded by local taxes and general obligation bonds requiring a two-thirds vote. The state provided funding for districts unable to raise sufficient funds locally because of low property values. These "low wealth" districts were bonded to the debt capacity established in the statute—1.25 percent of the assessed value of all taxable property in the district for elementary and high school districts, and 2.5 percent for unified districts. Educ. Code §§ 15102, 15106; *PGE v. Shasta Dam PUD* (1955) 135 Cal. App. 2d 463. The purpose of these debt-limitation statutes was to protect taxpayers from confiscatory taxation, and these debt capacity limits still apply today.

In June 1978, the property tax revolution hit California. Proposition 13 was enacted, placing limits on property taxes equal to one percent of assessed value, plus an additional amount

**STATE ALLOCATION BOARD
APPROVES $1.3 BILLION!!**

LPP = Lease-Purchase Program

In June 1978, the property tax revolution hit California. Proposition 13 was enacted, placing limits on property taxes equal to one percent of assessed value, plus an additional amount for pre-existing outstanding local debt.

for pre-existing outstanding local debt. It also prohibited local school districts from raising local taxes for school construction, and prohibited agencies from issuing bonds without a two-thirds vote. As a result, funding for school districts shifted from the local community to the state.

Eventually, new laws were passed and constitutional amendments approved authorizing local governments to levy developer fees to provide interim housing (portable classrooms) for fast-growing districts, and to pass local bonds by a two-thirds vote. Prop. 46, 1986.

However, in the meantime, the need for additional facility funding remained. Before the end of the decade, the legislature passed the Emergency School Classroom Law of 1979 and the New School Relief Act, and recognized the need for deferred maintenance funding. School districts typically set aside up to one-half of one percent of the school district's general fund to match the state funds for deferred maintenance needs.

The 1980s experienced another surge in school enrollment, with over 200,000 new students each year in California's K–12 public school system. By the mid-1980s, there was an increased demand for additional new school facilities, and the state was falling farther behind in its effort to meet that demand. At the same time, existing schools were aging and in need of repair.

1982—Mello-Roos Is Born

The Mello-Roos tax is based on mathematical formulas that take into account a home's square footage and parcel size, and the need for new school facilities attributable to new housing construction.

To assist school districts in raising funds, the Mello-Roos Community Facilities District Act was passed in 1982. Govt. Code §§ 53311–53368.3. Mello-Roos allows for a "special tax" to be levied on property owners of newly-constructed homes within a Community Facilities District (CFD), the formation of which must be approved by two-thirds of registered voters in the district. If there are fewer than 12 registered voters, the vote may be passed by current landowners. The special tax is not directly based on property value, but on mathematical formulas that take into account property characteristics, such as a home's square footage and parcel size, and the need or nexus for new school facilities attributable to the new housing construction.

In 1986, the passage of Prop. 46 gave school districts the authority to seek approval by two-thirds of qualified voters to issue general obligation bonds and parcel taxes.

Statewide general obligation bonds have been the primary source of funding for the state program. Unlike local school bonds that require super majority votes of two-thirds or 55 percent, only a majority vote (50 percent) is required for passing a statewide school facility bond. State bonds directly impact the state's general fund for bond debt repayment, yet it is local school bonds that are more likely to be perceived as a tax increase. Given this public perception and the lower voter approval percentage, statewide bonds will likely remain popular as a funding source for school facilities.

In an effort to make limited state bond money stretch further, the legislature enacted Assembly Bill 87 in 1990 to create a multi-tier priority system for new school construction funding under the LPP. First priority was given to districts with multi-track, year-round (MTYRE) school schedules and districts that could raise the 50 percent matching funds. The legislature's policy preference for relieving overcrowding with MTYRE programs was later revised. Today, the law offers incentives to get districts away from MTYRE programs.

Between 1982 and 1998, $17.5 billion in state bond funding was distributed to school districts. State bond measures have been placed on the ballot by the legislature, and passed by the voters of California nearly every two years. Only during the 1994 recession did a statewide bond measure fail to pass.

1996—Impact of Class Size Reduction on School Facilities

The Class Size Reduction Facilities Program, established in 1996, was designed to assist school districts with facilities-related costs associated with reducing class size to 20 pupils in K–3 grades. Educ. Code §§ 52120–52128.5; 5 C.C.R. § 15130 *et seq.* The program was funded with $200 million through one-time Prop. 98 funds, and provided $25,000 in grants for each new classroom needed to reduce class size The amount per grant was later increased to $40,000. With the passage of Prop. 1A in 1998, an additional $700 million for up to 17,500 additional grants of $40,000 per new classroom was made available to school districts that were not fully funded in previous years. After the depletion of that $700 million, however, no additional money has been provided for this program.

The Class Size Reduction Facilities Program, established in 1996, was designed to assist school districts with facilities-related costs associated with reducing class size to 20 pupils in K–3 grades.

1998—Another Watershed Year in State Funding: The LPP Becomes the SFP

In 1998, the Leroy F. Greene Lease-Purchase Program was replaced with the Leroy F. Greene State School Facilities Program (SFP) with new funding provided under Prop. 1A.

SFP = State School Facilities Program

In August 1998, SB 50 (Chapter 407, Statutes of 1998) was signed into law, establishing the SFP and enabling a bond issue to be placed on the ballot. In November 1998, Proposition 1A was passed. It provided $6.7 billion in state general obligation bond funds for K–12 school construction. This included $2.9 billion for new construction, $2.1 billion for modernization, $1 billion for hardship districts, and $700 million for new K–3 class size reduction facilities. The SFP replaced the LPP with a grant program where the state offered funding to districts in the form of grants to acquire school sites, construct new school facilities, or modernize existing school facilities. It also made significant reforms in the state school building program by streamlining the approval process for construction projects and establishing cost saving measures.

These reforms included adoption of a fixed matching grant per new pupil growth (based on 50 percent of the statewide average new construction cost), and a fixed grant per existing pupil for eligible modernization (based on 80 percent of the statewide average). The program also contained school district eligibility requirements to ensure that districts maintained their facilities and increased construction for facilities maintenance. It also provided funds for districts that face exceptional hardships and are unable to meet the local matching requirements. Finally, the program contained accountability provisions to ensure state facilities funds were expended in an appropriate and timely manner.

Table 2-1. Recent State School Bond History

Month	Year	Proposition no.	Amount in millions	Percent		Votes	
				YES	NO	YES	NO
November	1982	Prop. 1	$ 500	50.5	49.5	3,621,422	3,554,500
November	1984	Prop. 26	$ 450	60.7	39.3	5,190,887	3,354,902
November	1986	Prop. 53	$ 800	60.7	39.3	4,100,775	2,651,479
June	1988	Prop. 75	$ 800	65.0	35.0	3,519,902	1,899,245
November	1988	Prop. 79	$ 800	61.2	38.8	5,651,376	3,578,515
June	1990	Prop. 123	$ 800	57.5	42.5	2,781,974	2,054,386
November	1990	Prop. 146	$ 800	51.8	48.2	3,679,108	3,424,276
June	1992	Prop. 152	$ 1,900	52.9	47.1	3,119,411	2,774,699
November	1992	Prop. 155	$ 900	51.8	48.2	5,440,083	5,061,978
June	1994	Prop. 1B	$ 1,000	49.6	50.4	2,095,620	2,130,196
March	1996	Prop. 203	$ 3,025	61.8	38.2	3,258,442	2,009,983
November	1998	Prop. 1A	$ 9,200	62.0	37.5	4,522,509	2,721,959
November	2002	Prop. 47	$ 13,050	59.1	40.9	4,222,946	2,925,223
March	2004	Prop. 55	$ 12,300	50.9	49.7	3,239,706	3,130,921

Source: CASH website (www.cashnet.org), Secretary of State web site (www.ss.ca.gov)

This SFP also established a new process for determining the amount of fees developers may be charged to mitigate the impact of development on school facilities. Under this reform, a school district can charge fees above the statutory cap only under specified conditions, and then only up to the amount of funds that the district would be eligible to receive from the state.

Post-2002

In 2002, the California Legislature enacted AB 16, which authorized placement of Prop. 47 on the ballot in November 2002, authorized placement of another bond on the ballot in November 2004, and established new rules for the allocation of the new state bond money. The voters passed Prop. 47, and as a result, AB 16 governs this additional funding. Passage of Prop. 47 provided $13.05 billion for school construction projects. In March 2004, another bond measure passed and provided an additional $12.30 billion for school construction projects.

Recently, a greater understanding of the interface between academic achievement and the structure of the school facility has led to a push for equity in facilities.

More recently, a greater understanding of the interface between academic achievement and the structure of the school facility has led to a push for equity in facilities. The landmark *Williams v. State of California* case resulted in a settlement in 2004 that will provide nearly $1 billion for structural improvements in school facilities in the lowest academic performing schools. Additionally, new legislation was passed to fund pilot projects for the construction and reconfiguration of existing high schools into smaller schools of less than 500 students in 2006.

The Finance Team

More often than not, district staff is overloaded with other responsibilities and cannot take on additional burdens, such as evaluating state funding. Furthermore, the state process changes frequently, so to keep up with the constant flux, many districts rely on consultants with expertise in the related field of need. Many districts have sufficient expertise on staff to navigate the web of state funding, however, that staff person must stay current on state entitlement issues because changes to the program can interfere with planned projects. Larger districts have individuals on staff dedicated to state funding issues, but it may be more cost effective for small to medium size school districts to utilize consultants. If a district is able to seek state funding entitlements in-house, the same staff person should perform the analysis year to year, otherwise it would be in the district's best interest to hire a consultant to monitor the process.

It is advantageous for the district to assemble its team prior to the completion of the baseline eligibility determination because the eligibility can be shaped to meet the future needs of the planned or proposed projects. Once locked into place however, eligibility alterations to new construction baselines are rare, and consist of changes to existing law that affect facilities originally reported to the state at a particular grade level group (K–6, 7–8, 9–12). Additionally, a district may convert the new construction baseline from a district-wide basis to a high school attendance area (HSAA) basis if the district demonstrates that at least one of the HSAA has negative eligibility, and the district agrees to report future eligibility based on this method for at least five subsequent years.

Team members typically include an architect, a construction management firm, and specialty consultants for state eligibility and environmental issues. Once assembled, the team members should work together to facilitate the process.

If the planned project includes site acquisition, the site must be evaluated for possible toxic contamination. If further investigation is warranted, it is advisable to include special consultants who specialize is this area. Once a site is identified, plans and specifications will be developed by the architect and submitted to CDE and DSA for their approval. The architect or construction manager should work closely with the district staff or consultant seeking state funding eligibility to ensure the project complies with requirements of law regarding the district's eligibility. There are no guarantees when it comes to state funding. Rules change regularly, and funding is frequently exhausted.

CDE	= California Department of Education
DSA	= Division of the State Architect
G.O. Bonds	= General obligation bonds
HSAA	= High school attendance area

Team members typically include an architect, a construction management firm, and specialty consultants for state eligibility and environmental issues.

Bond Counsel

The bond counsel is responsible for drafting the legal documents under which the debt is issued, and for providing the legal opinion stating that the debt is validly issued and exempt from federal and state income taxes. The bond counsel advises districts on the options for election dates, and drafts ballot language for Mello-Roos and G.O. bonds (general obligation bonds). The bond counsel works with the financial advisor or underwriter to present the issuance of the debt.

Financial Advisor / Underwriter

The financial advisor formulates the district's funding plan for its school facility projects. Many of the duties of the financial advisor and underwriter overlap. However, only the underwriter purchases or underwrites debt. The financial advisor/underwriter is responsible for delivering debt to the market by calling prospective bidders, obtaining insurance, structuring the transaction, assessing bond market conditions, and selecting timing of offering in the market and on the forward calendar (the schedule of debt coming to the market), analyzing the viability of revenue streams, and recommending the maturity schedule. They are responsible for assessing the district's assets and determining the debt limit amount (determining if the district can raise enough money to fund its school facility project). Financial advisors and underwriters will also help secure the services of other needed professionals such as the rating analyst (who reviews the district's finances, local economy, insurance, etc., and rates the bond), the bond insurer (insured bonds get AAA rating and are easier to sell) and the dissemination agent (who submits the annual report regarding the district and its credit to the bond rating companies in New York).

Disclosure Counsel

SEC = Securities and Exchange Commission

Underwriters have traditionally prepared the "official statement," which is the offering document that provides a summary of the debt. However, since the rules of the Securities and Exchange Commission (SEC) require strict accuracy of the documents and are becoming more complex, more and more school districts are using disclosure counsel to prepare the official statement.

Sources of Money to Build Schools in California

This section describes the various pools of money and financing mechanisms available to California school districts to fund school facilities. The ability of a school district to take advantage of these options depends upon local resources, existing and future enrollments, and the condition and age of existing facilities.

Without local funding, a school district cannot meet the 50 percent funding requirement for new construction projects or the 40 percent matching requirement for modernization projects.

A school district must secure local funding for its share of the project. Without local funding, a school district cannot meet the 50 percent funding requirement for new construction projects or the 40 percent matching requirement for modernization projects.

Ideally, a district has developed a funding plan as part of its Facilities Master Plan identifying all the sources of money and financing mechanisms available to the district to meet its facilities needs. For most districts, obtaining a share of state bond funds will be critical to the ability to fund school facility projects.

State Bonds Under the SFP

AB 16/Propositions 47 and 55: 2002 and 2004 state bond. Early in 2002, AB 16 (authorizing the largest statewide bond measure in U.S. history, totalling $25 billion) was passed by the legislature and signed into law by the Governor. Kindergarten-University Public Education Facilities Bond Acts of 2002 and 2004. The bill placed a $13.05 billion bond measure before the voters in November 2002 and an additional $12.3 billion bond measure in March 2004. AB 16 made major changes to the School Facilities Program, and to the laws and regulations governing allocation and distribution of state bond money to local school districts.

Critically overcrowded schools. The Critically Overcrowded Schools Program (COS), which was launched in 2003, reserves funds for qualifying projects

COS = Critically Overcrowded Schools Program

Table 2-2. Comparison of School Facilities Bonds SB 50 (1998) and AB 16 (2002)

Subject	AB 16 (Hertzberg) April 2002	AB 50 (Greene) 1998
	The Kindergarten—University Public Education Facilities Bond Acts of 2002 and 2004 provide:	The Class Size Reduction Kindergarten–University Public Education Facilities Bond Act of 1998 provides:
General/Fiscal impact	• $25 billion in state bonds ($13,050,000,000 in 2002 and $12,300,000,000 in 2004)	• $9 billion for new state bonds
Composition of State Allocation Board	• Adds three members to SAB (for a total of ten): (1) One appointed by the Governor; (2) an additional Member from the Senate Minority Party; and (3) an additional member from the Assembly Minority Party • Requires that two members of the Senate and Assembly belong to the majority party and one to the minority party	• SAB has seven members: (1) Director of Finance, (2) Director of General Services, (3) Superintendent of Public Instruction, (4) two Members of the Senate, appointed by the Senate Committee on Rules, and (5) two Members of the Assembly, appointed by the Speaker of the Assembly
Developers fee	• Suspended the possible imposition of a Level III fee until November 2004	• Established Level I, II, and III fees. Authorizes imposition of higher fees if certain requirements met
	• Establishes a Homebuyer Downpayment Assistance Program to help pay the school facilities fee for affordable housing development • Creates Critically Overcrowded School Program	
Modifies rules for state funding process	• Modifies funding provisions related to: – Multi-track year-round schools – Supplemental apportionments for small schools	
	• Adjustments for densely populated urban areas • Eliminates priority points ranking mechanism • Revises the state to local cost share for modernization from 80/20 to 60/40 with the state contribution remaining the same	
Library and higher education facilities appropriations	• Appropriates $651,289,000 to the University of California, the California State University and the California Community Colleges for construction of education and library facilities	
Joint use	• $50 million for joint use facilities	
Energy	• Creates new energy efficiency supplemental grants	
Charter schools	• Sets aside funds ($100,000 in 2002; $300,000 in 2004) for Charter Schools	

for up to four years, with a potential extension of one year, if certain conditions are met. A total of $3.94 billion was reserved ($1.7 billion from Prop. 47 and $2.24 billion from Prop. 55). This program addresses the concerns that warranted the use of priority points. Its purpose is to allow school districts with extended site acquisition processes to have access to state funds. A district that has difficulty gaining access to state funds due to a lengthy site acquisition process is often compelled to add students to an existing site, which causes high site density. The COS program uses site density as the major criteria for eligibility. Funds under the COS are not available for the applicant district until all the criteria for a SFP new construction application have been approved. The program does not provide additional funding beyond the normal new construction grant. However, it does allow for a reservation of funds for the entire project, including

A district that has difficulty gaining access to state funds due to a lengthy site acquisition process is often compelled to add students to an existing site, which causes high site density.

Multi-story construction
at site-impacted high school

CBEDS = California Basic
Educational Data System
OPSC = Office of Public
School Construction

The COS program provides districts a reserved source of funding for up to four years, with a possible one-year extension, for site and project funding.

COS funding uses site density
as a qualifying criterion

site acquisition without DSA-approved plans, which is unique to this program. The funding reservation also includes an additional one-time 12 percent increase for inflation that may only be utilized to the extent such inflation is recognized by the state.

Source schools. Qualification for the COS program is determined through source schools, which are sites that meet the following criteria (equal to 210 percent of CDE guidelines for site capacity):

- Site density of 115 pupils/acre in grades K–6
- Site density of 90 pupils/acre in grades 7–12

The October 2001 California Basic Educational Data System (CBEDS) is the official enrollment used to determine eligibility for source school identification. Qualifying schools must be on the CDE source school list, which is determined by the usable site acreage for all sites owned by the district.

Once it is certified as a source school, eligibility for funding is based on the qualifying pupils (150 percent of CDE guidelines) at those sites. Utilizing the October 2001 CBEDS, qualifying pupils are determined by enrollment that exceeds the following:

- 86 pupils/acre in grades K–6
- 68 pupils/acre in grades 7–12

Although it may have qualifying pupils, a district must be eligible for new construction under the SFP to participate in the COS program.

The COS program provides districts a reserved source of funding for up to four years, with a possible one-year extension, for site and project funding. Since the district is not required to have a site purchased nor have DSA-approved plans to apply for COS funds, in order to apply to the Office of Public School Construction (OPSC) for an apportionment reservation, the following information is required:

- Preliminary appraisal of proposed site (less than 6 months old)
- Median cost of land using historical data
- Estimated relocation and Department of Toxic Substances Control costs

If land acquisition is part of the project, the district is entitled to a set aside of four percent of the value of the land or $50,000, whichever is greater. In addition, the new site must also comply with the following proximity criteria if the school is within:

- The attendance area of source school(s)
- One-mile radius of any source elementary school
- Three-mile radius of any middle or high school source school

COS funding. The COS program provided for two separate funding cycles:

- $1.7 billion in November 2002
- $2.44 billion in March 2004

Application for COS program. The OPSC must have received applications for the first round of COS funding between November 6, 2002 and May 1, 2003. The application for the March 2004 allocation must have been filed at least 60 days prior to and no more than 120 days after the election. If the applications exceeded available funding for either of the funding cycles, they would have been ranked according to onsite density. However, if the applications did not exceed available funding, a 15 percent contingency would have been reserved for future inflation or shortfalls in preliminary estimates, and the remainder would have been transferred into the new construction funding pool.

Although the reservation of money is marked as a preliminary apportionment, the COS program does not allow for advance funding prior to DSA-approved plans. The actual funding will be provided at the time of the final project apportionment, which indicates a DSA-approved plan or a biddable project. Please note that the final apportionment is still subject to the new construction eligibility and regulations governing the SFP at the time the project applies for funding. It should be stated again that the COS program is only a reservation of funds for up to five years, and was created solely to assist school districts with extended site acquisition issues. Once a site has been selected and potential clean up identified, the district is free to move forward with the development of the plans for the project. Although the district has up to five years to apply for project funding with OPSC, it is required to provide project status reports to the OPSC each year demonstrating progress on the project.

The COS program is a reservation of funds for up to five years that was created solely to assist school districts with extended site acquisition issues.

Joint use funding. The state legislature is interested in encouraging the exploration of collaborative projects between higher educational institutions. This is accomplished through AB 16, which provides $50 million for funding of joint use projects in November 2002, and another $50 million in March 2004. In order to receive joint use funding through the state, the joint use partner must fund at least 25 percent of the project cost. If the school district has passed a local bond that specifies that such funds are to be used for the joint use project, then the school may provide the full 50 percent share. The idea is to tap funding sources outside of the normal cycle for K–12 school construction. In the past, these joint use projects required matching funds, provided by either the joint use partner or the school district.

The AB 16 Joint Use program is divided into two separate categories: Types I and II. The two categories of projects will be funded in priority, with Type I applications funded first, then Type II projects. Districts may submit multiple applications. School districts cannot be funded for more than one project within each type until all applicant districts have received funding for one project. There are the two categories of funding:

Type I joint use. A district may request funding for a Type I joint use project if the following criteria are met:

Joint Use Performing Arts Center, Arroyo Valley High School, San Bernardino, California

- The plans and specifications for the joint use project are included in the plans and specifications for a new school, or an addition to an existing school for which the district has requested SFP new construction funding.
- The joint use project will be located on the same site as the SFP new construction project is located.
- The joint use project will increase the square feet and/or extra cost of a multi-use room, library, gymnasium, child care facility, or teacher education facility.
- At least one of the joint use partners is an institution of higher education, government agency, or nonprofit organization.
- The District has entered into a joint use agreement that meets the criteria in Education Code section 17077.42.
- The construction project for the joint use project was not executed prior to April 29, 2002.
- Both DSA and CDE have approved the plans and specifications.

Type II joint use. A district may request funding for a Type II joint use project if all of the following criteria are met:

- The joint use project proposes to reconfigure an existing school building as part of the modernization plans, or to construct new school buildings on an existing school site that doesn't have that type of facility.
- The joint use project will be located on the same site as the SFP new construction project is located.
- The joint use project will increase the square footage of and/or add extra cost to a multi-purpose room, gymnasium, childcare facility, library, or teacher-training facility.
- At least one of the joint use partners is a government agency, an institution of higher education, or a nonprofit organization.
- The district has demonstrated it has joint use square feet eligibility pursuant to section 1859.124(b) of Title 12 of the California Code of Regulations.
- The district has entered into a joint use agreement that meets the criteria in Education Code section 17077.42.
- The construction project for the joint use project was not executed prior to April 29, 2002.
- Both DSA and CDE have approved the plans and specifications.

The joint use project funding has a maximum of $1 million for an elementary school, $1.5 million for a middle school, and up to $2 million for a high school project.

The joint use project funding for each project is a maximum of $1 million for an elementary school project, $1.5 million for a middle school project, and up to $2 million for a high school project. If the joint use project serves more than one grade configuration or multiple school sites, the joint use eligibility and funding is based on the highest-grade level served by the facility.

For availability and the window of dates for submittal of applications, districts should monitor the OPSC website (www.opsc.dgs.ca.gov).

Eligibility. The eligible building area for each project is based on the CDE's Minimum Essential Facilities in Title 5 of the California Code of Regulations. If the project is a Type I project, the amount of eligible building area is determined based on the type of facility and grade levels. For Type II projects, the eligible area is determined by subtracting the area for the type of facility from the building area for the joint use building type in the project. If there is area in the project, the eligibility is zero. For example, consider a 15,000 square foot gymnasium addition to a 1,000 student middle school. The minimum essential facilities area for this project would be 1,000 students x 12.9 square foot per student or 12,900 square feet. The amount eligible for funding under joint use would be 2,100 square feet. The 12,900 square feet would be funded under the SFP if eligibility existed in that program. Proposed AB 16 regulations, § 1859.124.1, approved by the SAB September 25, 2002.

Funding. Funding for joint use projects is specified in Regulation section 1859.125. $173.30 per square foot is allowed for toilet facilities and $96.30 per square foot allowed for non-toilet facilities. These numbers represent the state's 50 percent share of the joint use project. These values cannot exceed $1.0 million per elementary school project, $1.5 million per middle school project, and $2.0 million per project for high schools.

Additional grant for energy efficiency. A byproduct of the state's energy crisis, AB 16 provides additional funding of up to five percent more for projects that meet the requirements for the Additional Grant for Energy Efficiency. Districts should note, however, that this additional grant is not eligible for projects in districts that have received funding from the Renewable Energy Program, because the pot of state money is quite small—$5.8 million for modernization and $14.2 million for new construction.

Districts are eligible for this additional grant for new construction projects where the design exceeds Title 24 energy standards by at least 15 percent. If so, then the district is eligible for a one percent increase in grant for each 2.5 percent increase in energy efficiency, but a maximum 5 percent increase in grant for greater than 25 percent increase in energy efficiency. Currently, the calculations are required to be done on a "whole building" methodology using EnergySoft's EnergyPro 3.1.™ However the requirements change frequently and districts are advised to consult the most recent Title 2 regulations for updates.

Districts are eligible for this additional grant for modernization projects where the design exceeds Title 24 energy standards by at least 10 percent. If so, then the district is eligible for a one percent increase in grant for each one percent increase in energy efficiency, but a maximum 5 percent increase in grant for greater than 15 percent increase in energy efficiency.

Methods to achieve these percentages include conservation, peak-load shifting, use of solar water heating technology, photovoltaics, and other technologies. DSA review is required and must concur that the requisite percentage of energy efficiency has been achieved. In early 2003, DSA and the California Energy Commission (CEC) developed the regulations to be used to implement this program. Applications, along with building performance calculations will be submitted to DSA for verification prior to funding by OPSC.

Modernization of 50-year-old buildings. Renovating older buildings usually involves extensive additional costs compared to newer buildings. AB 16

A byproduct of the state's energy crisis, AB 16 provides additional funding of up to five percent more for projects that meet the requirements for the Additional Grant for Energy Efficiency.

Renovation of Grand View Elementary School, Manhattan Beach, California

CASH = Coalition for Adequate School Housing
CEC = California Energy Commission
SAB = State Allocation Board

What Is a Priority Point?

A priority point mechanism is a method of apportioning state bond funds when demand exceeds available funding. Priority points separate district applications into two categories—those with enough points to receive project funding, and those with insufficient points. Under the Proposition 1A system, the level at which projects were funded fluctuated to allow approximately $126 million to be distributed each quarter. This system was rendered ineffective by AB 16.

Added by AB 562 in 1999 in response to the *Godinez* lawsuit, Education Code section 17072.25 requires the SAB to develop priority points (a mechanism for ranking approved applications for new construction funding) when:

- Total state funds necessary for funding all approved projects exceed the total state funds for allocation
- The actual amount of unallocated state bond proceeds available on or after July 1, 2000 for new construction is $300 million

Priority points are based on the percentages of current and projected unhoused pupils relative to the total population of the applicant district or attendance area, and the total number of currently and projected unhoused pupils in an applicant district or attendance area. Other factors are considered, but cannot constitute greater than a 10 percent weight in the overall priority ranking. ■

SAB Regulations; Title 2, C.C.R. §§ 1859.91, 1859.92

provides for an additional per-pupil allowance for the increased costs of modernizing buildings over 50 years old that have never been modernized with state funding. The age of a building is measured at DSA approval date, plus 12 months. In addition to the 50-year-old building grant, a project is allowed an additional grant for utility upgrades. The categories for utility upgrades include water, sewer, electrical, gas, and communication. The additional grant for utility upgrades will be the lesser of 60 percent of the cost of the eligible work or an amount not to exceed 20 percent of the pupil grant. Districts that have a mix of 25- and 50-year-old buildings will report the percentage of either classrooms or square footage of the portion attributable to the older buildings on the SAB application for funding. Districts will then receive a pro-rata share of the higher pupil grant amount for that portion of the project.

The current grant amounts are as follows:

Grade classification	Basic grant amount (2006)
Elementary pupil	$ 4,249
Middle school pupil	$ 4,494
High school pupil	$ 5,884
Special day class—non-severe	$ 9,056
Special day class—severe	$ 13,543

Note: These amounts represent the state's 60 percent share of the project, and will be adjusted annually. They only apply to facilities that house mainstream K–12 student enrollment.

Priority points. Passage of the November 1998 statewide school bond (Prop. 1A) allocated $9.2 billion. However, within a year controversy raged over how to distribute the already scarce funds among school districts, whose facility needs far exceeded the $9 billion. A priority points system was implemented to address the concerns over this lack of funds (*see* sidebar). Fortunately, with the passage of the November 2002 state school bond (Prop. 47), and its infusion of over $13 billion in funds, this controversy may become a mere historical anecdote.

With the passage of AB 16 and its injection of state bond funds, the controversy regarding priority points is once again on the back burner. Assembly Bill 16 establishes that priority points shall not apply to projects funded by state bonds approved by voters after January 1, 2002. However, priority points are not likely to be raised as an issue again until state bonds become scarce again.

Distributing state bond money to school districts

Role of OPSC and State Allocation Board. In order to navigate the process to successful acquisition of state funds, one must first understand the players involved in the process. The first and most important body to recognize is the State Allocation Board (SAB). Created in 1947 by the state legislature, the SAB is the authority responsible for determining the allocation of state resources, namely state general obligation bond issues and other available state funds used for new construction and modernization of local public school facilities. In addition, the SAB governs the State Relocatable Classroom, Deferred Maintenance, New Construction, Modernization, Energy Efficiency, COS, and Joint Use Programs.

The SAB generally meets monthly (every fourth Wednesday) at the state capitol. At each meeting, the SAB approves applications for eligibility and funding, rules on appeals, receives and considers public comments, and adopts policies and regulations pertaining to the programs the SAB administers. The SAB is comprised of ten members:

- Director of the Department of Finance or designee (traditionally the chairperson)
- Director of the Department of General Services or designee
- Superintendent of Public Instruction or designee
- Two state senators (by appointment)
- Two state Assembly members (by appointment)
- Minority party Assembly member (by appointment)
- Minority party senator (by appointment)
- Other appointee of the administration (Governor's Office)

The OPSC administers the State School Facilities Program in conjunction with the SAB. As staff to the SAB, the OPSC is responsible for managing all state funding and expenditures. OPSC prepares regulations, policies, and procedures for approval by the SAB.

Other agency approvals required to gain access to state funds for either new construction or modernization come from CDE, DSA, and DTSC. CDE approves proposed school sites and construction plans. The construction plan review focuses primarily on the educational adequacy of the proposed facility and conformance to Title 5 guidelines. DSA reviews construction plans and specifications to ensure compliance with California's building codes, namely seismic, fire and life safety, and access. Lastly, DTSC's involvement is limited to new construction projects, either new schools

The Allocation Controversy

A direct result of the use of priority points, the allocation controversy began when students, parents, and community organizations in the Los Angeles Unified School District filed a lawsuit to stop distribution of Prop. 1A funds. *Godinez et al. v. Davis et al.* The plaintiffs in *Godinez* alleged that the state had failed to carry out the voters' intent that funds be used to relieve overcrowding and accommodate student enrollment growth. They contended that the state had replaced the need-based priority system with a "first come, first served" system, and that this system was biased against overcrowded school districts in heavily congested urban areas due to the extraordinarily long site acquisition delays in funding and cleaning up potential school sites. As a result of the testimony presented in the case, the court directed the SAB to review its regulations regarding priority points. SAB Regulation sections 1859.91, 1859.92 (established the point approved on January 2, 2001).

Following the direction of the courts, in December 2000, the SAB adopted new emergency regulations that assigned priority points to each approved application based on need criteria. Most California school districts remained in disagreement with the court's ruling and SAB's court-directed regulations.

The new regulations rationed the remaining Prop. 1A funds through August 2002. Of the $1.32 billion remaining, $872 million was allocated in equal quarterly distributions, and $450 million was reserved for a final August 2002 allocation for projects approved by June 26, 2002. In any quarter, if all approved applicants did not receive apportionments based on available funds, the lower priority point applicants would have to wait until the next quarterly disbursement and compete with other approved applications. Unfortunately, many school districts that were prepared to construct new schools did not receive funding due to a lack of priority points.

Based on the adoption of the new regulations, the parties in *Godinez* agreed to settle the lawsuit contingent on the implementation of the priority point regulations. However, in November 2000, the Coalition for Adequate School Housing (CASH—an advocacy organization for member school districts) filed a separate lawsuit (*Corona-Norco v. State Allocation Board*) to challenge the new regulations. CASH alleged that the priority point regulations exceeded the SAB's authority, since approximately $300 million had been approved, but the new emergency regulations would allow only $125 million to be allocated in the first quarter. Unfortunately, the funding was exhausted before the *Corona* case could be settled. ■

Unfunded List

When state bond proceeds have been exhausted, SAB grants an unfunded approval to projects that have received all the required agency approvals for state funding and places them on a list.

A word of caution: Although it has historically recognized projects in the pipeline, the state has always made it clear that placement on an unfunded list is not a guarantee or commitment to future funding. ■

✍ **practice tip**

Caution should be exercised when establishing eligibility on an HSAA or super HSAA basis, since a subsequent boundary change could redistribute students elsewhere in the district.

SHSAA = Super high school
           attendance area

California Basic Educational Data System (CBEDS)

Official school district enrollment used for state eligibility determination is reported every October.

or additions to existing schools. The agency assists districts with assessments of possible contamination and, if necessary, with developing and implementing remediation plans.

Determining a district's entitlements to state bond funds. First and foremost, the district must determine its entitlement to state bond funds.

Determining eligibility for entitlements is complex. The laws and regulations governing distribution of state bond money change with the passage of each bond measure, and nearly every year in between. For instance, Chapter 12 of Title 1, Division 1, Part 10 of the Education Code explains the rules for allocation and distribution of the 1976 LPP program, whereas, Chapter 12.5 explains the rules for distribution of the 1998 SFP bond money. With the passage of AB 16 and Prop. 47 in 2002, new programs have been created with new rules to govern them.

Projects approved by the SAB and placed on an unfunded list have no promise of future funding unless the legislature specifically guarantees funding of projects in the pipeline. However, if we use past performance as our guide, the state has always honored projects placed on unfunded lists, and has fully funded them from future bond issuances.

Eligibility determination. The SFP provides state funding for two primary facilities programs: New Construction and Modernization. The new construction grant provides funding on a 50–50 state and local matching basis, while the modernization grant provides funding on a 60–40 state and local matching basis.

There are two main steps to the process for obtaining a district's allocation of state funds for these programs—an application for eligibility, and an application for funding. First, a district must get approval from the SAB on its applications for eligibility. Eligibility applications, however, do not secure state funding, nor do the applications place a project on any funding list. The eligibility approval by the SAB merely recognizes that the district or county office meets the criteria under law to receive its portion of state funding, and eligibility for new construction is only established until the annual October CBEDS report is complete, or a maximum of one year. Eligibility for modernization projects are locked in place, providing protection from possible enrollment declines or facility changes at particular sites. Happily, modernization eligibility may be adjusted upwards if warranted based on enrollment increases at the site.

New construction eligibility application process. In order to establish new construction eligibility in the SFP, a district must demonstrate in the SAB 50-01 Enrollment Project Certification form that its seating capacity is insufficient to house the existing and projected pupil enrollment for the next five years. Once the new construction eligibility is determined, a "baseline" is created that remains for all future applications. The baseline is adjusted only for enrollment fluctuations and for facilities added or lost to the district. Except for these adjustments, the baseline is established only once. If it can be demonstrated that errors were made to the initial baseline determination, or changes to regulations warrant adjustments to existing facility counts, then a district may file a new application to adjust the previously established baseline.

New construction eligibility can be filed on a district-wide or, if acceptable, on an HSAA or a super high school attendance area (SHSAA). For most districts, the district-wide basis is the most beneficial method. Conversely, if a district has isolated areas of growth and flat or declining enrollment, filing on an HSAA may be the most beneficial method. Filing on an HSAA is the same as a district-wide area, but the district is broken down into smaller districts that feed into an existing active high school. A district may also combine two or more adjacent HSAAs, commonly called a "super attendance area." Although a district may have filed on a district-wide basis for baseline determination purposes, it may elect to evaluate whether converting to an HSAA basis increases eligibility. In that case, the district must be able to demonstrate that at least one of the HSAA's has negative eligibility at any grade level in order to change the baseline determination. Continuation high schools may not be used for this purpose and there must be an existing high school in the area defined to qualify. Once a district elects either the district-wide or HSAA method, it must file all future new construction applications on that basis for five years, with the above situation as the only exception. Districts must therefore give serious consideration to the future impact of filing on this basis.

Establishing the district's baseline. Before asking "where's my cash?" a district must first establish a construction baseline and submit to OPSC the following three forms.

SAB 50-01—Enrollment certification/projection. The method of projecting future enrollment involves using current and historical California Basic Education Data System enrollment data for the district. The data collected is then projected using the cohort-survival projection into the future for five years—the more projected students, the greater the possibility of getting funds.

The following information is needed to complete the form:

- CBEDS (enrollment) by grade level for the current year and previous three years
- Special education enrollment for the current year by category and severity
- Continuation high school enrollment by grade level for the current year and previous three years
- Supplemental enrollment figures:
  - Dwelling Units included in approved subdivision maps or valid tentative subdivision maps for development in the district or HSAA. If the district elects to request this supplement, the district representative will need to have the following on file:
    - Approved dates of the maps by the city or county planning commission
    - The number of units to be built in the subdivision
    - A yield factor from the various types of subdivision housing; as an alternate, the district may accept the statewide average yield factor of 0.7, for unified districts, 0.5 for K–8 districts, and 0.2 for high school districts

SAB 50-02—Existing school building capacity. The SAB 50-02 is a record of the district's teaching stations. SFP Regulation sections 1859.31 and 1859.32 provide instructions on what spaces are to be included or excluded in the calculation of the district capacity.

Cohort Survival

State-recognized student projection methodology calculates the average change between grade levels for the previous four years, and projects that average change by grade level into future years. This method is based on the use of a weighted average. For example, a change in the kindergarten enrollment during the previous year will have a much greater effect than the same numerical change to high school enrollment four years earlier. ■

Adjusted Capacity

Gross teaching station capacity is reduced for classrooms qualified under Regulation section 1859.32.

Operational Grants

Operational funding is available for qualified MTYRE districts. However, grants for operation reduce that districts' eligibility for new construction funding.

✐ **practice tip**

Take great care when using the "house count" method to project enrollment. Due to a case of misuse, the SAB highly scrutinizes these applications. Houses that have been occupied may no longer be part of the count.

Use of final maps has a very narrow window. The district should make certain that all criteria for the final maps has been met.

✐ **practice tip**

Never establish a baseline when eligibility is negative. Doing so will lock a district into counting all of its facilities forever, limiting future options for disposition and eligibility for growth.

Changes can be made to a baseline that will affect eligibility, *e.g.*, removal of portables. A baseline that is established to *include* these facilities cannot be changed. If removed prior to establishing the baseline, they will not be included.

The process of calculating a district's existing school building capacity is to:

- Compile a gross inventory, per Regulation section 1859.31, of all spaces constructed or reconstructed to provide pupil instruction. The grade level of each classroom should also be identified.

- Make adjustments to the gross inventory, per Regulation section 1859.32, by excluding spaces that are not deemed available teaching stations. To determine pupil capacity, the remaining classrooms are multiplied by 25 for elementary and 27 for middle and high school classrooms.

- If the district or feeder elementary districts do not have at least 30 percent of its K–6 enrollment on a multi-track year-round schedule, a final calculation is done to increase the capacity of the district's K–6 enrollment to approximate a year-round schedule. The calculation is 6 percent of the districts adjusted K–6 capacity.

- A final adjustment occurs for those districts on a MTYRE schedule that receive MTYRE Operational Grants from the CDE. The district's capacity is increased by the number of Operational Grants it received from the CDE. The reduction to eligibility is always based on the previous years Operational Grant request.

Onsite reviews. As part of the inventory process, the district must submit records of existing teaching stations in the district. These records generally consist of the following:

- Diagrams of the facilities in each district school site. The diagrams must include all permanent and relocatable classrooms. Most districts use fire drill maps or 1A diagrams from the LPP. The diagrams must be included with the application.

- Documentation supporting any exclusions claimed from the gross inventory must be on file at the district.

SAB 50-03 eligibility determination. The SAB 50-02 (existing school building capacity) is subtracted from the SAB 50-01 (five-year enrollment projection) above. The number of pupils remaining, if any, are considered "unhoused" and comprise the district's new construction grant eligibility. If the existing school building capacity is larger than the district's projected enrollment, the district has negative new construction eligibility. These figures are calculated by grade categories (K–6, 7–8, 9–12, non-severe special education, severe special education), with each group receiving a different grant-funding factor.

New construction eligibility application approval. Once the district has completed SAB Forms 50-01, 50-02, and 50-03, it is ready to submit the eligibility application package. Before adding the application to the office workload list, the OPSC will conduct a preliminary review of the package to ensure all required documents have been received. Prior to presentation to the SAB, a more detailed review, including onsite visits, will be conducted by OPSC to ensure the accuracy of the facilities reported. When the review is complete and the OPSC has validated the eligibility calculations, the item is presented to the SAB for consideration of approval. The district will now have official new construction eligibility based on "unhoused" pupils, until the next October CBEDS.

At that time, the district will have to evaluate enrollment changes in the grade level categories to assess new construction eligibility fluctuations—only small school districts with total enrollments of less that 2,500 are protected from such fluctuations. Qualifying small school districts have their new construction eligibility protected for a three-year period.

Modernization project grant funding. As with the new construction grant, the modernization basic grant provides all essential project costs. Modernization grant funding may be used for all project expenditures, excluding new building area. It may not be used for new construction or new site development; however, the funds may be used for additional toilet facilities necessary to comply with the Americans with Disabilities Act (ADA), replacement in kind of permanent and portable construction, as long as no new additional area is provided, and replacement in kind of existing site development work.

The basic grant is determined by multiplying the number of pupils assigned to the project times the per-pupil grant amount. In some instances, this is the total enrollment at the site, but for sites that have buildings that do not qualify for modernization, the number will be less than the total enrollment. SAB adjusts the per-pupil grant every January, based on the change in the Marshall Swift Class B Construction Cost Index. The 2006 grant amounts, which represent the state's 60 percent share of the project, are as follows:

Grade classification	Basic grant amount (2006)
Elementary pupil	$ 3,059
Middle school pupil	$ 3,236
High school pupil	$ 4,236
Special day class—non-severe	$ 6,521
Special day class—severe	$ 9,746

Modernization eligibility application process. Modernization eligibility is much easier to calculate than new construction, because it involves only one school as opposed to the entire district's facilities. Applications are submitted on a site-by-site rather than a district-wide or HSAA basis. To be eligible, a building must be age qualified (at least 25 years old for a permanent building and at least 20 years old for a relocatable building) or modernized with state funds (at least 25 or 20 years ago). In addition, the district must demonstrate that students enrolled at the site are or will be using the facilities to be modernized. Closed schools may be eligible, but the district must assign students immediately to establish the planned enrollment.

SAB 50-03—Eligibility determination. This is the same form used for new construction applications. In order to complete the form, the district representative will need a completed site diagram for the applicable school that contains the following information:

- Number of permanent buildings
- Number of portable classrooms
- Ages of all facilities on site
- Most recent CBEDS enrollment at the site

Euclid Elementary School modernization, Ontario, California

Eligibility is determined by utilizing one of three methods:

- Option A. All age-qualified teaching stations are loaded by a factor of 25 (elementary) or 27 (middle and high school students) to calculate the maximum students eligible for modernization.

- Option B. Option B compares two prorated methods, and the method that calculates the greatest eligibility is entered under this heading. Using the first method, the district takes all the age-qualified teaching station facilities and divides them by the total teaching stations at the site, to determine the percentage of age-qualified facilities. That percentage is then multiplied by the current CBEDS site enrollment to calculate the eligibility. The second method is similar to the classroom prorated method, but utilizes building area as the percentage factor. All building area, excluding open corridor square footage, for age-qualified facilities is compared to the total site building area. The resulting percentage factor is then multiplied by the current CBEDS site enrollment to ascertain the eligible modernization grants. The method that yields the larger grant figure is selected under this option. If the district selects this method, it will be necessary to provide square footage information on the site diagrams as well.

- CBEDS enrollment. The final modernization eligibility is determined by the lesser of the age-qualified capacity (the greater of Option A or Option B above), or the actual site CBEDS enrollment.

Modernization eligibility application approval. After completing the SAB 50-03, the district may submit an application for modernization eligibility, which is similar to the application for new construction. Prior to the district's presentation of its package to the SAB, the OPSC conducts a preliminary review to ensure that all required documents have been received and then does a more detailed review, including onsite visits, to ensure the accuracy of the facilities reported in the application. Once the review is complete and the OPSC has verified the eligibility calculations, the district may apply to the SAB for consideration of approval. The school site for which the application was approved will now have its eligibility locked in, and this can only be changed if the district submits an amended application to increase the current eligibility already on file for the school site.

New construction project grant funding. When the district has established its new construction baseline, and determined it has new construction eligibility, it may request funding for the design and construction of the planned project. Under most circumstances, the grant is approved only after the district has received site approval from the CDE and the plans and specifications have been reviewed and approved by DSA and the CDE.

A new construction project grant consists of a basic grant and any supplemental grants for which a project qualifies.

A new construction project grant consists of a basic grant and any supplemental grants for which a project qualifies. Based on the grade level, the basic grant funds the design, construction, inspection, testing, furniture, equipment, and any other cost associated with the construction and completion of the planned project, but not *land* acquisition costs. For instance, the basic grant does not provide for site acquisition, site utilities, service site, or offsite development costs, although supplemental grants adjust the basic grant for geographical variances in costs.

New construction basic grant. The new construction basic grant is based on the number of pupils assigned to the project. The district must determine the number of basic grants to request for the project. The most common methodology determines the grade level to be served and the number of classrooms to be constructed in the project. Typically, K–6 classrooms are loaded at 25, 7–12 classrooms are loaded at 27, Non-severe Special Education classrooms are loaded at 13, and Severe Special Education classrooms are loaded at 9.

As an example, assume the district is eligible to construct a new elementary school with 25 classrooms. This will equate to the following:

$$25 \text{ (CRs)} \times 25 \text{ (K–6 state loading standard)} = 625$$

In the example above, the district may request different basic grants: the actual loading of 625 or less than 625. If a district can complete the project for less than the 625 basic grants, it may do so. However, the district must comply with the requirements found in Regulation section 1859.51(i)(1)–(6).

The basic grant is determined by multiplying the pupils assigned to the project by the per-pupil grant established in law. The grant is adjusted annually by the SAB every January, based on the change in the Marshall Swift Class B Construction Cost Index. The 2006 grant amounts are as follows:

Grade classification	Basic grant amount (2006)
Elementary pupil	$ 7,082
Middle school pupil	$ 7,490
High school pupil	$ 9,805
Special day cass—non-severe	$ 15,096
Special day class—severe	$ 22,572

New construction supplemental grant. A new construction supplemental grant is designated for a unique project, certain geographic locations, and special project needs. It is based on formulas set forth in the SFP Regulations. The following is a list of supplemental grants:

Special education (therapy). This grant is only available for facilities that serve severely disabled individuals with exceptional needs. The basic grant is increased for the area of therapy rooms, not to exceed 3,000 square feet, plus 750 square feet per additional special day class classroom. The following unit costs, which are adjusted annually, are the state's 50 percent share per square foot of therapy area:

- $236 per square foot for toilet facilities
- $130 per square foot for other facilities

Multi-level construction. This grant is available to construct multi-level facilities on small sites. A project qualifies if its usable acreage is less than 75 percent of the site size the CDE recommends for the master-planned project capacity. Qualifying projects receive an increase of 12 percent for each pupil housed in a multi-level building.

What Is Master Planned Capacity?

The planned capacity of the school site in the near future is not necessarily the current designed capacity. *See* discussion of Facilities Master Plan in chapter 3.

The Short Life of the "Use of Grants" Regulation

The School Facilities Program, established by SB 50 in 1998, significantly changed the method of determining the funding available to a school district for the construction of new schools. The Lease Purchase Program had a long history of funding schools on the basis of a set building area for each unhoused student, and a set allowance for the cost of varying types of building area. The SFP changed the method to a more straightforward per pupil grant amount. The SFP loads existing facilities at a loading standard established in law: 25 students per teaching station at the K–6 level; and 27 students per teaching station at the 7–12 grade levels. However, the law was silent concerning loading standards used in *new* facilities. This allowed districts with alternative loading standards or with alternative educational methodologies some flexibility to apply for the number of students that would *actually* be housed in the newly designed facilities. The number of pupil grants in the application would be indicated on the district's baseline and deducted from the eligibility. The state considered these grants as "full and final" and that it was the responsibility of the school district to manage the grants and the construction costs.

That was the theory. Most school districts soon discovered that the grant amounts in the SFP were considerably less than the LPP allowed. Several chose to supplement the project budget by *adding additional grants.* For many school districts, specifically those experiencing hardship, this was the only method available to build projects of quality and longevity. Districts also learned they had more flexibility to use grants from one grade level to fund construction of a school for another grade level instead of waiting for full eligibility.

The SAB considered this an inappropriate use of the grants and a method for some districts to receive more than their share of state money from the limited funds. For the first time in mid-2001, the SAB adopted regulations to limit a district's ability ➡

Site acquisition. This grant is available to acquire and develop a new school site for a planned new school or addition to an existing school, or to reimburse or credit the district for 50 percent of the site acquisition costs originally expended by the district. The state will only recognize 50 percent of the lesser of the appraised value or the original purchase price of the site. Eligible costs for site acquisition are as follows:

- Fifty percent of the relocation cost (Residential and Business occupants)
- Two percent of the site's value, with a minimum of $25,000
- Fifty percent of costs related to the DTSC review and oversight
- Fifty percent of hazardous waste removal (no more than 150 percent of the appraised value; no less than four percent of the appraised value)

Eligible expenditures for hazardous waste removal cannot exceed the difference between the actual purchase price and the appraised value of the site.

Site development. This supplemental grant is available for the purpose of developing the site where the project is located, authorized in Regulation section 1859.76. DSA approved plans and detailed cost estimates must be submitted to OPSC to qualify for this grant. Fifty percent of the following costs are available for both new and addition projects:

- **Utility services.** Improvements of water, sewer, gas, electric, and telephone from the point of connection (utility connection) to the project site meter or major building lateral location.
- **Offsite development.** Improvements located along the perimeter of two adjacent sides of the site, including street grading and paving, storm drainage lines, curbs, gutters, sidewalks, and street lighting. Local entities having jurisdiction over such improvements must approve the plans and specifications prior to the district seeking supplemental grant funding. If local approval has not been obtained, a letter from the approving agency can be submitted indicating that all offsite improvements are consistent with local requirements.
- **Service site development.** Improvements performed within school property lines that may include site clearance, rough grading, soil compaction, drainage, and eligible erosion control. This work is to be completed prior to general site development and construction of buildings.

Replaced facilities. This supplemental grant is available to school districts that demolish single-story facilities in order to increase pupil capacity on the same site. To qualify, the school must be on a multi-track year-round schedule, the site size must be less than 75 percent of the size recommended by the CDE, and the school's student capacity must be increased. Furthermore, the cost of the demolition and replacement facilities must be less than the state's cost to provide new facilities at another site. If the project qualifies, the state will fund 50 percent of the replacement cost of the single-story facility(s) to be replaced.

Geographic location. This supplemental grant is available to remote, difficult-to-access districts with a lack of qualified contractors. School districts may request an augmentation to the basic grant pursuant to Regulation section 1859.83 (a), based on geographic location or regional variations in construction costs.

Small-size projects. This grant is available to school districts with projects that house no more than 200 students. The basic grant can be augmented by 12 percent for projects that house fewer than 101 students, and by 4 percent for projects that house more than 100, but not more than 200 students.

New school projects. This grant is available to districts that build a new school on a site with no existing facilities. Smaller construction projects may not have enough classrooms to generate the appropriate funding for essential school facilities; consequently, pursuant to Regulation section 1859.83(c), districts may qualify for supplemental funding to provide these facilities.

Urban-impacted sites. This supplemental grant is available to new school projects where the usable site acreage for the project is less than 60 percent of the recommended site size per CDE guidelines for the master-planned project capacity. It was originally developed and intended to be available for urban school districts dealing with impacted sites, high property values, and high population density; however, in recent years any new school site meeting minimum site requirements qualified for the basic grant adjustment. The State Allocation Board amended and adopted Regulation section 1859 on January 22, 2003, changing the qualifications. Districts must now meet all of the following conditions:

- The usable acres of the site for the project are 60 percent or less of the CDE recommended site size based on the the existing enrollment at the site, or the existing enrollment, plus the greater of the school building capacity of the DSA approved plans or the pupil grant requested in the new construction project.
- At least 60 percent of the classrooms in the new construction plans are in multi-story facilities for any type of new construction project.
- The value of the site being acquired for the new construction project is at least $750,000 per acre.

to apply for more grants than a project would house, and to provide a method of determining how the cross grade grants could be used. This was called the Use of Grants. OPSC Reg. section 1859.77.2. Initially, districts were limited to applying for grants for no more than 150 percent of the number of students housed in the project using the loading standards established in SB 50. In March 2001, this was further reduced to 135 percent. If a district applies for a project and does not have sufficient eligibility for grants at that grade level configuration (K–6, 7–8, 9–12), it must first use the eligible grants at the grade level of the school, then the available grants at the next lowest grade level, before using a grant from a higher level. This significantly reduces a school district's flexibility in design and its ability to use the grants to compensate for an inadequate level of funding provided in the grants and for the phasing of projects.

To qualify for a Use of Grants, the district was required to submit a housing plan to the CDE indicating how the additional students would be housed. Many districts indicated that they would use either multi-track, year-round education or portable buildings to house the excess students. This was in direct conflict with legislative priorities since the SB 50 provisions and later legislation contained strong policy preferences to reduce the use of MTYRE as a method for housing students and reduce the use of portable classrooms. Unfortunately, the rules the legislation established gave incentives to school districts to take actions in direct contravention of its policy goals. In recognition of this incongruous result, the SAB in December 2002 instituted *a total ban on the use of additional grants* to fund a project, regardless of the housing plan (2 C.C.R. §§ 1859.77.2, 1859.77.3). However, cross grade loading may still be allowed, but only at the state loading standards and under the guidelines previously mentioned. ■

If the conditions are met, the increase shall be:

- **Modernization projects.** Equal to 15 percent of the Modernization grant and 15 percent of the funding provided by the small size project adjustment (Regulation § 1859.83(b)), plus 0.333 percent for each percentage decrease of the CDE recommended site size.
- **New construction projects.** Equal to 15 percent of the new construction grant and 15 percent of the funding provided by the small size project adjustment (Regulation § 1859.83(b)), and the excessive cost to construct a new school project, plus 1.166 percent for each percentage decrease of the CDE recommended site size. For example:

CDE site size	Percentage of new construction	modernization
60	15.0	15.0
50	26.6	18.3
40	38.2	23.6
30	50.0	27.0
20	61.4	30.3
10	73.0	33.6

For districts that qualify for a financial hardship grant, certain special apportionments may be available.

Financial hardship. As stated previously, the grant is approved only after the district has received site approval from the CDE, and the plans and specifications have been reviewed and approved by the DSA. However for districts that qualify for a financial hardship grant, the following are available:

- **Separate design.** Qualifying financial hardship districts may receive a separate apportionment for design costs (40 percent for new construction; 25 percent for modernization), that are intended to allow a district to contract with a design professional to prepare project plans for DSA approval. Once the plans have received DSA approval, the district can request the remaining new construction funding.
- **Separate site.** Qualifying financial hardship districts may receive a separate apportionment for site acquisition, which is intended to allow a district to acquire a site for the project.
- **Separate site—Environmental hardship.** No-financial hardship districts may also receive a separate site apportionment if the DTSC certifies by letter that the time necessary to complete the remediation or removal of hazardous waste on site will exceed 180 days. Under this circumstance the district becomes eligible for a separate apportionment for site acquisition, even though the district does not qualify for financial hardship assistance.

60 Percent Rule

The work contained on the plans must be at least 60 percent of the total project grant.

New construction application for funding. Once the eligibility for a district has been established, and plans and specifications have received agency approval from both the CDE (discussed in chapter 4) and DSA (discussed in chapter 5), the district may apply for funding by submitting a funding package to the OPSC.

The following should be included in the district's request for funding:

- Appraisal of property to be acquired (only if application includes site purchase). Appraisal cannot be older than six months.

- Final escrow closing statement or court order (only if application includes site purchase)
- CDE approval of site (only if application includes site purchase)
- Final DSA Plan and Specifications Approval
- Cost estimate for entire project. (Portions of the project that are not going to be state funded do not need to be included.)
- Detailed cost estimate for site development required if the district is requesting additional grants for new construction funding:
  - Utilities cost estimate
  - Offsite cost estimate—requires local agency jurisdiction sign-off
  - Service site cost estimate
- CDE approval of plans (SFID 4.09)
- SAB 50-04 (OPSC funding application form) that includes information about:
  - Grade level of the project
  - Pupil grants requested
  - Site acquisition
  - Additional or supplemental grants being requested
  - District Certifications regarding:
    - Establishment of restricted maintenance account
    - Contracts for professional services
    - District contribution
  - Architect certifications regarding:
    - Date of DSA review and approval of plans and specs
    - Cost estimate that complies with the OPSC 60 percent rule

Special State Funding Programs

Charter school facilities. As discussed previously, AB 16 (Propositions 47 and 55) created a new $400 million fund for charter schools ($100 million from the 2002 state bond money and an additional $300 million from the 2004 bond). In January 2003, AB 14 (Goldberg) in conjunction with AB 16, added new duties for school districts and charter schools for gaining access to the new state bond fund money. Educ. Code § 17078.50 *et seq.* A new state regulatory agency was added to the layer of oversight as charter schools must seek funding eligibility and certification as a financially sound school from the California Schools Finance Authority, who must in turn coordinate with SAB.

In 2003, three new pieces of legislation created a greater incentive for school districts to provide for and include charter schools in the funding plans: Proposition 39, AB 14 (Goldberg), and AB 16 (Hertzberg). As part of Proposition 39, section 47614 of the Education Code was amended regarding the district's obligations to provide facilities to charter schools. The effective application date of this amendment is either three years after the passage of Proposition 39 (*i.e.*, November 8, 2003), or, if a school district passed a school bond prior to that time, the July 1 following the measures passage.

In 2003, three new pieces of legislation created a greater incentive for school districts to provide for and include charter schools in the funding plans.

In November 2003, each district had to begin providing charter schools with contiguous, furnished, equipped facilities sufficient to accommodate all students attending the charter schools located within the district's boundaries.

Facilities provided should be reasonably equivalent to those for other students in the district, and should be contiguous, furnished, equipped, and remain the school district's property. The district should make a reasonable effort to place the charter school near where it wishes to be, and not move it unnecessarily.

The district may charge the charter school a *pro rata* share based on the ratio of space the school district allocates to the charter school divided by the total space in the district for those facilities costs the school district pays from unrestricted general fund revenues. No charter school should be otherwise charged for the use of its facilities. The district is not required to use unrestricted general fund revenues to rent, buy, or lease facilities for a charter school. Each year the charter school must reasonably project its average daily classroom attendance by in-district students for the following year, and the district must use this projection to allocate facilities. If its average daily attendance is less than predicted, the charter school must reimburse the district for the over-allocated space as specified by regulation. If the projected average daily attendance for an operating charter is less than 80 percent, the district may deny the facilities' request.

In November 2003, each district had to begin providing charter schools with contiguous, furnished, equipped facilities sufficient to accommodate all in-district students. The conditions had to be equivalent to those of other district schools. If a bond election was held before 2003, those obligations also began sooner, and a district may be able to charge the charter school rent.

Since this legislation is relatively new, the SAB and OPSC will be developing emergency regulations to implement its provisions, and school districts should anticipate a state of flux as this evolves. Districts should carefully review their funding plans and eligibility documents with their charter schools. For instance, a school district may claim the entire pupil attendance of a charter school that is physically located within its geographical jurisdiction. Educ. Code § 17070.73. Where coordination is lacking, districts risk losing a percentage of their eligibility to charter schools. Since districts and charter schools sometimes view each other as competitors, coordination may be hard to achieve. For that reason, the SAB is proposing to regulate mediation between the two in funding disputes.

Multi-track year-round educational operation grants. These year-round grants are allocated to school districts that are implementing or planning to implement MTYRE at individual school sites. To qualify, a district must demonstrate substantial district-level overcrowding (5 percent over capacity) in the district or high school attendance areas, as demonstrated by current enrollment, capacity of facilities, and growth projections. The district must also demonstrate substantial school site overcrowding (5 percent over capacity). Lastly, the district must have new construction eligibility in the SFP or it cannot apply for an Operational Grant.

School site level eligibility criteria

- Education Code section 42267 requires school districts participating in the SFP to report the number of pupils enrolled for whom they claim Operational Grant payments. Districts must certify that the number of pupils enrolled at a school site will be housed in excess of traditional or single-track capacity as a result of MTYRE programs.

- The minimum reduction specified at the school site level increases progressively from 5 percent in the first year to 10 percent in the second year and 15 percent in the third and each subsequent year of participation in the Operational Grant program. School sites can exceed these minimums at any time in applying for grant funding. For districts participating in the SFP, these percentages will be used to reduce new construction eligibility whether they are achieved or not. For districts not participating, the immediate practical effect of the progressive reduction of SFP new construction eligibility is inconsequential, although it may affect future participation.

- A school site may certify fewer students than the actual number determined to be in excess of the school facility capacity, but may not fall below a 5 percent school site excess capacity minimum. Conversely, a school site may certify all students in excess of capacity, resulting in a greater reduction in building eligibility.

School site level funding. Based on the percentage of pupils certified in excess of facility capacity and pursuant to Education Code section 42263(c), the district would receive funding according to the table below. The table is subject to SAB calculation (Educ. Code § 42263(d)), annual state legislative action, and state budget language.

Percent of pupils housed in excess of school facility capacity based on loading standards	Percentage of payment based on a cost avoided figure of $1,353	Portion of $1,649 per excess pupil
0 to 4	0	$ 0.00
5 to 9	50	$ 824.50
10 to 14	67	$1,104.83
15 to 19	75	$1,236.75
20 to 24	85	$1,401.65
25+	90	$1,484.10

Many more school districts are participating in the Operational Grant Program since the passage of SB 50 in 1998. Prior to SB 50, school districts were required to reduce their new construction eligibility by the highest number of students applying for Operational Grant Funding in any prior year, which never was decreased; consequently, districts had to contemplate the trade off between actual and anticipated grant funding in current and future years, while assessing the loss of new construction eligibility for applying for such funds. As a result of this, many school districts opted out of the Operational Grant Program because they did not anticipate requesting the same level of grant funding, but would continue to lose the highest level for determination of new construction funding eligibility.

With SB 50 and the SFP, school districts now have the opportunity to jump in and out of the Operational Grant program, and not adversely affect future new construction eligibility. School districts are now required to reduce their new construction eligibility only by the previous year's Operational Grant request, and not the highest request. This significant change in the program has increased the number of school districts participating in the program, and consequently reduced the funding available to school districts requesting Operational Grants.

With SB 50 and the SFP, school districts now have the opportunity to jump in and out of the Operational Grant program, and not adversely affect future new construction eligibility.

If the funding appropriated in the Budget Act of 2002 was insufficient to meet the demand for the 2002–2003 fiscal year, grants would have been proportionately reduced. In recent years, the percentage of allocations has been as follows:

Years	Percentage
1997–1998	96
1998–1999	86
1999–2000	65
2000–2001	35
2001–2002	26
2002–2003	44
2003–2004	23

The chart illustrates the increasing draw on these limited funds. Moreover, districts must reduce their new construction eligibility by the prior year's operational grant request, based on the number applied for, not the number actually funded.

Timeline for the operational grant application process (bi-annually)

September (year 1)	By September of each year, the districts applying for grants must complete and submit the following forms:

- 2003/04 school district enrollment calculation (OP-04)
- 2003/04 operational grant certification (OP-08)
- 2003/04 multi-track year-round school projected enrollment calculation (OP-09)

December (year 1)	CDE begins notification of award level based on available funding.
May (year 2)	CDE mails out Final School Site Certification Excess Capacity Enrollment forms to school districts receiving operational grants.
June (year 2)	School district reports and makes adjustments, if any, to the number of pupils claimed based on enrollment data.

The CDE Operational Grant Forms (OP-04, 08/09) are relatively easy to complete and can be found at the CDE website (www.cde.ca.gov/facilities). The forms include current district enrollment information (OP-04), the number of Operational Grants being requested (OP-08), and the projected MTYRE enrollment (OP-09). These reported enrollment figures are updated prior to June 30 of the following year if enrollment has increased over projections and the district wishes to apply for the higher figures.

Class size reduction. The Class Size Reduction (CSR) Program and the CSR Facilities Funding Program represent the single largest appropriation ever—nearly $1 billion for the initial year for educational reform. California Education Code §§ 52120–52128.5 and 17200–17207. The goal of the K–3 CSR Program is to increase student achievement, particularly in reading and mathematics, by decreasing the size of K–3 classes to 20 or fewer students per certificated teacher. Districts receive $650 for each student in grades K–3 that

CSR = Class size reduction

The CSR Program and the CSR Facilities Funding Program represent the single largest appropriation ever—nearly $1 billion for the initial year for educational reform.

participated in a class of 20 or fewer students (only three grade levels per school could participate in the first year). Districts operating half-day programs for smaller classes received $325 per pupil. In 1997–98, school districts received $800 per pupil for the full day program (Option One); and $400 per pupil for the half-day program (Option Two). In 1999–2000, school districts received $844 per pupil for full day, and $422 per pupil for half day. Unfortunately, due to a severe budget crisis in California, no funding remains for the CSR program. Between 1996–97, $771 million was allocated for operation costs (hiring teachers), and $200 million was allocated for school facilities to districts that implemented CSR. To fully implement CSR, the Program requires an annual allocation of approximately $1.5 billion.

To fully implement Class Size Reduction, the Program requires an annual allocation of approximately $1.5 billion.

Since the CSR Program is a "voluntary" incentive program, the lack of operational money may make it unlikely that districts can continue to offer it, even though political and community pressures at the local level make it extremely difficult for a district to avoid adopting CSR.

State Relocatable Classroom Program. The State Relocatable Classroom Program provides school districts with classroom facilities to house kindergarten through 12th grade enrollment. Since the supply is limited, the state has created a priority system to determine the order in which buildings will be approved for placement. The priority levels for placement are:

- **Facility hardship.** Eligibility based on the district having a SAB approved LPP hardship project, or an SFP facility hardship project, or
- **Standard eligibility.** Eligibility based on the standard eligibility formula using basic teaching station loading standards and a one-year projection for average daily attendance (ADA), as determined by the state's enrollment projection for SAB 50-01, or

  ADA = Average daily attendance

  - The district application for state relocatable classroom(s) may be based on "the number of teaching stations approved (but not yet constructed) pursuant to the SFP"
  - Eligibility based on unhoused community day pupils
  - Eligibility based on the district agreeing to hire an additional teacher for the relocatable classroom
  - Eligibility based on interim housing needs during a modernization project
  - Eligibility based on:
    - Licensed child day care programs; or
    - Recreation and enrichment activity programs for school-age children on a school site

Application process. The district must first establish eligibility and submit a completed SAB 25-1 (Eligibility Worksheet) to OPSC. Additionally, the completed form SAB 50-01 (Enrollment Certification) establishes the one-year enrollment figures to be used in the determination of need. Lastly, the district submits form 25-2 (Application to Lease State Relocatable Classroom(s)), and certifies that it meets the conditions outlined on the form, namely:

- The governing board has passed a resolution supporting the application
- School district has title to the site

- School district will hire an architect and a DSA-approved inspector for the project
- District has completed a feasibility study for implementing district a year-round multi-track educational program
- Annual fee of $4,000 per classroom will be paid to the SAB
- Project meets CEQA requirements
- Classroom will be used for K–12 instruction purposes
- Facility, furniture, and equipment will be maintained at district expense
- Property and liability insurance will be provided at district expense
- Classroom will be connected to a fire alarm system, pursuant to current law

Once a project is SAB-approved, the time limit for delivery applies. The district must submit the completed site and building plans to DSA within 60 days of receiving the manufacturer's building plans from the OPSC, or the building may be reassigned to another district. Additionally, the district must accept delivery of the relocatable classroom(s) within 60 days after the OPSC makes it available, or the building assignment may be reallocated. The documents to submit after SAB approval are SAB 25-3 (Site Readiness Certification), which requires DSA approval of the plans, and district certifications of the building location, availability of the location for placement of building, and the adequacy of drainage. The form SAB 25-4 (Certification for Reimbursement), which entitles the district to reimbursement of $9,450 for a standard classroom, $15,650 for infant preschool facility, or $13,500 for a childcare facility, is also submitted. To the extent that the expenditures exceeded these allowances, the district bears the additional expense.

Making use of a state relocatable building has a few drawbacks—one is that a district may not make any alterations or modifications to the facility without prior written approval by the OPSC.

Making use of a state relocatable building has a few drawbacks, one of which is that a district may not make any alterations or modifications to the facility without prior written approval by the OPSC. Additionally, if the district desires to relocate the building to another campus, it must do so at its own expense, notifying OPSC prior to relocation and obtaining DSA approval for the new site. Lastly, the district is stuck with the building even if it is unused until such a time that the state needs to remove it for delivery to another district. The cost of returning the building will be borne by the state. However, the district is responsible for returning the building in new condition.

District purchase or buyout. Education Code section 17089.2 allows school districts and county superintendents to purchase state relocatable classrooms that were under lease on or prior to December 1, 1991, either by outright purchase or by a nine year interest free installment payment plan. Installment payment minimums are as follows:

- **Year 1** $2,500
- **Year 2** $2,750
- **Years 3–9** $3,000 or until paid off

The actual purchase price is based on the SAB's base purchase price table, reduced by the rental payments made by the district, but the purchase price may never be less than $4,000 per classroom.

School year	Base price	School year	Base price
09/80–08/81	$ 32,500	09/86–08/87	$ 35,500
09/81–08/82	$ 33,000	09/87–08/88	$ 36,000
09/82–08/83	$ 33,500	09/88–08/89	$ 36,500
09/83–08/84	$ 34,000	09/89–08/90	$ 37,000
09/84–08/85	$ 34,500	09/90–08/91	$ 37,500
09/85–08/86	$ 35,000	09/91–12/01/91	$ 38,000

The documentation required to be submitted to OPSC for the buyout are Forms SAB 25-46 (Application to Purchase State Relocatable Classroom(s)) and SAB 25-46A (Application to Purchase State Relocatable Classroom(s) Attachment A). These forms identify the district's intention to purchase the state relocatable classroom(s), their location(s), and the method of payment.

State-deferred maintenance program. The intent of the program is to provide state-matching funds on a dollar-for-dollar basis and to assist districts with expenditures for major repair and replacement of existing school building components. Typically this includes plumbing, heating, air conditioning, electrical systems, roofing, interior and exterior painting, and floor systems.

Application process. In order for a project to be funded under this program, the district must complete a Five Year Plan (Form SAB 40-01) and submit it to OPSC no later than May 30 for the current fiscal year. The plan details the district's schedule to accomplish the major repair or replacement work over a five-year period. This plan must be submitted or be on file with the OPSC for the current fiscal year in which funding is sought. The plan may remain in place for the entire five years or can be amended as needed, but only once per fiscal year, unless an unanticipated emergency project exists.

Additionally, the district must certify that pursuant to Education Code section 17584.1(a), the district's governing board has discussed the proposals and plans for fund expenditures of the deferred maintenance for school district facilities at a regularly scheduled public hearing.

District funding. The SAB approves the plan and proposed projects but does not fund projects on the district's five-year plan. However, a project may not use deferred maintenance dollars unless it is identified on the five-year plan. The maximum state funding allowed is based on a calculation set out in Education Code section 17584(b) and certified to the OPSC by the CDE.

All districts with a current and SAB-approved five-year plan are eligible for a basic apportionment for the Deferred Maintenance Program, which is funded in arrears. Based on the amount of funds available, the district will either receive its full apportionment or a prorated amount. The latter is usually the case, and the apportionment is subject to the district matching the available funding.

No additional forms need to be filed to receive an apportionment. The district must ensure that the funding is used for projects identified on the plan only.

District deposit. The governing board of the district is required to establish a restricted fund designated for the deposit of district and state matching funds. The fund is referred to as the "district deferred maintenance fund."

Annual deposits of district funds are required by the date specified of each fiscal year. All monies deposited into the fund and all interest earned must be used

All districts with a current and SAB-approved five-year plan are eligible for a basic apportionment for the Deferred Maintenance Program.

on the listed project in the SAB approved five year plan. If a district elects not to deposit the maximum amount calculated by the CDE, the district's governing board is required to provide a report to the legislature by the following March 1. The report should contain a schedule of the deferred maintenance needs for the current fiscal year and an explanation of how the district plans on meeting its current need, without depositing the maximum amount as calculated by the CDE.

More often than not, districts receive prorated apportionments, leaving unmatched state funds in the district deferred maintenance fund. A district is allowed under Education Code section 17583 to transfer unmatched state funds to other expenditure classifications in the district. However, if the purpose is for other than deferred maintenance, a school board resolution approving the transfer by a two-thirds vote is required. On the other hand, if the district does not wish to transfer the unmatched state funds, it may carry over the funds to offset some or the entire match required for the subsequent fiscal year.

Criticial hardship funding. Critical hardship applications may be submitted at any time throughout the year, but must be deemed complete by OPSC prior to May 30 and the start of construction in order to be considered for funding for the fiscal year. A critical hardship exists when the SAB determines the existence of all of the following:

* The district has deposited the required basic contribution in its deferred maintenance fund.
* The district has a project on its approved five-year plan that, if not completed in one year, could result in serious damage to the remainder of the facility, or could result in a serious health and safety hazard to the pupils.
* The total funds deposited by the district and the state for the basic apportionment are insufficient to complete the critical hardship project.

The OPSC will perform a site visit to determine if a critical hardship actually exists and if the application should be approved. Once a project has received approval, the following funding requirements apply:

* **First project.** The district is required only to have made its maximum deposit into the deferred maintenance fund.
* **Second project.** The district is required to contribute 50 percent of the cost of the project, or agree to pay its 50 percent share by an offset to future basic apportionments.
* **Third and subsequent projects.** The district is required to contribute a 50 percent cash contribution for each project.

The following is the state's prioritization for critical hardship requests:

* **Priority 1.** Resolution passed by the local school board to close the school or a portion of the school pending repairs. (School closure must happen when school is in session.)
* **Priority 2.** Project involves underground toxic/contaminated tank cleanup and removal, roofing, plumbing (water/sewer), heating/air-conditioning, and electrical.
* **Priority 3.** All other items; *e.g.*, wall systems, floor systems, and paving.

Critical Hardship Application. The district must revise its five-year plan, including the critical hardship project, or provide a copy of the district's current plan identifying the project. The district must also complete the Critical Hardship Application form (SAB 40-5), and provide a detailed cost estimate with unit cost breakdowns for the proposed work. Additionally, the application must include an architect or engineer's report detailing how the project qualifies as a hardship, the recommended solution, and a detailed description of the work to be completed.

Ineligible Critical Hardship expenditures. Enhancements are not allowed with these funds, meaning repairs should be like for like unless prohibited by DSA or by local ordinance. Additional ineligible items are service warranties, equipment rentals, work done on facilities not owned by the district, repairs made to portable buildings that exceed 50 percent of the replacement costs, and cost to abate friable asbestos encountered as a result of construction.

Small high schools. In September 2004, California Governor Arnold Schwarzenegger signed legislation to create incentives and funding for small high schools on a pilot basis. AB 1465: Chapter 04-894; Educ. Code §§ 17070.10, 17070.15, 17070.30, 17070.32, and 17070.99. The new law sets aside $25 million in school construction bonds to create an incentive for school districts to build new small high schools and to reconfigure large high schools into smaller communities of 500 students or less.

Districts seeking to build small high schools on a pilot basis as part of an academic reform strategy focusing on the positive outcomes that small schools encourage are eligible to apply. Beginning January 1, 2006, the SAB is required to adjust the maximum total new construction grant to 120 percent of the standard eligibility for new construction, and lower the match percentage for districts proposing small high schools from 50 to 40 percent, thus increasing the state apportionment share from 50 to 60 percent. For detailed information on application requirements and timelines, districts should consult the OPSC website (www.opsc.dgs.ca.gov). The program sunsets in 2008, and includes a requirement that CDE conduct evaluations of the its effectiveness in improving academic achievement in order to inform the direction of future school facilities funding policies and measures.

Williams settlement: Equity in facility funding for schools with low academic achievement. The 2004 *Williams* case resulted in a landmark Superior Court settlement. *Eliezer Williams et al. v. State of California et al. (Williams)* was filed as a class action suit in 2000 in San Francisco County Superior Court. Plaintiffs include nearly 100 San Francisco County students who filed suit against the State of California and state education agencies. The basis of the lawsuit was that the agencies failed to provide public school students with equal access to instructional materials, safe and decent school facilities, and qualified teachers.

In 2004, the San Francisco Superior Court approved the notice of Governor Schwarzenegger's settlement of the case. A package of legislation adopted in 2004, along with the governor's budget allocations, implements the *Williams* settlement, including issues related to facilities funding, instructional materials, teacher credentialing and assignment monitoring, public reporting in the School Accountability Report Cards, and year-round schools operating on the Concept 6 calendar. In

In September 2004, California Governor Arnold Schwarzenegger signed legislation to create incentives and funding for small high schools on a pilot basis.

API = Academic
Performance Index

the settlement, $138 million in additional funding was allocated for standards-aligned instructional materials for schools in the lowest ranks (first and second ranks—known as deciles), as determined through the 2003 Academic Performance Index (API) Base. The settlement also includes $50 million for implementation costs and other oversight-related activities for schools in deciles one through three (2003 API Base). Another $800 million will be provided for critical repair of facilities in future years for schools in deciles one through three (2003 API Base).

Meanwhile, SB 550 and AB 2727 establish minimum standards and accountability system to enforce those standards, and AB 1550 phases out the Concept 6 multi-track year-round school calendar system into a shorter academic year by 2012.

Pursuant to the Williams *settlement, the County Superintendents have increased responsibilities for school district oversight.*

New duties for County Superintendents. Pursuant to the *Williams* settlement, the County Superintendents have increased responsibilities for school district oversight. Expanding the requirements in Education Code section 1240, every county superintendent must "visit and examine" each school in his or her county at reasonable intervals, and annually must present a report to the governing board of each district, the county board of education, and the board of supervisors in that county describing the "state of the schools" ranked in deciles 1–3 of the 2003 API base. The visits must be conducted at least annually and no less than 25 percent of the visits may be unannounced. The purpose of the visits is to:

- Ensure that students have access to "sufficient" instructional materials
- Assess compliance with facilities maintenance to determine the condition of a facility that "poses an emergency or urgent threat to the health or safety of pupils or staff"
- Determine if the school has provided accurate data for the annual school accountability report card related to instructional materials and facilities maintenance

New duties for districts. Each district or county office must post a notice or summary of the *Williams* settlement requirements in its main office and on its web site, which must also link to the CDE web site (**www.cde.ca.gov**) and publish CDE's toll-free number (1-877-532-2533).

With respect to the facilities issues, the class of inadequate facilities in the notice includes:

[I]nadequate, unsafe and unhealthful school facilities such that (1) the student attends classes in one or more rooms in which the temperature falls outside the 65–80 degrees Fahrenheit range; or (2) the student attends classes in one or more rooms in which the ambient or external noise levels regularly impede verbal communication between students and teachers; or (3) there are insufficient numbers of clean, stocked and functioning toilets and bathrooms; or (4) there are unsanitary and unhealthful conditions, including the presence of vermin, mildew or rotting organic material;

overcrowded schools such that (1) the student is subject to a year-round, multi- track schedule that provides for fewer days of annual instruction than schools on a traditional calendar provide; or (2) the student is bused excessive distances from his or her neighborhood school; or (3) the student attends classes in one or more rooms that are so overcrowded that there are insufficient seats for each enrolled student to have his or her own seat or where the average square footage per student is less than 25 square feet.

CDE Notice of Class Action Settlement (www.cde.ca.gov/eo/ce/wc/notice english.asp)

As part of the school accountability report card, school districts and county offices of education are required to make specified assessments of school conditions including the safety, cleanliness, and adequacy of school facilities and needed maintenance to ensure good repair. In addition, each school district or county office of education participating in the School Facility Program or the Deferred Maintenance Program is required to develop a school facility inspection system to ensure facilities are kept in good repair. Good repair is defined to mean that the facility is maintained in a manner that ensures that it is clean, safe, and functional as determined pursuant to an " interim evaluation instrument" developed by the Office of Public School Construction pursuant to section 17002(d)(1) of the Education Code. This tool is intended to assist school districts and county offices of education in that determination. It is available on-line at the OPSC website (www.opsc.dgs.ca.gov).

In addition, section 35186 of the Education Code requires that districts use a Uniform Complaint Procedure. CDE has provided a sample form on its web site. Sections 1859.300 through 1859.329 of the OPSC regulations and SAB Forms 61-01, 61-02, and 61-03 govern the new district's compliance with the School Facilities Needs Assessment Grant Program and Emergency Repair Program Regulations. Since regulations, forms, and guidelines to implement the settlement are new, in development, and in flux, districts with schools in the bottom three deciles of academic achievement should closely monitor the OPSC and CDE web site.

Local Bonds

School district debt financing. Debt financing converts expected future income—tax receipts, rental income, state and federal grants, and other sources—into available income, with the agreement to repay the financing mechanism over time with interest. Essentially, the school district issues debt in the form of a bond. Investors then make a loan to the district by purchasing their bonds—that generate tax-exempt interest income for the investors. School districts use debt financing to acquire land, construct new buildings, improve existing ones, install improvements and facilities, and acquire equipment. Debt financing can also be employed to provide school districts with working capital.

Debt financing converts future income—tax receipts, rental income, state and federal grants, and other sources—into available income, with the agreement to repay the financing mechanism over time with interest.

A number of techniques are used for debt financing, and the ones used are generally determined by the school district's need. For example, working capital may only be financed through tax and revenue anticipation notes. However, in most instances, more than one technique can be used to achieve the desired debt financing.

The four most commonly used debt-financing techniques for school districts are:

- General obligation bonds
- Mello-Roos special tax bonds (Mello-Roos bonds)

✒ practice tip

The agency issuing a G.O. bond can levy an *ad valorem* property tax at the rate necessary to repay the principal and interest of the bond. Property tax used to repay a G.O. bond issue is not subject to the usual *ad valorem* limitations based on property tax rates; however, special overall limitations exist to avoid excessive G.O. debt:

- A city has a maximum G.O. debt limit of 15 percent of the assessed valuation of all property within its boundaries

- A county has a maximum G.O. debt limit of 5 percent of assessed valuation

- A unified school district has a maximum G.O. debt limit of 2.5 percent of assessed valuation

- Elementary and high school districts have a maximum G.O. debt limit of 1.25 percent of assessed valuation

What Is a General Obligation Bond?

A G.O. bond is an instrument used by cities, counties, and school districts to finance acquisition and construction of public facilities and land.

- Lease-financing (Certificates of Participation (COPs))
- Tax and revenue anticipation notes (TRANs)

The selection and implementation of one or more debt-financing mechanisms for public school districts must be approved by the Board.

General obligation bonds. In June 1986, California voters approved Proposition 46, a constitutional amendment that restored the authority to issue general obligation bonds to counties, cities, and school districts. General obligation bonds, also called G.O. bonds, are backed by the full faith and credit of the issuing agency and are paid for by increasing local property taxes above the limit imposed by Proposition 13. Because they involve an increase in property taxes, they require voter approval.

The California Constitution and the Education Code authorize school districts to issue general obligation bonds for capital outlay purposes. Cal. Const., Art. XIII, section 1(b); Art. XVI, section 18; Educ. Code § 15100 *et seq.* These bonds can include the purchase of property, construction on that property, the purchase of existing school sites and/or buildings, the improvement of current school sites and/or buildings; and costs associated with bond issuance and management. They may be used to finance land acquisition, construction or acquisition of school buildings and facilities, the expansion, restoration, remodeling, or improvement of school facilities, and the permanent improvement of school grounds. They cannot be used to finance operation or maintenance expenses. Nor can they be used for acquisition of furnishings, vehicles, or equipment (unless the equipment is affixed to real property and is treated as real property for legal purposes).

Traditionally, local general obligation bond elections require two-thirds voter approval for passage. As a result of the passage of Prop. 39 in November 2000, school districts now have the opportunity to seek local G.O. bonds with a 55 percent voter approval. The alternate 55 percent vote G.O. bond does not replace existing law that provides for the issuance of general obligation bonds approved by a two-thirds vote, but it allows the governing board to make a choice between the existing and new procedures at the time it calls the election. A school board may only proceed under the 55 percent election process upon a two-thirds vote of the board members. Once a board decides to utilize the 55 percent bond option, it may not subsequently opt out of that procedure, even if the proposition ultimately obtains two-thirds voter approval. This lower voter approval authorization comes with several conditions of use.

The repayment of general obligation bonds are secured by an *ad valorem* tax on all taxable property within the school district's boundary. The charge on the property tax bill will continue until the bonds have been paid off in full. This is one of the main reasons they are seen as a safe alternative funding source for school facilities. As long as the tax rate is set properly, the repayment of the principal and interest should have no burden on the school district funds because the *ad valorem* tax creates a new revenue stream.

If a district successfully passes a G.O. Bond, it will be necessary to establish two funds. One is a bond interest and redemption fund for the collection of taxes and the subsequent payment of the principal and interest. The second is a building fund for the receipt of the sale of bonds and the related capital outlay expenditures. These are established in cooperation with both the County Office of Education and the county auditor-tax collector.

Of all the financing techniques available, G.O. bonds provide the lowest borrowing cost to school districts because investors consider them minimal risk. These bonds are repaid with revenues from increased property taxes. They may be used to finance land acquisition, construction or acquisition of school buildings and facilities, the expansion, restoration, remodeling, or improvement of school facilities, and the permanent improvement of school grounds. They cannot be used to finance operation or maintenance expenses. Acquisition of furnishings, vehicles, or equipment (unless the equipment is affixed to real property and is treated as real property for legal purposes), is not permitted under the two-thirds vote option, but may be funded with Prop. 39 (55 percent) bond proceeds.

Of all the financing techniques available, G.O. bonds provide the lowest borrowing cost to school districts because investors consider them minimal risk.

School Facilities Improvement District. The School Facilities Improvement District Law (SFID Law) (Educ. Code § 15300 *et seq.*) provides a method for school districts to issue G.O. bonds for a portion of rather than the entire district.

SFID = School Facilities Improvement District

Once an SFID is formed, the governing board of the school district, acting as the governing board of the SFID, may call for a special election or submit the G.O. bond proposition at the next statewide general election.

Within the newly formed improvement district, a bond election can be held and, if approved by either a two-thirds or 55 percent (pursuant to Prop. 39) of those voting, the general obligation bonds may be issued by the county on behalf of the improvement district. The law governing SFID G.O. bonds is nearly identical to the statutes governing school district G.O. bonds. Educ. Code § 15300 *et seq.*

Traditional two-thirds vote G.O. bonds. At the time it decides to call an election, a district must decide whether it will hold a traditional G.O. bond election that requires a two-thirds vote or a new Prop. 39 G.O. bond election that requires a 55 percent vote. The procedures for the two types of G.O. bonds are quite different. Before the district makes its selection, it should consider the likelihood of attaining a two-thirds majority. When it determines to hold a two-thirds vote G.O. bond election, the school district orders county superintendent of schools to call an election. Permissible election dates are any Tuesday during the year except the day before, day after, or day of a state or federal holiday. An election notice must be posted in every school and in three public places within the school district. The county registrar of voters must submit to each registered voter a sample ballot, a voter's pamphlet containing the bond measure text, the tax rates projection required to repay the G.O. bonds, a county counsel legal analysis, and, if submitted, arguments for and against the G.O. bonds. If the bond receives approval from at least two-thirds of the votes, then the school board adopts a resolution and requests the county board of supervisors to sell and issue all or a portion of the authorized amount of the G.O. bond. The board of supervisors then adopts a resolution authorizing the issuance and sale of the school district G.O. bonds, which may be sold at a competitive or negotiated sale.

A district must decide whether it will hold a traditional G.O. bond election requiring a two-thirds vote or a new Prop. 39 G.O. bond election requiring 55 percent.

Prop. 39—55 percent vote G.O. bonds. In contrast to this relatively simple procedure, there are many steps and procedures to take advantage of the lower 55 percent vote G.O. bond authorized by Prop. 39. In addition, due to its

Ad Valorem Tax

The term *ad valorem* is Latin for "according to value." An *ad valorem* tax is based on the assessed value of real estate or personal property. It can be a property tax or even duty on imported items. *Ad valorem* tax is often used interchangeably with property tax. Property *ad valorem* taxes are the major source of revenues for state and municipal governments.

For districts that have not been able to gain support from two-thirds of the voters, the 55 percent vote G.O. bond procedure may enable them to pass a bond successfully.

newness, there is some uncertainty regarding the scope of its requirements (*e.g.*, the duties of the bond oversight committee).

The total amount of outstanding and new G.O. bond debt to be issued may not exceed 2.5 percent of the assessed value of taxable property within a unified school district; the limit for other school districts is 1.25 percent. The assessed value is determined *only* at the time of issuance; subsequent changes in assessed value are not relevant.

In anticipation of G.O. bond financing, there is no statutory authority for districts to issue notes for interim construction financing, and they are not permitted to use G.O. bond proceeds to finance bond interest during the construction period.

G.O. bonds must be sold and issued sufficiently early in the fiscal year (usually no later than mid-August), in order for the county auditor-controller to calculate the required property taxes for the coming year. The maximum interest rate allowed by law on G.O. bonds is 12 percent per year. G.O. bonds typically mature no later than 25 years from the date of the bonds, however, the Education Code does allow issuance of 40-year-term G.O. bonds. In many cases, the full 25 years may not be available: for example, the final maturity date for G.O. Bonds dated January 1, 2002 and fixed to mature on July 1 of each year may be no later than July 1, 2026—or 24.5 instead of 25 years after their date.

Advantages of the 55 percent vote G.O. bond. The most obvious advantage of Prop. 39 G.O. bonds is reduction in the voter approval threshold. For districts that have not been able to gain support from two-thirds of the voters, this procedure may enable them to pass a bond successfully. The second main advantage is the broader scope of expenses covered. Specifically, Prop. 39 permits the financing of furnishing and equipping of school facilities. Under the two-thirds vote G.O. bond, furnishings or equipment are covered only when attached or fixed and they can be characterized as improvements to real property.

Disadvantages of the 55 percent vote G.O. bond

Fewer and infrequent election dates. A Prop. 39 bond election is limited to statewide primary or general elections (March and November of even-numbered years, respectively) or a regularly scheduled local or statewide special election.

In contrast, under the two-thirds vote traditional G.O. bond, an election may be held on any Tuesday during the year except the day before, day after, or day of a state holiday.

Authorized facilities list. Under Proposition 39, the board is required to establish a list of specific school facilities projected to be funded (the "authorized facilities list"), and certify that the board has evaluated safety, class size reduction, and information technology needs in developing the authorized facilities list. This requirement to disclose the facility for which the bond proceeds will be spent does not require that only those projects that promote the safety, class size reduction, or information technology needs be funded.

The 55 percent bond measure must contain the specific project list, certified by the board after an evaluation of safety, class size reduction, and information technology needs. This list becomes part of the measure, and is essentially cast in stone by a successful 55 percent vote. Thus, careful drafting is critical to ensure the ability to deal with escalating project costs or changing priorities. Too much flexibility may make a bond measure unconstitutional from the start—such as reserving the right to substitute or add projects or to spend leftover money on projects not on the list.

Limit on the authorized bonded indebtedness under the 55 percent vote procedures. The total amount for bonds that may be issued under both the traditional two-thirds vote G.O. bond and the Prop. 39 55 percent vote G.O. bond shall not exceed 1.25 percent of the taxable property of the applicable elementary or high school district or 2.5 percent of the taxable property of the applicable unified school district. However, under the Prop. 39 G.O. bond, the bonds may only be issued if the tax rate levied to pay debt service would not exceed $30 per $100,000 of taxable property of the applicable elementary or high school district, $60 per $100,000 of taxable property of the applicable unified school district, or $25 per $100,000 of taxable property of the applicable community college district, when the school district projects assessed valuation to increase in accordance with Article XIIIA of the California Constitution. The practical effect of this limitation is to reduce the maximum potential bond authorization by approximately 50 percent.

New accounting and audit requirements. With a Prop. 39 G.O. bond, a district's board must conduct an annual independent performance audit to ensure that funds have been expended only on specific projects on the authorized facilities list. It must also conduct an annual independent financial audit of the proceeds from the sale of the bonds until all of the proceeds have been expended.

Bond oversight committee. The board is required to appoint an independent citizen's oversight committee within 60 days of the date that the governing board certifies the results of the election. Educ. Code § 15278(a). With a two-thirds G.O. bond there is no legal requirement to appoint a bond oversight committee to monitor the expenditures, but some districts choose to anyway.

The bond oversight committee must consist of at least seven members, including one representative of a taxpayers' association, a representative of a senior citizens' organization, one parent or guardian of a child enrolled in the school district, and one member who is a parent or guardian of a child enrolled in the school district and is active in a parent-teacher organization. It may not include any school district employee or official, vendor, contractor, or consultant.

The purpose of the bond oversight committee is to inform the public about bond proceeds expenditures, and to alert the public to waste or improper spending. It is obliged to advise the public as to whether the school district is in compliance with the requirements of Article XIIIA, Section 1(b)(3), and to issue annual reports. The district's board is required to provide technical administrative assistance and sufficient resources to the committee to publicize its conclusions in a report and on the district's website, even though those expenses are not covered by bond funds. Educ. Code § 15280(b).

Bond oversight committee meetings must be open to the public and held in accordance with the Brown Act, which governs open meetings for local government bodies. Govt. Code § 54950 *et seq.*

The bond oversight committee must ensure that bond funds are spent as proposed on the ballot, and none are spent on school district salaries or operating

The purpose of the bond oversight committee is to inform the public about bond proceeds expenditures, and to alert the public to waste or improper spending.

expenses. The committee can also file a court appeal to stop expenditures and halt construction projects if it believes funds are being improperly spent.

It is the responsibility of the school district or community college board to order annual performance and financial audits of the bond funds, and to provide the information to the bond oversight committee.

Litigation risk. Proposition 39 creates a new form of legal action that may be brought by a citizen against the school district.

A citizen residing in a school district who is assessed and liable to pay an *ad valorem* tax on real property within the district, or who has paid such a tax within one year before the commencement of an action, may bring a "School Bond Waste Prevention Action" to obtain an order restraining and preventing an expenditure of bond proceeds by the school district that were authorized by the 55 percent vote procedure. Educ. Code § 15284. In order to prevail, the action must show that:

- The expenditure is not in compliance with the law, or
- An expenditure will produce waste or great irreparable injury, or
- The governing board of the school district has willfully failed to appoint an oversight committee

In contrast, there is no such cause of action for bonds passed under the traditional two-thirds vote process. If successful, the citizen is eligible for an award of attorney's fees from the court.

Proposition 39 also states that upon receipt of allegations of waste or misuse of bond funds, appropriate law enforcement officials shall expeditiously pursue the investigation and prosecution of the violation. Thus, a citizen or the district attorney can serve as the enforcing authority.

G.O. bonds—Advantages and disadvantages. G.O. bonds offer many advantages to districts over other forms of debt financing. They are relatively secure and simple in structure and they require minimal school district staff time compared to other financing methods.

However, the total amount of capital that can be generated is limited by the statutory debt limits of 1.25 and 2.5 percent (for unified school districts). The election requirements impose a long delay between initiation of proceedings and the school district's receipt of bond proceeds. The two-thirds vote can only

Table 2-3. General Obligation Bonds	
Two-thirds vote G.O. bond	**55 percent vote G.O. bond**
two-thirds vote	55 percent vote
real property	real property and furnishings and equipment
more flexibility	"authorized facilities list" only
elections any Tuesday (except day before, during, and after holidays)	elections in March or November of even-numbered years
1.25 / 2.5 percent debt limits	bond oversight committee
	authority requirements
	litigation risks

be used to finance real property acquisition and improvements. And, unlike the Mello-Roos Bond financing technique, there is no flexibility in establishing the tax formula—the tax must be levied based on a uniform percentage of the assessed value of each parcel within the school district.

Mello-Roos Community Facilities Districts

The Mello-Roos Community Facilities District Act (Govt. Code § 53311 *et seq.*) allows school districts to form a Mello-Roos Community Facilities District to issue bonds to acquire school sites and construct school facilities. The repayment of these bonds is secured by a special tax within the boundaries of a Mello-Roos Community Facilities District, where property owners are assessed a special tax to finance specific improvements within that district. Mello-Roos special taxes must be approved by two-thirds of the voters within the proposed CFD or, when the district has fewer than 12 property owners, by a majority vote of the owners. Property owner elections may be held by mailed ballot when approved by the county registrar of voters. Proceeds from a Mello-Roos tax can be used to directly fund improvements such as new schools and also, if bonds have been issued, to pay debt service on those bonds.

The main advantage of the Mello-Roos Community Facilities District Act over other financing is that it allows a school district to establish a financing district that does not include all the land within its boundaries. The boundaries can be any size—the whole school district, the area around a single school site, or a combination of inclusions and exclusions so that certain areas within the Mello-Roos district are not included in the tax base. This means that newly developing areas, where demand for additional school facilities is greatest, can be isolated from those parts of the district in which facilities are adequate or where demand is otherwise low. The more successful Mello-Roos elections have been those that create a Mello-Roos district that is undeveloped but may be developed quickly. In these "bare-land" Mello-Roos elections, the landowners and developers hold the votes, and generally want school construction.

Mello-Roos Community Facilities Districts are a separate legal entity from the school district's governing board, and the accounting should not be co-mingled with the district's activities.

The use of Mello-Roos taxes for seismic safety improvements is subject to certain limitations. First, only that work certified by local building officials as necessary to meet seismic safety regulations can be financed. Second, no dismantling of an existing building or construction of any new or substantially new building can be financed. Third, if improvements to private buildings are to be financed, the CFD must have unanimous approval of the affected land owners. Fourth, work on private buildings is limited to those that need seismic safety retrofitting or were destroyed by the October 17, 1989 Loma Prieta earthquake.

In addition, within the counties declared disaster areas as a result of the Loma Prieta quake, a CFD may be formed to pay for any work needed to rebuild, repair, or replace public or private buildings damaged or destroyed in that quake. Work financed under this provision of Government Code section

Case Study I

The Rocklin Unified School District used the case study method in February 1989 when it created a 4,454-acre Mello-Roos district to fund school construction in a rural area slated for rapid development. This taxing district will help finance six new K–6 schools and cost future homeowners up to $400 per year. ■

Case Study II

Sacramento County's Elk Grove Unified School District made good use of the Mello-Roos Act case study method when faced with neighborhood opposition to its proposed special tax and school bonds.

After its first attempt to form a Mello-Roos CFD failed narrowly, Elk Grove redrew the boundaries of the proposed financing district to eliminate mobile home parks where citizens tended to be elderly and generally in opposition to the special tax. On its second attempt, the Mello-Roos district and its maximum bond issue limit of $70 million were successfully ratified. Proceeds of the CFD are to be used in conjunction with developer fees and state funds to meet the district's planned facility needs. ■

Source: Constantine Baranoff, Elk Grove Unified School District

Ad Valorem Tax vs. Mello-Roos Special Tax

The annual Mello-Roos levy, collected through the county property tax bill, is an amount determined by lot size or square footage of the home and its nexus to new school facilities needs. Unlike the basic property tax, it is not an *ad valorem* tax. For example, in one community it might be $840 per year for a standard lot and $1,200 per year for an oversized or premium lot.

53313.5(h) is limited to those buildings that have been specifically identified in the resolution of intention to establish the CFD. The resolution must have been adopted before October 17, 1994.

A Mello-Roos tax can pay for the planning and design work directly related to improvements being financed. Mello-Roos proceeds may also pay fixed special assessment liens or repay indebtedness secured by a tax, fee, charge, or assessment levied within the CFD. Govt. Code § 53313.5.

A Mello-Roos CFD may also fund the following services on a pay-as-you-go basis:

- Police protection (including the provision of jails and detention facilities)
- Fire protection and suppression
- Ambulance and paramedics
- Flood protection
- Recreation program, library services, and additional funds for the operation and maintenance of parks, parkways, open space, museums, and cultural facilities (this final service cannot be approved through a landowner election), and
- Removal or remedial action for cleanup of any hazardous substance.

Govt. Code § 53313

A CFD tax approved by landowners' vote (*i.e.*, when there are fewer than 12 registered voters in the proposed district) can only finance the above services when they are in addition to services already provided to the area before the district was formed. Govt. Code § 53313.

Bonds may be issued to finance infrastructure (but not services) under the Mello-Roos Act, with debt service paid from the proceeds of the district. However, in order to avoid defaults, the legislative body must determine before the sale of bonds that the value of the real property subject to the special tax will be at least three times the total principal amount of the bonds to be sold and the principal amount of all other outstanding bonds within the CFD boundaries. This rule and exceptions to it may be found in Government Code section 53345.8.

Issuing bonds secured by the proceeds of the CFD has become quite popular, because they provide an immediate source of cash that can be repaid over time. Refer to Government Code section 53345 for the procedure for issuing bonds. As with all special taxes, Mello-Roos taxes are subject to reduction or repeal by initiative.

Proposition 218 does not specify whether the qualifying signatures for an initiative must be gathered jurisdiction-wide and the question put to jurisdiction-wide vote, or whether the initiative is limited to that portion of the jurisdiction within the boundaries of the CFD.

Legal issues related to special taxes. School districts may impose special taxes in the same manner as counties and cities, provided that the tax applies uniformly to all taxpayers or all real property within the district. This rule of uniformity contains an exception allowing taxpayers 65 years of age or older to be exempted from this kind of special tax. Under the provisions of Government Code section 50079, "qualified special taxes" (also called parcel taxes) may only be imposed when two-thirds of the school district's voters approve the proposal.

Under Prop. 218, a school district is a "special district" for purposes of defining the type of tax it may impose and the voting requirements for that tax. Under Article XIIIC of the California Constitution, a district "shall have no power to levy general taxes." Any such tax, even if placed into the school district's general fund, is considered a "special tax" that cannot be imposed, extended, or increased without approval of two-thirds of the district's voters.

According to information compiled by the School Service of California and Cal-Tax, 63 special tax elections for schools were held during the period between 1983 and April 1988 with one in three approved. Taxes proposed since that time have fared similarly.

California Building Industry Association v. Newhall School District (1988) 206 Cal. App. 3d 212, illustrates how careful school districts must be when creating a special tax. In overturning alleged special taxes in five Santa Clarita Valley school districts, the Court of Appeal concluded that they were not special taxes because: (1) they applied solely to developers rather than uniformly to all taxpayers or landowners in the district; (2) they could be characterized as a development fee because they did not exceed the cost of contemplated school facilities and were imposed solely on those who were seeking to develop land; and, (3) at that time, school districts had no specific legislative authorization to levy special taxes (this has since been rectified by Government Code section 50079). Furthermore, the court held that because the exaction exceeded the limits imposed on development fees by Government Code section 65995, it was not valid as a development fee either.

Grupe Development Co. v. Superior Court (1993) 4 Cal. 4th 911, ruled out the use of special taxes in districts that have levied full developer fees. In overturning a special tax levied by the Chino Unified School District, the state Supreme Court concluded that Government Code section 65995 preempts all school district authorities to levy special taxes for school construction if the taxes would cause the district to exceed the fee cap stipulated in the code, even though special taxes, except for Mello-Roos taxes, are not explicitly mentioned in the code. The decision was based on the language of section 65995, which placed a cap on fees of $1.50 per square foot of accessible space in residential dwellings. While exempting Mello-Roos taxes from this limit, the court concluded that, as a matter of statutory construction, the explicit exemption of Mello-Roos special taxes indicated that the cap applied to all other special taxes. The court held that the intent of the legislature was to strike a balance between the need for adequate school facilities and affordable housing. The court said "It would manifestly upset that balance to construe section 65995 to allow school districts to collect—as the District does here—special taxes to offset development costs in addition to the maximum amount authorized" under the code.

Lease Financing

Lease financing is becoming a popular alternative to outright purchase or issuing bonds to finance capital assets over a period of several years. It provides a

Between 1983 and April 1988, 63 special tax elections for schools were held, with one in three approved. Taxes proposed since that time have fared similarly.

good alternative to general obligation debt because it enables school districts to finance capital assets over a multi-year period without voter approval.

Tax-exempt lease financing uses one of the following arrangements:

- Direct lease
- Certificates of participation
- Lease revenue bonds

Direct lease. The direct lease method is most often used to finance the acquisition of equipment or relocatable classroom buildings. A school district will lease property from the lender, which may be the vendor of the property, a leasing company, or a bank. When the lease term expires, the title to the property is transferred to the school district. Since the interest is paid by a school district (part of the payment is designated as "interest"), the interest may qualify as tax-exempt income to the lender. The vendor, leasing company or bank may then transfer its interest in the lease to another party.

Certificates of participation. One of the easiest, but most fiscally dangerous, forms of creative financing is certificates of participation. The main problem is that COPs have no guaranteed payment source. The general fund can too easily become the final victim in poorly planned COPs. Even financial planners with the best of intentions have come up short on the "guaranteed income," such as developer fee revenues, originally offered to satisfy the issuance of the certificate.

Certificates of participation are not specifically authorized in the Education or Taxation Codes, nor do they require an election. They are merely a funding tool to enable school districts to lease or lease-purchase various capital outlay items.

The COPs method requires a school district to lease the property being acquired from a third-party lessor, usually a nonprofit corporation or joint powers agency. Lease payments made by the school district to the third-party lessor are assigned to the lender (the COPs owners) to repay the debt. Each COPs owner is entitled to a proportionate amount of the lease payments made by the school district, and the COPs represent this entitlement. As in direct lease financing, a portion of each payment is designated as interest and the owners of the COPs may receive tax-exempt interest payments. Similar to bonds, COPs are sold to investors.

What are COPs?

- COPs are receipts confirming ownership of a share in the school district lease. The lease is the school district obligation, and its payment generates tax-exempt interest. COPs have no independent legal existence or significance.
- COPs do not alter the character of the school district lease, which is basically the same in each of the three lease-financing structures.
- Because COPs are not part of a statute, they are not subject to statutory requirements that may affect debt obligation, including interest rate limitations, election restrictions, and other statutory limitations on bonds.

The most important item to keep in mind is that COPs have no guaranteed funding source for their repayment, as do bonds and Mello-Roos funds. Many districts might anticipate collecting enough developer fees or special agreement revenues to cover long-term COPs debt, but the actual debt is applicable to the school district's general fund should all other repayment sources dry up. This potential liability should be recognized as part of a budgetary contingency.

If it is still a participant in the LPP, a district must obtain a subordination of the state's lien before the COPs can be sold. This requirement, however, will only apply to districts participating under the SB 1795 Joint Use Program, which falls under the provisions of the Lease Purchase Program. All others fall under the provisions of the Lease Purchase Program. All other state-funded programs are subject to the School Facilities Program.

In order to realize cost savings and reduction in school district staff, pooled financing combines debt issuance by multiple borrowers into single financing. The pooling is achieved either by having a single issuer loan the proceeds of its bonds ("pool bonds") to multiple borrowers or by issuing COPs ("pool COPs"). The repayment of the pool bonds or the pool COPs is dependent on the repayment by each of the multiple borrowers, and can be rated only by the credit status of the weakest of the multiple borrowers. To overcome this challenge, pooled financing is unrated or includes credit enhancement in the form of a letter of credit or bond insurance. The credit enhancement device can secure either the pool bonds or the pool COPs, or the individual obligations of each of the multiple borrowers.

Lease revenue bonds. Lease revenue bonds are issued by a joint powers authority or nonprofit corporation that meets certain federal tax law qualifications for the issuance of tax-exempt bonds (commonly known as a "63–20 corporation" after the original U.S. Treasury Revenue Ruling in which such qualifications are described—*see* Rev. Proc. 82-86). In lease revenue bond financing, the bond proceeds are used to finance the school district project. The bonds are secured by and payable solely from lease payments made by the school district to the joint powers authority or 63-20 corporation. In contrast to the direct lease and COP structures, the lease payments in a lease revenue bond structure need not contain a designated interest component—the tax-exempt obligations are the bonds themselves.

Lease revenue bonds may be issued by a nonprofit corporation under the Nonprofit Public Benefit Corporation Law (Corp. Code § 5110 *et seq.*) and the Public Leaseback Act (Govt. Code § 54240 *et seq.*), a parking authority created under the Parking Law of 1949 (Streets & Highways Code § 32500 *et seq.*), a redevelopment agency (Health & Safety Code § 33000 *et seq.*), or a joint powers authority under the Joint Exercise of Powers Act (Govt. Code § 6500 *et seq.*). In general, lease revenue bonds may be more expensive to issue than general obligation bonds, but their advantage includes the lack of a public vote requirement.

Article XVI, Section 18 of the California Constitution states that a school district may not incur any indebtedness (that it cannot repay in the year incurred) without approval by two-thirds of the electorate voting on the matter at an election held for that purpose. In lease financing, however, the district's obligations under the lease are designated to avoid classification as indebtedness for purposes of this constitutional restriction. This is usually accomplished in the following ways:

- Using a long-term lease containing a rental abatement provision. Under a long-term lease, the payment is contingent upon the school district's having use and occupancy of the premises during the period for which the lease payment is due. The district's obligation to make lease payments is abated,

Lease revenue bonds are issued by a joint powers authority or nonprofit corporation that meets certain federal tax law qualifications for the issuance of tax-exempt bonds.

or reduced, during any period in which the school district does not have full beneficial use and occupancy of the property. These are often referred to as "Offner-Dean" leases, after two leading California court cases holding that such leases do not constitute debt for California Constitutional purposes. In order for lease payments to remain contingent, as the courts require, Offner-Dean leases must not provide for the acceleration of lease payments upon the lessee's default, and should not have a lease term that extends beyond the anticipated useful life of the property.

- **Annual appropriation lease.** Under this lease the school district is obligated only for payments due in the then current fiscal year. The school district has the right, at least once during each fiscal year, to unilaterally terminate the lease by not appropriating the lease payments for the following year. Annual appropriation obligations may be structured as leases, installment sale agreements, or lease-purchase agreements, and still avoid the constitutional debt limit.

Tax and Revenue Anticipation Notes

Tax and Revenue Anticipation Notes are short-term obligations (approximately one year) a district issues to provide immediate funding for cash flow deficits. Unlike a G.O. Bond or Mello-Roos CFD, no new revenue stream is created. Pooling the TRANs issued by several school districts offers each one simple, cost-effective market access, even for relatively small notes. The most popular TRANs program in California is sponsored by the California School Boards Association, which acquires TRANs from several school districts simultaneously at the beginning of July, resulting in pool bonds being issued in the pool of TRANs required.

Special Assessments

The Landscaping and Lighting Act of 1972 authorizes a school district to levy assessments for maintenance of an auditorium, meeting room, gym, stadium, recreation facilities, and civic center for the surrounding community.

Under the Landscaping and Lighting Act of 1972, school districts are authorized to levy assessments to pay for the maintenance of school auditoriums, meeting rooms, gyms, stadiums, recreation facilities, and civic centers for the surrounding community. *Howard Jarvis Taxpayers Association v. Whittier Union School District* (1993) 15 Cal. App. 4th 730.

The court held that a school district is a special district for purposes of the 1972 Act. In addition, the levy of this special assessment by the districts does not violate the *Serrano* principle, which limits the imposition of *ad valorem* property taxes that make the quality of educational opportunity dependent upon the wealth of the school district's property owners. The assessment is not based on property value, but rather on the relative degree of benefit that a parcel derives from the community facilities provided by the school.

In this case, the assessments were not levied for educational purposes (which was not approved by the court), but to finance recreational improvements to benefit the community. The districts demonstrated this by limiting their assessments to that portion of the facility used for community activities.

This case does not offer carte blanche to school districts for the use of the Landscaping and Lighting Act. It does illustrate that a carefully designed assessment, limited strictly to financing those community facilities that the school provides, may offer an alternative financing method.

These assessments are subject to the voting requirements and are limited by Prop. 218 to properties that can be shown to derive a "special benefit" from the assessment. Proposition 218 raises a substantial hurdle for districts that wish to use the Landscaping and Lighting Act.

The fee nexus and accounting requirements of the Mitigation Fee Act (Govt. Code § 66000 *et seq.*) apply to all school district exactions. The court in *Shapell Industries v. Governing Board of the Milpitas Unified School District* (1991) 1 Cal. App. 4th 218, holding that the developer is responsible only for that share of school need caused by new development, set forth a three-part method for determining fees. First, since the fee is to be assessed per square foot of development, there must be a projection of the total amount of new housing expected to be built within the district. Second, in order to measure the extent of the burden new development imposes on schools, the district must determine approximately how many students the new housing will generate. And finally, the district must estimate the cost of providing the necessary school facilities for that approximate number of new students. However, the *Loyola Marymount* court held that the higher scrutiny of the two-part *Nollan/Dolan* test does not apply to school fees.

The fee cap established under these laws is the total amount of fees that may be levied for school facilities. Govt. Code § 65995. This includes fees intended to mitigate an environmental effect under the California Environmental Quality Act (CEQA). Govt. Code § 65996. The fee cap does not apply to special taxes imposed under the Mello-Roos Community Facilities Act. Gov't. Code § 65995; *Western/California Ltd. v. Dry Creek Joint Elementary School District* (1996) 50 Cal. App. 4th 1461.

When a school district establishes a Mello-Roos Community Facilities District to finance the acquisition or improvement of school facilities, the property within that CFD is exempted from paying "any fee or other requirement" levied to benefit another school district if the fee was levied after the resolution of formation of the CFD was adopted. The affected school districts can, however, mutually agree upon other arrangements. This law took effect on September 30, 1989. Govt. Code § 53313.4.

Fees imposed on any mobile home or manufactured home located within a mobile home park or mobile home subdivision that is limited to residence by older persons cannot exceed those imposed on commercial or industrial development. If such a mobile home park or mobile home subdivision subsequently decides to permit residents other than older persons, it must notify the affected school district. Subsequent home installations for younger persons will be subject to residential fees. Govt. Code § 65995.2.

Assessment district formation procedure. Proposition 218 establishes a common formation and ratification procedure for all special assessment districts as defined by Section 4, Article XIII D of the California Constitution. These requirements apply to all special assessments, to the exclusion of any conflicting laws.

All assessments must be supported by a report prepared by a registered professional engineer. The report must contain the total amount of money chargeable

The fee nexus and accounting requirements of the Mitigation Fee Act apply to all school district exactions.

CEQA = California Environmental Quality Act

The fee cap established under these laws is the total amount of fees that may be levied for school facilities. This includes fees intended to mitigate an environmental effect under CEQA.

to the assessment district, the amount chargeable to each parcel in the district, the duration of the payments, the reason for the assessment, and the basis upon which the proposed assessment was calculated. Section 4(c), Article XIII D, California Constitution. Although not explicitly mandated by Prop. 218, the report should also include a description of the improvements or services to be financed through the special assessment, the proposed district boundaries, and a description of the special benefit that each parcel receives as a result of the assessment.

Prior to creating an assessment district, the city, county, or special district must hold a public hearing and receive approval from a majority of the affected property owners casting ballots.

Prior to creating an assessment district, the city, county, or special district (*e.g.*, school district) must hold a public hearing and receive approval from a majority of the affected property owners casting ballots. All owners of property within the assessment district must be mailed a detailed notice of the public hearing and a ballot with which to voice their approval or disapproval of the proposed district at least 45 days prior to the hearing. Section 4(e), Article XIII D, California Constitution. The notice must contain: the total amount of money chargeable to the assessment district; the amount chargeable to each parcel in the district; the duration of the payments; the reason for the assessment; the basis upon which the proposed assessment was calculated; a summary of the ballot procedure; and the date, time, and location of the public hearing. The notice must also disclose that a majority protest will result in the assessment not being imposed.

At the hearing, the agency's governing body must consider all protests to district formation. Assessment district proceedings must be abandoned if a majority of the ballots received by the conclusion of the hearing protest creation of the district. Ballots are to be weighted according to the proportional financial obligation of the affected property: the larger the l obligation, the greater the weight must be assigned to the property. Unlike previous law, the governing body cannot overrule the property owner's vote. No other form of election is required. Once created, an assessment may be repealed or reduced by popular initiative.

A key practical question about the ballot process under Proposition 218 is who votes when a property is held in multiple ownership (or multiple renters are directly liable for payment of the assessment), or when the property is owned by a public agency?

A district must clearly identify the special benefit being conferred to the parcels being assessed, excluding any identified general benefit. The district must apportion the assessment on an individual basis to parcels within the district. Where an assessment is challenged in court, Proposition 218 specifies that the district carries the burden of proof in showing that the property is receiving a special benefit and the amount assessed is proportional to, and no greater than, the special benefits conferred. Most importantly, a district will have to educate property owners about the advantages of the prospective assessment. The ballot process established by Prop. 218 favors those property owners who oppose the assessment (since they are generally the most motivated to return a ballot).

A district will have to educate property owners about the advantages of the prospective assessment, because the ballot process established by Prop. 218 favors those property owners who oppose the assessment.

Land Banks

In order to meet school site requirements at lower cost, school districts located in high-growth areas use Land Bank programs, which provide a method for school districts to acquire parcels of land in convenient neighborhood locations before they are developed. A variation on the lease financing technique, the Land Bank program helps a school district control the cost of land by replacing the uncertain rate of future land appreciation with the current long-term tax-exempt interest rate. Land Banks are particularly useful whenever a district has a confirmed need for land for a future project or projects, and an appropriate property is available for negotiated purchase, but funds for the purchase are not yet available due to lack of resources or regulatory restrictions on their expenditure. *See* the Land Bank discussion in chapter 4.

A Land Bank is particularly useful when a district has a confirmed need for land for a future project, and an appropriate property is available, but funds to purchase the property are not yet available.

Land Banks are typically nonprofit corporations owned by school districts (often the same corporations used for COPs financing), which may take title to properties likely to be developed as a school in the future. A property in a land bank may be purchased by a school district once that district has funds available and is authorized to use them for property acquisition—generally after proper project approvals and full regulatory compliance.

Developer Fees: SB 50 and AB 16

For school districts experiencing growth due to new residential or commercial development, developer fees can provide another source of monies to help fund school facilities. Unfortunately, many urban school districts in California are experiencing population growth without corresponding growth in new housing and are not able to tap into this source of funding.

In 1998, the California Legislature passed SB 50, also known as the Leroy F. Greene School Facilities Act of 1998. In addition to replacing the LPP state funding program with the SFP, the bill authorized school districts to charge traditional or alternative and much higher fees on new residential construction, if certain requirements are met—known as Level 1, 2, or 3 fees. Govt. Code §§ 65995.5–65995.7. The fees can only be imposed for facilities necessitated by new development. SB 50 also placed new limitations on the power of cities and counties to require mitigation of school facility impacts from new development, suspending the applicability of a series of court cases known as *Mira/Hart/Murrieta*.

SB 50 developer fees. SB 50 provides authority for school districts to charge three different levels of fees. Education Code section 17620 provides the basic authority for school districts to levy fees against construction for the purpose of funding construction or reconstruction of school facilities, subject to limits set forth in Government Code section 65995. Administrative regulations adopted by the SAB do not directly affect requirements for studies, but guide how certain variables are calculated. Title 2, Calif. Code Regulations.

Level 1 fees. Govt. Code § 65995. As established by the School Facilities Act of 1986 and unchanged by SB 50, a district may charge Level 1 fees as long as they are justified by the school district's development fee justification study (required by Educ. Code § 17621 and Govt. Code § 66001). In 1998, Level 1 fees were an inflation-adjusted $1.93 for residential construction and an inflation-adjusted $0.31 for commercial or industrial construction. In 2006, the fees became $2.63 and $0.42, respectively.

Level 2 fees and Level 3 fees. Govt. Code § 65995.5, Govt. Code § 65995.7. Before a school district can charge higher Level 2 fees and capture up to 50 percent

Timely Application

The term "timely application" refers to the use of Form SAB 50-04. The content of SAB 50-04 is based on information in Forms SAB 50-01 and SAB 50-03. In order to secure Step One and its ability to charge higher developer's fees, some districts file SAB Form 50-04 for at least one project concurrently with filing SAB Forms 50-01, 50-02, and 50-03, or as soon as possible thereafter. Although the SAB requires DSA approval of all project plans and specifications for which funding is sought, some districts file a qualifying SAB Form 50-04 (and requested funding) for a single relocatable structure.

Brief History of Developer Fees

Prior to 1998, the maximum fee that could be charged by school districts was $1.50 per square foot for residential development and $0.25 per square foot for commercial and industrial development, with modest inflationary adjustments ($1.93 and $0.31 in 1998, $2.14 and $0.34 in 2002). Govt. Code §§ 65995.5–65995.7.

While many read the 1986 law as prohibiting municipalities from levying fees in excess of the statutory maximum amounts to fund schools, or denying requests for development because of the lack of school facilities, court interpretations of the law have allowed assessment of much larger fees.

In *Mira Development Corp. v. City of San Diego* (1988), 205 Cal. App. 3d 1201 *("Mira"); William S. Hart Union High School District v. Regional Planning Commission* (1991) 226 Cal. App. 3d 1612, *("Hart"); and Murrieta Valley Unified School District v. County of Riverside* (1991) 228 Cal. App. 3d 1212 *("Murrieta"),* the courts held that the limitations of the School Facilities Law of 1986 only applied to adjudicative decisions of local governments, not legislative decisions (such as general plan amendments, zoning changes, and development agreements). The courts held that when a local government made a legislative decision concerning land use under its general police powers and duties to mitigate environmental impacts under CEQA, it could consider the impacts of that decision on school facilities and condition its approval on mitigation measures—even if the mitigation measures exceeded the limits of what school districts could require on their own.

At its core, and in response to the perceived excesses resulting from the *Mira/Hart/Murietta* decisions, SB 50 removed the ability of local governments to impose developer fees or other demands in excess of statutorily set maximum amounts to help fund school facilities. Specifically, SB 50 amended Govt. Code § 65995(a) to provide that only those fees expressly authorized by Educ. Code § 17620 or Govt. Code § 65970 *et seq.* (the traditional facilities fees), may be charged as a condition of any legislative or adjudicative act approved by a local government, and states that these fees are "full and complete mitigation of the impacts of any legislative or adjudicative act…on the provision of adequate school facilities." Govt. Code § 65995(h). Further, SB 50 prohibited local government from refusing to approve legislative or adjudicative acts involving development "on the basis of a person's refusal to provide school facilities mitigation that exceeds the amounts authorized [by SB 50]." Govt. Code § 65995(i).

The amounts of the Level III fees are set forth in a district's School Facility Needs Analysis, and the fee may vary from district to district. ■

of its site acquisition costs, and up to twice the amount funded by the SAB for its site development costs, several requirements must be met.

To collect Level 2 fees (and Level 3, if triggered) a district must:

- Apply for new construction funding to establish its eligibility
- Meet two of the four threshold tests
- Calculate the fee
- Follow certain specified procedures, including yearly rejustification and readoption

The following sets forth and describes the statutory procedures for each of the four steps required to implement developers fees. Due to the intense scrutiny and review that the public and the development community gives this process, the district should ensure that it is carried out by an experienced staff member or consultant.

Step one: Apply for state bond funding. The school district files a "timely application" to the SAB for new construction funding, and the SAB determines if the school district meets the eligibility requirements set forth in Education Code sections 17071.10 *et seq.* and section 17071.75 *et seq.* Govt. Code § 65995.5(b)(1).

Step two: Satisfy threshold test. The school district must satisfy at least two of the four following threshold requirements that are found in Government Code section 65995.5(b)(3):

- Meets substantial enrollment requirement (percent of students on MTYRE)
- Received at least 50 percent voter support for a general obligation bond within past four years
- Meets specified level of outstanding debt
- At least 20 percent of classrooms are portables

The detailed criteria for the four threshold requirements are as follows:

- Multi-track year-round education requirement:
  - At least 30 percent of K–6 enrollment in high school attendance area of growth are on MTYRE for unified and elementary school districts, or
  - At least 30 percent of high school district enrollment are on MTYRE, or
  - At least 40 percent of K–12 enrollment within the boundaries of the high school attendance area for which the district is applying for funding are on MTYRE
- School district has placed a local bond measure on the ballot in the past four years that has received a vote of at least 50 percent plus one
- School district meets one of the following criteria:
  - District has issued debt or incurred obligations for capital outlay equal to 15 percent of local bonding capacity including indebtedness repaid from:
    - Property taxes
    - Parcel taxes
    - District's general fund
    - Special taxes levied by cities, counties, and special districts, approved by a two-thirds vote of the qualified electors pursuant to Article XII A, section 4, of the California Constitution
    - Special taxes levied pursuant to the Mello-Roos Community Facilities Act of 1982 that are approved by a vote of registered voters
    - Special taxes levied pursuant to the Mello-Roos Community Facilities Act of 1982 that were approved by a vote of landowners prior to November 4, 1998
    - Revenues received pursuant to the Community Redevelopment Law (pass-through funds, tax-increment funds), or
  - The district has issued debt or incurred obligations for capital outlay equal to 30 percent of local bonding capacity, including indebtedness repaid from:
    - Property taxes
    - Parcel taxes
    - School district's general fund
    - Special taxes levied by cities, counties, and special districts, approved by a two-thirds vote of the qualified electors pursuant to Article XII A, section 4, of the California Constitution
    - Special taxes levied pursuant to the Mello-Roos Community Facilities Act that are approved by a vote of registered voters
    - Special taxes levied pursuant to the Mello-Roos Community Facilities Act approved by vote of landowners after November 4, 1998; and
    - Revenues received pursuant to the Community Redevelopment Law (pass-through funds, tax-increment funds)
  - Within a school district, at least 20 percent of teaching stations pursuant to Education Code section 17071.25 are relocatable classrooms.

✍ **practice tip**

Make sure your Level 1 fee justification is in effect and current, since residential additions, commercial-industrial, and other projects are not subject to Level 2 or Level 3 fees.

Step three: Calculate fee. The school district must calculate the Level 2 or 3 fee.

How to calculate Level 2 fees. The Level 2 fee is the number of unhoused students identified in the needs analysis, multiplied by the regular grant amount per each grade level, plus the sum of site acquisition and development costs, less local funds "dedicated" by the governing board for school facilities slotted for new construction, divided by the projected residential units' square footage to be constructed during the next five years. Govt. Code § 65995.5(c).

Local funds are dedicated by the governing board to provide facilities necessitated by new construction, including commercial and industrial fees. Govt. Code § 65995.5(c)(2). Districts may refer to Annual and Five Year Developer Fee Reports required per Government Code sections 66001 and 66006 to identify the dedicated funds.

Projected square footage shall be determined by information from the city or county where the new residential units are to be constructed, or by a market report prepared by an independent third party.

State funding received will be less than the amount required to provide adequate facilities, and developer fees will most likely be necessary to satisfy the deficiency.

The regular grant amount is a per unhoused pupil grant that excludes the cost of interim housing, central administration, and other site specific facilities. Therefore, state funding received will be less than the amount required to provide adequate facilities, and developer fees will most likely be necessary to satisfy the deficiency.

Elementary and high school districts that split developer fees (Educ. Code § 17623) must satisfy requirements to levy the alternative statutory fee described above. Govt. Code § 65995.5(d).

Level 2 Fees may only be used to finance school facilities that have to accommodate students generated by new residential construction. Govt. Code § 65995.5(f). The district's share of the Level 1 fee will be deducted from the Level 2 Fee to determine the funds available for administrative costs.

How to calculate a Level 3 fee. Govt. Code § 65995.7. If authorized, Level 3 fees can be charged to capture 100 percent of a school district's facility costs due to increased growth. Govt. Code § 65995.7.

The Level 3 fee is the amount of local funds dedicated for school facilities to accommodate new growth, including the Level 2 commercial/industrial fee. Govt. Code § 65995.7(a). The maximum total Level 3 fee that may be levied is equal to the sum of this amount, and the Level 2 fee.

Level 3 fees may only be used to finance the school facilities as required to accommodate students generated by new residential construction. Govt. Code § 65995.5(f). The district's share of the Level 1 fee will be deducted from the Level 3 fee to determine the funds available to spend on administrative costs.

When is a Level 3 fee imposed? Before a Level 3 fee can be imposed, two requirements must be met. First, state funding must not be available. Govt. Code § 65995.7(a). Second, the school district must have already adopted the Level 2 fee.

A school district knows that state funding is not available when two actions take place: The SAB has notified the Secretary of the Senate and the Chief Clerk of the Assembly, in writing, of the determination that funds are no longer available (Educ. Code § 17072.20.); and the SAB "shall declare that state funds are insufficient when" the grant requests ready for apportionment exceed the amount of state funds available. The state Attorney General has opined that, as long as state funds are available and the SAB is still approving apportionments (not when new construction grant requests exceed available funds), school districts may not increase their school impact fees from Level 2 to Level 3. Cal. Op. Atty. Gen. No. 01-803 (February 13, 2002). This declaration serves as the mechanism for the SAB to notify the legislature for purposes of the Level 3 fee. Regulation § 1859.91.

Step four: Prepare and adopt a School Facility Needs Analysis. In order to charge Level 2 or Level 3 fees, a school district must adopt a School Facility Needs Analysis (SFNA) in accordance with Government Code section 65995.6. Though the SFNA is similar to the Fee Justification Study, the legal requirements differ (Table 2-4). The purpose of the SFNA is to determine the need for new school facilities attributable to growth from new residential development. Govt. Code § 65995.6. The SFNA documents that the district has met prerequisite eligibility tests and calculates the fee per square foot of new development, using the formula prescribed in state regulations. Since SFNAs are increasingly subject to legal challenges, districts should use empirical data to backup their conclusions. *Coalition for Affordable Housing in Los Angeles v. LAUSD* (May 31, 2002) L.A. Superior Court Case No. BC 260529 (court found SFNA failed to rely on adequate data).

As a practical matter, the fee justification study and needs analysis may be combined into a single document, so long as it contains the data elements for both studies.

Conduct preliminary review before preparing the SFNA. A preliminary estimate of eligibility should be prepared using SAB Forms. First, the district should perform an estimate to determine if the Level 2 fee calculation exceeds the current Level 1 fee. In 2004, the statutorily set Level 1 fee rose to $2.24 per square foot for new residential development and $0.36 per square foot for new commercial and industrial development. Second, the district should review to determine if the district can satisfy at least two of the four requirements for eligibility.

The district should confirm that it possesses a current eligibility determination from SAB or can complete the requirements to obtain eligibility before the district can adopt an SFNA. The district must be eligible *at the time* the governing board adopts a resolution establishing Level 2 or 3 fees. Thus, the district must make sure its eligibility application is current when ready to adopt the Level 2 or 3 resolution.

The district should also possess an adequate capital improvement plan covering at least the next five years. This is not the Level 1 fee study and not the facilities master plan (although the capital improvement plan may be a part of the facilities master plan).

Content of needs analysis. Govt. Code § 65995.6(a) and (b). The first content requirement is a projection of the number of "unhoused pupils" generated by "new residential units" based upon the historical student generation rates of new residential units constructed during the previous five years and upon relevant planning agency information that may modify the historical figures.

New homes expected in the next five years. When providing the numbers and types of homes expected in the next five years, districts should be cautious of unrealistic projections, especially those by regional agencies (ABAG, SCAG,

SFNA = School Facility Needs Analysis

As a practical matter, the fee justification study and needs analysis may be combined into a single document.

The district should possess an adequate capital improvement plan covering at least the next five years.

Table 2-4. Fee Justification Study vs. SFNA Legal Requirements

Fee Justification Study § 66001	School Facilities Needs Analysis § 65995.6
Identify purpose of the fee	Purpose of fee is to reimburse school district for new school facilities needed to house pupils attributable to new residential development
Identify use to which the fee is to be put (public facilities must be identified)	Project the number of unhoused elementary, middle, and high school pupils generated by new residential units, in each category of pupils enrolled in the district (based on the five-year historical student generation rates)
Determine whether a reasonable relationship exists between the fee's use and the type of development project on which the fee is imposed	Calculate existing school building capacity, including additional capacity created by the multi-track year-round schedule
Determine whether a reasonable relationship exists between the need for the public facility and the type of development project on which the fee is imposed	Identify and consider any surplus property the district owns that can be used as a school site or that is available for sale to finance school facilities
	Identify and consider the extent to which projected enrollment growth may be accommodated by excess capacity in existing facilities
	Identify and consider local sources other than fees, charges, dedications, or other requirements imposed on residential construction available

SACOG, etc.) that may conflict with locally adopted plans. The SFNA should include a discussion of the reasonableness of agency projections. If mobile homes are to be subject to Level 2 or 3 fees, they should also be included in the SFNA.

Pupil-per-home yield rate (by grade level by type). If local district data is unavailable, the SFNA cannot use statewide averages and must yield rates from other districts in the city or county, carefully establishing why these other ratios are sufficiently similar (*e.g.*, type of housing unit) to rely upon.

The SFNA must establish that the yield rate is based on units built in the last five years, which is similar to units expected in the next five years. Districts must be careful not to gerrymander the information to enable artificially higher fees. For example, if the only multi-family project was for affordable housing, the ratios may not reflect market-rate units proposed in the next five years. The SFNA can include continuation high school and special education enrollment in the respective grade level yield factor, or it can be tracked separately by grade level group.

Some SFNAs adjust yield rates to augment low numbers from recently built homes and the tendency for new homes to have younger students. Rates that are arbitrarily changed are easy to challenge. Any adjustments should be based on hard empirical data with extensive backup.

Unhoused pupils in next five years (by grade level). In most cases, the fifth year projection includes students from approved tract maps. Districts should be careful to not double count by subtracting the fifth year projection from capacity, and then subtracting the students from new homes (many of which are the same on the tract map adjustment as the 50-01 projection).

Available capacity (by grade level). Available capacity may be calculated with the same process used for completing the districts SAB Form 50-02.

Districts should use the form to reflect conditions at the time the resolution authorizing the Level 2 or 3 fee is adopted, not as of the date the district last submitted the SAB Form 50-02.

Alternate sites available for use or sale. If the district has surplus sites or alternate sites, the SFNA must demonstrate that another site is not usable for the proposed project or is not available for sale to finance the project. If a site is not needed in the five-year window, then it could be considered surplus and the potential value deducted from the cost basis for Level 2 or 3 fees.

Note that "surplus" as used here means "available" rather than the formal process defined in the Education Code for disposition of surplus property.

The Needs Analysis must answer each of the following questions:

- Does the district own any surplus property that can be used as a school site or is available for sale to finance school facilities?
- To what extent can projected enrollment be accommodated by excess capacity in existing facilities?
- Are local sources—other than fees, charges, dedications, or other requirements for residential construction—available to finance the construction or reconstruction of school facilities?
- Are there school facilities that could be constructed to accommodate new growth? Compare proposed facilities with annual and five-year developer fee reports to ensure consistency.

The SFNA must establish a nexus or reasonable relationship between Level 2 and the impact of new residential development.

Procedure for adopting the SFNA. The SFNA must be provided to the local government and available for comment 45 days prior to a public hearing. Govt. Code § 65352.2. The time and place of the hearing, including location and procedure for requesting a copy of the SFNA, must be published in a newspaper of *general circulation* at least 30 days prior to the public hearing. Govt. Code § 65995.6(d).

Also, at least 30 days prior to the public hearing, the district must mail the SFNA to any person who has made a written request at least 45 days before the date of the public hearing.

Prior to adoption of the SFNA at the public hearing, the governing board must respond to any written comments received. There is no legal requirement for the response to be in writing, and a district may respond to comments orally at the public hearing. Finally, the board must adopt the SFNA by resolution and make a finding that the SFNA is exempt from CEQA.

Government Code section 65995.6(g) provides that CEQA "may not" apply to the adoption of the needs analysis, whereas Education Code section 17621 specifically exempts the adoption of the fee justification study from CEQA. Although this language adds some confusion, most SFNAs, as studies that do not commit the district to a direct or indirect physical change in the environment, are exempt from CEQA.

Effective date. The Level 2 fee (or Level 3 fee) is effective immediately upon adoption by the governing board. Govt. Code § 65995.6(f). Alternative school fees (Level 2 and Level 3 fees), supported by an SFNA, are valid for one year.

If the district has surplus or alternate sites, the SFNA must demonstrate that another site is not usable or is not available for sale to finance the project.

Annual recalculation of existing school building capacity. An annual update of a needs analysis must include a revision of a school district's eligibility. As a prerequisite to the preparation of an initial needs analysis, a school district must file an application for state Funding using Forms SAB 50-01, 50-02, and 50-03. For this annual update, a school district must recalculate its existing school building capacity. Although a district is not required to adjust its original baseline determination by resubmission of Forms SAB 50-01, 50-02, and 50-03 to OPSC, for purposes of demonstrating current eligibility these forms are often updated to reflect current five-year enrollment projections, as well as updated facility capacities (*i.e.*, classroom capacity). The only form submitted to OPSC on an annual basis to update eligibility is the SAB 50-01. All other adjustments to the district's capacity to house students is updated on what is called the New Construction Eligibility Worksheet, which is an internal spreadsheet kept by OPSC.

Site acquisition and development costs. The statute requires that land be necessary for the project in order to include the site acquisition cost. The burden is on the SFNA to prove that land is needed. Land purchase is not justified if only one or two classrooms are needed in the next five years. In contrast, land purchase is reasonable if two-thirds more students from new residential development are expected to enroll. Districts should carefully prorate land cost if less than a full site is justified. Before concluding that additional land is required for mitigation, storm water retention, or other reasons, a district will want the SFNA carefully reviewed to determine the legality of that fee.

The SFNA should also include good supporting documentation for the cost of land. The SFNA should document that site development costs included in the cost calculation are necessary. The cost basis used should be reasonable and well documented.

Government Code sections 66006–66007 require public agencies levying fees on new development to identify the projects to be funded in whole or in part. Thus, it is important that the SFNA contain a project list that matches the projects listed in the district's capital improvement plan.

Relationship between developer fees and Mello-Roos CFDs. The use of Mello-Roos financing for schools as a condition of approval of any legislative or adjudicative action is prohibited by law. A person's refusal to participate in a Mello-Roos school funding program may not be taken into account when considering any legislative or adjudicative action relating to land development. If a person voluntarily participates in a Mello-Roos program approved by landowner vote, the present value of the taxes to be paid are to be calculated as an amount per square foot of assessable space and credited against any developer fee liability.

To comply with SB 50 however, the taxes need to be approved by two-thirds of the registered voters within the boundaries of a Mello-Roos district created by the school district (which could include the entire school district territory). Because registered voters rather than landowners approve the tax, the amount of the tax is not an offset to developer fees (although it would be taken into account in the justification studies done for the developer fees). It may also be possible for a school district to propose to its voters that they approve a Mello-Roos tax that is levied on any property that receives approval

Districts should carefully prorate land cost if less than a full site is justified.

Using Mello-Roos financing for schools as a condition of approval of any legislative or adjudicative action is prohibited by law.

for a development that will lead to increased enrollment. The theory is that the tax is not a condition of approval for the development; it is a consequence of that approval.

Reporting requirements. Districts have annual and five-year reporting requirements. Govt. Code §§ 66001 and 66006. These reports must be prepared and completed no later than one hundred eighty days after the last day of each fiscal year, to account for the various types of fees received, interest earned, and how the fees have been expended regarding the applicable statutory provisions.

Effective January 1, 2001, the legislature established a similar reporting requirement for proceeds of bonds of school districts. SB 165.

Costs allowed in the SFNA. Government Code section 65995.5(f) restricts use of Level 2 and Level 3 funds to costs identified in the SFNA. Fees may be used to pay the direct cost of preparing the SFNA and administering the fee collection program. Districts should be very cautious about spending Level 2 or Level 3 fees on COPs or leases of existing buildings.

Only costs related in an SFNA to new residential construction in the next five years may be included, and these may be included only as prescribed in sections 65995.5 and 65995.6. Costs and projects need to match capital improvement plans or construction schedules.

The district should review the SFNA to ensure consistency with the district's Level 1 fee justification study and its capital improvement plan. If the commercial/industrial fee is justified based on unfunded cost from new residential construction, and if commercial/industrial fees will reduce that unfunded cost, those revenues may reduce the district's Level 2 fee. Similarly, Level 1 fees based on new residential construction may reduce the district's Level 2 fee.

The issues related to preparation of an SFNA can be quite tricky, particularly where the district has a Mello-Roos or other income stream or some of the homes expected in the next five years are covered by existing contracts.

Other Sources of School Facility Funds

Redevelopment agencies. A redevelopment agency is usually created to alleviate conditions of blight in older, urban areas. The redevelopment agency is able to use special legal and financial mechanisms to eliminate blight and improve economic and physical conditions in designated areas. This authority is conferred on the agency through California's Health & Safety Code section 33000 *et. seq.*, also known as the California Community Redevelopment Law.

The basic need and purpose of redevelopment is the existence "in many communities of blighted areas which constitute physical and economic liabilities, requiring redevelopment in the interests of the health, safety and general welfare of the people of these communities and of the state." Redevelopment or "blighted" areas are established to maintain and increase the supply of housing for low and moderate income households, renovate or remove and replace deteriorated and dilapidated structures, foster job creation, and establish a climate that will attract and sustain private investment, and eliminate "blight."

The law contains additional statements of state policy that are the basis for the powers made available to redevelopment agencies, as follows:

Issues related to preparing an SFNA can be quite tricky, particularly where the district has a Mello-Roos or other income stream or some of the homes expected in the next five years are covered by existing contracts.

- The blighted areas present difficulties and handicaps, which are beyond remedy and control solely by regulatory processes in the exercise of the police power.

- The blighted areas contribute substantially and increasingly to the problems of, and necessitate excessive and disproportionate expenditures for, crime prevention, correction, prosecution, and punishment, the treatment of juvenile delinquency, the preservation of the public health and safety, and the maintaining of adequate police, fire and accident protection and other public services and facilities.

- The conditions of blight tend to further accelerate and magnify the obsolescence, deterioration, and disuse because of the lack of incentive to the individual landowner and his inability to improve, modernize, or rehabilitate his property while the condition of the neighboring properties remains unchanged.

- The redevelopment of blighted areas and the provisions for appropriate continuing land use and construction policies applicable to them constitute public uses and purposes for which public money may be advanced or expended and private property acquired, and are governmental functions of state concern in the interest of health, safety, and welfare of the people of the state and of the communities in which the blighted areas exist.

Although a redevelopment Agency is a separate legal entity, a city council or board of supervisors usually serves as its legislative body. This legislative body makes all policy determinations for the implementation of the agency's programs, such as state law governing a minimum of 20 percent of the revenues accruing to a redevelopment agency be set aside for maintaining and expanding the supply of housing for low and moderate income households.

The agency's funding is derived primarily from four sources:

- **Property tax increment**—the mainstay of redevelopment financing, but a limited resource even in the best of times because of Prop. 13

- **Tax allocation bond proceeds**

- **Grants**

- **Other general revenues**—includes proceeds from land sales, developer payments, rental income, loan repayments, and investment income

A survey area is an area under study to determine the feasibility of a redevelopment project designation. A project area is a designated redevelopment area.

A survey area is an area under study to determine the feasibility of a redevelopment project designation. A project area is a designated redevelopment area.

Once a project is identified or need is established, how is it funded? Projects are funded through resource allocations, including those for staff. The basis for these allocations relies largely on the positive impact a project or program has on the agency. Evaluation criteria might include:

- How effective will the project or program be in creating a catalytic change in the community and to what extent will it lead to the community becoming more self-sustaining?

- How effective will the project be in generating additional resources for the agency, especially discretionary resources?

- How effective will the project or program be in leveraging resources from other sources?
- How will the project maintain a visible agency presence for positive change in the affected community?
- How does a district gain access to money?
- When will it happen? Redevelopment plans are long-term with 40-year horizons. Districts need to be aware that the money is dependent on other variables in the community and may not be generated for 15 years or more.

Surplus property disposition. Most land owners are free to sell their property at will to any buyer and use the proceeds of the sale as they wish. School districts are not. The laws governing disposition of school district property are complex and require that very specific procedures be followed at each step. Educ. Code § 17388 *et seq.* The main requirements are summarized below.

The laws governing disposition of school district property are complex and require that very specific procedures be followed at each step.

A school district may only offer its properties for sale to potential buyers as provided for in the Education Code. Districts must first send written offers to local, regional, and state park and recreation authorities. Educ. Code § 17464; Govt. Code § 54220. Then the district must follow a detailed and sequenced notice procedure to other public agencies and the former property owner by specified methods. *See, e.g.,* Educ. Code § 17470.

Initially, and prior to the offering of district-owned property for sale, a district must appoint an advisory committee of between 7 to 11 members who represent the community's ethnic and socio-economic composition. The committee should include tenants and landowners, business leaders, teachers, parents, and experts in real estate, construction, environmental matters, and the law.

The advisory committee must examine demographic enrollment data, capacity of existing facilities, etc., in order to establish a list of surplus property eligible for sale and disposition.

The governing board must adopt a resolution of intention with the specific content requirements of sections 17468 and 35161 of the Education Code, and publish it for three successive weeks in a newspaper of general circulation. Notice must also be provided to the local planning commission. Govt. Code § 65402.

The bid process for sale of surplus property is similarly detailed. *See* Educ. Code §§ 17455–17484.

The use of the funds from the sale of surplus property is restricted. Proceeds must be used for capital outlay or property maintenance costs with a recurrence of less than five years. Educ. Code § 17462.

Sale of surplus property is not only a potential source of funds—it is a required component of a district's SFNA, necessary to charge Level 2 developer fees. Where a district has found property to be surplus, the amount of the Level 2 fee must be decreased.

Sale of surplus property is not only a potential source of funds—it is a required component of a district's SFNA, necessary to charge Level 2 developer fees.

Special rules for lease of surplus property. A school may not construct a facility on leased land using state funds. Educ. Code § 17070.70; 2 C.C.R. § 1859.74.1.

Exchange. A far more streamlined process applies when districts seek to merely exchange property, rather than sell it. Educ. Code §§ 17536 and 17538. The board must merely adopt by a two-thirds vote a resolution of its intent to exchange the property.

Select Federal Grant Programs

Federal school renovation program (Omnibus Appropriations Act). This is a federal $1.2 billion program for all 50 states, of which California is eligible for the $138 million Omnibus Appropriates Act. Seventy-five percent, or $103 million, is allocated toward urgently needed renovations. The distribution of this pot of federal money is administered by OPSC. Twenty-five percent, or $35 million, is allocated toward the Individuals with Disabilities Education Act (IDEA), technology needs related to school renovation, and charter school facility financing. The IDEA and technology funds are distributed by CDE, while the charter school facility money is distributed by the federal government.

The funds were released in two phases, in 2002 and in 2004. Future funding availability is subject to federal budget decisions.

OPSC requires a simple one-page application that does not have to include plans or cost estimates. It is a district-wide grant, not a project-specific grant. The maximum grant is $275,000 per 10,000 students. There is no matching requirement. In order to be eligible, the district must provide proof that it notified all charter nonprofits of the funds availability, provide current student enrollment numbers in the district (not including the charter schools), and identify the district's percentage of bond indebtedness and percentage of charter schools. *See* SAB Forms 60-01, 02, 03.

The QZAB is a federal program to help strengthen schools serving large concentrations of low-income families.

Qualified Zone Academy Bonds. The QZAB is a federal program to help strengthen schools serving large concentrations of low-income families. 26 U.S.C. § 1397E. Created by the Taxpayer Relief Act of 1997, QZABs are obligations issued by state or local governments to renovate and improve certain eligible public schools. The QZAB is a loan that must be repaid within a specified time. The rate of the tax credit and the maximum term of the bond are determined by the United States Treasury Department. The tax credit mechanism eliminates the cost of interest only, not the bond principal.

Schools can use the QZAB to address infrastructure, health and safety, environmental, and energy efficiency issues associated with aging and overcrowded schools. New building construction cannot be funded with QZAB.

Eligibility. An eligible school either:

- Is located in an empowerment zone or an enterprise community, or
- Has at least 35 percent of its students eligible for free or reduced-cost lunches under the National School Lunch Act, and
- Has an education program designed in cooperation with business and receives a private business contribution that is not less than 10 percent of the proceeds of the bond

QZABs can be only used for:

- Rehabilitating or repairing the public school facility
- Providing equipment for use at the facility
- Developing course materials for education to be provided in the school, or
- Training teachers and other school personnel in the specified site(s)

In 2002, President Bush signed the Economic Stimulus Package, including a two-year extension of QZAB funds. California received approximately $50 to

$55 million each year for 2002 and 2003. Charter schools are eligible to apply either directly or through the district in which they are located under the same conditions that other school districts are eligible. 5 C.C.R. § 15132(a).

Federal E-rate program/California Teleconnect Fund. E-rate is a Federal Communications Commission (FCC) program that provides eligible K–12 public schools and libraries 20 to 90 percent discounts on approved telecommunications, Internet access, and internal connections costs. Similar to the QZAB program, E-rate discounts are based on the number of students eligible for the National Free Lunch Program. Schools and libraries in low-income urban communities and rural areas qualify for higher discounts.

California Teleconnect Fund (CTF) is a California Public Utilities Commission (CPUC) program. While the E-rate program includes discounts for a wider range of telecommunications services, CTF offers discounts for measured business service as well as high bandwidth data lines. Although offering a smaller menu of eligible services, the CTF application process is simpler than E-rate. Applications for CTF discounts are submitted to a telecommunications carrier, who will submit the completed eligible application to the CPUC. When CTF discounts are approved the telecommunications carrier will discount the telecommunications to the school.

For school facility projects, both sources of funds can assist in providing the technology infrastructure needed in new construction and modernization projects. For more information and application materials, districts should consult CDE's Education Technology Planning Guide (www.cde.ca.gov/ctl/edtech-plan.pdf), the FCC website (www.fcc.gov/ccb/universal_service/schoolsandlibs.html), and the CPUC website (www.cpuc.ca.gov/published/rulings/1622.htm).

CPUC = California Public Utilities Commission

CTF = California Teleconnect Fund

FCC = Federal Communications Commission

chapter 3

Planning and Design

The planning and design of school facilities occurs in two stages, with the first taking place at the district-wide level. A facilities master plan is developed to ensure that the district's educational program is supported by its school facilities. It involves a team approach to defining the educational program—examining the existing and projected student body and its learning needs, assessing the capacity of existing facilities to support the current and projected future educational program, and developing priority recommendations and a plan to implement and finance those priorities.

The second stage of planning takes place at the site-specific level. A district develops the educational specifications to translate the education program needs into building spaces. Early coordination with local government planning agencies and state regulatory agencies is required, and is well-advised to help ensure the site will meet the numerous regulatory requirements.

At both levels, a district is likely to call upon expert assistance in one or more disciplines. Selection of those experts is critical to assuring school facilities that deliver the district's educational program to the students. Indeed, compliance with the laws governing planning and designing of school facilities will not necessarily ensure that the district's educational program is supported and enhanced by its facilities. The most critical ingredients to guaranteeing a successful project is the collaboration between educators, district administrators, architects, and education specialists.

The most critical ingredients to guaranteeing a successful project is the collaboration between educators, district administrators, architects, and education specialists.

Planning Team

Due to the complexity and wide variety of expertise (*e.g.*, education, architecture, finance) required to site and build a school facility in California in the twenty-first century, the first step in developing a facilities master plan is to form a team of professionals. Many school districts have staff with the expertise to create a facilities master plan, others must employ outside assistance. Members of the team can include the superintendent, assistant superintendents, board members, directors, school principals, facility planning staff, maintenance staff, district finance staff, district architect(s), demographers, and outside consultants. CDE is charged with the duty of assisting school districts in their comprehensive planning efforts, and will provide sources of expertise upon request. Educ. Code § 16322.

Team Activities

Initial team activities will include gathering and analyzing data related to the educational programs and the facilities needed to support them, the use, capacity, and condition of existing facilities, and the district's demographics and future enrollments. The team also may choose to interview residents living near the school to understand how the school is perceived in the neighborhood. Typically, the district's educational planner, demographer, and architect collect the educational program data, assess the condition of the facilities, and compile the district's demographics.

The team then focuses on activities that define the current and future educational programs and facilities, and the equipment needed to accommodate and support them. Next, the team develops a financing plan, and establishes a framework for future facilities improvements. Finally, the team focuses on communicating the needs to the district's constituency and building support for financing school facilities.

Educational Facility Planners

The educational planner or planners conduct preliminary research concerning the district's educational needs, and develop the educational program and specifications. Usually they are district employees, but some districts hire educators, planners, or architects who specialize in developing facilities master plans.

Design Professional in Charge (Architect/Engineer of Record)

State law requires that a licensed architect or engineer prepare drawings and specifications before they are submitted to DSA for review. This individual is also responsible for observing construction, interpreting drawings and specifications, administering required testing and inspection processes, and preparing change orders. In most cases, only California licensed architects or structural engineers may act as the "Design Professional in General Responsible Charge" of a school construction project. Licensed mechanical and electrical engineers may serve on projects limited primarily to mechanical or electrical alterations.

The architect converts the district's facilities master plan and educational specifications into school facilities. He or she also provides input on the facilities' capacity, and the feasibility of constructing new or modifying existing facilities to meet the ed specs. The architect is not an educator and should not lead the educational program phase. Depending upon the project delivery method selected (*see* chapter 5), the district will have to retain the services of an architect to develop the detailed design for the project. The architect is typically selected pursuant to a competitive proposal process, and is involved in developing the design, obtaining design approvals, issuing plans and specifications for

The Planning Team

- Educational facility planner(s)
- Design professional in charge (architect/engineer of record)
- School board members
- District superintendent
- School principal
- Project manager
- Construction manager
- Engineers and specialty consultants

The architect converts the district's facilities master plan and educational specifications into school facilities.

construction, advising the district regarding the award of the construction contract, responding to submittals and questions relating to the design from the construction contractor, and completing the project.

If the district selects the "Design/Bid/Build" delivery system, the architect will be responsible for a complete and accurate project design. Since design problems are one of the most common causes of "problem projects," sufficient care must be taken in selecting an architect and ensuring the design is complete before construction of the project begins. Because of the unique regulatory requirements in California, it is advisable to retain an architectural firm that has experience designing schools in California.

Since design problems are one of the most common causes of "problem projects," sufficient care must be taken in selecting an architect and ensuring the design is complete before construction begins.

School Board Members

The role of the board is to set policy and leverage resources to support its policy goals. Most board members rely on a dedicated professional staff to run their facilities program. However, with respect to the planning and design of school facilities, either one board member represents the board as an active member of the core planning team, or the full board may be involved by receiving periodic updates. In either case, the core planning team should hold a series of workshops with the board at regular intervals throughout the process to consider policy and budget issues.

District Superintendent

The superintendent's office has critical leadership functions to fulfill. The superintendent, or deputy superintendent must be actively engaged in the facilities planning process.

School Principal

The school principal provides input regarding the school's day-to-day operation, educational, process, and security considerations. In addition, each principal may form a school-based facilities committee, which will inform the district-wide facilities team. This committee may consist of teachers, technology staff, custodial, maintenance and/or operations staff, parents; school advisory counsel and PTA members, students, local business supporters, and representatives of groups that use the grounds and/or facilities. The team evaluates the school's specific needs and develops priorities to be incorporated into the facilities master plan.

Project Manager

The project manager acts as the district's agent by managing the allocation of funding for the various projects, and overseeing the selection of designers, construction managers and contractors. The project manager's ultimate responsibility is to ensure that the district's construction program is properly planned and implemented in accordance with the budget and schedule. Sometimes this role is shared by two people—one who oversees preconstruction or planning and design, and one who oversees construction, including bidding. The district may choose to hire a consultant to manage the planning if it does not have sufficient in-house staff resources.

The project manager's ultimate responsibility is to ensure that the district's construction program is properly planned and implemented in accordance with the budget and schedule.

Construction Manager

A construction manager may be a team member depending upon the project delivery method chosen by the district. In lieu of a general contractor, the construction manager acts as the district's agent in the management of the construction subcontractors. Education Code sections 17019.3 and 17070.98 authorize a district to retain a construction manager. Ideally, the construction manager has a track record of successful school plan review, construction, and cost estimating. The construction manager may be involved in performing "constructability" reviews of the design before the project goes out for bid, managing the bid process for the project, advising the district on the selection of a bidder, developing and implementing procedures for the construction management process, overseeing and communicating with the contractor(s) during construction to insure that the project is built according to the specifications and the project schedule, and closing out the project.

Engineers and Specialty Consultants

These consultants typically work directly for the architect. Their services are usually provided to the owner as part of the architect's services. They are also known as subconsultants and are responsible for designing specific components of the building and site. These include:

- Structural engineer—Major building structure and seismic resisting components
- Mechanical engineer—Heating, ventilating, cooling, and plumbing systems
- Electrical engineer—Power, lighting, data, and communication systems
- Civil engineer—Grading and drainage systems
- Food service consultant—Kitchen and food service design components
- Landscape architect—Design of landscaping and grounds
- Interior design—Design of interior finish materials and colors

Facilities Master Plan

A comprehensive facilities master plan helps ensure that the district's school facilities support current and future education programs. It serves as a guide for assessing the need for facility improvements and capital investments, and determines the scope of repairs, modernization, upgrades, and new construction needed to achieve the educational program. It will also assess the federal, state, and local funding sources and financing options available to the district and assess how the projects can be accomplished with available funds.

Importance of the Facilities Master Plan

In order to obtain approvals for a school site from CDE, and therefore state funding, a district must establish why the site is justified with a facilities master plan, developer fee justification study, or five-year plan. 5 C.C.R. § 14011. The district must demonstrate that the classrooms at the new school site have adequate space to perform the curriculum functions for the planned enrollment (5 C.C.R. § 14030). Districts certifying that state funding will only be used on existing school sites containing a school building, or that they only maintain one school, are exempt from the requirement to prepare a facilities master plan. Educ. Code § 16322(d).

A facilities master plan is most useful for the school system's internal planning—it helps a district decide the building sites it needs to buy or retain. It can also be a reference tool for districts when weighing the impact of changing school organization, for example, changing from a junior high school to a middle school structure.

Coordination with Local Government and Community

It is advisable for a district to coordinate with local government planning agencies early and often during the development of its facilities master plan. Minimal coordination is mandated by law—at least 45 days prior to completion of a facilities master plan (or long range plan or school facilities needs analysis), a district must provide a copy to the local planning agency for review, and if requested by the district, the local government must grant a meeting within 15 days. Govt. Code § 65352.2.

Early coordination with local government planning agencies can help assure that zoning plans allocate space for school sites near housing developments, uncover possible joint-use opportunities or site acquisitions, and discover possible construction or operational funding assistance. Development of the district's facilities master plan provides a public forum for discussing the needs of the various community groups who use or have an interest in school facilities. Community involvement can also be useful for resolving politically sensitive issues such as school openings, closings, or attendance boundary adjustments. With the increasing need for districts to generate matching funds of 50 percent or greater for facility improvements, the facilities master plan can assist the superintendent and board to gain community support for

✎ **note**

Many of the suggestions in this section are derived from the article "Blueprint for Growth" that appeared in *The Executive Director* (December 1991) and are reprinted with permission here. The authors are Glen Ovard, Professor, Brigham Young University; Salt Lake City, Utah; Dr. Joel Kirschenstein, President, Sage Institute, Inc. (which specializes in school planning in Westlake Village, California); and Dr. Kelvin Lee, Superintendent, Dry Creek Elementary School District, Roseville, California.

A facilities master plan is most useful for a school system's internal planning—it helps a district decide the building sites it needs to buy or retain.

Development of the district's facilities master plan provides a public forum for discussing the needs of the various community groups who use or have an interest in school facilities.

financing—whether through a local voter-approved funding measure, or with political, financial, or technical support.

School districts can also play an important role in local government planning by actively participating in the development of general plan updates, specific plans, and community plans. By participating in the development of these plans and their components (such as the traffic circulation and housing elements), districts can help ensure that land use plans adequately address the need for safe, accessible, and adequate school facilities. School districts can also actively participate in the local government review of individual development projects to ensure that they are compatible with and do not impose burdens on school facility needs.

School districts can play an important role in local government planning by actively participating in the development of general plan updates, specific plans, and community plans.

Contents of the Facilities Master Plan

Each district should tailor the contents of the plan to its own requirements. At a minimum, the facilities master plan must contain the requirements in the California Education Code. Under sections 16011 and 16322 of the Education Code, a facilities master plan must contain:

- **Educational program**—An evaluation of the current and future educational program
- **Existing school facilities**—An analysis of existing school facilities and how each must be reconstructed or replaced to better support current and future educational programs and code requirements
- **Demographics**—An evaluation of how existing demographics and future population trends will impact facilities
- **Policy statement**—A description of equal educational opportunities
- **Priorities**—A prioritization of current and future school facility needs
- **Policy statement**—An explanation regarding the cooperation with local government to achieve community development
- **Continuous review**—A plan for continuous review and updating of the facilities master plan

While not required by law, most school districts also include a finance section and an implementation section in their master plan.

- **Finance and Implementation**—An analysis of financing options available to the district and detailed plans for implementation of the district's priorities

The facilities master plan should inform the board and public of the grade configuration, enrollment levels, and the maximum capacity each district campus will expect to house if expansion is necessary.

When completed, the facilities master plan should ultimately inform the board and the public as to the grade configuration (*e.g.*, K–6, 6–8, 9–12, or K–5, 6–9, and 10–12) to be served, the enrollment levels expected, and the maximum capacity each district campus will expect to house if expansion is necessary. CDE also provides guidance for developing a master plan on its web site (www.cde.ca.gov). Many districts also include the sections described below.

District history and background. A history is valuable to citizens and can demonstrate to potential voters that the district has changed—for example, transforming from being a railroad town to a high-tech community changes demographics and justifies why changes are needed (*e.g.*, increase public support for expenditures at a high-tech school). This section might describe the evolving educational needs for students to meet the needs of a shifting community, as well as society as a whole.

The history section should outline any boundary changes over the past decade caused by consolidation or unification and describe current boundaries. It should also describe mandatory busing plans, past enrollment patterns, buildings, and modification in the district's grade structure and curriculum, and include a map showing the district's existing schools and properties acquired for school sites.

Community factors. A short description of the community should be included. This section describes its size, general geography and significant geographic features, employment patterns, and major employers, as well as industrial and population growth, major government agencies and planning departments, important district committees, recreational jurisdictions, and agencies with bonding or joint agreements with the school system. It should also identify economic trends, socio-economic makeup, and the community's residential areas.

Educational program. This section should sketch both current and planned programs and goals. It should set forth the district's board-approved philosophy and goals, including size of schools, grade configuration, and location of schools. Of particular importance are explanations of the teaching methodologies that will be used. For example, project-based learning and decentralized administrative functions could increase building areas required to meet the educational program. This section should also identify enrichment programs for in-room versus pull-out programs, computer and related technologies, and unique requirements for each school level—such as federal programs for students with special needs, summer school, vocational centers, day care, regional occupational centers, school and business partnerships, and recreation programs shared with local governments.

It should identify the type of school district (elementary, secondary, unified, consolidated, joint, or county), the grade configuration, and the organizational structure, and briefly describe each grade's curriculum. This section should also describe the assumptions used to prepare the plan; for example, expanding school sites due to growth, city/county demographic data, future land use assumptions, and unification. Ideally, a summary chart or supporting document should provide the educational specifications for each grade configuration.

This section should also list the criteria used for school sites, including maximum and minimum school size and enrollment, maximum distances from school to students' homes, maximum number of students in academic and physical education classrooms, staff-to-student ratios, and professional qualifications of the staff.

As current programs change or new programs develop, instructional methods and the facilities that best support them need redefining. These spaces may vary from small group rooms to large group lectures. Finally, this section should describe the policies and operation of the instructional support services— such as school and district libraries and audiovisual centers, health and guidance, and support services, including administration, transportation, planning, food,

The educational program section should describe assumptions used to prepare the plan: expanding school sites due to growth, city/ county demographic data, future land use assumptions, and unification.

ADA = Americans with
Disabilities Act

custodial, and maintenance services. These factors form
the basis for facility improvements, and incorporate the
equipment and the systems needed to support the educational processes.

Existing school facilities. This section evaluates
the physical condition and use of every school and building the district owns. Schools are designed to house elementary, middle, junior high or intermediate, and high
school grade configurations and implement the educational trends of the time. After a while, enrollment and/or
program definition at a campus may change, causing
existing facilities to become less suited to support the
ongoing activities of new programs.

Current uses and capacity of each school site.
The facilities master plan assesses each site's current
physical condition, the uses to which it is being put, and
its existing capacity. It is helpful to prepare a site map
showing the grounds, buildings, and rooms for each site.

This section should rate how each building, and
each part of each building, is used throughout the typical school day. To measure this, the team should look at
both frequency of use and capacity. Proper capacity depends in part on how a space is utilized—for example,
a kindergarten classroom where varied activities take
place requires more space than a lecture room. The capacity must also conform to building and fire codes,
legal or contractual requirements, and the needs of new
technologies the district might be planning to introduce.
The team can obtain model evaluation forms from national organizations and architectural firms. *See* Council
of Educational Facility Planners (www.cefpi.org).

Since some schools are used for more than just
the district's educational program, the other uses of the
school should also be identified. For instance, the playfields and play courts may also be used as supplemental
parks and recreational facilities, and the buildings may
be used for meetings and other activities.

Code compliance and safety. Each site should
be reviewed for code compliance and safety. Older school
buildings were designed with less stringent codes and
ordinances compared to today's requirements. Construction codes have become increasingly rigorous with regard
to life safety and equal access. Structural design regulations for earthquake resistance are also more rigorous.
Additionally, fire codes have changed, and the Americans with Disabilities Act (ADA) has new regulations.

Demographics in Depth

Demography is "the statistical study of human population, especially with reference to size and density, distribution and vital statistics." One purpose of a school district demographic study is to provide insight about enrollments regarding size, grade organization, location, and the timing of a school's long-range facility planning. Its goal is to provide sufficient information to set policies and make decisions. Short-term projections needed for budget preparation must be precise, aiming for less than one percent error. But even more important is the summary of major factors affecting school enrollments, so that, when new information is available, adjustments can be made to an earlier projection. Forecasting must be a continuous effort if planning crises are to be avoided.

Many demographic study methods are available that have been used for a variety of purposes. This particular method concentrates on micro-demographics, which is the study of small population bases utilizing time series analysis, as opposed to mathematically oriented models that have been applied to large populations. Mathematical models developed for projecting populations, such as equations that include adjustments for mortality and fertility rates, have some validity for large population bases. However, they are insensitive to the large deviations encountered at local levels and are therefore not useful regarding factors that affect school district enrollment.

Time-series analysis is a statistical method that considers cyclical, seasonal, and irregular population trends. These components can be seen in a school district's enrollment history. The trend factor is an upward- or downward-moving enrollment, usually in close correlation with the total population. The cyclical factor can be seen in the "waves of children" that pass through grade levels, with some levels decreasing while other increase. The seasonal factors include migrant children who enter school in the fall but leave after a few months; declining high school enrollments throughout the school year due to mid-year graduation, students turning 18 and dropping out of school, and truancy. The irregular factor can best be seen in a community's major economic occurrences, such as new housing development that brings in new residents, new industries hiring new workers, and major construction projects.

Cohort-Survival Method

One of the most commonly used methods used in time-series analysis is called cohort survival. This method incorporates trend and cyclical factors within its algorithm by using enrollment data from prior years to project the statistical survival rate of student groups as they pass through grade levels. With cohort survival, the changes in enrollment resulting from students entering and leaving school or being held back a grade are calculated automatically. When the number of kindergarten children projected to enter school is included in the data by using outside information, the projections are generally reliable for several years.

One great deficiency of this method is that numerical results remain accurate only when a district is experiencing a constant rate of change in population. Sudden periods of rapid growth or rapid decline cannot be predicted. Nor can attitudinal changes that result in a sudden enrollment drop, such as increasing high school dropout rates. The projection deficiency exists because the survival factor is averaged, producing a level line for adjusting future cohorts. One attempt to account for changing rates is made by applying a weighted mean, whereby greater emphasis is given to more recent data. However, this and other methods simply cannot overcome the problem of using a straight line when the change occurs as a curved line. Nevertheless, cohort-survival does keep the cyclical nature of the enrollment curve intact, and only its numerical values become slightly distorted.

Micro-Demographic Analysis Method

A second method for series analysis ignores historical school enrollments and begins with data relating to population and housing units. Occupancy rates per housing unit and the percentage of the total population representing school age children follow a trend and cyclical pattern that can usually be derived with a reasonable degree of accuracy. Likewise, the percentage of school-age children attending public schools, which usually remains fairly constant over a short period of time, can be obtained. Then, it's possible to project public school enrollment by projecting population and housing units using data that planning ➡

departments and developers provide. By refining the data at each step along the way, greater accuracy for various areas within a school district may be obtained. For example, housing unit projects, occupancy rates, and pupil yield factors can be broken down by study areas. Pupil yield factors can be further broken down into various housing types if a special study is needed to determine the short-range impact of an apartment complex.

The time-series analysis method, like all projection methods, requires a detailed, accurate historical database. Nonetheless, the only purpose for an accurate database is to derive the trend and cyclical nature of the underlying statistical factors, such as occupancy rates, pupil yield factors, and public school percentages. Once they are known, past and present factors can be used to predict the future with reasonable accuracy—regardless of actual future population and housing that materializes. The unknown factor that most contributes to error is the projection of housing units to be built over a specified period in each study area. Here, the predictor is at the mercy of many external changes in a dynamic world. These include decisions by planning commissions and other government agencies, availability of utility lines, interest rates and other

economic issues affecting external and internal growth, availability of construction money, and the changing plans of developers. However, the need for a new school in a given neighborhood can usually be determined quite accurately from the potential development possibilities, although *when* the school will be needed may vary according to when the housing units are actually built.

With a rapidly growing school district, or one that has not maintained a constant rate of growth from year to year, time-series analysis has the advantage of factoring in irregularity. In this situation, both time-series and cohort projection should be used, with both sets of results correlated. If the comparison yields a strong positive correlation, a school district may proceed knowing it has identified a range of probable enrollment sufficiently accurate for making decisions. But regardless of possible numerical errors when using only time-series analysis, the trend and cyclical components usually remain intact, thus permitting corrections to annual or semi-annual projections. Other methods that a school district might consider—including the "least-square method" or the "constant pupil yield method"—are subject to large errors because they do not take into account the dynamic nature of aging communities that change patterns of age distribution. ■

Moreover, districts should check for asbestos and other hazardous materials.

A list of improvements or modifications required for each school site should be prepared, including upgrading older structures to meet current codes, installing a new fire alarm system, structural improvements, and new ADA access ramps, hardware, and accessible toilet room design. All building systems, including the mechanical, electrical, and plumbing systems, need to be evaluated for condition, ability to meet current uses, and the district's projected technology needs.

Demographics of the district. Demographic analysis is designed to provide a district with detailed descriptions of its resident population, existing student base, and projected future enrollment. Information needed for demographic analysis includes trends in population growth, employment, language, and the district's ethnic composition, as well as detailed descriptions of residential housing tenure, unit types, and major geographical or topographical features of the city and county in which the district is located.

Modern demographic analysis begins with a computerized map of the district's territory, which provides the basis for analyzing study areas and/or attendance boundaries, projecting enrollments, and forecasting future development. Additionally, it can be used to extract U.S. Census data and California Department of Finance data. It helps to define areas of population and housing from which students are generated for the proposed school enrollment and identify the district voting constituency. Information from other surrounding cities and districts may be included when relevant.

Demographic studies present data and information in simple, easy-to-read tables and charts that help determine when future enrollment growth will exhaust school capacities, or when enrollment decline may permit reorganization of facilities to save costs. Charts are printed in color to facilitate analysis.

If a community's growth pattern seems to be accelerating or fluctuating, a more detailed analysis of the causes and effects of the changes and their impact on future enrollments will have to be made. If enrollment is dropping, more time is available to make adjustments, and fewer or no new facilities will be needed. But if developers are building large new housing tracts, projections will be needed in advance.

Projecting enrollment. The most common method for projecting future enrollment, called "cohort survival," is based on school enrollment data for the previous three to five years. The most useful projection technique for communities that are growing rapidly is called "mapping," because it breaks down the district into subareas.

A common way to project future enrollment is to use SAB Form 50-01 with the cohort survival method. Typically, districts rely on numbers from the same date each year (usually from fall enrollment or the first report period), to determine the change in the number of students in each grade one year and in the next higher grade in the following year (for example, the number of fourth-graders in the 1989–90 school year and fifth-graders in 1990–91 school year). It is difficult to obtain a reliable count of children expected to enroll in kindergarten—districts typically estimate enrollment based on how kindergarten enrollments have changed in recent years. They then calculate the percentage of change for each grade level and apply that ratio to the known number of students in the grade as they move to the next grade.

Mapping. In areas of rapid population growth, a technique called "mapping" works well. With mapping, the school district is divided into smaller planning units, or subareas, that are organized by the preferred size for a single enrollment area. Whenever possible, major geographic features, such as highways or railroads, should serve as boundaries for the subareas.

In each subarea the district determines the existing number of houses and apartments and the "yield rates" or "generation factors" for those dwellings—that is, how many students, by grade level, live in each type of dwelling, based on past enrollment. If the houses or apartments being built are similar to the ones already there (check for similar zoning by the planning board), the yield rates should not change. If yield rates for a specific area are not known, the district may use the state default levels established in SAB Form 50-01 of 0.7 students per household for K–12, 0.5 students per household for K–8, and 0.2 students per household for grades 9–10.

These generation factors are used to project the number of children in each grade expected from the new homes. If the zoning status or the quality and type of housing are changing, it is necessary to calculate a new yield rate for each grade level for all the planned houses and apartments. Multiplying the yield rate of each type of dwelling unit by the number of new units being constructed, plus the existing units, will provide the subarea's anticipated enrollment figures.

The final step is to compile the subarea enrollment projections into a single projection that encompasses the entire school district.

If a community's growth pattern seems to be accelerating or fluctuating, a detailed analysis of the causes and effects of the changes and their impact on future enrollments will have to be made.

✍ **practice tip**

Since the state uses the cohort survival method to determine eligibility for funding, its use in the district's facilities master plan will facilitate the use of data for eligibility purposes.

2 C.C.R. § 1859.42

With mapping, the school district is divided into smaller planning units, or subareas, organized by the preferred size for a single enrollment area.

The owner gets upset when the state tells them the forms aren't in.
I had a project where the inspector died...
I couldn't get him to sign the 6A form.

Taking into account the adequacy of existing schools, the district determines new school zones based on enrollment projections and subarea analysis, and selects new building sites as close as possible to the center of the new zones.

Priorities. Once current conditions, future trends, and the educational program have been assessed and identified, the school district should analyze and define its priorities. Since funding resources for facilities are usually very limited, this section should make a complete list of its facility requirements, ranking them in order of recommended implementation. This information is useful in determining the projects to execute first.

Finance and implementation plan. Once the tasks of assembling the data regarding facility needs are completed, the team must determine how to finance and implement the district's facilities priorities. If the district lacks expertise on staff, a financial advisor or a state program specialist should be hired to provide funding options for the district to consider.

Ideally, the planners, educators, architect, and demographer developed a comprehensive list of existing school improvements that are needed, an estimate of predicted new school facilities that will serve future residential development, and the estimated costs of these improvements.

This list should be based on the information the team has gathered to determine the type and number of schools the district will need, the board policy decisions about school sizes, walking distances, and busing, the enrollment projections for district subareas, and the map of current schools to determine approximate attendance and where future schools should be located. Some districts chart their projections for each grade level and subarea by using transparent sheets over an enlarged district map. Additionally, using another transparent overlay can show proposed attendance boundaries.

Taking into account the adequacy of existing schools, the district determines new school zones based on the enrollment projections and subarea analysis, and selects new building sites as close as possible to the center of the new school zones. These mapped zones will serve as a guide when the district's real estate personnel or brokers are seeking a suitable site to acquire. It will also limit the search for alternative sites outside the zone, since they will not meet the facilities master plan or educational program objectives.

In this section of the facilities master plan, the federal, state, and local funding sources should be identified. If available funds are sufficient to pay for all future schools and needed improvements, then the district may implement its plan. Most likely these financial resources will be insufficient, and other local resources, such as a general obligation bond, may be needed.

Following development of the district-wide facilities master plan, a realistic assessment of the district's financial picture and schedules for siting and construction work will require a site-specific plan.

Educational Specifications

What Are "Ed Specs"?

Educational specifications guide the planning and construction of a school facility by converting curriculum into space. They are a collection of objectives relating to the community needs, education, and policies, as well as statements on primary and support programs outlining what local educators want to achieve regarding people, activities, and relationships. Educational specifications are a written means of communication between educators and design professionals.

Educational specifications guide the planning and construction of a school facility by converting curriculum into space.

Educational specifications, also known as the architectural program, contain, at a minimum, the following:

- The spaces to be included in the project
- A description of the functions to take place in those spaces
- Relationships between the spaces
- Building area required
- Relationships of the site functions
- Detailed space requirements such as mechanical, electrical, technological, and furnishings

Another part of this equation also needs to be considered: the teaching methodologies or pedagogy to be used in each facility. When developing the educational specifications, it is important to consider that curriculum trends and teaching methodologies change frequently. Since it is more difficult to change the facilities than the curriculum, the design should include flexibility.

For school facilities to meet a community's needs, educational programming should precede architectural programming. It should be developed and written by educators, and the educational specifications should be developed with the input from all the major groups using the proposed facilities. Architects trained in facilitating the process of collecting the data for ed specs can provide valuable input on how educational concepts can be translated into the physical environment. Caution should be exercised, however, to avoid designing during the programming process, because it can limit input and potential solutions. Although related, educational programs and educational specifications are quite different, and neither educators nor architects are capable of performing both tasks.

For school facilities to meet a community's needs, educational programming should precede architectural programming.

Why Develop Ed Specs?

In California, the overriding reason to prepare ed specs is that they are required by law. All school districts, whether state- or locally-funded, are required to prepare minimum educational specifications. 5 C.C.R. § 14030.

It is important to understand the distinction between the educational program and the educational specifications. The program defines the goals of the district's educational philosophy, the process, and the expected outcome. The specifications define in detail the requirements of the facilities needed to deliver that curriculum.

State-funded school districts must seek CDE approval of their ed specs twice, but locally-funded school districts do not need to seek CDE approval. The state-funded districts first must submit preliminary plans and ed specs to CDE prior to preparation of final plans for approval. 5 C.C.R. § 14031(a). Later, these districts must seek CDE approval of final plans, including any alterations to the ed specs. 5 C.C.R. § 14031(b). Waivers or exemptions from these requirements may be granted by the State Superintendent of Public Instruction.

The primary purpose of educational specifications is to give the project designer detailed criteria for the design. However, ed specs can also have a number of secondary purposes. As the architect develops the plan, ed specs can verify that the design has met the users' intent. Meetings should be held periodically with the ed spec committee for the purpose of reviewing specifications to be certain the design is meeting its educational goals.

Building a school facility is a lengthy process, and end users are often not involved in developing the design. For these people, ed specs documentation can serve as something of an "operator's manual." While the documentation may not always change opinions, at least the reasoning behind the design will be clear. In any capital improvement program, it's important to engage the public. Involving key members of the community and local officials increases the possibility of "buy-in," and may result in greater support for local bond measures and agency approvals.

Developing Ed Specs

Experience has shown that written educational specifications will yield the best product if they are prepared by the school staff and educational specialists.

They should be based on the school district's goals, objectives, and policies, and on community input, as defined in section 14030 of Title 5 of the California Code of Regulations. The list is long and exhaustive. For instance, ed specs must define parent drop-off and pick-up areas, special education rooms, gymnasiums, lockers, showers in lockers, placement of water fountains, trash pickup, secure storage areas, counter tops accessible for an age-appropriate population both at a standing and wheelchair level, placement of clerical staff so that they have a clear view of the nurse's office, and fixtures for lighting. It's also required that "classrooms at new school sites shall have adequate space to perform the curriculum functions for the planned enrollment as described in the school district's Facilities Master Plan." Other specifications are prepared by CDE, such as for mobile classrooms for physically handicapped students. Educ. Code §§ 16197, 56836, 17251. While identifying minimum content requirements, the law does not specify a method for developing educational specifications, leaving school districts a great deal of flexibility.

While identifying minimum content requirements, the law does not specify a method for developing educational specifications, leaving school districts a great deal of flexibility.

Methods for
Developing Ed Specs

Since it takes time to develop the vision and define features specific to a school site, many districts begin developing ed specs one to three years before a school facility is designed. Although many educational facility planners recommend that specs be developed in tandem with the architect, some school districts choose not to involve the architect or designer in the initial planning. Many districts find that a good first step is forming a committee of school administrators, teachers, parents, and other specialists, such as special ed teachers, curriculum planners, and librarians, to incorporate the ideas of people who will be using the facility. For instance, a committee member for an elementary school might offer good reasons why kindergarten classrooms should be separate from the rest of the campus, or that the plan should include two different playgrounds for younger and middle students. This type of expertise can be very helpful when developing facilities that enhance the learning environment.

Many facility planners recommend the following questions be asked when developing ed specs.

- What is the philosophy behind the program?
- What type of curriculum and/or programs will be offered?
- Who should be involved?
- What are the important time lines in the proposed project?
- What are the current teaching styles that will be utilized by the teachers?
- What are the current learning styles employed by students?
- What role will technology play in the educational process?
- How will the community use the building?

Form of Ed Specs

Once they are developed, detailed ed specs are written into a document. "Bubble" diagrams or drawings are developed to illustrate desired area relationships. *See* Figure 3-1. Others create a matrix to serve as a guide. Ed specs are not absolute, but are the essential first step in the process of designing a school.

Ed specs are not absolute, but are the essential first step in the process of designing a school.

Contents of Ed Specs

Ed Specs should include:

- A description of each instructional or activity space, including function and type of space
- Approximate square footage or size of each space
- Student capacity
- Special design considerations;
- Functional relationships between spaces

In addition, the document should comprise:

- Teaching and student learning styles
- Instructional program information and objectives
- Existing and projected enrollment analyses
- Required land and facility resources

Section 14030 of the California Code of Regulations lists the complete requirements.

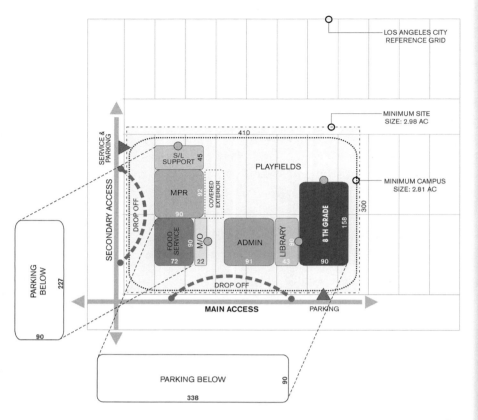

Ground Level — First Floor

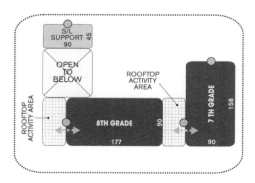

Level 2 — Second Floor

Figure 3-1
Typical Bubble Diagram

School boards can request an exemption for an ed spec standard from the State Superintendent of Public Instruction if the district can demonstrate that the "educational appropriateness" and the "safety of the school design" would not be compromised by an alternative to that standard. 5 C.C.R. § 14030 (r). When seeking an exemption or requiring clarification of CDE standards, a district should contact the CDE field services consultant responsible for schools in its county. The process is rather informal. The Department of Education staff is sensitive to constraints school districts face in providing needed facilities and can help a district find alternative ways to comply with its standards, particularly where the standards are difficult or impossible to accommodate.

The specific needs of education in California are continually changing. So too are the facilities. They must be planned, designed, and constructed to reflect the community they serve. Educational specifications provide specific design directions and are the most effective means of communications between the educational client and the architect.

Coordination with State Government Regulatory and Planning Agencies

Good planning for a school facility requires understanding the role of state agencies and the criteria they use in approving potential school sites. School districts may need state agency approval to receive state funding for siting and construction of a school facility.

Safety and Welfare for School District Workers

California's Department of Industrial Relations (DIR) was established to improve working conditions for wage earners. DIR regulates school districts, as employers, to ensure safe and healthy working conditions for their *employees* under the Occupational Safety and Health Act (Cal-OSHA) of 1973. Labor Code §§ 6300–6719. DIR enforces prevailing wage requirements applicable to school facility construction projects as public works projects. With the passage of AB 1506 (Wesson), districts seeking state bond funding for their projects must initiate and enforce a labor compliance program. Labor Code §§ 1771.5, 1771.7. DIR is authorized to grant or revoke approval of a compliance program. Title 8, C.C.R. §§ 16425–16439. OSHA and labor compliance program requirements for school facilities are also addressed in chapter 5.

Protection of the Environment from School Facility Use

For each school facility construction project, a district must comply with CEQA requirements (Pub. Res. Code § 21000 *et seq.*). CEQA sets out an information disclosure process enabling a district to avoid or mitigate significant environmental impacts that may result from siting and construction. No state agency enforces CEQA. Citizens bring lawsuits to enforce its provisions, and each district must certify its own compliance. CEQA requirements related to school facilities are discussed in chapter 4.

School districts are also responsible for protecting the state's waters from pollution in storm water runoff from school sites. The State Water Resources Control Board (SWRCB) and its Regional Water Quality Control Boards (RWQCBs) are responsible for protecting water quality in California. The SWRCB has adopted general permits to regulate storm water runoff from construction and industrial activities and MS4s. School districts engaged in certain categories of construction must comply with the Construction Activities Storm Water General Permit (General Construction Permit). In 2003, the SWRCB adopted the Small MS4 Permit, which requires school districts to develop, implement, and maintain a storm water management program (SWMP) for each school within the district. Requirements of the SWRCB related to school facilities are discussed in chapter 5.

State Role in Ensuring That State Funds Are Expended Wisely (OPSC/SAB)

While the state regulatory role in the siting and construction of school facilities has been traditionally one of ensuring that the school building is conducive to learning and free of health and

CEQA = California Environmental Quality Act
DIR = Department of Industrial Relations
OPSC = Office of Public School Construction
OSHA = Occupational Safety and Health Act
RWQCB = Regional Water Quality Control Board
SAB = State Allocation Board
SWMP = Storm water management program
SWRCB = State Water Resources Control Board

For each school facility construction project, a district must comply with CEQA requirements.

The legal problem ...there's so many players you don't know which donkey to pin the tail on.

State Role in Ensuring That Schools Are Safe

Earthquake and Structural Safety, Fire Safety, and Equal Access for the Disabled

Historically, the state's interests in school facilities concern health and safety. The Field Act of 1933 established structural standards and state oversight of design and construction to ensure that school children would be safe from damage caused by earthquakes. The DSA, part of the California Department of General Services, is the state agency that administers the Field Act. The DSA must review and approve plans for new schools, regardless of their funding source, and requires a more rigorous review of plans and construction than the Uniform Building Code. Among the differences is that the DSA inspector must personally observe that construction standards are met. In addition to Field Act requirements, the DSA reviews for compliance with the state fire safety requirements and with Title 24 accessibility standards (related to the Americans with Disabilities Act requirements). DSA requirements are discussed in detail in this chapter and in chapter 5.

Safety from Surrounding Uses and Environment and Educational Design (CDE)

The state's interest in health and safety now includes requirements regarding proximity to incompatible land uses and exposure to environmental hazards. The School Facilities Planning Division of the CDE reviews and approves sites and building plans for new school facilities. The agency also reviews potential sites for safety issues, including proximity to railroads, power lines, traffic congestion, exposure to hazardous materials, seismic land stability, and other potential hazardous land uses.

CDE also reviews school building plans to determine if its educational design standards are met. Although the standards must be met on all projects, this review is required only if state funds are used and optional when local funds are used. CDE's educational design standards include minimum parcel size, class size, location of bathrooms, water fountains, etc. CDE site requirements are discussed in more detail in chapter 4.

Safety from Toxic Soil (DTSC)

In 2000, the state's interest in health and safety expanded to include ensuring that school sites do not pose any environmental health risk due to contaminated soil. DTSC reviews and oversees the environmental assessment of soil in Phase I or the more detailed Preliminary Environmental Assessment, and removal or remediation if any is required. DTSC requirements for school facilities are discussed in detail in chapter 4. ■

We found it was best to have Arthur at the presentation ...when the design is outrageous and costs a fortune

safety risks, the growing dependency on the state for funds is accompanied by a growing role in monitoring their expenditure. As explained in chapter 2, the OPSC within the Department of General Services determines whether school districts are eligible for state funds. The SAB was created in 1947 to allocate state funds to poor districts in the wake of the post-WWII baby boom. The SAB is a small state agency, primarily a decision-making body comprised of legislators and department officials, staffed by the OPSC. Because the funds available has never matched the need, school districts have competed for state funding. The rules for allocating scarce state funds are constantly changing with each new lawsuit, new court ruling, new piece of legislation, and adoption of emergency regulations. OPSC and SAB requirements are discussed in chapter 2.

Coordination with Local Government Agencies

Maintaining good relationships with the local authorities is essential when developing a school project. Although public school districts may exempt themselves by a two-thirds' majority vote of the school board from most local planning, zoning, and building department requirements, the local agencies *do* have jurisdiction over street development, landscaping, sidewalks, and utilities outside the district's property. Local planning departments also have the authority to review and approve drainage plans for school sites, and road improvements and grading plans affecting drainage. Govt. Code § 53097. The approval of these elements of the project could be withheld if other requirements are not met. It is important for the district to discuss the project with the local authorities early on to get their support and, where possible, meet local standards. When a district requests an early coordination meeting, the local planning agency is obligated to meet with the district within 15 days. Govt. Code § 65352.2(b). School districts may also proactively work with local agencies to obtain dedications of elementary school sites from developers seeking tentative tract map approvals. Govt. Code § 66478.

Local Zoning Agency

Local school boards can exempt themselves from local requirements within the property of the school project by a two-thirds majority vote of the board, after complying with the notice requirements of Government Code section 65352.2 and section 21151.2 of the Public Resources Code. With this two-thirds vote, local planning departments cannot require schools to meet planning and zoning requirements within the school site boundaries, and local building departments have no right to review public school plans and specifications. However, the ability to exempt a project from local ordinances does not apply to nonclassroom facilities, including, but not limited to, warehouses, administrative buildings, and automotive storage and repair buildings. Govt. Code § 53094.

While local government zoning authority can be limited by a school board's vote, this limit does not apply to work outside those lines or offsite. Conversely, districts need not seek state agency approvals for offsite work since local governments retain their jurisdiction outside the district's property lines.

Notice Requirement

In 2001, AB 1367 (Wiggins) modified the local school board exemption from local requirements. This law modified California Government Code sections 53091 and 53094 and added section 65352.2. School districts are now required to notify the local planning department 45 days prior to the completion of a district master plan, long range plan, or school facilities needs analysis, and to supply such documents to the local planning agency for review. The local planning agency may request, and must be granted within 15 days, a meeting with the school district to discuss the documents. The school district may also request a meeting with the local planning agency, which must be granted within 15 days. Only after this process is complete may the school board take action by a two-thirds majority vote to exempt a project from local planning requirements.

State vs. Local Role in Public Education

Since its admission to the Union, California has assumed responsibility for a statewide public education system open to all. The Constitution of 1849 directed the Legislature to "provide for a system of common schools, by which a school shall be kept up and supported in each district …." Cal. Const. of 1849, art. IX, § 3. That constitutional command, with the additional proviso that the school maintained by each district be "free," has persisted to the present day. Cal. Const., art. IX, § 5.

In furtherance of the state system of free public education, the Constitution also created state and county educational offices, including a Superintendent of Public Instruction and a State Board of Education. Cal. Const. art. IX, § 2–3.3, 7. It authorized the formation of local school districts (Cal. Const., art. IX, § 6½, 14), required that all public elementary and secondary schools be administered within the public school system (Cal. Const. art IX, § 6), established a State School Fund (Cal. Const., art. IX, § 4), reserved a minimum portion of state revenues for allocation to the Fund (Cal. Const. art. XVI, § 8, 8.5), guaranteed minimum allocations from the Fund for each public school (Cal. Const. art. IX, § 6), specified minimum salaries for public school teachers, authorized the State Board of Education to approve public school textbooks (§ 7.5), and permitted the Legislature to grant local districts such authority over their affairs as does not "conflict with the laws and purposes for which school districts are established." § 14.

Accordingly, California courts have adhered to the following principles: Public education is an obligation that the state assumed by adopting the Constitution. *San Francisco Unified School Dist. v. Johnson* (1971) 3 Cal. 3d 937, 951–952; *Piper v. Big Pine School Dist.* (1924) 193 Cal. 664, 669. The public school system, although administered through local districts created by the Legislature, is "one system…applicable to all the common schools…." *Kennedy v. Miller* (1893) 97 Cal. 429, 432. "In view of the importance of education to society and to the individual child, the opportunity to receive the schooling furnished by the state must be made available to all on an equal basis…." *Jackson v. Pasadena City School Dist.* ➡

Public Education

continued

(1963) 59 Cal. 2d 876, 880. "[M]anagement and control of the public schools [is] a matter of state[, not local,] care and supervision...." *Hall v. City of Taft* (1956) 47 Cal. 2d 177, 181; *California Teachers Assn. v. Huff* (1992) 5 Cal. App. 4th 1513, 1523–1524. The Legislature's "plenary" power over public education is subject only to constitutional restrictions. *Hall v. City of Taft*, supra, at pp. 180–181; *Tinsley v. Palo Alto Unified School Dist.* (1979) 91 Cal. App. 3d 871, 903–904. Local districts are the state's agents for local operation of the common school system (*Hall v. City of Taft*, *supra*, at p. 181; *San Francisco Unified School Dist. v. Johnson*, *supra*, 3 Cal. 3d at p. 952; *California Teachers Assn.*, *supra*), and the state's ultimate responsibility for public education cannot be delegated to any other entity. *Hall v. City of Taft*, supra; *Piper v. Big Pine School Dist.*, *supra*, 193 Cal. 669.

While the Legislature has assigned much of the governance of public schools to local districts (*e.g.*, §§ 14000, 35160 *et seq.*, 35160.1) that operate under officials who are locally elected and appointed (§§ 35020, 35100 *et seq.*), for some purposes the districts are separate political entities. For example, *Johnson v. San Diego Unified School Dist.* (1990) 217 Cal. App. 3d 692, 698–700 (general theory of respondeat superior does not make state liable for torts of local district or its employees); *Gonzales v. State of California* (1972) 29 Cal. App. 3d 585, 590–592; *First Interstate Bank v. State of California* (1987) 197 Cal. App. 3d 627, 633–634 (state not vicariously liable for district's breach of

contract); *Board of Education v. Calderon* (1973) 35 Cal. App. 3d 490, 496 (local district is not the "state" or the "People," so as to be civilly bound in dismissal proceedings by teacher's acquittal of criminal sex offense under principles of res judicata).

With respect to funding local schools, the existence of the local-district system has not prevented recognition that the state has broad responsibility to ensure basic educational equality under the California Constitution. Because access to a public education is a uniquely fundamental personal interest in California, our courts have consistently found that the state charter accords broader rights against state-maintained educational discrimination than does federal law. Despite contrary federal authority, California constitutional principles require state assistance to correct basic "interdistrict" disparities in the system of common schools, even when the discriminatory effect was not produced by the purposeful conduct of the state or its agents.

In *Serrano v. Priest* (1971) 5 Cal. 3d 584 (*Serrano I*), the court struck down the existing state public school financing scheme, which caused the amount of basic revenues per pupil to vary substantially among the respective districts, depending on their taxable property values. *Serrano I* concluded that such a scheme violated both state and federal equal protection guarantees because it discriminated against a fundamental interest—education—on the basis of a suspect classification—district wealth—and could not be justified by a compelling state interest under the strict scrutiny test thus applicable. Pages 596–619. ▪

Local Health Agency

Local health departments associated with the county of jurisdiction are authorized to approve the kitchen facilities and some swimming pools in a school project. Educ. Code § 49403. Since these vary, it is advisable to contact the health department to determine specific requirements. Copies of local codes and/or regulations can usually be obtained from the agency. It is essential to meet these requirements and obtain documented approval prior to DSA submittal. Local health departments, similar to local fire marshals, may inspect kitchen facilities at any time. If discrepancies are found or if approvals have not been obtained, these agencies can prohibit a school from using the kitchen.

Local Fire Authority

The relationship and distribution of power between the local fire authority, the Office of the State Fire Marshal, and the DSA is confusing. On the one hand the DSA is the approving agency for all fire detection and protection systems in a public school. The requirements for new and modernized facilities are in the California Code of Regulations, Title 24. DSA must enforce these requirements as approved by the California Building Standards Commission.

On the other hand, the local fire department has jurisdiction over the facilities immediately upon occupancy of the facilities, and may have very different and more restrictive requirements. 19 C.C.R. §§ 3.05, 3.18. To make matters even more complex, the local fire department, unlike the local building department, has the right to close a facility any time there is a significant violation of the fire ordinances. There have been instances when a project met state standards through DSA, and then was closed by the local fire department for lack of fire suppression equipment. These instances are rare, but they demonstrate the need for a strong relationship with the local fire department.

The Office of the State Fire Marshal (OSFM) now has limited involvement in the school approval process. In the past, the OSFM assigned personnel to DSA to complete the fire and life safety portion of the plan check. Now DSA personnel are assigned to that task. The OSFM is still responsible for the development of regulations through which the projects are approved, however. The OSFM also has authority over all local fire departments, although they seem reluctant to use that authority. There have been many attempts by the state to bring consistency to local fire department standards and treatment of school facilities, but they haven't been successful. If the school district is having difficulty with a local fire department's treatment of a new facility, it may appeal to the OSFM.

Local fire marshals do have authority over access to school sites for fire department equipment, requirements for adequate water flow to the site, and the number and placement of fire hydrants. Fire-Flow Requirements for Buildings, section 903.3 and Appendix III-AA, Uniform Fire Code; Fire Hydrant Locations and Distribution, section 903.4.2, Appendix III-BB, Uniform Fire Code.

Fire fighting equipment varies from jurisdiction to jurisdiction. To protect the facilities adequately, the equipment must be able to reach all buildings on a school campus. A general rule of thumb is that all portions of a building must be within 150 feet of a fire access road. With some variations, the standard length of a fire hose is 150 feet, and fire fighters must be able to connect to a piece of equipment on the access road and reach every building. In some cases, fire department requirements consider fire hydrants pieces of equipment for this purpose.

Fire departments must also have the ability to open all gates and remove obstructions easily from fire access roads in case of emergency. If gates must be locked at any time, the fire department may be required to have access to keys. One method used is a Knox box, a device containing keys to padlocks on gates to buildings that can be made part of a building or welded to a fence close to a gate. The fire department can then use one key to gain access to all the keys for a site. More often than not, if the gate has a padlock, the fire department will simply use a set of bolt cutters to remove the lock. In any case, the district should coordinate with the local fire department about its particular requirements.

The fire department must also approve the design of the fire access road. Since the turning radius and pavement section requirement for each piece of equipment may vary, fire department standards should be reviewed prior to beginning the site layout. While the fire department may have a certain pavement section as its standard, in many cases the project's civil engineer can demonstrate that the standard is excessive, and a design that supports the equipment should be approved. Also, most fire departments do not like dead-end access

✍ practice tip

Notice to the local planning commission is due at least 45 days prior to completion of the master plan, long-range plan, or school facility needs analysis.

OSFM = Office of the
State Fire Marshal

A general rule of thumb is that all portions of a building must be within 150 feet of a fire access road.

roads because backing up and turning around a large piece of equipment can be difficult. Since turn-around areas take up a considerable amount of land, an access road that loops the site is preferred.

Street and Other Offsite Improvements: Funding Considerations

Generally, the local planning department sets the standards for the street width, pavement section, and the curb, gutter, and sidewalk design. These agencies may also have landscaping and lighting standards for the public right-of-way. It is up to the school district to negotiate how they must comply with these standards. The state will pay only a limited portion of the offsite development, and this can sometimes be used as an effective negotiating tool to reduce the requirements.

Section 1859.76 of the OPSC Regulations outlines the extent to which the state will participate in funding offsite development. The school district must understand that, unless the qualifications for financial hardship can be met, more than half the cost of the work will be the district's responsibility. Currently, the work eligible for funding includes development along two adjacent sides of the school site. This development includes the cost of one-half of the locally mandated street width. The state will pay 50 percent of one-half of the street improvements required by local ordinance. If the district is required to develop more than half of the required street width, the additional work will be at the district's expense. The state will also participate in the development of any sidewalks, landscaping, or street lighting that may be required by local ordinance. OPSC does require the submittal of these ordinances to substantiate the requirement, and will also participate in street signage, traffic signals, and offsite development fees if these are required by ordinance.

A portion of the cost of storm drainage, water lines, and sanitary sewers will be paid by the state to the point of connection. Above what the state pays, this can be a significant local cost for some districts.

Street utilities are also allowed if they directly benefit the school. Storm drainage, water lines, and sanitary sewers will be paid by the state to the point of connection. Above what the state pays, this can be a significant local cost for some districts. For example, if a 4-inch water line is required to serve the school site and the local public works department requires an 8-inch line to serve the surrounding community, OPSC would only pay the state's 50 percent of the cost of a 4-inch pipe. The district would then be required to pay the additional cost or negotiate a lower cost with the local agency. In some cases it may be able to establish a reimbursement agreement with the local agency, which can return some of the development cost to the district as additional users tap into the services. Ideally, the local agency would establish the agreement and assume the responsibility for the financing of the services. The district would then only be responsible for their portion of the work.

OPSC will pay the state's 50 percent share of utilities to the point of connection, an important consideration when selecting a site.

OPSC will also pay the state's 50 percent share of the utilities to the point of connection, an important consideration when selecting a site. If the district selects a site that is remote from utility connections, the cost could be substantial. Even if the state pays 50 percent of the allowable costs, the district's 50 percent plus any additional requirements that may be imposed by the local public works department could be significant.

The project must also be designed to local utility company standards. Connections for electricity, gas, telephone, and cable TV must be approved by the these companies, and the standards and approval process for utility companies vary across the state.

To verify the costs of offsite utility services and service site development, the OPSC requires completed and approved drawings accompanied by a detailed cost estimate. This has posed serious problems for districts where local jurisdictions are slow in approving those plans. In many cases, the plan check and connection fees will not be developed by the agency until the construction contract is signed. Or the fees may change when the contract is signed. This could be after the OPSC final apportionment is made, leaving the district solely responsible for the additional cost. The OPSC has agreed to allow school districts to submit unapproved plans and associated cost estimate with the application for funding if accompanied by a letter from the local agency or utility company indicating that the work in the drawings is required for approval.

To avoid potential problems with the project schedule and state budgets, the district and the project architect should work closely with the local public works agency and utility companies early in the process.

To avoid potential problems with the project schedule and the state budgets, the district and the project architect should work closely with the local public works agency and utility companies early in the design process.

Planning and Designing the School Facility

Building or modernizing a school facility is a great opportunity for a school district to have a positive impact on students, staff, and the community for many decades. Good design can greatly support learning, save on maintenance costs, and reduce operation costs. However, school districts too often perceive the design process as an added burden rather than a significant opportunity. This is understandable—many districts do not have the resources to become as involved as they should with the design and construction process. The state program does not allow construction funds to pay the staff salaries needed to manage capital improvement programs. Though not as strict, local bond funds also have restrictions on staff expenditures. Yet, despite these disincentives, the design process can make the difference between a liability and a valued resource.

A well-designed facility can benefit the school district in many ways and cost the same or often less than a poorly designed facility. Active participation by the district and its staff will accrue benefits for many years because the finished school will better respond to the district's needs. This participation is most critical in the educational specifications, pre-design planning, schematics, and design development process. Most major decisions are made during these times, and by the time construction documents and construction are executed, relatively few decisions are left to be made.

Design and siting of a school can occur simultaneously, however at times, the design is largely completed before a site is selected, and then is tailored to the site. Other times, however, a school district already possesses a site before the design process begins. *See* the discussion in chapter 4 about whether or not the siting process should precede the design process.

Design Process Overview

This section summarizes the typical design process for a new campus, an addition, and/or modernization project. The design process begins with a set of design criteria (the educational specifications), and ends with an extensive set of detailed instructions to the contractor (the construction documents).

Educational specifications. As discussed above, ed specs establish the project's design criteria, and tell the architect and engineers what should go into the building. As schools take on more responsibilities—such as special education, child care, and joint-use functions—the need for more detailed educational specifications increases.

Predesign planning. At this point, the district and architect analyze the project requirements and define how the processes will be executed. Also covered are project budget, schedule, site information, and educational specifications. This effort can move more quickly if the district retained the architect to prepare or take part in the preparation of the educational specifications. If not, the architect will need additional time to become familiar with the educational specifications, and project site, and to verify the project budget.

Schematic design. This is where the architect develops a design or design options from the district's educational specifications, and ideas become drawings that represent the building. In order to ensure the project conforms to the district's needs, active involvement and review by the district is very important in this phase. This is the time to move walls, try different layouts, and then make a final decision on the size, shape, and look of the buildings. Changes made after this phase can be time-consuming and costly.

A preliminary cost estimate is prepared, and then drawings illustrating floor plans, a site plan, and exterior elevations are developed. For state-funded projects, preliminary plans should be submitted to CDE for review and approval. This is also the point where a preliminary plan review or preliminary conference with DSA can be scheduled. The review is optional and is intended to help resolve questions of code interpretation and special project design or site conditions. The preliminary conference is especially beneficial for complex projects and for architects and engineers who have not worked with DSA in the past. This conference can also be scheduled during the design development and during the construction document phase.

Design development. At this stage, the design is refined and generalities become specifics. Decisions are made about building materials, heating ventilation and cooling systems, electrical systems, structural system, and a more detailed cost estimate is developed.

Construction documents. Construction documents, or "blueprints," include drawings and technical specifications for every system, detail, and material of the building. The technical specifications establish the type and quality level for the products and work on the project. The drawings include plans, elevations, sections, and schedules that define the quantity and location of building components. Usually grouped by design discipline, they include civil, architectural, structural, heating ventilation and air conditioning (HVAC), plumbing, electrical, and landscape sections. Though the district's involvement is usually less in this phase, it is

The design process begins with a set of design criteria (the educational specifications), and ends with an extensive set of detailed instructions to the contractor (the construction documents).

The Design Process

- Educational specifications
- Predesign planning
- Schematic design
- Design development
- Construction documents

HVAC = Heating ventilation and air conditioning

critical that the district stay involved to answer questions and make the decisions required to complete the documents. It is important that a representative from the design committee review the construction documents for conformity with the district's requirements. This is the opportunity to verify details such as the location of light switches, computer network outlets, door locations, and the location of built-in furniture. These drawings will have a greater level of detail than the educational specifications, and this is the last opportunity prior to the project being built to verify that everything has been included and is correctly placed. An updated cost estimate is also prepared. The cost estimate and the drawings should be reviewed by the district, its design committee, and others involved in the process, such as the maintenance and operations staff. When complete, the drawings are submitted to DSA for construction approval and to CDE for final plan approval. DSA-approved drawings are then submitted to CDE and OPSC for construction funding on state-funded projects.

Title 5 establishes minimum standards for K–12 public school facilities, requiring that the general design:

- Evolve from a statement of educational program requirements reflecting the school district's educational goals and objectives
- Be master-planned to provide for maximum site enrollment
- Be located on a site that meets CDE standards (specified in § 14010)
- Provide occupants environmental comfort and work efficiency
- Require a practical minimum of maintenance
- Meet federal, state, and local statutory requirements for structure, fire, and public safety
- Be engineered with flexibility to accommodate future needs

Design Committee

The design committee interprets the district's educational specifications and reviews and monitors the design work of the architect, which is critical to the success of the capital improvement project. Consisting of several members, the design committee is supported by others who lend their expertise depending upon the scope and phase of a project.

Ideally, the design committee would include one member who is responsible for writing and revising the educational specifications. In many districts it is the facilities planner or director who heads the design committee. Another key member would have sufficient authority and trust to make important decisions regarding school design without asking the board to approve each decision. This might be the district superintendent, an assistant/associate superintendent, or another high-level person in the district. A third key member might be the school principal or someone equally familiar with day-to-day operations of the facility being designed. This person could evaluate the basic operational needs of a design, such as educational and security procedures.

The design committee interprets the district's educational specifications and reviews and monitors the architect's, which is critical to the success of the capital improvement project.

A design committee at work

Table 3-1. Educational Facility Area Standards
Summary of Minimum Size Areas Title 5, C.C.R. § 14030

Room / Facility type	Minimum sizes	Selected special requirements (see Title 5)
Kindergarten classrooms	1350 sq. ft. per classroom	Dedicated restrooms, includes restrooms, teacher prep rooms and storage
Kindergarten outdoor play space	2:1 Ratio	Conduit and cabling outlets for networks or stand alone equipment
General classrooms grades 1–12	960 sq. ft. per classroom	
Specialized classrooms		
Resource specialist program	240 sq. ft. per room	
Speech and language program	200 sq. ft. per room	
Psychologist office		Provides confidentiality
Special day classrooms	See Educ. Code § 17747(a) for size req'ts	Properly equipped for age and type of condition
Laboratories		
Science laboratory	1300 sq. ft. per room	Includes storage and teacher prep area
Consumer home economics	1300 sq. ft. per room	
Industrial technology education	Varies	
Computer instructional support area	960 sq. ft. per room	Sufficient outlets, power sources, network links
Auxiliary areas		
Gymnasium	Varies	
Multi-purpose rooms		
Elementary	5.3 sq. ft. per unit of a.d.a. 3500 sq. ft. minimum	
Middle	5.3 sq. ft. per unit of a.d.a. 4500 sq. ft. minimum	
High school	6.3 sq. ft. per unit of a.d.a. 7500 sq. ft. minimum total	
Food service area		
Elementary	2 sq. ft. per unit of a.d.a. 400 sq. ft. minimum 1480 sq. ft. maximum	
Middle	2 sq. ft. per unit of a.d.a. 400 sq. ft. minimum 1880 sq. ft. maximum	
High school	3 sq. ft. per unit of a.d.a. 600 sq. ft. minimum 3975 sq. ft. maximum	
Administrative offices	Varies	
Library/Media center and technology	960 sq. ft. minimum	Circulation desk has proper visual of study areas, stack space, and student work areas
Elementary	960 sq. ft. minimum	
Middle	21 sq. ft. per unit of a.d.a.	
High school	4 sq. ft. per unit of a.d.a.	

Title 5 Plumbing fixture guidelines

People served	Fixture quantity	
Kindergarten 1–20	1 Toilet	
Kindergarten 21–50	2 Toilets	after 50, one toilet for every 50 students
Elementary students	1 Toilet per 25 female students 1 Toilet per 30 male students 1 Urinal per 75 male students	
Secondary students	1 Toilet per 40 male students 1 Urinal per 35 male students 1 Toilet per 30 female students	
Staff	1 Toilet	
1–15	2 Toilets	
16–35	3 Toilets	
36–55	1 Toilet per add. 40 women	
Over 55	1 Toilet per add. 40 men 1 Urinal per add. 50 men	

Others added to the team when their particular area of concern is being reviewed would include maintenance staff, department heads, program directors, physical education staff, a teachers' representative, the food service director, and representatives from the community.

The design committee should monitor and review the architect's work on a regular basis and make decisions in a timely manner so that the project can stay on schedule. The district's design team leader should also solicit contributions from district personnel—such as maintenance, custodial, and computer network staff—who have specialized knowledge of building system preferences. The architect should be given these preferences at the beginning of the process, and the preferences should be reviewed regularly. The committee's involvement is necessary during the design phase because the process is linear and builds upon itself—advancing from the general to the specific, and from the preliminary to the exact. If design committee decisions are later reversed, a significant amount of time and effort will be lost.

The design process can take several weeks to more than a year, depending on the project's size and complexity. Reviews should happen regularly, from the beginning to the end of the project. At a minimum, the district should conduct thorough reviews of the architect's and design team's work at the end of schematic design, design development, and construction documents. Since every subsequent phase will have a much larger amount of information, extra time for review should be scheduled.

Selecting the architect. The selection of the architect and design team is one of the most critical decisions a school district will make. A good architect can save significant costs in construction and operation and provide facilities that meet educational needs far into the future. An unskilled architect or one unfamiliar with California school facilities may cost the district that same amount. The design professional controls the quality of the design and construction documents. Well-designed facilities will meet educational needs, and good quality construction documents will save the district money in claims during construction.

Special rules apply to California school districts when procuring architectural and engineering services. When state funds are being used, school districts must comply with the provisions of California Government Code section 4525 *et seq*. Educ. Code § 17070.50.

Legal requirements for selecting architects. SB 50, enabled by Proposition 1A as approved in November 1998, added section 17070.50 to the Education Code requiring school districts seeking state funding to use a competitive process in selecting design professionals.

Proposition 35 added section 4529.10 *et seq*. to the Government Code, including section 4529.12, which now requires school districts to obtain architectural, landscape architectural, engineering, environmental, land surveying, or construction project management services through a fair, competitive selection process that avoids conflicts of interest.

Government Code section 4526 requires that the selection of any individual, firm, partnership, corporation, association, or other legal entity providing services be "on the basis of demonstrated competence and on the professional

The design process can take several weeks to more than a year, depending on the project's size and complexity.

Proposition 35

Passed in November 2002, Prop. 35 amended the California Constitution to remove restrictions on public agencies that contract for architectural, engineering, surveying, environmental, and construction management services. Prop. 35 requires that procurement of these professional services employ "a fair and competitive process." The statute does not further define the meaning of "fair and competitive."

Qualifications-Based Selection

Using the QBS method, professional service proposals are weighted first on competence, creativity, and performance and second on negotiation of a fair and reasonable price. When this procedure is used, several professional firms submit qualifications and performance records for the district's review. Key elements to consider in this review include:

- Technical qualifications
- Experience with similar projects
- Reputation with existing clients
- Current workload
- Performance incentive fee
- Compatibility

QBS = Qualification-based selection
RFQ = Request for qualifications
RFP = Request for proposal

qualifications necessary for the satisfactory performance of the services required." This is sometimes described as a qualification-based selection (QBS) process. Government Code section 4528 requires that state agencies attempt to negotiate a satisfactory contract—*i.e.*, one at a fair and reasonable price—with the firm considered the most qualified; only when that attempt fails may they negotiate with the next most qualified. Government Code sections 4526, 4527, and 4528 do not require local agencies to adopt the same procedures as those sections mandate for state agencies.

Many school districts use the QBS method to select architects, as required of state agencies. Others interpret "competitive process" to mean that the services must go to the firm with the lowest fees. Government Code section 4525 requires that selection by state agencies made on the basis of qualifications, and the fee is determined by negotiation after the selection has been made. However, other school districts, in the interest of saving time, do not follow this bifurcated process (first ranking firms solely on the basis of qualifications and then negotiating in that order about price and other conditions of employment). Many districts do not interpret section 4526 to require selection of the most qualified firm, as long as the one selected meets the level of competence and qualifications necessary for the job. Since section 4526 requires that the services be engaged "at fair and reasonable prices," many districts have concluded that price can and should be a factor in the process itself.

Government Code section 4529.12 requires a "fair, competitive selection process," but does not specify or limit the factors to be considered. At a minimum, a district's determination of each firm's relative competitiveness to perform these services can be based on the three factors identified in Government Code section 4526:

- Demonstrated competence
- Professional qualifications
- Fairness and reasonableness of the estimated price

The selection process

Request for qualifications. One of the first steps in selecting an architect is a solicitation, either by advertising or in a letter, to a select list of respondents. Two terms are commonly associated with the solicitation, the request for qualifications (RFQ) and the request for proposals (RFP). Although often used interchangeably, these terms are different. An RFQ is a request for a statement of qualifications from the respondent, whereas an RFP is a request for the proposed cost for a given scope of work. Since professional services of the architect, engineers, or land surveyors must be selected on the basis of qualifications, only the RFQ would be used to solicit these services.

Contents of an RFQ. An RFQ should require that the submitting firm include a statement of qualifications to assist the district in evaluating the firm's creativity and level of experience. The format for this information should be the same for all RFQs so that each submission can be evaluated on an equal basis.

It is not generally recommended that a district require design as part of its selection process. A firm might submit a design that looks wonderful, but has little to do with the district's needs or its educational program. Also, a competition of this sort may have little or no incentive to work within a budget, either in costs or building area.

The RFQ should include a cover letter that summarizes the firm's history, vital statistics, and interest in the projects.

Advertisement. Typically, a district will announce its need for professional services in relevant publications. Govt. Code § 4527(a). While no minimum advertising period is specified, the district will want to advertise for at least a two-month period to ensure a good response.

The interview. A screening of the RFQs should result in a short list of qualified firms, but for practical purposes the interview list should be limited to five or six. Govt. Code § 4527(a). If the district is selecting architects for several projects, the number interviewed may be greater. Because the district needs to develop a strong working relationship with the firm, assessing team dynamics should be the primary focus of the interview panel. Bear in mind, however, that almost every firm will have a good presenter, even they may not be the best choice for the team. Interview panels should choose members who have the best qualifications for the project.

It is also important to note that a district electing to use the standard OPSC requirements should allow sufficient time for a submitting firm to meet the advertising requirements of the process. Public Contract Code section 10140 requires a 24-day minimum.

The district should give at least two weeks' notice prior to the date of the interview. This will allow each firm to prepare an electronic or visual presentation specific to the projects.

The panel. The interview panel should be made up of district staff who will be working with the design team. These may include primarily the facilities and school site staff. Remember, the interview's primary purpose is to gauge the level of comfort the district has with the individuals on the design team. The superintendent and a school board member may also wish to be involved, but the panel should be limited to six or eight people to keep the discussions and the selection process manageable.

The format. A typical interview format will allocate approximately 20 minutes for a firm to present its work and qualifications. This is followed by a period of approximately 20 minutes for questions from the interview panel.

The district should take control of the entire selection process, from the pre-qualification questionnaire to the recommendation to the school board. The district should establish the interview framework and format, and the interview team should create an interview guide and evaluation form to ensure that each firm is responding to identical questions. Questions should be designed to measure the design team's knowledge of the process and of school architecture.

Final step. Under the QBS method, price is a factor only after the most qualified professional firm has been identified and agreement on the scope of services is reached.

The Pitfalls of Shopping Price

Shopping price for professional services eliminates desirable "give and take" and puts the school district in the position of saying, "here's what I want done by whoever will do it the cheapest." In this way, the district denies itself access to the most valuable asset a professional has to offer—creative technical knowledge and experience applied to develop functional, cost-effective, solid solutions.

An RFP written solely by the client regarding the scope of work to be performed frequently contains insufficient detail to serve as a valid basis for price. In fact, in those instances where a price quotation is mandated, firms bidding on the same job almost invariably arrive at differing interpretations of what is a presumably adequate scope of work with wide variations in cost estimates and even greater variations in quality.

Price competition for professional services can also limit the resources a professional has available to analyze the problem in detail and search for innovative solutions. In the short run, the school district may save a few dollars, but in the long run the project may carry a huge price tag, including the often hidden cost of public denial and rejection.

In addition, when shopping price for professional services, the result may be a significant increase in the cost of construction as well as the long-term costs of operation and maintenance. ∎

DVBE/MBE/WBE

In 1996, California passed Prop. 209, which barred race or gender from being considered in state hiring or contracting decisions. As a result, participation of a Minority Business Enterprise (MBE) and Women's Business Enterprise (WBE) is no longer a prerequisite for state funding for school districts.

Additionally, a Disabled Veteran Business Enterprise (DVBE) is no longer required on a project-by-project basis, but districts must meet a DVBE participation goal of three percent district-wide or demonstrate that a good faith effort has been made to meet the goal. DVBE programs remain intact since they are not race or gender-based. If it chooses, a school district may not require submitting firms to participate in these programs. However, it may choose to make participation a local requirement, and, if so, that condition must be included in the RFQ.

Historically, many school districts have informed the submitting firms in the RFQ that data will be collected over the course of the project related to the participation of DVBE, MBE, or WBE firms. ■

DVBE = Disabled Veteran
           Business Enterprise
MBE = Minority Business Enterprise
WBE = Women's Business Enterprise

The district ranks the most qualified firms or individuals numerically in order of preference and then negotiates the scope of services, the personnel it will commit, and the schedule by which the work is to be completed. After agreeing to its scope, the district and the firm negotiate a fee that is fair and reasonable to both parties. If an agreement on compensation is achieved, a contract is signed. Should no agreement be reached, negotiations are terminated, and the district begins negotiating with the second-ranked firm.

The district should give notice that each firm should contact a single designated district representative so that every participant in the process receives the same information.

The most common fee structures are fixed, cost plus, and percentage of construction. While the perception may linger that the fee scale recommended by the OLA in 1979 and kept as a part of the LPP is still valid, the scope of services required to complete a project at that time was less than what is required today.

The Government Code procurement procedures do *not* specify the contents or nature of the agreement ultimately to be entered into between the local agency and architect.

Modernization and Additions

Performing construction at a site with students and existing facilities, particularly when school is in session, adds an additional complexity to the process. The following issues should be considered for these types of projects.

Record drawings. Record drawings, or "as-builts," are the documents from which original buildings and subsequent alterations were constructed. They can be a valuable source of information for the architect, engineers, and contractors during the design of a remodel or an addition to a project. Ideally, the district has kept record drawings in good condition for reference, but all too often they are lost or severely damaged.

Providing this information in a complete and accurate manner can save a significant amount of time and cost when a project involves altering existing facilities. Also, these documents can be a valuable resource for ongoing facility maintenance and repair.

Access compliance. The Americans with Disabilities Act is a federal law that mandates specific requirements for public agencies to make their services and facilities accessible to persons with disabilities. 42 U.S.C. § 12101 *et seq.*, 29 C.F.R. § 1630.1 *et seq.* At the beginning of a modernization project, the owner/district should review its responsibilities under ADA to be sure they have been fulfilled in order to facilitate DSA access compliance, plan review, and approval. The ADA requires that a modernization project make older buildings accessible to persons with disabilities. This includes adding elevators to multi-story buildings, ramps on sites with stairways, wheelchair lifts to stage areas, accessible parking lots, and larger toilet stalls and new door hardware that is easier to use. Since these improvements are usually required for any significant remodel and can consume a large portion of the budget, the work should be mapped out early in the project.

Hazardous materials. If not identified early in the design process, hazardous materials in existing buildings can create delays and added costs. A district should provide the architect with any completed hazardous materials surveys and consider having them redone to reflect the specific scope of a project. Asbestos, lead, PCB, and other materials should be properly identified and abated or contained in areas where construction will occur.

Safety. Construction activities at a site with concurrent operations require particular consideration, and special requirements must be established to protect the safety of students and staff. Barricades, fences, contractor staging areas, contractor access, testing schedules, hours of construction, and contractor interaction with students and staff should be clearly defined in the bid and contract documents before construction begins. Construction activities should be reviewed with the CDE school facilities consultant in detail well in advance of bidding, so that all safety requirements are identified and communicated to the contractor. Requirements added after engaging the contractor and beginning construction could be costly and delay project completion.

Phasing and temporary facilities. Depending on the size and scope of the modernization, existing facilities may be unavailable for use during school hours. Some types of projects can be scheduled during vacation, but many will require temporary, relocatable buildings to replace facilities that are being renovated.

The duration of use and extent of temporary facilities should be reviewed carefully with school site staff to minimize disruption to ongoing site activities. All phasing and limitations of building access should be clearly communicated to the contractor so its bid price reflects all phasing and work schedule requirements.

Project delivery methods. How the project design and construction team is structured and what is agreed to by all parties is called the project delivery method. Ideally, this decision is made at the very start of a project, so that the design process is executed efficiently. *See* chapter 5 for more details.

Cost Control—A Critical Concern

Managing the cost of the construction process is critical to ensuring the success of a capital improvement project. Most projects have budgets that fall short of important needs, so active participation in cost control throughout the entire duration of a project is essential.

Many of the decisions made in the course of designing and building a school facility have an effect on cost, and before a major decision is made, the cost impact should be considered. Tracking costs is a daunting task because there is no single source, and they can fluctuate greatly. It takes a coordinated effort and regular updates to maintain an accurate project cost estimate.

The various forms of cost and budgeting information can make communicating costs accurately difficult, so great care should be taken in understanding the type and accuracy of budget data.

Cost estimate or budget? The terms *cost estimate* and *budget* are often used interchangeably and cause confusion. The *budget* is the amount the project's owner has available to spend. The *cost estimate* is a projection of what the design or program may cost. Ideally these two numbers will coincide or, better

Transition Plan and ADA Coordinator

The Americans with Disabilities Act requires that school districts prepare and adopt a transition plan and designate an ADA Coordinator. With these in place, DSA may allow more latitude with access improvements, saving construction funds for higher-priority items.

U.S.C. §§ 12101

Managing the cost of the construction process is critical to ensuring the success of a capital improvement project.

yet, the final total cost will be less than the budget. But it takes a lot of effort and cooperation from the entire project team to achieve this goal.

Because the design criteria or "wish list" is often complex and long, the cost estimate may exceed the budget. Estimates should be reviewed at appropriate milestones, since discrepancies are easier to reconcile in the planning and design phase than during the preparation of construction documents and construction itself. At the beginning of the project, the person responsible for preparing the estimates should identify the level of detail required. Most contracts stipulate the architect as the responsible party. However, the services of a cost-estimating consultant may be necessary, and architects can include this service for an additional fee. Some construction managers and contractors are able to project their costs based on detailed construction documents and specifications, but most are not set up to offer such a detailed breakdown.

Cost estimate. The total cost of a construction project can be broken down into three separate components: site acquisition costs, soft costs, and hard costs.

Site acquisition costs. Site acquisition costs include land purchase costs, real estate fees and CEQA mitigation costs, and other costs associated with acquiring land for a project. This project-specific cost can vary greatly from project to project. Some projects have no land cost component because the land is already owned (*e.g.*, modernization projects on existing facilities.) For other projects land costs are a significant part of the total project cost because of high real estate values or because environmental clean-up costs associated with the land are substantial. For this reason, the cost of land is often excluded from project cost summaries and estimates and tracked separately.

Soft costs. These include fees and all other costs that are not paid to the contractor or construction manager to build the building. They include plan check fees, architecture and professional service fees, inspection and testing fees, and furniture and equipment.

Hard costs. These include construction management fees and work in the contractor's bid such as site improvement work (parking lots and landscaping), offsite improvement construction (roads, waterlines, traffic signals, etc.), and building construction (all aspects of construction from floor to roof). Both labor and materials are included in the hard cost estimate.

Budget. The project budget should also be tracked, reviewed, and updated regularly with revenue sources identified and maximized for each project.

Depending on the source of funds, available money could be reallocated during the course of a project based on other funding priorities that affect the final project budget. In general, reductions in the project budget after the design is completed tend to be more difficult and expensive the later they are made. As much as possible, a realistic budget should be established at the beginning of a project and not changed. It should stand as the target for the design team to meet.

For most projects, eligibility for state funding is a key factor that should be performed by someone familiar with the intricacies of the programs available. For state-funded new construction, the architect and the design committee should be aware of any factors that could affect the amount the state will contribute. Site size, location, and development as well as multi-level construction

The total cost of a construction project can be broken down into three separate components: site acquisition costs, soft costs, and hard costs.

and special education rooms can provide supplemental funding for a project. The modernization program, while less complex, has very few supplemental funding opportunities (*see* chapter 2).

To the extent possible, changes that require redesign or revisions to the contractor's scope of work should be avoided, because they can significantly increase design fees and costs of construction.

Cost-Saving Considerations

Use of consulting services. As a portion of total cost, consulting services are a small part of the picture, but the decisions they make or fail to make can affect every aspect of a project to an extent much greater than design fees alone. In a word, investing in a top-quality consultant may yield a return many times over in cost savings and time.

Hiring a qualified consultant is critical to project success. To use these services efficiently, a district must understand the consultant's responsibilities and monitor its progress. Due to the complexity and multiple disciplinary expertise required to plan, fund, site, and construct a school building, a district rarely has a full complement of expert staff to complete the job. School facilities are team projects, but districts are responsible for knowing the team members that are required for each phase. Because a large number of consultants are needed, a district should watch for overlap and conflict to avoid duplication of effort and services.

For example, if an experienced and capable architect is retained to perform design and planning services, an additional program manager or project manager consultant may be unnecessary. A district should understand what specific work product or "deliverable" each consultant will provide. Services that are vague or subjective—to "monitor progress" or "control" the work of another consultant or "provide regular reports"—may be a waste of money or, even worse, lead to serious cost overruns.

Anticipating needs. Keeping an eye on future facility needs can have a big impact on a project's cost. By tracking enrollment, growth, and demographics regularly, a district may be able to start the school facility site acquisition process much sooner. As a result, the district may have a broader array of choices and lower prices for land in advance of need.

Cost of the site. While site acquisition costs may be the most significant part of total project cost, districts are advised not to purchase the lowest cost site without considering the site conditions. The site with the lowest purchase price may have so many expensive problems that the construction costs could exceed the savings of cheap land.

It's important to consider the site conditions that can negatively affect the cost of construction, such as subsurface geological conditions, environmental clean-up, site slope, site improvements, and offsite improvements. A site with a higher purchase price on which it is less expensive to build could end up saving the district millions of dollars in construction costs. *See* chapter 4 for information relating to site acquisition practices.

Savings in design. During design and construction, the district will develop alternatives and make many critical decisions. The process is one of compromises

The Real Cost of Building a School

The cost to build a typical elementary school can exceed $12 million, but the cost of operating and maintaining that school for 40 years can exceed $100 million. Initial construction cost investments such as energy-efficient lighting and durable building materials can save a school district millions of dollars over the life of a school facility. When establishing design criteria and construction budgets, and selecting building materials, it is important to consider the construction cost and the total cost of operation. ■

It's important to consider site conditions that can negatively affect the cost of construction: subsurface geological conditions, environmental clean-up, slope, and site/offsite improvements.

and balancing conflicting priorities. The district should require that consultants provide enough information to allow for reasoned decisions, and representatives of the district should understand and communicate the district's priorities clearly to the architect and the design team.

In construction, building area is roughly proportional to cost. If the size of a new library is doubled, for example, the cost will be doubled. If the number of trees in a courtyard is tripled, the expense for that change may triple. This simple concept can significantly affect the cost of construction. If the size of a facility can be reduced, or a room or function eliminated, meaningful savings can be achieved. Analysis of this type is rarely explored thoroughly until late in the process, when the cost overrun is apparent but there's little time left for major redesign. A thorough ed specs process can set design criteria and maximize design efficiencies.

Ideally, the district should critically review the building area program and the educational specifications to weed out what is unnecessary in the preliminary plans. Before beginning the schematic design, the district should attempt to control what is often an ever-increasing project wish list. While the design team or building user groups may have developed these items in good-faith brain-storming sessions, the list may greatly increase the budget. The district must re-establish the priorities, relating each item back to the list of objectives of the facilities master plan and ed specs, eliminating what is not required to fulfill the district's educational program goals.

Items that are desirable but not essential can be identified as a bid alternate. Then the contractor will provide a price, and the district can later choose whether to include it. Ideally, each project should have only a few alternates that are identified early in the process, preferably during design development.

Because construction prices fluctuate daily based on the cost of materials, the availability of labor, and the amount of construction activity in a region, change is an inevitable part of the process. Moreover, cost estimating itself is inherently inexact. The budget should provide for these unanticipated possibilities in the form of a contingency that could range from 3 to 25 percent of the original estimate, depending on project phase and complexity.

The grade configuration of a K–12 facility can also affect cost, with high schools more expensive than middle schools and middle schools more expensive than elementary schools. For example, facilities for a district with a grade 10–12 high school and a K–8 elementary school will cost less than facilities for one with a grade 9–12 high school, a grade 6–8 middle school, and K–5 elementary because in the latter case more students are housed in the more expensive facilities.

How a facility is used may also affect its cost. If used for double sessions, extended days, and year-round school, a new facility may require less area overall.

Controlling costs is an activity that is critical to the success of a design and construction process, but unfortunately, many other priorities compete for a district's attention. When addressed early and regularly in a project, cost control can save a significant amount of time and money for all involved. Pursuant to section 17070.33 of the Education Code, the SAB has published a handbook for school districts struggling with this issue, entitled "Public School Construction: Cost

When addressed early and regularly in a project, cost control can save a significant amount of time and money for all involved.

Reductions Guidelines," which is available on its website (www.opsc.dgs.ca.gov).

Value engineering. Sometimes mistakenly equated with cost reduction at the expense of building performance and quality, some interpretations of value engineering ignore the fact that an inferior alternative may result in high long-term costs for maintenance and operations. But by exploring lower-cost design alternatives that do not diminish the project's function or quality, value engineering can be a beneficial exercise when executed early in the design process.

Reuse of plans. When strict guidelines are followed, reuse of an existing design and building plan can provide a small reduction in the cost of construction and the time needed to deliver a school project. Section 17070.33 of the Education Code requires that SAB adopt recommendations regarding the use of cost-effective, efficient, reusable facility plans. Section 17261 of the Education Code requires CDE to maintain plan pools and specifications for rural school buildings to be made available to school districts at a minor fee for the purpose of reuse. SAB maintains a stockpile of plans appropriate for various climates and geographic conditions throughout California.

To fulfill these requirements, OPSC has devoted part of its website to examples of school projects architects have submitted. When a project appears to meet the needs of a particular community, the school district may negotiate with the architect for a reuse of the plans. This concept is not new but, to be most effective, reuse of the plans must be accomplished with few if any modifications. Site conditions and orientation must be similar, the condition of the soils must be comparable, and, most importantly, the educational programs must be the same. Without this last provision, a school district may find that the facility drives the educational program, rather than the program driving the facility.

Typically, the most effective application of plan reuse is *within* a school district. Many rapidly growing school districts have developed prototypical plans and have reused the designs several times. One of the most notable is Clark County School District in Las Vegas. As one of the most rapidly growing districts in the country (an average of ten schools opening per year), the district effectively uses prototypical plans for most of their facilities.

Typically, the most effective application of plan reuse is within a school district.

Schedules can be compressed with plan reuse. The time for preparing documents can be reduced if the required changes are limited. Close contact should be maintained with DSA to ensure that the changes made will *not trigger a full* check of the plans. The current policy is that if a set of plans can be checked, sheet for sheet, with a previously approved set of drawings within a two hour counter check, the project will be treated *as a reuse* and stamped out at the end of the two-hour time frame. If the comparative check cannot be completed *within the two hours* it must be submitted for a full check. This procedure makes it very difficult, particularly on larger projects, to obtain a reduced plan check time for any project. Each project should be reviewed at an early stage with the DSA to determine the applicability of a reduced plan check time.

Reuse of plans can also reduce the construction costs due to change orders. Through trial and error, as the plans are reused, problems with the documents or the program can be rectified and eliminated in subsequent reuse of the plans. Such advantages increase if the same contractor is used on all projects.

Site topography will affect how a building responds to level changes.

While intended to yield significant savings in design fees, in reality, a direct reuse of plans may reduce total cost only slightly, and result in a project that may not fit the district's needs.

When designing a project, the architect takes into account a wide variety of factors specific to the site. For example:

- Site topography will affect how a building responds to level changes
- Accessibility is a key consideration with changes in elevation, and the design will need to respond to this
- The design must respond to the site's orientation
- The west face will need to be treated differently than the north face
- Site configuration may determine a building's location and configuration
- A long narrow site may require a different design than a site that is square
- Where to locate vehicular and pedestrian access is a factor in planning and design
- If any of these or other factors change in a reuse, the design may need to be modified significantly

Engineering determinants must also be taken into consideration in a reuse. If the soil type and/or bearing capacity changes, the specifications for the foundation or building structure may need to change. Shifting the orientation will affect the design of mechanical and electrical systems. This shift will also influence heat loss/heat gain calculations, and the mechanical units may require a different design or size. This in turn may affect electrical and related specifications.

The design for the site, street access, parking, hardcourt, and playfields can seldom be reused. For reuse to be successful, site configurations and soil conditions must be similar, and this is rare. The landscape itself may require alteration, possibly resulting in the need for new offsite and utility connections. When reuse is the preferred option, serious consideration should be given to the configuration of the site. One with conditions similar to that of the original will require the fewest changes and provide the most effective reuse.

While reuse is generally intended to yield significant savings in design fees, in reality, a direct reuse of plans may reduce the architect's fees by one to ten percent. This amounts to approximately 0.5 percent to 0.7 percent of the total cost—a relatively small savings for a project that may not fit the district's needs. Moreover, this savings will only be achieved if the district makes *no* changes.

The concept that plans can be taken off the shelf and immediately put out to bid for a new site with little or no additional expenditure is a fallacy. School districts must consider all of these factors when contemplating reuse of plans. The true impact on cost, schedule and, most importantly, the educational program should be evaluated before making that decision.

chapter 4

Siting: Site Selection and Approval

To site a school, a district first must select sites that can meet the district's educational program goals described in the Facilities Master Plan and Ed Specs, as well as the ever-growing array of regulatory requirements. The typical siting process, parts of which can occur concurrently, can be roughly outlined as follows:

- District site selection team *selects sites* that meet Facilities Master Plan goals and Ed Specs

- District *obtains CDE initial and final approval* of sites that meet CDE's educational, health, and safety requirements

- District *obtains DTSC approval of sites* that meet DTSC's health and safety requirements

- District *complies with CEQA* (reports any adverse environmental consequences from siting and construction of school, and ways of avoiding or mitigating where feasible)

- District *acquires site*

This chapter discusses the legal requirements and recommended state policies that districts should follow for each step of the siting process. It also reviews some special siting issues for schools located in the coastal zone, in agricultural areas, or where wetlands or endangered species exist, and discusses special issues for small school sites, joint use of schools with other public and private land uses, and playgrounds.

While the three main environmental and site review processes required of school districts were developed separately, each has its own specific procedural steps. However, the processes overlap, and some requirements can be accomplished concurrently. For instance, geological studies required for the CDE site selection review can be conducted as part of the CEQA review. Also, state law expressly states that the DTSC and CEQA review processes may occur concurrently.

CDE = California Department of Education

CEQA = California Environmental Quality Act

DTSC = Department of Toxic Substances Control

This chapter discusses the legal requirements and recommended state policies that districts should follow during the siting process.

Playground, San Pasquel
K-8 School, Escondido, California

PEA = Preliminary endangerment assessment
RAP = Remedial action plan
RAW = Removal action workplan
REA = Registered environmental assessor

There's an old saying:
If your horse dies... Get off!
In education we get a bigger
whip, ride for longer times,
change riders, blame the horse's
parents or study sites where
dead horses are ridden in style.

Site Selection Team

CDE recommends that districts form a "site selection team" to recommend sites to the district's board. *School Site Selection and Approval Guide*, School Facilities Planning Division, California Department of Education (2000) (*"Selection Guide"*). CDE recommends that the team include community members, teachers, administrators, public officials, and the architect the school district selects to design the project. At a minimum, the team should involve the district's facilities planner, a real estate appraiser, a civil engineer, environmental consultants for both CEQA and DTSC issue-spotting (who will often supply the traffic engineer and other environmental and engineering specialities), legal counsel specializing in real estate acquisitions and environmental law, and the school facilities consultant assigned to the district at CDE (if the district is seeking CDE written approval of the site).

Environmental Consultant

School siting can involve rigorous environmental review under many different laws. Since most districts do not have specialized staff to conduct these reviews, consultants should be engaged early in the process. At least two types of services may be needed, one for the preliminary assessment and another to prepare CEQA documentation.

The preliminary review process for DTSC involves what is known as the Phase I or preliminary endangerment assessment (PEA) and possibly also the removal action workplan (RAW)/remedial action plan (RAP). This environmental consultant must be qualified and licensed as one of the following:

- Registered geologist/certified engineering geologist
- Professional engineer
- Class II registered environmental assessor (REA)
- Licensed hazardous substance contractor

The second service, preparation of CEQA documentation, can often be performed by the first environmental consultant, since many are qualified to provide both DTSC- and CEQA-related services. That same consultant might also prepare the documents necessary to meet CDE's environmental and site selection review. Generally, however, a firm will specialize in one type of service or the other.

Regulatory Compliance— CDE Criteria

Site Selection Factors

The typical site selection process begins with

- Identification of important site factors
- Search for sites exhibiting those factors
- Preliminary review of those sites as suitable for selection

- Regulatory compliance for those sites
- Acquisition of sites that have passed or are expected to pass all regulatory clearances

For each need identified in the Facilities Master Plan, CDE recommends that a district find a minimum of three suitable sites.

The list of important site factors should be based on:

- School district's Facilities Master Plan and Ed Specs
- Criteria for CDE approval
- Criteria and standards of the other regulatory agencies

The state regulatory agency and legal requirements involved in selecting and approving school sites are described in detail below.

Ideally, a school district's Facilities Master Plan reflects the district's demographics, potential growth rates, and existing school sites capacities. This information will be the primary guide in selecting the location of potential school sites. The Facilities Master Plan should indicate when a district will need a new school and in what general area. In some cases, the Facilities Master Plan also has influenced the applicable general plan, community plan, or specific plan to ensure that potential school sites are consistent with the Facilities Master Plan's needs, and surrounded by compatible land uses. For each need identified in the Facilities Master Plan, CDE recommends that a district find a minimum of three suitable sites.

To assist in the identification of the important site factors, CDE has prepared School Facilities Planning Division (SFPD) Form 4.0, *Initial School Site Evaluation*, for use by the district's site selection team. This form should be used in conjunction with the Facilities Master Plan during site selection. As discussed further in this chapter, the Education Code and its implementing regulations in Title 5 contain prohibitions that bar schools from locating near certain hazards.

SFPD = School Facilities Planning Division

Ultimately, the most crucial question facing a district searching for school sites is: Will the site fulfill the goals of the educational plan?

The most crucial question facing a district searching for a school site is: Will the site fulfill the goals of the educational plan?

Site Utilization Study: Early Design Considerations

The purpose of a site utilization study is to determine as accurately as possible the amount of land needed for the school in question. The district planner or architect should prepare the site utilization study prior to the purchase of a site. As discussed in more detail in chapter 3 under Planning and Design of the School Facility, early design studies such as the site utilization plan should be based on the district's Facilities Master Plan, its Ed Specs, and the formulas recommended by CDE. The site utilization study should include a preliminary layout of the proposed buildings and grounds, parking area and roads, and playground areas. The utilization study can help determine whether the site has linkage to local and regional transportation, whether it is accessible on at least two sides, whether walking routes to school are safe, whether the utility services are adequate, etc. It can help the district decide whether the site and its physical characteristics can accommodate the school.

Preliminary Title Report

Once sites meeting the requirements of the Facilities Master Plan and Ed Specs are identified, the site selection team should obtain a preliminary title report. A preliminary title report will indicate factors that may present challenges or cause delays associated with the acquisition of the property. For instance, a preliminary title report will identify the owners, easement holders, other parties with interests in the property, debts held on the property (including those of state and federal tax agency lienholders), and the existence of any blanket lien. The more parties with interests in the property, the more time may be required to negotiate the purchase. The site selection team can use the preliminary title report to determine the likelihood of a willing seller or the need for eminent domain.

The preliminary title report will also help detect any potential difficulties with the site; for example, an easement for railroad tracks or a hazardous materials pipeline, or may disclose that the property a district proposes to acquire is an agricultural preserve under a Williamson Act contract. Govt. Code § 51200 *et seq.* If so, the district must advise both the Director of the California Department of Conservation and the local city or county of its intention to consider the location of a school facility. Govt. Code § 51291(b). School districts are prohibited from locating a school facility in an agricultural preserve "based primarily in consideration of the lower cost of acquiring land in an agricultural preserve" or when the school facility can be located in another reasonable place. Govt. Code § 51292.

Site Search

The search for sites can be done by district staff or by a land broker. If a broker is used, the broker should be part of the site selection team, and should understand the criteria for the educational program and the regulatory constraints on site selection. Often districts will have staff review sites by aerial maps, local government planning documents (*e.g.*, general plan, specific plan, or community plan), tract maps of the building or engineering departments of local government, driving around the area and visiting sites, and informally consulting with local entities such as the local planning department, real estate brokers, and community groups.

As previously indicated, CDE recommends that at least three suitable sites be found for each school. The details of land acquisition are covered in the Land Acquisition section found later in this chapter. However, one point worth making at this early stage is that once a potentially suitable site is found, it is advisable to have a land broker make the initial contact with the landowner in order to maintain the confidentiality of the district as a potential buyer, particularly regarding negotiation over price.

Preliminary Review of CDE and District Siting Criteria

The site selection team should assess potential sites against the district criteria it has developed, in addition to CDE criteria. Certain sites may be eliminated out of hand for failing to meet mandatory CDE site selection criteria. For instance, any sites containing pipelines carrying hazardous materials should be eliminated.

Questions to ask include:

- Does the topography provide suitable usable acreage?
- Does the site contain anything unusual (*e.g.*, existing structures) that would greatly increase costs of development?
- Does the area have major potential hazards (*i.e.*, nearby railroad tracks, power lines, airports)?

If the information is available, the team should identify utility providers and the closest connection points, the sewer depth, or the need for a pump station. Engaging a traffic engineer at this stage may also benefit the site selection process. While detailed traffic analysis is not necessary at the initial planning stage, traffic-related issues may be a key concern for other agencies and for the community. If the district has engaged a traffic engineer, the team should walk the site and its surroundings to identify safe routes to school. Surroundings should be examined to determine if street improvements (*e.g.*, sidewalk, curb and gutter, paving, lighting, fire hydrants) would be required. The district might also ask the local air district to identify any locations of hazard-emitting facilities that would rule out a site. Finally, the district might consider whether a CEQA review is appropriate at this point so that potential environmental and siting issues could be identified in advance of selection. For an in-depth discussion of this, see Earlier Timing of CEQA below.

Consultation with Local Government

Consultation with the city or county in which the site is located should also occur concurrently with the site selection process. The district should meet with the city or county to discuss the sites under consideration, identifying any issues related to these sites. This initial outreach should not be confused with the formal notice the district must provide to the planning commission for sites within its jurisdiction that the district is seeking to acquire for a new school, or for an addition to an existing school, consistent with Public Resources Code section 21151.2. *See also* Govt. Code §§ 53094, 65402(c). That formal notice should be completed after the sites have received initial CDE evaluation, in order to reduce the potential for the planning commission to review sites CDE cannot approve. This can be part of the CEQA process, described in more detail below.

The traffic engineer can meet with the city or county traffic department to determine key intersections that need evaluation, and the potential for significant traffic improvements.

The team should walk the site and its surroundings to determine whether there are safe routes to school. The surroundings should be examined to determine if street improvements (*e.g.*, sidewalk, curb and gutter, paving, lighting, fire hydrants) would be required.

Community and political support for the site should also be examined. For instance, through community outreach, the team may discover whether the site is desired for some other use (*e.g.*, baseball field, park) by the community or local politicians. Community outreach will formally be required as part of the CEQA process. However, informal consultation at this stage could occur

Consultation with the city or county in which the site is located should occur concurrently with the site selection process.

through a district "open house" meeting or a portion of time set aside for public comment during a regular board meeting.

Procedures for Obtaining Preliminary Site Approval from CDE

Once potential sites have been identified, the site selection team may seek initial site evaluation to ensure that each site meets CDE criteria before beginning an in-depth review. Where the district will be using state funds and CDE site approval is required, a preliminary review will help ensure that the district will be able to secure final approval. CDE's initial approval can potentially save a district costly investigations and studies, or lost time on sites that have no possibility of meeting CDE's strict criteria. If no state funds are to be used, then CDE initial evaluation and approval are optional. However, a district may voluntarily seek endorsement from CDE, giving the district an added level of security and providing flexibility for reimbursement or state funding if revenue sources change in the future.

Whether or not state funds are used, the board must hold a public hearing to evaluate properties using CDE's site selection standards in Title 5 of California Code of Regulations before commencing the acquisition of real property for school sites. Educ. Code § 17211. Typically, the site selection team will provide a report on each site to the board.

In order to obtain a preliminary site approval from CDE the district must:

- Schedule a field visit with the CDE consultant
- If the site is within two nautical miles of an airport runway, request that CDE arrange an investigation of the site by Caltrans
- Provide the CDE consultant with maps of three approvable sites identified by the district for review purposes

The CDE consultant will view the sites and provide the district a written evaluation of the site(s) on SFPD Form 4.0, "Initial School Site Evaluation." The consultant will provide the district with three forms required for final approval (Educ. Code § 17251, 14 C.C.R. § 14010 *et seq.*, SAB Reg. § 3863). The forms are as follows:

- SFPD Form 4.01 *School Site Approval Procedures*
- SFPD Form 4.02 *School Site Report*
- SFPD Form 4.03 *School Site Certification*

Even if CDE's approval is not obtained, the district should make sure that these forms contain all the information CDE requires for written approval of the site.

Once the district has narrowed its list of suitable sites and receives CDE's initial evaluation, an in-depth review should be conducted. A Phase I environmental assessment is relatively inexpensive and could have been undertaken during the initial evaluation to narrow the possibilities. If it was not, the assessment should be conducted before the more costly CEQA review or before extensive PEA or remediation efforts are performed, after a site has cleared the CDE list. Because they are long and complicated, the CEQA and DTSC review processes are covered in more detail below. A full description of CDE site selection criteria, to ensure initial evaluation and final approval by CDE, is also described below.

Preliminary approval by CDE can save a district costly investigations and studies, or lost time on sites that have no possibility of meeting CDE's strict criteria.

✎ **note**

Districts with locally funded projects are not required to obtain CDE approval, but must follow the procedures and criteria listed in Title 5, Section 14012.

A Phase I environmental assessment is relatively inexpensive and can be undertaken during the initial evaluation to narrow the possibilities.

Site size. CDE's School Facilities Planning Division publishes the *Guide to School Site Analysis and Development* to help districts determine the amount of land and square footage needed to support their educational programs in accordance with the goals in the Facilities Master Plan, Ed Specs, and federal and state law (available at www.cde.ca.gov/facilities/sfpdpublications.htm). The Guide provides detailed quantitative information for each grade level, unusual site conditions, physical education requirements, parking, and access roads, with tables, graphic layouts, and steps to follow.

The *Guide* was updated in 2000 to reflect recent changes in recommended site acreage that are primarily the result of legislation regarding class size reduction and gender equity issues. Education Amendments of 1972, Title IX.

More classrooms are required to implement class size reduction. For example, an elementary school with 300 pupils in grades one through three with class sizes of 30 would require ten classrooms for those grades; whereas class sizes of 20 would require 15 classrooms. A reduction in the number of pupils per classroom does not equal a reduction in the size of the classroom itself, since CDE maintains its policy of 960 square feet for a standard classroom and 1,350 square feet for a kindergarten room.

The physical education program has long been the most influential factor in determining how much land is necessary to construct a school. This factor has achieved even more importance as a result of Title IX, which mandates equal access for female athletes. The acreage requirements for physical education in grades 9 through 12 have been increased to include additional softball/soccer fields. The playfield area can increase from 1.4 acres to 3.4 acres. Other playground requirements are discussed in detail at the end of this chapter.

The physical education program has long been the most influential factor in determining how much land is necessary to construct a school.

The *Guide* has been organized according to CDE's regulations (14 C.C.R. § 14010), which is a great help to the district's architect when computing the area required. Some of its most basic guidance is reproduced here for easy reference.

At the state level there has been a growing recognition of the difficulty local school districts experience in meeting these requirements—due to scarce land, increasing student population, and rising real estate prices. CDE's regulations provide for deviations from the *Guide's* minimum requirements under certain "unusual or exceptional" conditions. For an in-depth discussion of the regulations in these special situations, see Small School Sites at the end of this chapter.

The basic minimum building area requirements are as follows:

- Kindergarten and grades 1–6   59 square feet per pupil
- Grades 7–8   80 square feet per pupil
- Grades 9–12   92 square feet per pupil

However, the *Guide* contains many more minimum areas, tables, formulas, and sample layouts for a school facility planner or architect to determine precise site size requirements.

Safety. After a site is screened to meet the Facilities Master Plan, educational program goals, Ed Specs, and CDE minimum size requirements, safety, the next important consideration, is regulated. The CDE safety criteria include the soil and toxics review DTSC conducts, CEQA review of the potential site, and DSA review to ensure the school building's structural safety and soundness. The CDE, DTSC, and CEQA requirements, triggered at the siting selection phase, are discussed in this chapter, while the DSA requirements, triggered at the design and construction phases, are discussed in chapters 3 and 5. Due to the overlap between the environmental and land use site reviews required of school districts, all three reviews can be conducted concurrently rather than consecutively.

For some hazards, the Education Code requires additional studies or procedures to determine if the hazards present safety risks.

The Education Code contains prohibitions that bar locating schools near certain hazards. For other hazards, the Education Code requires additional studies or procedures to determine if the hazards present safety risks. A district should determine if one of these hazards exists in the pre-screening process.

Sites containing or within 1,500 feet of hazardous pipelines. Acquisition of a school site is prohibited if the site:

> [C]ontains one or more pipelines, situated underground or aboveground, which carries hazardous substances, acutely hazardous materials, or hazardous wastes, unless the pipeline is a natural gas line which is used only to supply natural gas to that school or neighborhood.
>
> Educ. Code § 17213; 5 C.C.R. § 14010[h]; Pub. Res. Code § 21151.8 (a)(1)(c)

A school may not be located within 1,500 feet of an underground or aboveground pipeline if the pipeline is a safety hazard, determined by a risk analysis study. Title 5, C.C.R. § 14010(h). If the school is within 1,500 feet of a pipeline (pressurized above 80 psi), a risk analysis is required to examine the potential for pipeline failure to occur, and the potential for a fatality resulting from that failure. CDE then evaluates the results of the study to determine if the risk is within acceptable limits. CDE periodically revises the risk analysis protocols, which can be found in the School Site Selection and Approval Guide.

Prior to acquisition, the Caltrans Division of Aeronautics must approve any site within two miles of an existing or potential runway.

Airport runway proximity. A district should determine a potential school site's proximity to an airport runway. Prior to acquisition, the Caltrans Division of Aeronautics must approve any site within two nautical miles of an existing or potential runway, measured by direct air line to the nearest part of the site. Educ. Code § 17215. To obtain approval, the district must submit the requisite information to CDE, which acts as intermediary between the district and Caltrans. Because this can take awhile, the district should give the request for review high priority.

The district must submit two maps:

- A dated vicinity map of architectural or cartographic quality (drawn to scale of 1 inch = 1,000 feet, 1 inch = 2,000 feet, or 1 inch = 3,000 feet, that can be measured by an engineer's scale shown in the legend). The map must clearly depict the proposed site's boundaries and airport runway(s).
- A separate dated schematic that clearly depicts the layout and boundaries of the proposed facility (drawn to the same standards as the vicinity map with a recommended scale of 1 inch = 500 feet), delineating all existing and proposed property boundaries and/or streets.

Upon receipt, CDE must submit the maps to Caltrans. Caltrans is required to seek the comments of the owner and operator of the airport and return a written report of its recommendations to CDE within 30 working days.

CDE then has ten days to forward the report to the district. If Caltrans does not favor the site, then no state or local funds can be used to acquire or expand any school building on that site. (However, additions and expansions can be made to sites acquired prior to January 1, 1966. *See* SFPD Advisory 00-05.) If Caltrans favors the site, the district must hold a public hearing prior to acquisition. This hearing can be combined with any public hearing the district is holding regarding potential acquisition of the site. Districts must also identify whether the site is within two miles of a helioport, for which a special study is typically not required.

Railroad track proximity. A school does not have to be set back a specific distance from a railroad track. However, if the site proposed is within 1,500 feet of a railroad track easement, a competent professional must prepare a safety study. 5 C.C.R. § 14010(d). The study should assess cargo manifests, frequency, speed, railroad traffic. schedule, grade, curves, type, and condition of track, need for sound or safety barriers, pedestrian and vehicle safeguards at railroad crossing, presence of high pressure gas lines, and its evacuation plan. In addition to the analysis, reasonable mitigation measures must be identified.

If the site is within 1,500 feet of a railroad track easement, a competent professional must prepare a safety study.

Proximity to high-voltage transmission lines. Electric power transmission lines maintained by power companies may or may not be hazardous to human health. However, given the uncertainty of our scientific knowledge, CDE has established conservative limits and grants limited exceptions. No school site property line may be located closer than:

- 100 feet from the edge of an easement for a 50–133 kV line
- 150 feet from the edge of an easement for a 220–230 kV line, or
- 350 feet from the edge of an easement for a 500–550 kV line

In addition to ensuring that the potential school site complies with these limits, the district should contact the utility company regarding its plans to increase transmission line voltage or expand its use of high voltage power transmission lines on the easement. 5 C.C.R. § 14010(c).

Proximity of site to former landfills, hazardous release, or waste sites. Sites on former landfills, hazardous waste, or release sites cannot be approved unless the wastes have been removed. The district site selection team should determine if the site is within one-fourth of a mile of:

Sites on former landfills, hazardous waste, or release sites cannot be approved unless the wastes have been removed.

- A former dump or landfill area
- A chemical plant
- An oil field
- A refinery
- A fuel storage facility
- A nuclear generating plant
- An abandoned farm, agricultural area where pesticides and fertilizer have been used, or where naturally occurring hazardous materials, such as asbestos, oil, and gas are present

Educ. Code § 17213; Pub. Res. Code § 21151.8; 5 C.C.R. § 14011

The CEQA document prepared for a proposed school site must identify potentially hazardous facilities near the site. It must identify whether the site:

- Is a former hazardous waste disposal or solid waste disposal site and, if so, whether the wastes have been removed.

- Is a hazardous substance release site (list available at www.dtsc.ca.gov/database/Calsites/Cortese_List.cfm).
- Contains one or more pipelines situated underground or aboveground that carries hazardous substances, acutely hazardous materials, or hazardous wastes, unless the pipeline is a natural gas line that is used only to supply natural gas to that school or neighborhood.

Additionally, the district must notify and consult with the air pollution control district or air quality management district to determine if there are the facilities within ¼ mile of the proposed school site that could potentially emit hazardous emissions or produce hazardous or acutely hazardous materials, substances, or waste. Educ. Code § 17213; Pub. Res. Code § 21151.4. The relevant air quality district generally takes about six weeks to respond to the request for this information, so this timeframe should be built into the schedule.

Districts must identify and review the impacts of hazardous air emitters and hazardous material handlers within one-quarter mile of a new school site.

Proximity to hazardous air emissions (2003 SB 352 requirements). School districts must identify and review the impacts of hazardous air emitters and hazardous material handlers within one-quarter mile of a new school site. In 2003, this requirement was added to apply to any school sites within 500 feet of a busy freeway or traffic corridor (defined as averaging more than 50,000 vehicles per day in rural areas and 100,00 vehicles per day in urban areas), large agricultural operations, and rail yards, or any other facility "whose process or operation is identified as an emission source pursuant to the most recent list of source categories published by the California Air Resources Board." SB 352, Chapter 668, Statutes of 2003; Educ. Code § 17213; Pub. Res. Code § 21151.8.

If a proposed site boundary is within 500 feet of such a roadway, the district must determine, through specified analysis, if the air quality at the site poses a significant health risk to pupils. The school district must follow new and more stringent procedural criteria. Most significantly, SB 352 limits the ability of school districts to use a CEQA Statement of Overriding Considerations to approve a project despite the presence of environmental risks. Where such facilities are present, CDE will require the school district to certify compliance with the current statutes (on SFPD Form 4.03) by submitting all of the following:

- A school district governing board-adopted determination, as supported by information included in the project's adopted CEQA document (or other document adopted by reference in the CEQA document) stating whether the site boundary is within 500 feet of the edge of the closest traffic lane of a freeway or other busy traffic corridor, and that the site is not a waste disposal site, a hazardous substance release site, or a site that contains pipelines that carry hazardous substances.
- A school district governing board-adopted finding stating that based upon written notice to and consultation with the administering agency (*i.e.,* for hazardous material handlers) and the appropriate air pollution control district or air quality management district to identify permitted and non-permitted "facilities" within ¼ mile of the proposed school site, either:
  - Consultation identified none of the facilities or other significant pollution sources specified in Education Code section 17213 or Public Resources Code section 21151.8, or

- Facilities or other pollution sources specified in Education Code section 17213 or Public Resources Code section 21151.8 exist, but either:
  - Health risks from the facilities or other pollution sources do not and will not constitute an actual or potential endangerment of public health to persons who would attend or be employed at the school, or
  - Corrective measures required under an existing order by another governmental entity that has jurisdiction over the facilities or other pollution sources will, before the school is occupied, result in the mitigation of all chronic or accidental hazardous air emissions to levels that do not constitute an actual or potential endangerment of public health to persons who would attend or be employed at the school

- If the site boundary is determined by the school district governing board to be within 500 feet of a freeway or busy traffic corridor, the school district is required to submit the school district's governing board-adopted finding that states:

  If the site boundary is within 500 feet of a freeway or busy traffic corridor, the district must submit a finding that exposure to the site's air quality will not pose short- or long-term significant health risks to the pupils.

    The school district governing board determines through analysis pursuant to paragraph two of Health and Safety Code Section 44360(b), based upon appropriate air dispersion modeling, and after considering any potential mitigation measure, that the air quality at the proposed site is such that neither short-term nor long-term exposure poses significant health risks to pupils.

- If the applicable code conditions listed above cannot be met (*e.g.*, the site is within ¼ mile of a pollution source(s) and/or is within 500 feet of a freeway or traffic corridor, and either source will be a significant health risk), the district may instead submit school district governing board-adopted findings stating that:
  - Pollution sources exist, but specified code conditions cannot be met
  - School district is unable to locate an alternative site due to a severe shortage of sites that meet the requirements of Education Code section 17213(a)
  - District board has adopted a Statement of Overriding Consideration as part of the project's environmental impact report (EIR) pursuant to CEQA Guidelines section 15093

Resources that can help a school district comply with SB 352.

- Traffic count information for state maintained roads is available from the California Department of Transportation (www.dot.ca.gov/hq/traffops/saferesr/trafdata/index.htm). Cities and counties can provide traffic counts for their non-state maintained roads.
- The Office of Environmental Health Hazard Assessment (OEHHA) Air Toxics Hot Spots Program Guidance Manual for Preparation of Health Risk Assessments is available at the OEHHA web site (www.oehha.ca.gov/air/hotspots/HRQguide final.html).
- The air dispersion computer model known as Hotspots Analysis and Report Program (HARP), developed by the California Air Resources Board (CARB) as a tool to implement the OEHHA guidance manual, is available at the CARB web site (www.arb.ca.gov/toxics/harp.htm).

CARB = California Air Resources Board
EIR = Environmental impact report
HARP = Hotspots Analysis and Report Program
OEHHA = Office of Environmental Health Hazard Assessment

APCD = Air Pollution
Control District
AQMD = Air Quality
Management District
BZHWP = Border Zone/Hazardous
Waste Property

The CARB web site also has a list of emission source categories (www.arb.ca.gov/emisinv/emsmain.htm) and local Air Quality Management Districts (AQMDs) and Air Pollution Control Districts (APCDs) (www.arb.ca.gov/capcoa/roster.htm).

Usually, the proximity of a proposed school site to such hazardous facilities is not identified until a preferred site is selected, Phase I is conducted, and the EIR is prepared. To assist in evaluating potential school sites and avoid pursuing ones that may be hazardous, the site selection team should send a list of all the potential school sites to the local air district as early as possible. If a listed school site is near such a hazardous facility, the district may still acquire that site if the board makes one of the following written findings:

- No hazardous facilities existed.
- Hazardous facilities exist, but
  - Health risks from the facilities do not and will not constitute an actual or potential endangerment of public health to persons who would attend or be employed at the proposed school, *or*
  - Corrective measures required under an existing order by another agency having jurisdiction over the facilities will, before the school is occupied, result in the mitigation of all chronic or accidental hazardous air emissions to levels that do not constitute an actual or potential endangerment of public health to persons who would attend or be employed at the proposed school, *and* prior to occupancy of the school, the board makes a subsequent finding that emissions have been so mitigated

A determination that a site does not meet the above criteria must be based on a CEQA analysis and in a written document confirmed by the board. To save time and money, a district should instruct the environmental assessor to include this information in the Phase I environmental assessment. Both the CEQA document and the board's written findings must be included in the submission to CDE.

Presence of toxic and hazardous substances. The presence of potentially toxic or hazardous substances on or in the vicinity of a prospective school site is another concern. If the proposed land has been designated a border zone property (BZHWP—Border Zone/Hazardous Waste Property) by DTSC, then a school may not be located on the site without a variance written by DTSC. Health & Safety Code §§ 25220–25241. A list of designated border zone properties is available on the DTSC web site (www.dtsc.ca.gov).

If the proposed land has been designated a border zone property, a school may not be located on the site without a DTSC variance.

On January 1, 2000, Education Code sections 17070.50, 17072.13, 17210, 17210.1, 17213.1–3, and 17268 became effective. Together with subsequent amendments to these laws, AB 972 (2002) and AB 14 (2003), a new environmental review and approval process for assessments of toxic and hazardous materials was established with DTSC oversight. Final site approval from CDE and state funding are conditional upon receiving a clean bill of health from DTSC in the form of a "no action" or "no further action" letter. A detailed explanation of the new DTSC review process is contained below.

Downwind of a compost facility, rendering plant, or other noxious facility. While not required by law, the district will want to determine if any potential nuisance-creating facilities interfere with the learning environment.

These include stockyard, fertilizer plant, soil-processing operation, auto dismantling facility, sewage treatment plant, or other noxious or hazardous facility.

High-pressure/high volume water pipelines. If a proposed school site
is within 1,500 feet of an above-ground or underground water pipeline easement
that poses a safety hazard, the district should obtain the following information
from the water pipeline owner or operator:

- Pipeline alignment, size, type of pipe, depth of cover
- Operating water pressures in pipelines near the proposed school site
- Estimated volume of water that might be released from the pipeline
  should a rupture occur on the site
- Owner's assessment of the structural condition of the pipeline (periodic
  reassessment would be appropriate as long as both the pipeline and the
  school remain operational)
- School districts should determine from topographic maps and by consulting local officials the general direction water released from the pipeline
  would drain

*While not required by law, the dis-
trict will want to determine if any
potential nuisance-creating facilities would interfere with the learning environment.*

While designs of such pipelines include a wide margin of safety for the operating water pressures within the pipe, a sudden rupture from a high-pressure
pipeline during an earthquake can result in the release of a large volume of water
and fragments of concrete pipe hurled throughout the immediate area. Subsequent flooding along the path of drainage to lower ground levels might occur. If a
site is selected that contains such pipelines, CDE advises that districts seek to:

- Avoid or minimize student use of ground surfaces above or in close proximity to the buried pipeline
- Locate facilities safely or provide safeguards to preclude flooding in the
  event of a pipeline failure
- Prepare and implement emergency response plans for the safety of students and faculty in the event of pipeline failure and flooding

Proximity to above-ground tanks. A district should evaluate safety in the
event of a fire from or explosion of a nearby propane tank. CDE typically seeks
information about the number and capacity of the tanks, and their distance from
the proposed site, and recommends that school districts consult the state fire marshall or the Public Utilities Commission (PUC) for an expert evaluation. *State
Fire Marshall (916) 445-8200; Public Utilities Commission (415) 445-8477.*

PUC = Public Utilities
    Commission

Proximity to major roadways or noise sources. A school site "shall not
be adjacent to a road or freeway that any site-related traffic and sound level studies have determined will have safety problems or sound levels which adversely
affect the educational program." 5 C.C.R. § 14010(e).

Noise is sound that is too loud, distracting, or, even worse, injurious. The
loudness of sound is measured in decibels and each decibel level equals the
amount of acoustical energy necessary to produce that level of sound. The normal
range of conversation is between 34 and 66 decibels. Between 70 and 90 decibels,
sound is distracting and presents an obstacle to conversation, thinking, or learning. Above 90 decibels, sound can cause permanent hearing loss. Caltrans considers sound at 50 decibels in the vicinity of schools to be the point at which it

will take corrective action for noise generated by freeways. Streets & Highway Code §§ 216 and 216.1. The noise element of the applicable city or county general plan may contain different or more stringent noise levels. For instance, many require that interior noise levels not exceed 45 decibels, even though in an urban area this may be a difficult, if not impossible, standard to meet.

When considering a site near a freeway or other source of noise, the school district should hire an acoustical engineer to determine the location's sound level and assist in designing the school's acoustics should that site be chosen.

Close proximity to a roadway can also expose the site to hazardous materials. Trucks traveling on public roads—including interstate freeways, state highways, and local roads—often contain the same hazardous materials that railway cars contain. Although the quantities trucks carry are smaller in comparison to a railcar, trucks have a greater incidence of accidents, spills, and explosions. Moreover, the truck's protective enclosures are not as strong as are those of a railcar.

When evaluating a site near a major roadway, a school district needs to ask questions similar to those used when evaluating risk from rail lines:

- What is the distance from the near edge of the roadway right-of-way to the site?
- How many trucks carrying freight use the roadway when students and staff are present?
- Is a safety or sound barrier necessary?
- How will students coming across the highway get to school safely?

Like railroad setbacks, highway setbacks from schools are not established by law. However, CDE recommends the following setbacks from highways:

- At least 2,500 feet where explosives are transported
- At least 1,500 feet where gasoline, diesel, propane, chlorine, oxygen, pesticides, and other combustible or poisonous gases are transported

School Site Selection and Approval Guide, SFPD, CDE (2000)

Geological or flood hazards. New facilities may not be located on sites that:

- Contain an active earthquake fault or fault trace. 5 C.C.R. § 14010(f). Fault Zone maps are available at the California Department of Conservation web site (www.consrv.ca.gov) or by calling the department, (916) 324-7299.
- May be subject to moderate-to-high liquefaction or landslides. 5 C.C.R. § 14010(f). Seismic Hazard Zone maps are available at the California Department of Conservation web site (www.consrv.ca.gov) or by contacting the CDC, DMG, telephone (916) 323-8569. Maps are also available from BPS Reprographic Services, San Francisco, CA 94105, (415) 512-6550.
- Are within an area of flood or dam inundation unless the cost of mitigating the impact is reasonable. 5 C.C.R. § 14010(g). Flood maps are available from the Federal Emergency Management Agency (www.fema.gov) or from the local flood control agency or Map Service Center at P.O. Box 1038, Jessup, MD 20794-1038, (800) 358-9616.

As a condition of final site approval, the CDE consultant may require a hydrologic study or other means of confirming that the site will not be subject to flooding, or of the proposed mitigation measures and their estimated costs.

This detailed study can be completed as part of the CEQA analysis for the project. Districts should also note that designation of seismic zone on the seismic maps will affect the structural safety design features required for the project's construction approval phase, as required by the DSA under the Field Act.

What is the Alquist-Priolo Act? The 1972 Alquist-Priolo Earthquake Fault Zoning Act's main purpose is to prevent the construction of buildings used for human occupancy on the surface trace of active faults. This state law was a direct result of the 1971 San Fernando Earthquake, which was associated with extensive surface fault ruptures that damaged numerous homes, commercial buildings, and other structures. Surface rupture is the most easily avoided seismic hazard. The Act only addresses surface fault rupture and not other earthquake hazards. The Seismic Hazards Mapping Act, passed in 1990, addresses non-surface fault rupture earthquake hazards, including liquefaction and seismically induced landslides.

The main purpose of Alquist-Priolo is to prevent the construction of buildings used for human occupancy on the surface trace of active faults.

How does the law work? What are Alquist-Priolo special studies zones? The law requires the State Geologist to establish regulatory zones around the surface traces of active faults and to issue appropriate maps. (Renamed in 1994, "Earthquake Fault Zones" are still referred to by their original name "Special Studies Zone.") The maps are distributed to all *affected cities, counties,* and state agencies for their use in planning and controlling new or renewed construction.

Earthquake Fault Zone maps can be studied at local planning departments or at offices of the California Geological Survey. These maps show most streets, drainages, and other features. Local government may have already transferred Earthquake Fault Zone boundaries to parcel maps, so the relationship of the Zone to each parcel can easily be determined. A list of affected cities and counties is available on the web at www.consrv.ca.gov.

Geological and soils analysis. If the prospective school site is located within the boundaries of any Alquist-Priolo special studies zone, or within an area designated as geologically hazardous in the safety element of the local general plan (as provided in Government Code section 65302(g)), Education Code sections 17212 and 17212.5 require a geological study and soils analysis that assess the potential for an earthquake or other geological hazard damage.

The law states that "no school building shall be constructed, reconstructed, or relocated on the trace of a geological fault along which surface rupture can be reasonably expected to occur within the life of the school building." 5 C.C.R. § 14011(g). However, because California is seismically active and new faults are still being discovered, CDE and DSA require that all proposed school sites have geological studies and soils analyses completed. For the primary factors that must be included, *see* the sidebar on page 125. To save time and prevent duplication, this study can be completed as part of the CEQA analysis for the project.

Because California is seismically active, CDE and DSA require geological studies and soils analyses for all proposed sites.

Traffic and school bus safety conditions. The school facility should be situated so that students can enter and depart the buildings and grounds safely. As the number of schools providing child care and extended day classes increases, it is important that schools ensure the safe flow of buses and other traffic through designated areas of the grounds. When analyzing a potential site, the selection team should consider how its size and shape affect traffic flow, and the placement of pickup and drop-off points for parents.

Parent drop-off area

Land Use Authority: K–12 vs. Community College Facilities

In contrast to K–12 school districts, community colleges must comply with all applicable city and county zoning, building, and health regulations.

Educ. Code § 81951

Some local governments include potential future locations of school sites in their general plans, specific plans, and/or community plans.

CDP = Coastal development permit
ESHA = Ecologically-sensitive habitat area
FHWA = Federal Highway Administration
LCP = Local coastal plan

When designing pickup and drop-off points, the team should remember to separate bus traffic from all other traffic. Roads servicing the area that are off the main thoroughfare must be wide enough to load and unload pupils. The need for left turn lanes must be determined, and driveway openings must conform to local ordinances or regulations. CDE publishes a school bus driveway evaluation checklist. The district should also consult with the local traffic department and its CDE consultant to help evaluate issues of ingress and egress.

Safe routes to schools. CDE recommends that the site selection team walk the area surrounding each proposed site. If the walking routes are unsatisfactory, the school district should consider another site or work with the city or county to have safe walking routes installed before opening the school. CDE has published a "Walkability Checklist," using excerpts from the National Safety Council (available at www.nsc.org/walkable.htm).

Caltrans is responsible for distributing the guidelines for the Safe Routes to Schools program. More information about the program is available on the Caltrans web site (www.dot.ca.gov or www.dot.ca.gov/hq/traffops).

Federal Highway Administration (FHWA) funds may be available to help make school access safer for pedestrians and cyclists. AB 1475 (Chapter 663, Statutes of 1999) transfers FHWA safety funds to a program entitled Safe Routes to Schools. On September 9, 2004, Governor Schwarzenegger signed SB 1087 (Soto) extending this program until January 1, 2008.

Land use issues. Cities and counties are responsible for adopting local ordinances, policies, plans, and zoning maps related to allowed and prohibited land uses. Some local governments include potential future locations of school sites in their general plans, specific plans, and/or community plans. Ideally, a school district can coordinate its Facilities Master Plan with the local government to prevent conflicts. Land use issues are considered part of the district's compliance with CEQA. However, due to the difficulties inherent in such coordination, the legislature has authorized school boards to overrule local zoning and general plan land use designations with a two-thirds majority vote. If local planning jurisdictions object to the land acquisition of a school site, the board may override the zoning law by a two-thirds vote, provided the override is not arbitrary or capricious. Govt. Code § 53094; *City of Santa Cruz v. Santa Cruz City School Board of Education* (1989) 210 Cal. App. 3d.

Other Land Use Laws That May Govern School Siting

Coastal Act

The California Coastal Act established a 12-member statewide commission that governs land use decisions in the coastal zone. Pub. Res. Code §§ 30000–30900 and C.C.R., Title 14, §§ 13001–13666.4. School districts with school siting and construction projects in the coastal zone may have to obtain a coastal development permit (CDP) from either the local government, Commission, or both, depending on whether the local government has adopted a local coastal plan (LCP). The coastal zone extends three miles seaward and 1,000 feet inland of the mean high tide line. Pub. Res. Code § 30103(a). A school district should consult maps maintained by the Coastal Commission to determine if potential school sites are located within the coastal zone.

Once it determines that a potential school site is in the coastal zone, a school district should determine whether an LCP has been adopted for the jurisdiction, and the land use designation of the potential school site. Under the Coastal Act, cities and counties in the coastal zone are to adopt LCPs, which often act as a specific plan under the jurisdiction's general plan and must be certified by the Coastal Commission. LCPs are to give special emphasis to land uses valued in the Coastal Act, such as maximizing public access to coastal and public recreation areas. Pub. Res. Code § 30500.

Unlike general or specific plan designations in noncoastal jurisdictions, a school district does not have the ability to override LCP designations or zoning requirements established by the LCP or the Commission. Certain land uses have higher values in the coastal zone than in noncoastal areas—unfortunately, school uses are not among them. If the potential school site is in a zone designated as an "ecologically-sensitive habitat area" (ESHA), it is highly unlikely that the school district could obtain a zone change or LCP amendment to use it for a school. *Bolsa Chica Land Trust v. Superior Court* (1999) 71 Cal. App. 4th 493. Similarly, if the potential site is designated for a tourist, recreational, marine-related, or open-space—which are highly valued land uses in the coastal zone—the likelihood of a zone change or LCP amendment is even lower.

If an LCP has been adopted, its provisions govern land use for the site. The LCP designates areas where the Commission has original jurisdiction (if any), where the city has sole jurisdiction, or where the city is responsible for issuing a CDP. However, the Commission can appeal. Many jurisdictions along the coast have not adopted an LCP and may be a single-jurisdiction zone (district applies to Commission for a CDP) or dual-jurisdiction zone (district applies to both local government and Commission for a CDP).

Geological and Environmental Hazards Report

Site Description

- Identify location by street name, lot number(s), or other site specific descriptors
- Description of site reconnaissance, including vegetation (describe type), and previous site usage

Seismic and Fault Hazard

- Describe whether the site is in Alquist-Priolo zone, situated on or near a pressure ridge, geological fault, or fault trace that may rupture during the life of the building, and what the student risk factor is
- Location's potential for ground shaking from nearby faults or fault traces; discussion of field inspection and reconnaissance
- Known subsurface conditions based on existing subsurface explorations and/or literature review

Liquefaction Subsidence or Expansive Potential

- Discussion of subsoil condition relative to ground water and potential for liquefaction
- Mitigating factors

Dam or Flood Inundation and Street Flooding

- Site location in relation to flood zones and dam inundation areas
- If in flood zone, give year, type, and potential hazard
- Potential for sheet flooding, street flooding, and dam or flood inundation

Slope Stability

- If located on or near a slope
- Discuss potential for instability and landslides

Mitigations

- Discuss mitigations concerning student safety and staff use

*The precise land uses and per-
mitting requirements allowed for
each site should be identified at
the outset.*

The precise land uses and permitting requirements allowed for each site should be identified at the outset. While there is no guarantee that the 12-member Commission will grant a permit, the school district should consult with Commission staff and key Commission decisionmakers to determine whether a permit can be issued. Once satisfied that the possibility is strong, the district should start the process, since applying for single-jurisdiction can take six months to one year and dual-permit jurisdiction from 18 months to two years.

Agricultural Land Issues

State law also encourages public agencies, including school districts, to avoid acquiring land that is designated in the general plan and zoned for agricultural use, or sites that fall under the Williamson Act agricultural preserves and contracts. Districts should also note that due to the use of pesticides on agricultural land, special soil testing may be required by DTSC.

The California Land Conservation Act of 1965 (Govt. Code §§ 51200–51298, commonly called the Williamson Act), provides for the preservation of land through the establishment of agricultural preserves and restricts that land to agricultural or compatible use. A landowner who enters into a long-term contract with local government voluntarily restricts land use in exchange for reduced taxes.

A school district wishing to site a school on land restricted to agricultural use under a Williamson Act contract can cancel the contract in two ways. The landowner can file a notice of nonrenewal, which will phase out the tax breaks and end the contract in ten years. Alternatively, to make cancellation occur more quickly, the district can petition the local government to make certain public policy findings and pay a cancellation fee.

Should acquisition of agricultural land be necessary, however, districts must follow the procedures described in Education Code section 17215.5 and Government Code sections 51290 *et seq.*

Endangered Species Acts

The Endangered Species Act of 1973 (16 U.S.C. § 1531 *et seq.*) and the California Endangered Species Act (Fish & Game Code § 2050 *et seq.*) establish federal and state protections for fish, wildlife, and plants that are threatened or endangered. The state Act also protects candidate species or those species eligible for listing.

*A school district must investigate
the possibility that a threatened,
candidate, or endangered species
may be present on the property.*

As purchaser or owner of real property for development and construction of a school, a district must investigate the possibility that a threatened, candidate, or endangered species may be present on the property and plan in advance how the project can be designed to avoid or minimize those effects. If the facility will have an impact on a listed species, the district may have to obtain an incidental take permit from either or both the United States Fish and Wildlife Service (USFWS) or the California Department of Fish and Game (DFG).

DFG   = Department of
            Fish and Game
USFWS = United States Fish
            and Wildlife Service

Wetlands

Special regulatory requirements are applicable to school projects built on wetlands. Wetlands are characterized by unique physical, chemical, and biological features, including distinctive hydrology, soils, and vegetation. An environmental consultant retained early in the process can help eliminate sites with potential wetlands during the district's preliminary site review. However, it is often the case that a district does not screen for environmental conditions such as these at an early stage, and consequently wetlands are not detected until the district conducts its CEQA review for a favored site.

Unlike most natural resources regulated by environmental law in California, wetlands are regulated primarily by the federal government. The U.S. Army Corps of Engineer's administers Section 404 of the Clean Water Act. Section 404 requires that developers obtain a permit from the Corps before the deposit, referred to as "discharge," of dredged or fill materials into waters of the United States, which include wetlands. If a Section 404 permit may affect a listed threatened or endangered species, then formal consultation with USFWS and the National Marine Fisheries Service (NMFS) is required under the federal Endangered Species Act.

NMFS = National Marine Fisheries Service

DFG has jurisdiction over wetland resources associated with rivers, streams, and lakes under Fish & Game Code §§ 1600–1607, regulating the activities of school districts under Fish & Game Code § 1601. DFG is authorized to regulate work that will substantially divert, obstruct, or change the natural flow of a river, stream, or lake, substantially change the bed, channel, or bank of a river, stream, or lake, or use material from a streambed. Because its jurisdiction includes streamside habitats that under the federal definition may not qualify as wetlands on a particular project site, DFG's jurisdiction may be broader than that of the Corps.

A school district with a project that might affect wetland resources must seek a Section 404 permit from the Corps, notify DFG, and enter into a streambed alteration agreement, agreeing to certain conditions to ensure no net loss of wetland values or acreage. Districts in areas containing wetlands of special importance—such as the coastal zone, Lake Tahoe basin, or San Joaquin/Sacramento delta—may also have additional legal requirements.

A district with a project that might affect wetland resources must seek a Section 404 permit from the Corps, notify DFG, and enter into a streambed alteration agreement.

Department of Toxic Substances Control Review Compliance[1]

To address concerns regarding placement of new schools on contaminated properties, the legislature requires that the California Department of Toxic Substances Control provide oversight of review for contaminants where state funds will be used for acquisition or construction on proposed new school sites.

AB 387 and SB 162, the first two pieces of legislation creating the new review process, became effective in January 2000, and the process has been amended several times. The original bills contained detailed procedural steps and requirements, and subsequent amendments streamlined each step without sacrificing standards for environmental safety and health of children. Each bill is summarized below.

Exemptions from DTSC Review

No state funding? The DTSC review process is only required for property acquisition or facility construction projects that use state bond funding.

1. This DTSC review section was written by David J. Jensen, P.E., Camp Dresser & McKee, Inc.

Assembly Bill 972

Effective October 14, 2001, AB 972 was enacted to fine-tune the DTSC review process that AB 387, SB 192, and AB 2644 defined. The most significant change affects the public review and DTSC approval process for PEAs. The changes include:

- Delegation to the school district to perform public participation activities for the PEA concurrently with the CEQA process. The district may now choose one of two options for making a PEA available to the public.

Option A—Review of PEA independent of CEQA process.
Under Option A, the district makes the PEA available for public comment for 30 days at the same time as submittal to DTSC, and holds a public hearing on the PEA. DTSC completes its review of the PEA within 30 days after the close of the public comment period.

Option B—Review of PEA concurrent with CEQA review.
Under Option B, DTSC completes review of the PEA within 60 days of receipt. Provided DTSC concurs that it is adequate, the district shall then make the PEA available to the public in the same manner the draft CEQA document (either the EIR or the mitigated negative declaration) is made available, and will hold a public hearing on the PEA. DTSC will issue its final determination on the PEA within 30 days after the district adopts the CEQA document.

If the CEQA document will not be available until after 90 days of DTSC issuing its concurrence, the district shall make the PEA available to the public within 60 days of DTSC's concurrence.

- Addition of a requirement that residents in the immediate area be notified prior to initiation of work for a PEA in a format developed by DTSC.

Amended sections 17210.1 and 17213.1 of the California Education Code

Assembly Bill 2644

Effective September 13, 2000, AB 2644 was enacted to provide clarification of the DTSC review process for new schools defined in AB 387 and SB 162. Substantive changes to the DTSC review process include:

- Addition of the requirement that school districts perform public participation activities for the PEA concurrent with the CEQA process.

- Expansion of the acceptable qualifications for an environmental assessor to include professional engineers, registered geologists, and certified engineering geologists registered in the State of California. Minimum experience levels were also established. Prior to AB 2644, only Class II registered environmental assessors and licensed hazardous substance contractors were deemed qualified.

- Modification of the review process for a Phase 1 ESA by DTSC.

- Addition of requirement that residents be notified prior to the commencement of field work for a PEA.

Amended sections 17210, 17210.1, 17213.1, and 17213.2 of the California Education Code and added section 17072.18

Categorically exempt under CEQA? A minor addition to a school for a categorical exemption under CEQA is also exempt from DTSC review. Examples of projects that may be eligible include minor enhancements to classrooms, modernization, reconstruction of damaged property, and the addition of playground facilities or a limited number of new classrooms. When a project is exempt under CEQA, the district should exercise caution before proceeding without DTSC oversight. Be aware that a small change in project scope, a change in district or CEQA policy, or a third-party challenge may result in a project losing its exempt status. In the event of any change, a previously exempt project may require a new DTSC review.

Initiating DTSC review late in a project's development could cause serious delay because additional investigation may be required.

CDE policy regarding land acquisition. If the project involves land acquisition or a new school site, districts should also be aware that current CDE policy requires DTSC review, regardless of CEQA status.

DTSC Review Process

Depending on the quality of the information learned at each stage of the investigation, the DTSC review process (see Figure 4-1) may include the following:

- Phase 1 Environmental Site Assessment
- Preliminary Environmental Assessment
- Remediation

Remediation activities include Supplemental Site Investigation (SSI), Removal Action Workplan, or Remedial

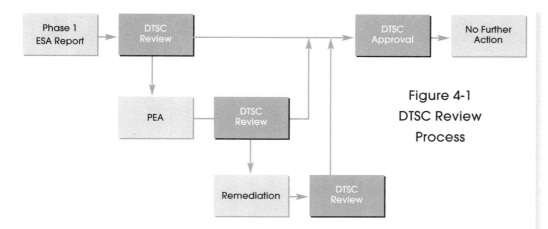

Figure 4-1
DTSC Review
Process

Action Workplan. Not each of these steps will be completed for each potential new school a district is considering.

The district will not have to complete all these steps for each potential school site. After each step, the information yielded may result in a determination by DTSC that no toxic risks are present and therefore DTSC will issue a letter stating that "no further action" is warranted (an NFA Letter). Often a Phase I ESA will result in a finding of "no action" and eliminate the need for PEA field sampling.

Phase 1 Environmental Site Assessment

The purpose of a Phase 1 ESA is to determine if recognized environmental conditions exist at a site. The term "recognized environmental conditions" refers to the presence, or likely presence, of hazardous materials in which the release or material threat of a release of hazardous materials may damage human health or the environment is a possibility. In terms of the DTSC review process, the purpose of the Phase 1 ESA can be simply thought of as an assessment to determine if further investigation (*i.e.*, sampling) is required.

The California Education Code, as amended by AB 2644, requires that school districts perform Phase 1 ESAs for potential new school sites in accordance with the ASTM standards E 1527 or E 1528. ASTM E 1527 and E 1528 represent the industry standard for Phase 1 ESAs prepared for commercial real estate. In addition, DTSC has guidelines that expand the ASTM requirements.

Contents of a Phase I ESA. The major components of a completed ASTM E 1527 Phase 1 ESA are:

- A review of available records for the site
- Site reconnaissance visit
- Interviews with owners, occupants, and local government officials
- Phase 1 ESA report

The ASTM standard fully describes these components. Completion of a comprehensive Phase 1 ESA helps demonstrate that potential environmental hazards pose no risk to human health or the environment, without having to perform a more costly and time-consuming PEA.

Assembly Bill 387 Senate Bill 162

Effective January 1, 2000, AB 387 (Wildman) and SB 162 (Escutia) were designed to provide a comprehensive program for addressing potential hazardous material contamination at a proposed new school site. Under the legislation, DTSC must be involved in the environmental review when state funds are to be used. Prior to obtaining state funding for property acquisition and/or construction of a new school facility, a school district must perform an environmental review with DTSC oversight. ■

Amended sections 17070.50 and 17268 of the California Education Code

Added six new sections: 17210, 17210.1, 17213.1, 17213.2, and 17213.3

Assembly Bill 14

Effective January 1, 2003, AB 14 was enacted to modify the process for submitting a Phase 1 ESA report for review. Under AB 14, a Phase 1 report that recommends no further investigation is sent directly to DTSC along with a check to cover the fee. Previously, this was submitted to CDE, and CDE would then forward the report to DTSC. ■

EA = Environmental assessment
NA = No action
NFA = No further action

Collecting Samples

The ASTM standard does not include collecting samples as part of the Phase 1 review. However, DTSC recognizes that, with the collection of a limited amount of samples, certain environmental conditions can be addressed during the Phase 1 review.

DTSC has developed additional guidance and regulations that allow districts to include samples for lead and PCBs in the Phase 1 ESA, or as an addendum. The purpose of this sampling would be to evaluate the potential impact to soil from lead-based paints or PCBs from leaking transformers without having to complete a PEA. If these constituents were not detected at significant levels, no further action would be required; otherwise, a PEA would be required. Districts should consult with DTSC before including these results in a Phase 1 ESA. ■

ACM = Asbestos-containing material
AHERA = Asbestos Hazard Emergency Response Act
EPA = Environmental Protection Agency
NESHAP = National Emissions Standards for Hazardous Air Pollutants
PCB = Polychlorinated biphenyl

Districts may choose to use previously prepared Phase 1 ESAs for a potential school site. DTSC will require that a new Phase 1 ESA be performed, or an addendum be prepared, if the previous report is more than 180 days old. This is necessary to determine if site conditions have changed.

Qualifications of an environmental assessor. The California Education Code defines the minimum qualifications for an environmental assessor performing Phase 1 ESAs as one of the following:

* Professional engineer, registered in California
* Certified engineering geologist, registered in California
* Geologist, registered in California
* Class II registered environmental assessor
* Licensed hazardous substance contractor

Consultants or contractors performing Phase 1 ESAs for school districts must have at least two years experience in the preparation of these assessments. An appropriately qualified person must sign the final Phase 1 ESA report to be reviewed by DTSC.

DTSC guidance. DTSC has developed procedures for performing Phase 1 ESAs, available on their website or from DTSC. This information clarifies the supporting documentation to be included, and what source areas for hazardous and naturally occurring materials may impact the site. DTSC's guidance goes beyond the scope of assessment detailed in the ASTM standard, and is intended to supplement, not replace, those standards.

Coordinating DTSC review with the CDE review. In addition to DTSC considerations, a district may wish to expand the scope of its Phase 1 ESA to include site selection criteria. The CDE has identified conditions that must be considered when evaluating properties in the site visit/review process. SFPD Form 4.0. Criteria related to safety and environmental concerns (*i.e.*, proximity rail lines, high voltage, and hazardous substance pipelines) identified in the Phase 1 ESA will help ensure that they are adequately addressed during the CEQA review.

Timing/Schedule/Costs

A Phase 1 ESA typically takes 30 to 60 days, excluding DTSC review time, which may add another 30 days. Completing a Phase 1 ESA, depending on the site's size and complexity, costs approximately $5,000 to $7,500.

Phase 1 results. Although its primary purpose is to identify recognized environmental conditions, a Phase 1 ESA performed as part of the potential new school site evaluation must also identify the next step in the DTSC review process. The results of the Phase 1 ESA should recommend one of the following:

* No action
* Further action (*i.e.*, investigation or sampling) is required
* Limited further action for lead-based paint and/or PCBs

If approved by DTSC, a no further action determination will close out the DTSC review process. A further action determination will result in a PEA being performed for the site. A limited further action applies to properties where the only potential sources of contamination are from lead-based paints and/or PCBs.

Factors for Success — General Considerations for a Successful DTSC Review

1 Active Participation in the Review Process

The district should play an active role in the DTSC review process. This is particularly important for districts with multiple projects.

To ensure that consultants performing the PEA are not recommending excessive work for the site, the district's project manager should participate in the scoping meeting with DTSC, be familiar with PEA field work and concur with recommendations, and participate in any public meetings.

Districts with multiple projects should ensure consistent requirements are being imposed among their sites since there can be a wide range of opinions on how to proceed with the investigation of a particular site.

2 Communication with DTSC

The district's project manager, or a senior management team member, should hold regular meetings with the DTSC Unit Chief project manager to discuss the project's status.

Project issues need to be identified early and discussed with DTSC as soon as possible (*e.g.,* notifying DTSC of changes in site configuration, conditions, and schedule requirements). District involvement may be needed to resolve differences between DTSC and consultants regarding technical issues.

3 Reliance on DTSC Guidance Documents

DTSC has developed several guidance documents related to the DTSC review process. Topics include:

- Environmental oversight agreements
- Phase 1 ESAs
- Sampling agricultural soils
- Preliminary environmental assessments
- Evaluating lead-based paints and PCBs
- Soil gas evaluations
- Clean imported fill
- Removal action workplans

Districts should avail themselves of these materials when developing approaches for evaluating potential new school sites.

4 Manage the Schedule

Completing the review and any necessary remediation may be prerequisite to property acquisition, the completion of CEQA, and school construction. A district embarking on a new school project needs to include the DTSC review process in its overall schedule. However, given the complex nature of some sites, identifying the steps in the review process may be difficult; *e.g.,* whether conducting a PEA or RAW versus a Phase 1 ESA will have a greater impact on the schedule.

Districts wishing to better manage and ensure timely completion of the process should:

- Define and track key project milestones
- Develop the PEA schedule with DTSC at the scoping meeting
- Document project schedules for PEAs and RAWs in the associated work plans
- Allow time for PEAs and RAWs when planning new school projects

- Define and reach agreement on the amount of time required by DTSC to review draft and final documents

DTSC is responsible for providing oversight of environmental reviews for all proposed new school projects within the state. To alleviate the possibility of delay resulting from DTSC resource limitations, a district should:

- Provide DTSC with advanced notice of proposed projects
- Request that DTSC assign a project manager early in the process
- Set a date for the scoping meeting well in advance
- Develop a detailed schedule, with DTSC concurrence on key milestones

While review times are mandated, a district can work with DTSC to accelerate the review period for a critical project. In addition, DTSC senior management should be notified when workplan reviews and reports are not completed in accordance with the project schedule.

5 Cost Control

Because the review is phased and site conditions are determined during review, the true cost of clearing a new school site may not be known until late in the process. This is especially true for a larger site with a complex history, and for a site where remediation will be required. As a consequence, the cost of a DTSC review can vary greatly, making it difficult for a district to develop a budget for the project before beginning the work. To allow for this uncertainty, contingencies for additional PEA sampling and RAW costs should be included in the budget.

The variability in project expenses also can make it challenging for ➥

a district to control contract costs. In particular, estimating the cost of a complete PEA is difficult when the amount of sampling required isn't defined until DTSC approves the workplan. An initial estimate for the PEA can significantly understate what is required, resulting in a large change order from the consultant. A district should take the following measures to control the cost of environmental review:

- Break up contracts/work authorizations into discrete components with clearly defined end points (*i.e.,* reports and plans). Examples include Phase 1 ESA, PEA scoping and workplan development, PEA field work and report, RAW workplan development, and RAW implementation. This approach gives a district more opportunities to control costs and evaluate a consultant's performance before continuing with the more costly phases of the project.

- When possible, obtain a fixed price bid from a consultant. A Phase 1 ESA and the PEA scoping and workplan development are amenable to this approach. Defining the work as a discrete project also makes it easier to obtain a fixed priced bid to implement approved PEA and RAW workplans.

The cost of environmental review can also be controlled by analyzing the viability of a proposed site at key decision points. This should include evaluating the estimated cost to complete the review and potential liabilities associated with the site. A district should try to determine the amount of each estimate, evaluating the project at the completion of each phase: *e.g.,* Phase 1 ESA, prior to initiating the PEA; completion of PEA, prior to initiating a RAW or RAP; and prior to implementing an approved RAW or RAP. By reviewing the economic viability of a proposed school site at each stage, a district may be able to avoid purchasing property with environmental liabilities that may be prohibitively expensive to remediate. ■

When Asbestos, Lead, or PCBs Are Present

Asbestos in schools. Asbestos is a fibrous mineral that has been used widely in construction materials, such as roofing and siding shingles, pipe and boiler insulation, and floor and ceiling tiles. In fact, asbestos-containing materials (ACM) generally do not pose a health risk. They may become hazardous and pose increased risk when damaged, disturbed in some manner, or deteriorate over time—and thus release asbestos fibers into building air.

AHERA. Under the federal Asbestos Hazard Emergency Response Act (AHERA), school districts have a responsibility as building owners to inspect their school facilities for ACM and prepare management plans to reduce health risks. 40 Code of Federal Regulations, Part 763, Subpart E. The U.S. EPA's school asbestos AHERA program and its guidance for other building owners is founded on the principle of ACM "in-place" management. This approach is designed to keep asbestos fiber levels low by teaching people how to recognize and actively manage asbestos-containing materials. Removal of ACM is not usually necessary unless the material is severely damaged or will be disturbed by a building demolition or renovation project.

Asbestos NESHAP. When planning to demolish or renovate school facilities or other buildings to build a school facility, a district must comply with the asbestos National Emissions Standards for Hazardous Air Pollutants (NESHAP) established by the U.S. EPA, pursuant to the federal Clean Air Act. 42 U.S.C. § 7401 *et seq.* Intended to minimize the release of asbestos fibers during activities involving its handling, NESHAP specifies work practices that must be followed during demolitions of all structures, installations, and facilities—regardless of the ACM amount—while renovating buildings that contain a certain threshold amount of friable asbestos (160 square feet in the facility or 260 linear feet on pipes).

A district must employ a person trained in provisions of the Asbestos NESHAP to supervise the methods and actions where ACM is stripped, removed, or otherwise handled during a demolition or renovation. For planned renovations and demolitions, a district must give both the U.S. EPA and the California Air Resources Board a 10-day notice. 40 C.F.R. Part 61 Subpart M, § 61.145(b).

Because California is a source of naturally-occurring asbestos, a school district located in an area where asbestos is found must take special care to prevent health risks during construction of school facilities. Serpentine and its parent material, ultramafic rock, often contain asbestos. Ultramafic rock has been used in some areas for surfacing unpaved roads, parking lots, playgrounds, and other open areas; therefore, some schools and daycare centers may currently have areas covered with this material. Ultramafic rock is found is especially abundant in the coastal ranges, the Klamath Mountains, and Sierra foothills of California, where it is commonly exposed near fault lines. The CARB regulates the construction, grading, and surface mining activities to control dust emissions that take place in areas with asbestos-containing rocks or soils. If naturally-occurring asbestos is identified at a school undergoing construction, the district should adopt the mitigation measures recommended by CARB in Fact Sheets (www.arb.ca.gov) and DTSC's interim guidelines.

The management of asbestos is generally outside the purview of DTSC. The district is responsible for the proper identification, management, and abatement of asbestos-containing materials under the federal laws discussed above. However, DTSC may request documentation that the abatement of asbestos-containing materials was properly performed.

Lead-based paint in schools. To address potential impacts from lead-based paints, DTSC requires that testing be performed at the site. Testing may include either soil sampling or analysis using XRF (x-ray fluorescence) technology. DTSC does not consider testing of structures to be sufficient.

DTSC has developed regulations to allow inclusion of limited soil sampling data for lead in soil from lead-based paint and/or PCBs in soil from electrical transformers in Phase I or a Phase I addendum. 22 C.C.R. §§ 69100–69107. DTSC has two fact sheets to assist school districts in the implementation of these regulations. *DTSC School Fact Sheet No. 5, Proposed Regulations on Preparation of Phase I Environmental Site Assessments*, and *Phase I Addendum: Lead-Based Paint and/or Electrical Transformer Investigation* (www.dtsc.ca.gov).

DTSC has also developed guidance for sampling the impacts of lead-based paint (www.dtsc.ca.gov). Soil sampling results may be submitted in the Phase 1 ESA as an addendum to a previous Phase 1 ESA or as a focused PEA. If a PEA has already determined that the site requires further action, the sample results can be submitted as part of a supplemental site investigation. The method of providing this data will depend on whether or not lead is detected in soils and the concentrations found. In the event elevated levels of lead are detected, generally 255 mg/kg soil, DTSC will require that the data be submitted as a PEA.

If DTSC notifies CDE that lead-based paints and/or PCBs are the only contaminants present, the district can apply for both site acquisition and construction funding before receiving a "no further action" determination from DTSC. The district and DTSC must submit Form 4.14 to CDE and jointly commit to complete response action prior to grading of the site. CDE SFPD Form 4.14, "Local Educational and Department of Toxic Substances Control Commitment to complete Lead-Based Paint and/or Polychlorinated Biphenyls Investigation and Related Response Action."

Submitting the Phase 1 ESA

If the Phase 1 ESA determines that no further investigation is required, the Phase 1 ESA report and a check for $1,500 must be submitted to DTSC:

Department of Toxic Substances Control, School Property Evaluation and Cleanup Division, 1011 North Grandview Avenue, Glendale, CA 91201

For a Phase 1 ESA that recommends no further action, DTSC has 30 calendar days to review the report. Based on this review, DTSC will either:

Benefits of Phase 1 ESA Completion

A district may choose to skip the Phase 1 stage, proceeding directly to the PEA. This approach may save time where the site condition or its historical use clearly suggest the need for a more thorough investigation. Even in those cases, however, completing a Phase 1 ESA is beneficial.

Information gleaned from a Phase 1 ESA can be used in the decision to pursue a site. It can also help estimate the cost to complete the PEA, at the same time assisting the district in its evaluation of the the Phase 1 ESA consultant's performance as it considers the larger PEA contract. ∎

U.S. EPA—Region IX

Asbestos NESHAP
Notification (Air 5)
75 Hawthorne Street
San Francisco, CA 94105

CARB Enforcement Division

Asbestos NESHAP Notification
Post Office Box 2815
Sacramento, CA 95812
Facsimile: (916) 445-5745

Phase 1 ESA

A consultant preparing the Phase 1 ESA will often identify a site's environmental conditions, without stating whether or not sampling is required. The consultant should be asked to provide a clear recommendation for either possibility. This will facilitate the report's review, reducing the possibility that DTSC will reject the Phase 1 ESA. ■

Figure 4-2
PEA Process

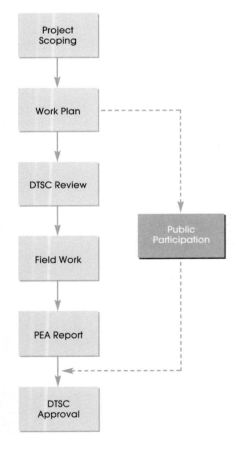

EOA = Environmental oversight agreement
SCA = School cleanup agreement
VCA = Voluntary cleanup agreement

- Approve the Phase 1 ESA and issue a "no action" letter
- Determine further investigation is required and issue a letter requiring that a PEA be conducted
- Determine that additional information is required to evaluate and approve the Phase 1 ESA

If more information is required to complete the review, DTSC must let the district know what is needed. DTSC will complete its review within 30 calendar days of the receipt of additional information.

Contacting DTSC during the Phase 1 ESA review may be useful to see if any issues have arisen that require additional information. This will expedite the process, reducing the possibility of DTSC determining that a PEA is required at a site with potential environmental hazards.

Environmental oversight agreement. In order to proceed with the investigation of a potential school site under oversight of DTSC, a school district must enter into an environmental oversight agreement (EOA). EOA is used for PEA, while a voluntary cleanup agreement (VCA) or school cleanup agreement (SCA) is generally required for any further action (SSI, RAW, or RAP) beyond PEA.

The purpose of the EOA is to identify PEA activities, schedule, and contacts to provide a mechanism for the district to reimburse DTSC for the cost of its oversight activities. In addition, under the EOA, all subsequent investigations and/or remedial activities must be performed in compliance with the California Health and Safety Code.

Districts with multiple projects should enter into a master EOA that covers all projects requiring DTSC oversight. This can reduce transaction time and cost, and simplify billing and payments.

Preliminary environmental assessment. The purpose of the PEA is to provide the information necessary to determine if a release or a threat of a release of hazardous materials exists at a site, and if that release poses a risk to human health and/or the environment. Figure 4-2 shows a flow chart for the PEA process. The major components of the PEA process include project scoping, work plan development, public notification, field work, report development, and public participation. Each of these components is described below. Additional information can be obtained from DTSC's guidance manual for the PEA process. DTSC 1994.

Project scoping and the scoping meeting. The project scoping phase is when the plan for investigating the site is conceptualized. This plan, which is formalized in the PEA work plan, is based on the results of the Phase 1 ESA and/or a review of other available information, such as previous Phase 1 ESAs, previous site investigations, and agency records.

The following must be considered during the PEA phase:

- Location and characteristics of the site
- Any previous investigations and/or remedial activities
- Current and historical land use
- Land use of the surrounding area

- Operations and chemical usage at existing businesses
- Agency records (*i.e.*, DTSC, RWQCB, and EPA)
- Maps and aerial photographs
- Observations from a site visit

Early in the scoping phase, the district should request that DTSC assign a project manager and schedule a scoping meeting. The DTSC project manager will assemble a team that usually consists of the project manager, a representative from the Geological Services Unit, and a toxicologist. The Phase 1 ESA for the site should be given to the DTSC project manager before that meeting.

The scoping meeting should establish the areas of concern at the site, the sampling approach needed to evaluate these areas, and procedures for managing the PEA process. Attendees should include a district representative, the consultant performing the PEA, the DTSC project manager, the GSU representative, and the DTSC toxicologist. If possible, particularly if this is the DTSC's first project with the district, the DTSC Branch Chief or School Unit Chief should attend.

Items covered in the scoping meeting should include:

- Review of the available background information for the site
- Identification of the areas of concern and potential chemicals involved
- Sampling locations, and number and type of samples to be collected
- Collection of background samples

The consultant performing the PEA should prepare a detailed schedule, that includes every major step in the process, the key milestones, and specific periods of time for DTSC review and response to DTSC comments.

PEA fieldwork notification. AB 972, in amending the public participation requirements of the DTSC review, requires that districts, prior to the start of work, notify residents in the immediate area. This notification, in a format approved by DTSC, must include:

- The name and location of the school project
- Purpose of the PEA
- Start and duration of field work
- Any planned disruptions to the community (*i.e.*, street closures)
- DTSC's role in the investigation
- A contact for questions regarding the PEA

To ensure that communities are made aware of proposed field activities, the PEA notification should be translated into the predominant language of the area. DTSC guidance recommends that the PEA notification be delivered to all residents with a clear line of sight to the property. Districts should also consider expanding their notification list to include district officials, local elected officials, and community stakeholders.

The notice should be provided prior to the start of any field work associated with the PEA. It does not have to be provided when the District selects the site or prior to the start of the Phase 1 ESA. A template for the PEA fieldwork notice can be obtained from DTSC.

GSU = Geological Services Unit

RWQCB = Regional Water Quality Control Board

✍ **practice tip**

Note in the public notification that performing the PEA does not mean the site is contaminated with hazardous waste. This will help prevent public misconception about the purpose of the investigation and conditions at the site.

To ensure that communities are made aware of proposed field activities, the PEA notification should be translated into the predominant language of the area.

The next step in the PEA process is to develop a workplan for the field investigation that details the sampling proposed for the site and the manner in which the data will be collected and analyzed. The workplan should address:

- Site description and background
- Conceptual site model
- Sampling strategy
- Analytical and quality assurance (QA)/quality control (QC) methods
- Health and safety plan
- Human health and ecological screening

The workplan should also provide a general discussion of how the analytical data collected during the field investigation will be incorporated into the human health screening provided in the PEA report.

While the primary focus of the PEA for a proposed new school site is to assess the potential for health risks to future students and staff, an ecological screening evaluation also must be performed. The purpose of the screening is to provide a qualitative assessment of the threat posed to biota or habitats by contaminants on the site.

OSHA requirements—Protecting the health and safety of workers. The draft PEA workplan should include a health and safety plan (HASP) for conducting a proposed field investigation. Health and safety requirements for workers investigating hazardous waste sites can be found at C.F.R. section 1920.120 and 8 C.C.R. section 5192. These OSHA requirements include training, participation in medical monitoring programs, and site specific safety measures.

While performing field activities for the district, the consultant is responsible for maintaining a safe work place during the site investigation. While it's important to review the consultant's HASP, the district should also discuss the matter with legal counsel to ensure that approval of a third-party HASP does not result in additional liability. For further discussion of OSHA requirements on project sites, see chapter 5.

Due to professional differences, the consultant and DTSC project managers may have difficulty reaching agreement on an issue regarding the PEA draft workplan. To avoid losing time during its preparation, outstanding issues should be discussed with the DTSC Unit or branch chief for timely resolution.

PEA workplan approval. A draft of the workplan will be submitted to DTSC for review and approval. Typically, DTSC will have comments that must be addressed before the workplan can be finalized and approved. The time required to prepare the final PEA workplan and obtain DTSC approval will depend on the capabilities of the consultant developing the plan, the complexity of the site, DTSC's work load on other school projects, and the amount of comments provided by DTSC staff. Generally, comments should be received from DTSC within 30 calendar days after submittal of the draft workplan.

DTSC strongly advises school districts to obtain PEA workplan approval prior to conducting field sampling. To speed up their schedule by approximately 30 to 45 days, a district may proceed with the field investigation program prior

DTSC advises that districts obtain PEA workplan approval prior to conducting field sampling.

to receiving formal DTSC approval of the PEA workplan, or even without submitting a workplan for approval. In those cases, the consultant should still prepare a site workplan and include it in the PEA report.

Proceeding without DTSC approval of the workplan has its risks. DTSC may not approve the sampling approach and may require additional sampling. This could potentially result in more time, and potentially more expense, being spent than would have been the case if the workplan were approved prior to initiating the field work.

Field Investigation

PEA report. The purpose of the PEA report is to analyze the data collected during the field investigation, evaluate the potential for threats to human health and the environment resulting from site conditions, and determine if further action is required for the site. In addition, the report provides a means to document the sampling activities performed at the site. In accordance with DTSC guidance, the following topics need to be included in the PEA report:

- Site description
- Site history and background information
- Apparent problems
- Environmental setting
- Sampling activities and results
- Human health screen
- Ecological screening
- Conclusions and recommendations

The site description, history, and background information can be taken from the Phase 1 ESA and/or the PEA workplan. The information to be provided to describe the site includes a written description, a map showing boundaries, address, acreage, assessors parcel numbers, current and surrounding land uses, and zoning. The site history and background section should include the physical setting (*i.e.*, topography, geology, and hydrology), operational history of current business, previous land uses, known environmental concerns, previous site investigations and remedial activities, and waste management activities.

A summary of the known and potential sources of contamination at the site, along with an identification of the potential chemicals of concern, should be provided in the site description section.

Environmental setting should include regional, local, and site specific topographic, geologic, hydrogeologic, and climate information. The discussion should be tailored to match the specific media (*i.e.*, soil, groundwater, and air) investigated during the PEA.

Sampling activities should describe the rationale for the strategy, collection points, and methods and procedures. Any deviations from the sampling methods and procedures need to be clearly noted and discussed. Include figures showing sampling locations and tabular summaries of analytical results along with a discussion of the results, laboratory reports, and QA/QC information.

To speed up the schedule, a district may proceed with the field investigation program prior to receiving formal DTSC approval of the PEA workplan, but this strategy has its risks.

A summary of known and potential sources of contamination at the site, along with identification of potential chemicals of concern, should be provided in the site description section.

Performing a Risk Assessment

For projects where the PEA is being conducted on an existing school site, it may be useful to perform the risk assessment using assumptions that reflect the true conditions at the school. This would include exposure durations based on student enrollment periods, and limiting or eliminating pathways of exposure when students and staff cannot be exposed to the chemicals of concern. The results of the school-based risk assessment can be helpful in determining if students and staff currently on campus are subject to actual risk and if immediate action is required. The assessment would be performed in addition to the residential-based risk assessment DTSC requires. ■

Risk Assessment

The probability that an event or action will damage human health or the environment.

The human health screening, often referred to as the risk assessment, is one of the most important elements of the PEA process. This is because risk assessment results are the primary factor in determining if further action is required at a site. The risk assessment is performed based on the conceptual model developed for the site and the results of the field investigation.

The results of the assessment are typically expressed as a risk estimate and a hazard estimate. The risk estimate represents the estimated excess lifetime cancer risk from carcinogenic compounds found at the site. The hazard estimate, commonly called the hazard index, assesses the potential threat from non-carcinogenic compounds found at the site. Risk assessment results are typically compared to screening levels of one-in-one-million ($1x10^{-6}$) for the risk estimate and 1.0 for the hazard index. DTSC considers results above these screening values elevated, and they trigger consideration for further action.

It is important to note that the risks calculated during the PEA process may not be, and most likely are not, the actual risks currently present at the site or the potential risk to future students and staff. This is because current DTSC guidance requires that potential school sites be evaluated as if it they are residential property. This is an inherently conservative analysis when evaluating school sites for the following reasons:

- The assessment assumes students and staff live at the site for a 70-year period, whereas student enrollment periods and staff career lengths are typically much shorter.
- The assessment assumes students and staff are present at the site 24 hours a day, as opposed to just during school hours. The actual time spent on site is further reduced by weekends, school breaks, and holidays.
- The assessment is based on the maximum concentrations for chemicals found at the site. In cases where sufficient field data has been collected, DTSC will allow the use of the 95 percent upper confidence limit concentration as opposed to the maximum value.
- The assessment assumes that all pathways of exposure exist regardless of where the chemicals of concern are located. For example, in the residential scenario, it is assumed students and staff would be exposed to elevated concentrations of lead in soils even if these concentrations were located well below ground or under building footprints or paved areas.

DTSC has developed a site-based guidance on performing risk assessments for proposed new school sites. According to the existing guidance, the PEA conclusions should address the following:

- Whether a release of hazardous substances occurred or the threat of one exists at the site
- If conditions pose a significant threat to public health or the environment
- If conditions are an immediate threat to public health or the environment

Based on these considerations, the PEA must provide a clear recommendation of either further action or no further action.

The decision to recommend further action is primarily based on the results of the human health screening. Sites with a risk estimate at or below $1x10^{-6}$ and a Hazard Index at or below 1.0 should require no further action. However, a site where these screening levels are exceeded does not automatically require further action. Some factors considered when determining the need for further action are the type of contaminants involved, their location and depth below ground, and the planned use of the area where the contamination was found.

Submitting the PEA Report

Once the draft PEA report is submitted to DTSC for review and approval, DTSC must make its determinations within the statutory timeframe. In most cases, DTSC's response will consist of comments that must be incorporated into the final PEA report before being resubmitted for review and approval.

For PEAs under the Option A process, DTSC must notify the district if it is likely to disapprove the PEA prior to the receipt of public comments. The notification includes the reasons why the PEA is likely to be disapproved and the actions that must be taken. It is highly recommended that a district representative review the PEA report with the consultant and be familiar with, and agree with, the conclusions before submitting the document to DTSC.

For PEAs under the Option B process, DTSC must complete its review within 60 days, while comments can be provided earlier. Review periods of 30 to 45 days or less are negotiable. In addition, DTSC's review and comment on the final report should require less time than required for the draft report.

PEA availability for public comment. Public participation is an integral component of the school site selection process. Districts must make the PEA report available for public review and hold a public hearing prior to obtaining final approval for property acquisition and construction. The procedural steps and their timing have been the subject of periodic legislative review. *See, e.g.,* AB 2644 (2001) and SB 972 (2002). Currently, the law provides for two methods of making the PEA available to the public: Option A, which is independent of the CEQA process; and Option B, which is linked to the CEQA process.

Option A. If Option A is selected, the district makes the PEA available for public comment for 30 days after submitting the report. DTSC must complete its PEA review within 30 calendar days after the close of the public comment period. *See* Figure 4-3 for a flowchart of Option A where an EIR is prepared.

Option A has the advantage of requiring less time for DTSC to review and approve the PEA than required by Option B. In addition, Option A allows the CEQA review process to be completed without DTSC involvement.

The potential drawback of selecting Option A is that the PEA report is made available to the public simultaneous with DTSC's review. AB 972 requires that DTSC notify a district when it is likely to disapprove the PEA prior to receiving public comments, and DTSC must define the actions necessary to obtain approval. If DTSC does not concur with or disapproves the PEA, the district may need to significantly modify the report, send out a second public notice of its availability, and hold another public hearing.

This potential problem can be avoided by consulting with DTSC prior to making the PEA available to the public. Consulting with DTSC prior to releasing the report for public review may add a week or two to the schedule, but

A conceptual site model identifies...

- Presence, source, and concentrations of hazardous materials
- Possible release or transport mechanisms for the hazardous materials, and
- Potential routes or pathways by which human or biological receptors could be exposed or environmental media (*e.g.,* soil, surface water, air) that hazardous materials could affect

✍ **practice tip**

Fatal flaws that could result in DTSC issuing a likely-to-disapprove notice include:

- Report not signed by a qualified professional, as defined in the regulations
- Not providing laboratory or QA/QC data
- An improperly performed risk assessment

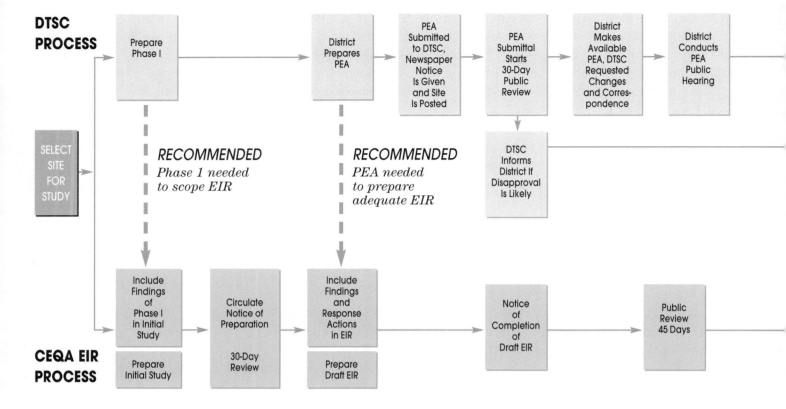

DTSC PROCESS

SELECT SITE FOR STUDY

Prepare Phase I

RECOMMENDED
Phase 1 needed to scope EIR

District Prepares PEA

RECOMMENDED
PEA needed to prepare adequate EIR

PEA Submitted to DTSC, Newspaper Notice Is Given and Site Is Posted

PEA Submittal Starts 30-Day Public Review

District Makes Available PEA, DTSC Requested Changes and Correspondence

District Conducts PEA Public Hearing

DTSC Informs District If Disapproval Is Likely

Include Findings of Phase I in Initial Study

Prepare Initial Study

Circulate Notice of Preparation

30-Day Review

Include Findings and Response Actions in EIR

Prepare Draft EIR

Notice of Completion of Draft EIR

Public Review 45 Days

CEQA EIR PROCESS

Figure 4-3
Option A Flow Chart
where an EIR is prepared

it will greatly reduce the chances of having to re-notice the availability of the PEA or of having to hold a second public meeting.

Option B. Under Option B, public review of the PEA report is linked to the CEQA review process. When this option is selected, DTSC has 60 calendar days to review the report and will either provide recommendations for modification of the report or concur with the adequacy of the report.

If DTSC concurs with the PEA, the PEA report is made available for public review concurrently with public review of the project's CEQA document. The district then holds a public hearing on both documents and submits all public comments to DTSC. Following the district's adoption of the CEQA document, DTSC issues its final determination on the PEA within 30 calendar days.

If the CEQA document will not be available until more than 90 days after DTSC issues its concurrence with the PEA, the district shall make the PEA available to public within 60 days of DTSC's concurrence. *See* Figure 4-4 for a Flowchart of Option B.

The main advantage of selecting Option B is that the PEA report has received preliminary approval from DTSC before it is made available to the public. In addition, districts can hold one public hearing instead of two. This can be advantageous for districts familiar with holding CEQA public hearings. However, Option A has no provision that the PEA hearing may not be held concurrently with the CEQA hearing should the district wish to do so. In this case, holding a joint meeting will allow the district to hold a single public hearing while retaining the accelerated review process under Option A.

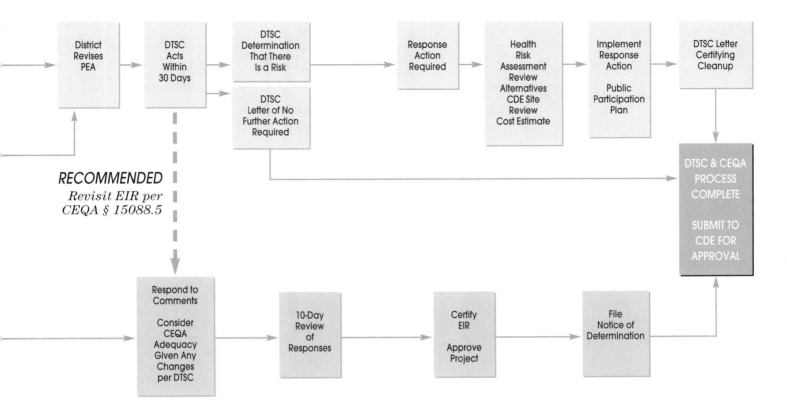

The main disadvantage is that the DTSC review under Option B takes significantly longer to complete. In addition, linking the DTSC and CEQA review processes creates the potential for delaying completion of the CEQA review.

When notifying DTSC that the public comment period has ended, send a letter to the DTSC project manager with the following information:

- Date of the public hearing
- Period of public review
- Statement that the CEQA document has been adopted (Option B only)
- Statement that the district has completed the PEA public participation requirement
- Any public comments received

Districts may provide DTSC public comments and any district responses in writing, as a transcript, or as a recording of the public hearing. A transcript is recommended as the most complete record of the meeting.

When selecting Option A or B, districts should carefully consider the timing of the project, the level of complexity of the PEA performed for the site, and the timing of the CEQA review. If the schedule for completing the DTSC review process is a key factor in the project's success, then Option A is most likely the best alternative for making the PEA available to the public.

PEA notice of availability. A formal notice of the availability of the PEA report for public review must be sent prior to the start of the public review period, and must include the following information:

Public Participation

A district may conduct the public comment and hearing on its own, or may request that assistance from DTSC. *See* DTSC's "Public Participation Guidelines for School District Staff Consultants." If a potential school site may require a response action, the district can request that DTSC assign a public participation specialist as early in the process as possible. ∎

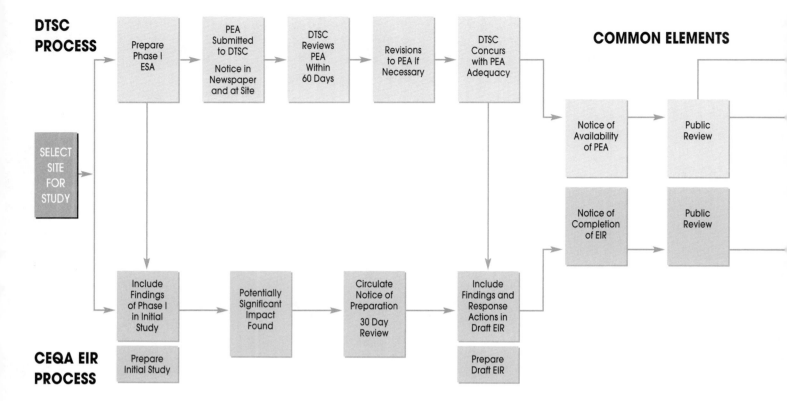

DTSC PROCESS

SELECT SITE FOR STUDY

Prepare Phase I ESA → PEA Submitted to DTSC — Notice in Newspaper and at Site → DTSC Reviews PEA Within 60 Days → Revisions to PEA If Necessary → DTSC Concurs with PEA Adequacy

COMMON ELEMENTS

Notice of Availability of PEA → Public Review

Notice of Completion of EIR → Public Review

CEQA EIR PROCESS

Prepare Initial Study

Include Findings of Phase I in Initial Study → Potentially Significant Impact Found → Circulate Notice of Preparation 30 Day Review → Include Findings and Response Actions in Draft EIR

Prepare Draft EIR

Figure 4-4
Option B Flow Chart
where an EIR is prepared

- Name and location of the school project
- Purpose of the PEA
- Notification option the district has chosen to use (A or B)
- Location of document repositories for the PEA report
- Date, time, and location of the PEA hearing
- DTSC's role in the investigation
- A contact for questions regarding the PEA

Notifying the public of the option selected can refer to the code section related to that option. An example of language that can be used to refer to Option A is "Pursuant to the California Education Code section 17213.1(a)(6)(A)...."

The availability notice should be sent to local residents and property owners. (The notification list should include all parties who received the PEA field work notice.) Posting a notice at the site and in local newspapers is also required. Districts should consider notifying district officials, local elected officials, and community stakeholders who are interested in the new school project. If Option B is chosen, the notice of availability of the PEA should be sent to all parties who receive notification regarding the CEQA document.

Document repositories. Copies of the PEA report must be made available during the public comment period. Recommended locations include:

- District headquarters or local office
- Local libraries
- Nearby schools
- School district's web site

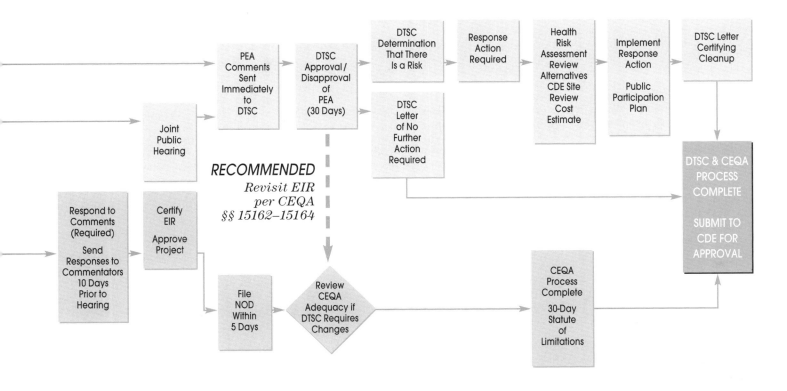

The document repository should include the PEA work plan and report, copies of DTSC comments, and revisions made to the PEA after the public hearing.

PEA Hearing

The purpose of the public hearing is to present the PEA results, receive public comments, and answer questions. The public should be informed of the date, time, and location of the hearing in the notice of availability.

Typically, the public review period for the PEA will be 30 calendar days, although in some special cases under Option B it can be shortened to 20 days. The public review period may be 45 days if the PEA public review period is linked to the CEQA process (Option B) and an EIR was prepared for the project. The public hearing may be held at any time during the public review period. Districts should consider holding the hearing approximately half-way through the public comment period, giving the public time to submit written comments after the hearing.

During the public hearing, the district should explain the role of DTSC in the review process. This is important because it will help bolster the public's confidence that the site has been thoroughly investigated, and let it know that the state, and not just the district, is approving the site.

PEA results. The purpose of the PEA is to determine if a release of hazardous materials has occurred at a site, and if that release poses a risk to human health and/or the environment. As is the case for the Phase 1 ESA, the PEA report must make a clear recommendation for the next step in the DTSC review process. The PEA results should include a recommendation for one of the following:

✎ **note**

Under certain limited conditions, CDE final approval may be obtained prior to implementation of the response action. *See* SFPD Form 4.15.

During the public hearing, the district should explain DTSC's role in the review process to help bolster the public's confidence that the site has been thoroughly investigated.

- No further action
- Further action (*i.e.*, remediation) required
- Limited further action for lead-based paint and/or PCBs

If approved by DTSC, a no-further-action determination will close out the DTSC review. A further action determination will result in a supplemental site investigation, removal action work plan, or remedial action plan. If a RAP is anticipated, a remedial investigation/feasibility study (RI/FS) may also be required.

An SSI involves collecting additional samples either to provide data confirming that remediation is required or to describe the affected soils to be removed. A RAW typically involves removing a defined volume of soil where the remediation cost is less than $2 million. A RAP is typically used to address remediation projects that are estimated to cost more than $2 million. Aside from cost, the primary difference between a RAW and RAP is that a RAP requires substantial further site characterization (a remedial investigation) and a more detailed evaluation of alternatives (a feasibility study) to select a remedy.

The limited further action result for lead and PCBs is generally unlikely, as the potential for lead-based paint impacts to the soil will typically be considered as part of the PEA. This may apply to residential property that the district chose not to sample during the PEA process. Based on the PEA results, districts will know if further action is required, and have a better idea about time and cost.

A district proceeding with acquisition and development of a site requiring remediation may be eligible for environmental hardship funding if remediation will take more than six months to complete.

If a district chooses to proceed with acquisition and development of the site requiring remediation, it may be eligible for environmental hardship funding if the remediation will take more than six months to complete. Districts planning on applying for environmental hardship funding should request that DTSC include language in the letter approving the PEA that recognizes further action will likely require more than six months to complete. Financial hardship funding is discussed in chapter 2.

Site Remediation Process

Prior to initiating any remedial activities, districts must enter into a voluntary cleanup agreement or a school cleanup agreement with DTSC. Like the EOA, the purpose of the VCA/SCA is to provide a mechanism for DTSC to identify PEA activities, schedule, and contacts to provide oversight, and for the district to reimburse DTSC for its cost. For districts with multiple projects, it may be useful to enter into a master agreement that covers all projects requiring DTSC oversight.

A district with multiple projects may find it useful to have a master agreement covering all projects requiring DTSC oversight.

The cost and time required to complete site remediation activities will very greatly, depending on site conditions and other factors such as obtaining access to or control of the property to be remediated. A simple SSI can be accomplished in several weeks, while a complex RAP can take two or more years to complete.

The district may seek full and final funding from the SAB prior to completion of response actions required by DTSC. The district must enter into and SCA—which includes stricter dispute resolution, termination, and penalties for noncompliance—than a VCA.

Documents and fact sheets regarding the SSI, RAW, and RAP processes are available at the DTSC website (www.dtsc.ca.gov).

The SSI, RAW, and RAP processes are discussed in greater detail in the following sections. Additional information can be obtained guidance documents and fact sheets available on the DTSC web site.

Supplemental site investigation. Before a removal action can be defined and implemented, the full extent of the contamination must be determined. However, while the results of the PEA may be sufficient to conclude that further action is required, the report may not provide a full characterization of its extent. In these cases an SSI will be necessary. If a RAP is anticipated, an RI/FS should be conducted instead of an SSI.

The purpose of the SSI is to define the extent of contamination for the RAW and to determine how much soil must be removed from the site. In some cases, collection of soil vapor or groundwater samples will be required, but extensive groundwater characterization will usually be performed as part of a RAP instead of a RAW. The data collected during the SSI can also demonstrate that no further action is required.

DTSC will typically require that a work plan or technical memorandum be prepared to define the scope of the SSI before the investigation begins. A technical memorandum, which costs less and takes less time to prepare, is an abbreviated work plan without full quality assurance/quality control information that supplements a previously approved work plan. Both documents must define the location, number, depth, and types of samples to be collected. DTSC approval of an SSI workplan is required if a new media type (such as groundwater or flux chamber sampling), further groundwater, or offsite investigation is necessary.

DTSC approval of an SSI workplan is required if data is needed for alternate evaluations including treatability or an FS. For sites with only additional or step-out sampling activities, the previously approved PEA workplan may be updated with an addendum (showing the number and locations of proposed samples), and incorporated into Section 3 of the SSI workplan with a reference. Without a previously approved PEA workplan, a separate SSI Workplan is required.

In consultation with DTSC, a previously approved PEA workplan may be updated with an addendum or a technical memorandum and incorporated into Section 4 of the SSI Workplan by reference. In this case, the use of a PEA screening risk evaluation process may be accepted by DTSC. *See* DTSC School Fact Sheet No. 4, June 2002. Consultation with DTSC or a more formal scoping meeting may be necessary before the scope of the SSI is defined.

Sampling during the SSI should be performed in a manner consistent with the field work performed during the PEA. This is beneficial because it will streamline DTSC's review of the sampling approach proposed for the SSI. In addition, it will reduce the cost of the SSI because the PEA Quality Assurance Plan and Health and Safety Plan can be used as opposed to developing new plans. The results of the SSI can be included in a separate SSI report or incorporated into the RAW.

Depending on the results from the PEA, the focus of the SSI will either be further delineation of "hot spot" concentrations or more generalized areas of contamination. "Hot spots" occur when a single sample, or limited number of samples, result in concentrations that are significantly higher than the nearby surrounding area. A key component of the SSI, particularly when addressing

Technical Memorandum

An abbreviated workplan without full quality assurance/quality control information that supplements the previously approved workplan

DTSC approval of an SSI workplan is required for existing school sites if data is needed for alternate evaluations including treatability or an FS.

✍ **practice tip**

To save time, provide a complete site characterization in the PEA. This eliminates the need to prepare and have DTSC review additional plans and reports during the SSI phase.

"hot spots," is determining how far to step out from existing data points in order to complete the delineation of the contamination. Collecting samples too close to existing data points may not provide a complete delineation and additional sampling, and more time, will be required. Conversely, collecting samples too far out will increase the amount of noncontaminated soil removed and will increase remediation costs.

The trade-off between potential remediation costs and schedule must be considered when developing the SSI sampling program. If schedule is the more critical issue, a larger step-out distance may be preferable. One method to balance these competing factors is to collect samples at two step-out distances and only analyze the samples from the closer distance. DTSC generally requires 10 feet horizontal step out samplings or 10 feet vertical intervals (or sometimes 5 feet for pesticides or total metals), from a hot spot. If this data does not provide a complete delineation, the second set of samples can be analyzed. This approach will increase the initial sampling costs, but in the end may save time by eliminating a second mobilization to the site.

If it is clear before the PEA report is finalized that a RAW will be required, the additional data collection can be performed as part of the PEA. Although this approach will increase the time and cost for the PEA, the additional work will be required regardless of which phase (PEA or SSI) it is performed in.

A district may be able to reduce the time required to complete the SSI by completing the delineation effort without receiving formal DTSC approval. The sampling methodology and results would be reviewed by DTSC as part of the RAW instead of as a separate SSI phase. While this approach will reduce the amount of time required, the district risks the possibility that DTSC will not concur that delineation is complete, and may subsequently not approve the RAW for implementation until additional sampling is performed. In that case, any initial time savings will be lost. It is generally preferable to obtain DTSC concurrence on the sampling approach before proceeding with field work.

If the risk calculated during the PEA process is primarily driven by "hot spots," not by more general site-wide contamination, the risk is only slightly elevated, and the results of the risk assessment should be reevaluated incorporating the SSI results. It is possible that the results of the revised risk assessment will justify a "no further action" determination from DTSC, which would be included in the SSI report and, if DTSC concurs, a RAW will no longer be required.

Districts seeking environmental hardship funding for sites requiring RAWs should wait for the SSI outcome before applying. If the SSI results in a "no further action" determination from DTSC before the application is filed, the environmental hardship application should not be submitted as an application for full funding can be submitted instead.

Removal action workplan. As noted previously, a RAW is used to address remedial activities costing less than $2 million. While the RAW process applies for all remedial actions under this amount, the most common remediations for proposed new school sites will be removal of contaminated soil. Figure 4-5 shows the major elements of the RAW process.

The trade-off between potential remediation costs and schedule must be considered when developing the SSI sampling program.

✎ **practice tip**

Complete the PEA as soon as possible. When further action is necessary, a district should apply for state funding and plan concurrently for that possibility.

While this may reduce the time required to complete an SSI, it increases the likelihood that DTSC will not agree that delineation is complete. In fact, DTSC might not approve the RAW until additional sampling has been performed.

Should that happen, the initial time savings is lost. Obtaining DTSC concurrence on the approach to sampling before proceeding with the field work is preferable.

The purpose of the RAW is to specify the selected remedial action, alternatives considered, and the method of implementation. The major elements include:

- A description of the contamination to be remediated
- Remedial action objectives (RAOs) for the RAW
- An assessment of the RAW's compliance with all applicable or relevant and appropriate requirements (ARARs)
- Engineering evaluation/cost analysis (EE/CA)
- Evaluation of alternatives
- Plan for RAW implementation
- Project schedule
- Public participation activities

The nature and extent of contamination, along with any background site information, should be consistent with that developed for the PEA and SSI reports. The RAW should focus on the remediation effort and information in the PEA or SSI.

It is important to develop specific RAOs and ARARs as part of the RAW. The purpose of the RAOs is to define criteria for certifying the implementation of the RAW, and they should be based on the risk levels identified in the PEA. Factors to consider when selecting ARARs include: air quality standards for soil removal actions (i.e., dust control), transporting waste material requirements, waste disposal requirements, local noise ordinances and restrictions during work hours, and worker health and safety requirements.

Typically, DTSC requires that the RAW contain a minimum of three alternative evaluations, with a "no action" scenario as one of the alternatives. The evaluation should be performed in a manner consistent with the EPA's engineering evaluation/cost analysis process, including a comparison based on three criteria: effectiveness, implementation, and cost.

The RAW implementation plan must define all of the key elements for conducting the removal action. This includes soil removal methods, worker health and safety, confirmation sampling, QA/QC plan for confirmation samples, air monitoring methods and dust control, and material transport and disposal.

Once complete, the draft RAW document is submitted to DTSC. Prior to approving the RAW as a final document, DTSC will carry out public participation activities and complete a review of the RAW under CEQA.

DTSC's objectives for a public participation program are:

- Ensuring the public is made aware of the project
- Defining public interest in the project
- Developing a community profile to ensure appropriate public involvement
- Providing fact sheets and other notices to keep the public informed
- Presenting an opportunity for public comment

Notifying the public can be accomplished through distributing a fact sheet to the local community and placing a notice in local newspapers. Distribution lists developed during the PEA process should be used and revised as necessary. All documents associated with the RAW must be available to the public. DTSC typically requests that a survey be performed to determine community interest, and then assesses whether a public participation plan and public meeting are required.

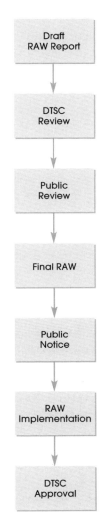

**Figure 4-5
RAW Process**

Draft RAW Report

DTSC Review

Public Review

Final RAW

Public Notice

RAW Implementation

DTSC Approval

ARAR = Applicable or relevant and appropriate requirements
CA = Cost Analysis
EE = Engineering Evaluation
RAO = Remedial action objective

DTSC typically requests that a survey be performed to determine community interest.

In most cases, DTSC will provide a public comment period and may hold a public meeting for the draft RAW. The comment period is usually 30 days, and may be extended based on the level of public interest. DTSC will prepare responses to comments and may require revisions in the draft RAW.

Because the approval is a discretionary decision made by a government agency, DTSC must complete a CEQA review before the RAW can be finalized and implemented. In many cases, RAWs for school sites are exempt from CEQA. If the project is not deemed to be CEQA-exempt, DTSC will complete an initial study to determine if a negative declaration (ND), mitigated negative declaration (MND), or EIR is required. DTSC will then prepare the necessary CEQA documentation and, if appropriate, hold a public comment period and public hearing.

It is not uncommon for the CEQA review to be the critical path toward completing the RAW process. While DTSC is the lead agency, the district may need to provide information for the initial preparation and other CEQA documentation. Districts should actively participate in the CEQA process to expedite completion.

Following preparation of the RAW, completion of public participation activities, and DTSC's CEQA review, the final RAW will be approved for implementation. Districts should notify DTSC in advance of the start of field activities and site access during the remedial action.

After completing the removal action, the district prepares a RAW completion report, documenting that the action was implemented in accordance with the approved RAW and requesting DTSC certification. At a minimum, the completion report should include the following:

- A description of the remedial work performed
- Results from confirmation sampling performed
- A statement that all remedial action objectives have been met

If it concurs that the RAW is complete, DTSC will notify the district of its approval and notify CDE that the RAW has been completed. DTSC certification that the RAW is complete is a prerequisite for initiating school construction.

Districts can obtain approval or "partial site approval" to proceed with construction on the non-impacted portions of the site if the area is limited. To proceed with construction before the remedial action is complete, the district must show that the site has been fully characterized, the remedial action will not impede environmental response actions, and construction and can be performed safely. DTSC certification of the RAW is required before the school can be opened.

Coordination with DSA. In some cases, the removal action will affect the school design, and DTSC will notify the DSA of special mitigation conditions that must be met. This is likely for sites where dangerous vapors, such as methane or hydrogen sulfide, may migrate. Typical mitigation measures include membrane barriers under buildings and in venting and monitoring systems.

The mitigation system design must be included in both the RAW and the final design the district submits to DSA. While it may approve the school design, DSA cannot approve the remedial action. DTSC is responsible for approving the effectiveness of the remedial action as part of the RAW approval, and will certify the completion of the RAW after the system has been constructed. Districts may be

MND = Mitigated negative declaration
ND = Negative declaration

It is not uncommon for CEQA review to be the critical path toward completing the RAW process.

practice tip

Most proposed school sites should be cleared either with a PEA or a RAW, with RAPs required in exceptional cases. A district should seriously consider whether to proceed with a site that requires the time and expense associated with a RAP.

responsible for ongoing operations and maintenance of mitigation which will require an operations and maintenance plan, scheduling periodic DTSC review for an indefinite period of time. Because the final certification occurs after the school is built, the district should provide sufficient design information to DTSC once the school design is approved and prior to beginning construction.

Because DTSC cannot certify the completion of the removal action workplan until school construction is complete, school districts will have to obtain CDE approval, and possibly state funding, prior to completing the DTSC review process. In these exceptional cases, CDE will approve the new school project, and state funding can be obtained—provided DTSC has notified CDE that the remedial action must be incorporated into the design. This notification can be provided as part of the PEA determination that specified further action is required.

Remedial action plan. A remedial action plan is typically required when the cost to remediate a site exceeds $2 million. Situations involving a RAP occur when the action involves more than soil removal—such as the design, construction, and operation of groundwater treatment or soil vapor extraction systems.

A remedial action plan is typically required when the cost to remediate a site exceeds $2 million.

Because of a RAP's complex nature and limited frequency, this section offers only a general description of the process. Major components include:

- Remedial investigation
- Feasibility study
- Public participation
- Remedial action plan document

The purpose of the RI is to provide a comprehensive characterization of the contaminants on the site. It is similar to the PEA in that it includes phases for project scoping, development of a RI workplan, field investigation, and the preparation of a RI report. The RI workplan will include a sampling plan, HASP, and QA/QC plan similar to the PEA workplan. The characterization conducted in the RI, however, is significantly more extensive, costly, and time consuming than that conducted during the PEA. Unlike the focus of the PEA, which is geared towards identifying if a release has occurred at the site, the RI provides sufficient information to design a remedial action. The results of the RI are often combined with the results of the FS in a comprehensive RI/FS report.

Unlike the focus of the PEA, the RI provides sufficient information to design a remedial action.

The FS process involves the identification of different remedial technologies for use at the site, the feasibility of remedial technologies, the development of remedial alternatives incorporating the feasible technologies, and a detailed evaluation of each remedial alternative. A "no action" alternative should always be included in the FS process.

Evaluation of remedial alternatives is based on the following nine criteria:

- Overall protection of human health and the environment
- Compliance with state and federal requirements
- Long-term effectiveness and permanence
- Reduction of toxicity, mobility, and volume
- Short-term effectiveness
- Implementability
- Regulatory agency acceptance

- Community acceptance
- Cost

The remedial alternatives are evaluated against the nine criteria, with the RI/FS report presenting the preferred alternative. While the FS identifies a preferred alternative, the RAP document presents the remedy.

The RAP process will require more extensive public participation activities than the one required for the PEA or RAW. DTSC requires a public participation plan and will typically hold public meetings to discuss the RI findings, present the FS results, and receive public comments on the draft RAP document.

The purpose of the RAP document is to formalize the selection of a remedy for the site. The document must, at a minimum, include a description of the preferred alternative, the rationale for its selection, a discussion of other alternatives considered, identification of RAOs and ARARs, and a summary of the findings from the RI and FS. Because it is not an engineering report, the RAP document need not include design details.

DTSC will review and approve the draft RAP, submit it to public review, and then finalize the document after the close of the public comment period. DTSC will complete any necessary CEQA documentation in conjunction with the draft development and final RAP. Prior to implementation of the RAP, the district may have to develop a remedial design (RD) document with engineering elements and design details. This may also include an OEM plan to insure the long-term effectiveness of the remedy.

It is important to note that a district is not responsible for remediating contaminated groundwater underneath a proposed new site unless the site is determined to be the source of contamination. However, if its presence beneath the site poses an unacceptable risk to the proposed school, a response will be required to make the site suitable for school use.

In such a case, a district can provide mitigation, perform groundwater remediation, or have the responsible party perform or fund these activities. These options, however, may result in the site being unsuitable given the time and cost associated with groundwater remediation and/or litigation.

OEM = Original equipment manufacturer
RD = Remedial design

CEQA Compliance Basics for School Facility Projects

CEQA requires that public agencies consider potential environmental implications of their actions when approving projects.

Enacted in 1970, CEQA requires public agencies to consider the potential environmental implications of their actions when approving projects. CEQA establishes a duty for public agencies, including school districts, to analyze, mitigate, or minimize foreseeable environmental damage. The California Environmental Quality Act is located in the Public Resources Code section 21000 *et seq.* CEQA Guidelines are regulations that guide public agencies on how to implement the very general directives in the CEQA statute. 14 C.C.R. §§ 1500 *et seq.* In other words, the CEQA Guidelines are a roadmap to CEQA compliance.

School districts must comply with both CEQA and DTSC environmental review requirements, regardless of the source of project funding, and also with the CDE environmental site review requirements when seeking state bond funding under the SFP. While similar, the environmental review processes have somewhat different purposes and outcomes. CEQA's purpose is to protect the environment from physical impacts caused by the construction and operation of a school facility. (In urban areas, this tends to be mainly construction-related air quality impacts, traffic impacts during operation, noise, and occasionally historic resources. In suburban or rural areas it can often also include impacts to agricultural resources, wetlands or endangered species). At the end of the CEQA process, a notice of exemption, a negative declaration, or an EIR is issued. An ND is adopted or an EIR is certified by the district's school board. The purpose of the DTSC review process is to protect the health of the students and staff at the school from toxic and hazardous substances that may exist in the soil, which is akin to the purpose of CDE's regulatory siting criteria—to provide a safe, healthy learning environment. At the end of the DTSC process, a "no action" letter or a "no further action" letter is issued. At the completion of the CDE process, CDE will provide approval of the site once their requirements have been satisfied.

This section provides a brief overview of CEQA's requirements, with a special focus on the CEQA issues that are raised concerning a school siting and construction project. For more information about CEQA, *see* Michael Remy *et al.*, *Guide to the California Environmental Quality Act* (Solano Press).

What Is the School District's Role in CEQA?

School district is the lead agency. As a public agency, a school district has a duty to determine whether its activities are "projects" under CEQA. Pub. Res. Code § 21065. Since school districts carry out their own projects—the siting and construction of school facilities—they are the lead agency responsible for complying with CEQA. Where the sole activity is a RAW or RAP, or where the district's EIR for the school facility project failed to include the potential that a RAW/RAP might be warranted in its project description, the DTSC may assume lead agency status. If the district determines that the activity involves discretion and has the potential to cause physical change in the environment, then the activity is a project subject to CEQA. For the most part, decisions to acquire school sites and approve construction are "projects" under CEQA.

As lead agency, a school districts is responsible for preparing an environmental review document under CEQA. Given the wide variety of topics to be evaluated, including air quality, traffic impact, noise, and historic resources, most school districts must hire an environmental consulting firm to prepare a sufficient analysis under CEQA.

As the lead agency, a school district is required to use independent judgment. This means that the district should review the environmental document prepared by the outside consultant and make its own independent conclusions about the significance of impacts and the feasibility of mitigation measures discussed in the environmental document. It also means that the school district should make informed, independent decisions about the level of review to be given each project under CEQA (whether an exemption, an ND, an MND, or an EIR).

Most importantly, using independent judgment as a lead agency means that it is the school district that self-certifies its compliance with CEQA. While many

As a public agency, a district has a duty to determine whether its activities are "projects" under CEQA.

Whether to Prepare CEQA Guidelines for the District

Each public agency must adopt its own guidelines, objectives, criteria, and procedures for complying with CEQA. *See* Pub. Res. Code § 21082. While some ambitious public agencies have developed CEQA Guidelines that specify the thresholds of significance they use or the activities approved that are categorically exempt, most agencies adopt the state CEQA Guidelines by reference. Many agencies that developed Guidelines more than a decade ago are now repealing ones that are outdated and adopting the state's by reference. ■

state regulatory agencies require evidence of CEQA compliance before they will issue their approval for the school project (*e.g.*, DTSC, CDE), it is the district that reviews and certifies its own compliance with CEQA.

School districts perform a wide variety of school siting and construction activities. Determining whether a CEQA review applies to any of these activities requires a case-by-case analysis.

What Is the CEQA Review Process?

Essentially CEQA has four phases of compliance: preliminary review, initial study, preparation of an environmental document, and project approval under CEQA. Phase I, termed "preliminary review" is the process in which a public agency determines whether the activity it is reviewing is a "project" subject to CEQA, and whether any exemptions apply. 14 C.C.R. §§ 15060–15062. If the activity is not a project or is exempt, then nothing further is required under CEQA. Phase II, termed "initial study," is the process in which a public agency determines the scope of, or defines, the project, and determines whether the project has the potential to result in significant environmental impacts. Phase III is preparation and review of an environmental document. The type of environmental document that is prepared depends on the outcome of the initial study. The document prepared is either an ND; an MND, or an EIR. Phase IV is the procedural requirements necessary to certify the environmental document and approve the project.

Defining the project. Defining the project, combined with determining the proper timing of review, may be the most difficult tasks in the entire CEQA process. This is greatly exacerbated by the length and complexity of school siting and construction projects. Generally, the overriding objective in defining the project is to capture the "whole of the action," or all the components of the action that have the potential to result in a physical change in the environment. 14 C.C.R. § 15378.

A common error is to assess project components by discretionary approvals. Another common error is to piecemeal the project by omitting project components that may have environmental impacts. The term "piecemealing" is used to describe a project that has been improperly broken into multiple parts, some or all of which may escape CEQA review. One common piecemealing error occurs when a public agency omits from the project's definition some reasonably foreseeable project components. Courts have required EIRs for projects that seemed limited, but that functioned as catalysts for foreseeable future development. For example, in *Fullerton Joint Union High School District v. State Board of Education* (1982) 32 Cal. 3d 779, the court held that environmental review was required prior to state approval of a plan to carve a new high school district out of a portion of an existing district because it would likely result in the siting of a new high school. And in *City of Antioch v. City Council* (1986) 187 Cal. App. 3d 1325, a court ordered a city to prepare an EIR to address future development that was a foreseeable consequence of the sewer lines and road it had approved.

A school district should include all reasonably foreseeable project components in a school siting and construction project. For school siting, the project definition should include all aspects of construction and occupancy, including site remediation where necessary. In addition, a plan for a school that includes reasonably foreseeable future additions or phased occupancy should be considered part of the project undergoing CEQA review. This might include remediation work such as a RAW or RAP that might be required by DTSC, later design work, later phases of construction, or plans to construct additions. In addition, the ultimate, maximum enrollment of the school should be addressed as part of the project. Even if, for budget reasons, the school project has temporarily been reduced in scale or phased occupancy is planned, a district should include all activities that will eventually be implemented. Distinguish, however, those aspects of a project that are merely wished for, but for which there are no actual plans to implement. Since the goal of CEQA is to provide realistic information so that a district can make better decisions regarding environmental impacts, only its actual planned activities and not its aspirations need to be analyzed.

Notice to planning commission. To ensure that time is not lost at the end of the CEQA process, the district should send the notice to the planning commission as early in the selection process as possible.

School districts are required by law to give notice to the planning commission for any sites within its jurisdiction the school is seeking to acquire title to for a new school or for any additions to existing school sites. Pub. Res. Code § 21151.2. The planning commission has 30 days to provide a written report, and the district must wait an additional 30 days after receiving the written report before acquiring title to the property. Starting the 60-day notice and comment process does not have to wait until final selection of a site. This 60-day period should begin early, concurrent with the district's other investigations regarding proposed school sites.

PHASE I: Preliminary Review

When does CEQA apply to a school siting and construction process? The first three steps in the CEQA compliance process, called the preliminary review, are determining: (1) whether the activity in question is a project, (2) whether the project is exempt from further review, and (3) if not exempt, whether the project has the potential to cause a significant effect on the environment.

When is an activity a project? What types of school siting and construction activities are projects subject to CEQA? An activity is a "project" subject to CEQA's environmental review requirements if it has three characteristics: it must be a *discretionary* decision by a *public agency* that will result in a direct or indirect *physical change in the environment*. Pub. Res. Code § 21065. In determining whether the activities contemplated by a school district trigger the requirement to proceed to Phase II of CEQA, a school district must determine whether the activity possesses these three characteristics and hence is a projects subject to CEQA. In many if not most cases,

School District Reorganization Issue and Lawsuit

In October 1998, various school districts asked the California Resources Agency to clarify that school district reorganizations are not subject to CEQA. In response, the Resources Agency adopted CEQA Guidelines § 15378(b)(5), which states that the following do not constitute "projects" for purposes of CEQA:

> Organizational and administrative activities of governments which are political and not physical changes in the environment (such as the reorganization of a school district or detachment of park land).
>
> 14 C.C.R. §15378(b)(5)

In *Communities for a Better Environment v. California Resources Agency* (2002) 103 Cal. App. 4th 98, the court found this regulation to be invalid and set it aside. As a result, school districts will no longer be able to rely on this CEQA Guideline to find that its purely organizational activities are not projects subject to CEQA.

In its decision, the court noted that political and organizational changes may cause direct or indirect physical changes to the environment (*e.g., Fullerton Joint Union High School Dist. v. State Bd. of Education* (1982) 32 Cal. 3d 779; *People ex rel. Younger v. LAFCO* (1978) 81 Cal. App. 3d 464). Thus, the court found that the decision to apply CEQA must be made on a case-by-case basis, and not by regulation.

School districts should review their internal organizational, administrative activities, and political boundary changes for compliance with CEQA. If the reorganization activity has the potential to result, whether directly or indirectly, in a physical change in the environment, the activity may qualify as a project under CEQA. ∎

the first two prongs will be met since a school district is a *public agency* and a school district's activities necessary to complete the Facilities Master Plan require "the exercise of judgment or deliberation" and hence discretion. The third prong is not always met. However, the activities necessary to make a site into a school usually involve physical changes in the environment. These include public works construction activities, clearing or grading of land, improvements to existing public structures, enactment and amendment of zoning ordinances, and adoption and amendment of local general plans.

When might a school district's school facility project be exempt from CEQA? CEQA's environmental review process has two sources of exemptions: statutory and categorical. A third, called the "common sense" exemption or general rule, also is available. The general rule is that CEQA applies only to projects with the potential for having a significant effect on the environment. When it is certain that the activity in question will have no possibility of having a significant effect on the environment, the activity is not subject to CEQA. *See* CEQA Guidelines § 15061(b)(3). Statutory exemptions are descriptions of types of projects for which the California Legislature has provided a blanket exemption from CEQA procedures and policies. Categorical exemptions are descriptions of types, or classes, of projects that the Secretary of the Resources Agency has determined do not have a significant effect on the environment. In contrast to statutory exemptions, categorical exemptions cannot be relied upon if certain conditions are present. For example, a categorical exemption is inappropriate where scenic resources or historic resources would be impacted.

In 2000, determining whether a project is exempt from CEQA took on a greater importance with the enactment of laws creating a toxic contamination review process under DTSC oversight. CEQA-exempt minor addition projects are also exempt from the DTSC review process. Educ. Code § 17268.

Statutory exemptions. The legislature has exempted only one specific school activity from CEQA, "the closing of any public school or the transfer of students from that public school to another school in which kindergarten or any grades 1 through 12 if the only physical changes involved are categorically exempt." Pub. Res. Code § 21081.18. Other statutory exemptions may apply to a school facility project. A comprehensive list of these exemptions can be found in sections 15260–15285 of Title 14, C.C.R.

Categorical exemptions. For a complete list of categorical exemptions, *see* Table 4-1 (those a school district is most likely to rely on are in italics).

Several categorical exemptions may apply to school siting and construction activities. Before relying on a categorical exemption, the district should make sure that the activity it is approving fits the criteria of the categorical exemption and that none of the exceptions listed in section 15300.2 exist. *East Peninsula Education Council, Inc. v. Palos Verdes Peninsula Unified School District* (1989) 210 Cal. App. 3d 155.

- Existing facilities. School activities at existing school sites should be reviewed under the Class 1 existing facilities exemption. Where such activities involve the "operation, maintenance, permitting, leasing, licensing, or minor alteration of existing public or private structures, facilities,

Guidelines section	Exempt activity	Guidelines section	Exempt activity
15301	Operation, repair, maintenance, or minor alteration of existing facilities; uses of structures are not expanded	15315	Subdivision of certain properties in urban areas into four or fewer parcels
15302	Replacement or reconstruction of existing structures or facilities on the same site having substantially the same purpose and capacity	15316	Certain acquisitions or sales of land in natural condition or containing cultural resource sites to establish a park
15303	New construction of limited small new facilities; installation of small, new equipment and facilities in small structures; and conversion of the use of small existing structures (e.g., construction of three or fewer single-family homes in urban areas)	15318	Designation of wilderness areas under the California Wilderness System
		15319	Annexations of certain areas containing existing structures and certain small parcels
		15320	Local government reorganizations requiring no changes in the areas where previous powers were exercised, such as the establishment of subsidiary districts, consolidations, and mergers
15304	Minor alterations in the condition of the land, such as grading, gardening, and landscaping, that do not affect sensitive resources		
15305	Minor alterations to land use limitations (that do not result in changes in land use or density), such as lot line adjustments, variances, and encroachment permits on land with a slope of less than 20 percent	15321	Actions by regulatory agencies to enforce a lease, permit license, or other entitlement; actions by law enforcement officials
		15322	Actions related to educational or training programs involving no exterior physical changes
15306	Basic data collection, research, experimental management, and resource evaluation activities that do not result in major disturbances to an environmental resource	15323	Normal operations of existing facilities for public gatherings for which the facilities were designed
		15324	Actions taken by regulatory agencies related to wages, hours, and working conditions
15307	Certain actions by regulatory agencies to maintain, restore, or enhance natural resources, other than construction activities, where the regulatory process includes procedures to protect the environment	15325	Transfers of interest in land to preserve open space
		15326	Actions needed to implement a housing assistance plan by acquiring an interest in housing units
15308	Certain actions by regulatory agencies to maintain, restore, or enhance the environment, other than construction activities, where the regulatory process includes procedures to protect the environment	15327	Leasing of new or unoccupied private facilities in a building exempt from CEQA
		15328	Installations of certain hydroelectric facilities of less than five megawatts capacity at existing facilities
15309	Inspections to check for the performance of an operation, or for quality, health, or safety of a project	15329	Installation of certain cogeneration equipment of less than 50 megawatts capacity at existing facilities
15310	Certain Department of Veterans Affairs loans and mortgages for purchases of certain existing structures	15330	Minor actions to prevent, minimize, stabilize, mitigate or eliminate the release or threat of release of hazardous waste or hazardous substances
15311	Accessory structures to existing facilities such as small parking lots, signs and seasonal uses		
15312	Sales of surplus government property, except in environmentally sensitive areas	15331	Restoration and rehabilitation of historical resources consistent with the Secretary of the Interior's Standards for the Treatment of Historic Properties
15313	Acquisition of land for fish and wildlife habitat conservation purposes		
15314	Minor additions to existing schools that do not increase capacity by more than 25 percent or 10 classrooms, whichever is less	15332	Certain infill development projects on sites of less than five acres

mechanical equipment, or topographical features, involving negligible or no expansion of use beyond that previously existing at the time of the lead agency's determination," those activities are exempt. 14 C.C.R. § 15301.

- **Replacement or reconstruction of existing schools.** This exemption covers "[r]eplacement or reconstruction of existing structures and facilities where the new structure will be located on the same site as the structure replaced and will have substantially the same purpose and capacity as the structure replaced." 14 C.C.R. § 15302. Capacity may be increased by up to 50 percent if replacement or reconstruction of existing schools is to provide earthquake resistant structures. 14 C.C.R. § 15302(a). This exemption can apply where portable classrooms are replaced with permanent structures.

- **New construction or conversion of small structures.** The class 3 categorical exemption consists of construction and location of limited numbers of new, small facilities or structures, installation of small new equipment and facilities in small structures, and the conversion of existing small structures from one use to another where only minor modifications are made in the exterior of the structure. 14 C.C.R. § 15303. This exemption might apply where a school district is converting existing office or storage buildings into classrooms, or might apply where a school district is constructing a small building or up to four buildings of less than 10,000 square feet on an existing school site.

- **Minor alterations to land.** Class 4 consists of minor public or private alterations in the condition of land, water, and/or vegetation that do not involve removal of healthy, mature, scenic trees except for forestry or agricultural purposes. 14 C.C.R. § 15304. Examples might include landscaping changes needed to convert a parking lot into a playground.

- **Minor additions to existing schools.** Minor additions to an existing school within existing school grounds are exempt where the addition does not increase original student capacity by more than 25 percent or ten classrooms, whichever is less. 14 C.C.R. § 15314. The addition of portable classrooms is included in this exemption.

- **Educational and training programs.** Class 22 exempts the adoption, alteration, or termination of educational or training programs that involve no physical alteration in the area affected or that involve physical changes only in the interior of existing school or training structures. 14 C.C.R. § 15322. Examples include but are not limited to development of or changes in curriculum or training methods, and changes in the school grade structure that do not result in changes in student transportation.

- **Leasing new facilities.** The Class 27 exemption consists of the leasing of a newly constructed or previously unoccupied privately owned facility by a local or state agency where the local governing authority determined that the building was exempt from CEQA. 14 C.C.R. §15327. To be exempt under this section, the proposed use of the facility shall:
  - Be in conformance with existing state plans and policies and with general, community, and specific plans for which an EIR or ND has been prepared

A minor addition to an existing school within existing school grounds is exempt where the addition does not increase original student capacity by more than 25 percent or ten classrooms, whichever is less.

- Be substantially the same as that originally proposed at the time the building permit was issued

- Not result in a traffic increase of greater than 10 percent of front access road capacity

- Include the provision of adequate employee and visitor parking

- **Minor remediation actions on school sites.** An exemption exists for minor cleanup actions—those that involve small or medium removal, costing $1 million or less—taken to prevent, minimize, stabilize, mitigate, or eliminate the release or threat of release of a hazardous waste or substance. 14 C.C.R. § 15331.

- **Specified infill development projects.** If it occurs within city limits on a project site of no more than five acres substantially surrounded by urban uses, the school site may be categorically exempt if it meets certain other requirements. It must be consistent with the applicable general plan designation, policies, zoning designation, and regulations. The site must have no value as habitat for endangered, rare, or threatened species, and project approval must not result in any significant effects relating to traffic, noise, air quality, or water quality. Finally, the site must be able to be adequately served by all required utilities and public services. 14 C.C.R. § 15332. Many school projects in highly urban environments would qualify for this exemption.

Exceptions to categorical exemptions. Certain categorical exemptions (Class 3, 4, 5, 6, and 11), however, may not be used for projects when one of the listed exceptions apply. 14 C.C.R. § 15300.2. For instance, a project that would cause a substantial adverse change in a historic or scenic resource,

Controversy Over the Application of the Class 14 Exemption

What is the appropriate starting point (or baseline) for measuring whether the proposed addition increases student capacity by more than 25 percent or ten classrooms?

According to the terms of the Class 14 exemption, the increase in student capacity or classrooms should be measured against the "original student capacity." The Guidelines do not interpret the term "original student capacity," thus allowing the interpretation to range anywhere from the capacity at the time the school was originally constructed to the capacity at the time the addition project is proposed. This distinction is critical to the application of the Class 14 exemption, as most of the schools in the district were built many decades ago and likely have already had their capacity expanded by more than ten classrooms or 25 percent since initial construction. If the baseline for qualifying for the Class 14 exemption is the capacity at the time the school was initially constructed, many proposed school addition projects would not qualify for a CEQA exemption. Under this narrow interpretation, projects as simple as the addition of a few portable classrooms on an existing school parking lot could be subjected to the often lengthy delays produced by CEQA review.

Until recently, a variety of interpretations existed. Many districts and EIR consultants have interpreted the phrase "original student capacity" to mean the aggregate of all school additions since the later of (1) the time at which the school was originally constructed or (2) the time at which the school was last subjected to CEQA review or (3) the time when CEQA was enacted (1970). These interpretations appear to be longstanding and are likely based on the indefinite case law and policy interpretations of CEQA "baselines" that have only recently been clarified. Revisions to the CEQA Guidelines in 1998 and recent case law support an interpretation of "original student capacity" that calculates capacity as at the time of the proposed project. 14 C.C.R. § 1525; *Bloom v. McGurk* (1994) 26 Cal. App. 4th 1307, *Fairview Neighbors v. County of Ventura* (1999) 70 Cal. App. 4th 238.

Due to the long-standing controversy, CDE requires that the district complete and sign a Form 4.07B certification indicating that the district has determined that its minor addition is exempt from CEQA and not subject to one of the listed exemptions in C.C.R. § 15300.2. ∎

or cause a cumulatively considerable impact, may not rely on a categorical exemption. Pub. Res. Code §§ 21084.1, 21084(b). Another example is a project located on a site that is included on the list of sites compiled by the DTSC known as the "Cortese List," known to have actual or suspected contamination by spills or leaks of hazardous substances. *See* dtsc.ca.gov for the most recent list.

What is an "unusual circumstance?" Districts typically rely on categorical exemptions for additions or modifications to an existing school site. However, even for relatively minor school projects, a categorical exemption cannot be relied upon if an unusual circumstance exists. The CEQA Guidelines do not define "unusual circumstance," and, as a result, it is very common for opponents of a school project to claim that an unusual circumstance exists. Therefore, it is useful to know the factual circumstances that a court has found unusual or usual. Generally speaking, courts have found that an unusual circumstance precluding reliance on a categorical exemption exists where scenic, biological, or nuisance conditions exist, but not where a project would exacerbate parking or traffic problems in built or urban environments. *See* Appendix B, page 247.

Phase 2: Initial Study

Once a school district has determined that their activity is a project, and that the project is *not* exempt, a CEQA Compliance Track is chosen. Some projects are clearly suitable for a particular CEQA compliance track, while others require more careful assessment of environmental, technical, and legal issues. Where it is clear that an activity qualifies for an exemption (*e.g.*, minor alterations to interior walls at an existing school) or requires preparation of an EIR (*e.g.*, acquisition and construction of a high school), the initial study does not need to be completed. However, even in the latter case, completing an initial study prior to preparing an EIR can narrow the focus of the EIR only to resources where a potential impact would occur. This is accomplished by demonstrating in the initial study that certain resources would experience no impact.

Where it is not clear, a school district must conduct an environmental self-assessment, commonly referred to as initial study, to determine the CEQA compliance track required. While CEQA prescribes no specific format for determining the compliance track to select, the Guidelines suggest use of the Environmental Checklist Form (Appendix G) for this purpose. 14 C.C.R. § 15063(f); Guidelines Appendix G. The Environmental Checklist Form is the overwhelmingly favorite tool for lead agencies in determining the appropriate CEQA compliance track. For that reason, the initial study process is now synonymous with the Environmental Checklist Form. Due to the fact that school facilities are subject to environmental requirements in excess of CEQA's requirements, a more comprehensive Initial Study Checklist is provided in Appendix E that encompasses CEQA, DTSC, and CDE environmental review criteria.

Three main CEQA compliance tracks do not qualify for an exemption:

- Where it can be fairly argued, based upon substantial evidence, that the project may result in significant unavoidable adverse impacts, a school district must prepare an EIR and comply with the specific public and agency notice and comment procedures and analysis that an EIR requires.

Districts typically rely on categorical exemptions for additions or modifications to an existing school site.

Initial Study

A preliminary analysis prepared by the lead agency to determine whether an EIR or an ND must be prepared, or to identify the significant environmental effects analyzed in an EIR.

- Where a school district determines that the project would not result in any significant impacts, it can prepare a negative declaration.
- Where the project will not result in significant impacts as a result of mitigation measures that can be imposed, a school district can prepare a MND.

Phase 3: Preparing the Environmental Document

Types of EIRs. If the district has decided during Phase II that preparation of an EIR is necessary, a district must decide the type of EIR that is most appropriate. Appendix J of the CEQA Guidelines is a handy, graphic tool that defines the many types of EIRs. *See* www.ceres.ca.gov/ceqa; 15 C.C.R. 15000 *et seq.*, Appendix J. CEQA recognizes that there are many types of projects, and that different tools may be needed to ensure adequate and timely environmental review. Most useful for this discussion are project EIRs, program EIRs, and tiered EIRs. These are discussed below.

Project EIR. The "project EIR" is the most common type of EIR. It examines the impacts that would result from a specific development proposal. 14 C.C.R. § 15161. School districts have typically prepared a project EIR to evaluate the environmental impacts of a specific school site and construction project. This is appropriate where a school district sites and constructs only one school per decade. However, site-specific project EIRs may not be the best choice for districts facing an urgent demand for numerous school facilities because of demographic growth and the class size reduction mandate.

Program EIR. A program EIR is prepared for a series of related actions that can be characterized as one large action, such as a general plan, master development plan, or regulatory program. 14 C.C.R. § 15168. It typically focuses on the impacts resulting from the program or plan that are not site-specific, such as loss of open space, and contains less detail than a Project EIR. It does not always include such site-specific issues as drainage, traffic patterns, or toxic levels in the soil at a particular location. Program EIRs can provide a more coherent basis than a Project EIR for assessing cumulative impacts and devising mitigation measures and alternatives to minimize and avoid cumulative impacts. They are often followed by project EIRs that then address the site-specific adverse environmental impacts of more discrete activities.

A program EIR may be appropriate if prepared to evaluate the needs analysis of a district's Facilities Master Plan. In fact, depending upon the content of the district's Facilities Master Plan, a program EIR may be required. The adoption of a plan is subject to CEQA when development or change in land use is a foreseeable consequence of the plan. It is well settled that general plans, specific plans, and rezoning ordinances require CEQA analysis. 14 C.C.R. § 15378(a)(1); *see, e.g.*, *Christward Ministry v. Superior Court* (1986) 184 Cal. App. 3d 180. In addition, courts have required CEQA compliance prior to certain plan-level actions by local agency formation commissions (LAFCOs), such as revising "sphere of influence guidelines" (*see City of Livermore v. Local Agency Formation Commission* (1986) 184 Cal. App. 3d 531), or approval of proposed annexation and deannexation of property slated for development (*see People ex rel. Younger v. LAFCO*

Negative Declaration

A negative declaration is a relatively brief document that describes the proposed project, presents the findings, and states the reasons why the district has concluded that there will be no significant impact. A completed initial study must be attached to an ND to support that determination.

Mitigated Negative Declaration

A mitigated negative declaration is the same as a Negative Declaration with the addition of identified mitigation measures and a mitigation monitoring program. An MND, rather than an ND, is prepared when an initial study has been prepared and a determination can be made that no significant environmental effects will occur because revisions to the project have been made or mitigation measures will be implemented to reduce all potentially significant impacts to less-than-significant levels.

Environmental Impact Report

An environmental impact report is a detailed and often lengthy document describing and analyzing a project's significant environmental effects, discussing ways to mitigate and/or avoid those effects.

LAFCO = Local agency formation commission

(1978) 81 Cal. App. 3d 464; *Bozung v. LAFCO* (1975) 13 Cal. 3d 263, 282). Other LAFCO actions have not been considered CEQA projects where they will not result in a foreseeable change in land use, such as detachment of land from a park district or denial of a city's application to expand its sphere of influence. *See Simi Valley Recreation and Park District v. LAFCO* (1975) 51 Cal. App. 3d 648; *City of Agoura Hills v. LAFCO* (1988) 198 Cal. App. 3d 480.

Even if not required, program EIRs can offer several advantages. If a program EIR identifies likely adverse environmental impacts and mitigation measures from school construction generally, then a later, site-specific project EIR would not need to be prepared for a site that presents no unique circumstances. The program EIR will require more investment by the district at the outset due to the range of sites and projects that will be covered in the document. However, preparation of a program EIR on the Facilities Master Plan can save the district time and expense in the future because it reduces the need for site-specific project EIRs as each school facility is individually proposed.

A site-specific project EIR may not always make the most sense nor provide the appropriate level or scope of environmental review under these circumstances. Continued use of the site-specific project EIR may consume the district's resources on repetitive and predictable environmental documents that draw the same conclusion time and again on issues such as noise or construction dust.

Tiering from plan-level documents. "Tiering" is a term of art under CEQA that refers to staging, or tiering, environmental impact analysis for separate but related projects from general issues to more specific issues as the stages become more focused and detailed. 14 C.C.R. §§ 15152, 15385. The legislature has determined that "environmental impact reports shall be tiered whenever feasible, as determined by the lead agency." Pub. Res. Code § 21093(b). The use of tiering is intended to allow agencies to avoid repetitiveness and wasted time on related projects. Pub. Res. Code §§ 21068.5, 21093(a); 14 C.C.R. §§ 15006, 15152. As one court has described it, "tiering is a process by which agencies can adopt programs, plans, policies, or ordinances with EIRs focusing on 'the big picture' and can use streamlined CEQA review for individual projects that are consistent with such...[first tier decisions] and are consistent with local agencies' governing general plans and zoning." *Koster v. County of San Joaquin* (1996) 47 Cal. App. 4th 29, 36.

Under certain circumstances, tiering may be an appropriate method for addressing the timing vulnerabilities of school siting and construction projects that take place in several stages during a five- to ten-year period. For example, it would be appropriate to prepare a first tier EIR for a school district's Facilities Master Plan and a second tier EIR for the later stage actions taken by the school district to implement the Plan.

By contrast, it would not be appropriate to prepare multi-tiered EIRs for a single school siting and construction project. That is, it would not be appropriate for each single site to undergo multiple CEQA reviews. Multiple reviews (or tiers of review) may be appropriate for projects that will proceed in phases, but this is not the case with most school siting proposals. The siting and construction of an individual school project itself is not phased. Instead a complex web

Under certain circumstances, tiering may be an appropriate method for addressing the timing vulnerabilities of school siting and construction projects that take place in several stages during a five- to ten-year period.

of governmental reviews exist that are strung out over a considerable length of time. Multiple CEQA reviews would prolong this arduous process, and nothing in CEQA or the statutes relating to school siting indicates that the legislature intended such a consequence.

Tiering from local government general or specific plan EIRs. With improved coordination of planning for schools with local governments, it may be possible for a district to achieve great efficiencies in the CEQA process. Where a local government has designated potential school sites in its general plan or specific plans and has evaluated and addressed the potential impacts from a school in that location, the school district may rely on that CEQA document to the extent that it addresses this potential future development.

The general plan is a comprehensive, long-term plan for the physical development of the county or city, and of any land outside its boundaries that in the planning agency's judgment bears relation to its planning. Govt. Code § 65300. A specific plan is a more detailed explanation of the systematic implementation of the general plan for all or part of the area covered by the General Plan. Govt. Code § 65450. The primary environmental impacts from school sites are related to land use compatibility, traffic (and related air quality issues), noise and construction-related impacts due to use of diesel equipment, grading, and dust control. To the extent that a general plan or specific plan EIR addressed the potential land use compatibility, traffic, air quality, and noise impacts, the district would be relieved of reexamining those issues.

Time pressure. The timing of CEQA review for school projects and other public agency projects has been controversial. Due to the amount of planning necessary for school facility projects, the numerous state regulatory reviews each facility must undergo, and the urgency for new facilities to meet class size reduction goals and population growth, the pressure is enormous to find ways to reduce the time to design and review a school facility. Since CEQA review can take up to 18 months to complete (six months at an absolute minimum), districts are constantly searching for ways to carry out the other regulatory review processes concurrently. While the DTSC environmental review process and CDE site selection review may occur concurrently with the CEQA process, often the other regulatory steps are predicated on a complete and final CEQA review, and thus must run consecutively, not concurrently.

Often predicated on a complete and final CEQA review, other regulatory steps must run consecutively, not concurrently.

The law. The CEQA statute itself does not specifically mandate the precise timing for preparation of the environmental review document. Nevertheless, the findings in Public Resources Code sections 21002 and 21003.1 express the legislature's general intent that the decision to approve, deny, or condition a project be based on a precedent environmental review, and that the review should be structured to "allow the lead agencies to identify, *at the earliest possible time* in the environmental review process, potential significant effects of a project, alternatives and mitigation measures which would substantially reduce the effects." Pub. Res. Code § 21003.1(a) (emphasis added).

Prior to 1998, the CEQA Guidelines addressed the question of timing very generally, with the basic admonition to conduct review "*as early as feasible*" in the planning process to enable environmental considerations to influence project program and design and *"yet late enough to provide meaningful information"* for environmental assessment. 14 C.C.R. § 15004(b).

In addition to the lack of specific guidance in statute and regulations, the case law has some uncertainty. For instance, a line of cases held that EIRs could not be deferred when an agency's action gave impetus to future foreseeable physical development projects. *See Bozung v. Local Agency Formation Commission of Ventura County* (1975) 13 Cal. 3d 263, 281; *City of Carmel-by-the-Sea v. Board of Supervisors of Monterey County* (1986) 183 Cal. App. 3d 229; *Christward Ministry v. Superior Court of San Diego County* (1986) 184 Cal. App. 3d 180. There were also cases that held that it was appropriate to defer the preparation of an EIR where early agency actions did not lead to specific, known physical development projects. *See Kaufman & Broad-South Bay, Inc. v. Morgan Hill Unified School Dist.* (1992) 9 Cal. App. 4th 464, 474, (formation of assessment district is not a "project" because it neither impels growth nor creates a need for construction of new school); *Schaeffer Land Trust v. San Jose City Council* (1989) 215 Cal. App. 3d 612, 624–626 (ND for plan amendment, future development contingent on compliance with traffic policy—plan had no present traffic consequences because "a specific development will require future environmental review," and "The decision leads City not one step closer to an ecological point of no return."). More recently, the court in *Burbank-Glendale-Pasadena Airport Authority v. Hensler* (2000) 83 Cal. App. 4th 556 held that an agency may not adopt a resolution of necessity for a condemnation action without completing CEQA.

One case is directly related to school facility projects. In *Stand Tall on Principles [STOP] v. Shasta Union High School District* (1991) 235 Cal. App. 3d 772, the court permitted a school district to identify a preferred site before preparing an EIR on the grounds that that act did not constitute an "approval" of the project. Although the holding of the court related only to the selection of a preferred site, the facts of the case, as recited in the opinion, suggest that the district had gone beyond the determination of a preferred site, to actual site selection, before CEQA review. The court stated:

> [I]f STOP contends an EIR is required prior to the ultimate selection of a particular site, that in effect is what is going to occur here when the district prepares the EIR on its preferred site in the context of a genuine and thorough assessment of all reasonable alternative sites. To us, this last option strikes the right balance in this case. We stress, however, that the EIR we envision must serve in a practical sense as an important contribution to the decision-making process and must not be used to rationalize or justify a decision already made.
>
> *Id.* at 783

The important question for the court in *STOP* was whether the district would have the benefit of an EIR before it grants final approval to a new high school site.

CEQA Guideline section 15004. In 1998, section 15004 of the CEQA Guidelines was revised to give specific guidance to lead agencies on the timing of CEQA review. Section 15004 clarifies that public agencies must consider a project's significant effects before taking an action that may limit their choice of potential

In 1991, the STOP court permitted a school district to identify a preferred site before preparing an EIR on the grounds that the act did not constitute "approval" of the project.

alternatives and mitigation measures, providing examples of how far the agency may proceed in its decisionmaking prior to initiating the CEQA process.

With respect to acquisition of land by public agencies, section 15004 states the general rule is "CEQA compliance *should* be completed prior to acquisition of a site for a public project." 14 C.C.R. § 15004(b)(1). The use of the word "should" was intentional, meaning that this particular Guideline is advisory, not mandatory. 14 C.C.R. § 15005(b). Where the Guidelines use the word "must" or "shall," they do so to identify a mandatory element of CEQA compliance that all public agencies are required to follow. 14 C.C.R. § 15005(a). In contrast, "should" identifies guidance based on policy considerations, legislative history, and federal court decisions that public agencies are advised to follow "in the absence of compelling, countervailing considerations." 14 C.C.R. § 15005(b).

After stating the general rule that public agencies *should* conduct the CEQA environmental review prior to site acquisition, the revised section 15004 not only incorporates the reasoning of *STOP*, but also specifies that the critical factor to CEQA timing is the point at which the public agency committed to a particular *use* for the site. Thus, section 15004 states that public agencies "shall not formally make a decision to proceed with the *use* of a site for facilities that would require CEQA review, *regardless of whether the agency has made any final purchase of the site for these facilities*." 14 C.C.R. § 15004(b)(2)(A) (emphasis added). As a result, a district "may designate a preferred site for CEQA review and may enter into land acquisition agreements when the agency has conditioned the agency's future *use* of the site on CEQA compliance." *Id.*

Earlier timing of CEQA review: Pre-site selection. The application of CEQA to the unique process of a school siting and construction project is extraordinarily complex. Conduct CEQA review too late, and the district fails to adequately inform itself of methods to avoid and minimize environmental impacts and risks a challenge that its CEQA review is a post-hoc rationalization. Too early, and it fails to foresee and evaluate changes required by later reviews, possibly wasting precious time and money if the preferred site fails to meet later state agency review requirements. A school district must balance these risks while observing the most basic principle of CEQA—that public agencies inform themselves of environmental impacts so that they can take actions to avoid or minimize those impacts.

To that end, the district might chose to commence CEQA review prior to site selection. Rather than select the site most likely to garner the five state regulatory review agencies' approval and then commence CEQA review for a school on that preferred site, the district may perform CEQA review concurrent with review of the site selection criteria of the other state regulatory agencies. Such environmental review would consider multiple sites, or variations on proposed use of each site. This would better inform the decision-making process and build in flexibility, allowing the district to accommodate changes, without needing to begin the CEQA process anew.

Specifically, a district could use the scoping process to inform itself of the other reviews that each school project must undergo. A lead agency will typically determine the proper scope of an EIR by consulting with responsible agencies,

Section 15004 of the Guidelines states that the general rule is that CEQA compliance should be completed prior to acquisition of a site for a public project.

✍️ **practice tip**

The timing of the CEQA environmental review is an issue of controversy among attorneys. School districts should consult legal counsel before proceeding.

Public Scoping Law

On January 1, 2002, a law governing the requirement to hold public scoping hearings became effective. Section 21083.9 of the Public Resources Code was added by AB 1502 (Stats. 2001, ch. 867, § 2), requiring a lead agency to hold at least one public scoping meeting on an environmental document if the project is "of statewide, regional, or areawide significance."

A project is of statewide, regional, or areawide significance under several criteria, including the following:

- The project is located in a sensitive area, such as the coastal zone, protected Williamson Act agricultural land, the Lake Tahoe Basin, within ¼ mile of a wild and scenic river, the Sacramento-San Joaquin Delta, the Santa Monica Mountains, or other sensitive habitat areas.

- The project has the potential for causing significant effects on the environment extending beyond the city or county in which the project would be located. An example of the effects include generating significant amounts of traffic that interfere with the attainment or maintenance of state or national air quality or water quality standards. 14 C.C.R. § 15206(b)(2), (b)(6)

- The project would provide occupancy for 500 people or more within ten miles of a nuclear power plant. 14 C.C.R. § 15206(b)(7)

trustee agencies, and any agency whose approval or funding the proposed project will need. Pub. Res. Code § 21080.4(a); 14 C.C.R. § 15082. A lead agency may, but is not required to, involve the public in the scoping process. 14 C.C.R. § 15083. Since school projects require state approvals, many districts have chosen to err on the side of caution and determined school projects to be "of statewide importance" and held public scoping hearings.

Even if not required, a public scoping hearing can have many benefits.

In developing its project definition, the district, as lead agency, should seek input from every public agency with specific expertise or statutory duties relating to the siting and construction of schools. These include public agencies that have not traditionally viewed themselves as "responsible agencies" per se, such as the School Facilities Planning Division of the California Department of Education; the Office of Public School Construction of the California Department of General Services, the State Allocation Board, and the Division of State Architect. The school district can use the CEQA scoping process to consult with these agencies and narrow the range of potential alternatives to be analyzed in its environmental review document, describing the facts and rationales by which rejected alternatives were deemed infeasible dictated by the Education Code requirements. *See Citizens of Goleta Valley v. Board of Supervisors* (1990) 52 Cal. 3d 553; 14 C.C.R. § 15126.6(c). In addition, school districts can take advantage of the CEQA scoping process to fold in its community outreach efforts and to incorporate public concerns in its site selection process. In this way, the school district's site selection process of continual winnowing down of potential sites will be subject to full public disclosure and evaluation, recorded in the environmental review document, and coordinated with the CEQA process.

New project definition emphasizing education mission. Typically, school districts have defined the project as a development proposal for a specific site (*e.g.*, a two-story middle school at parcel on corner of A and B streets.) In the past, where only one school was built per decade, this approach made sense. However it doesn't make sense for larger, overcrowded districts with a large number of schools to build in less than a decade—many of which are in the same geographically-confined area. More importantly, a school districts' role is not just to construct buildings. As discussed in previous chapters, the construction of school facilities is merely one of the means and component of educating children. A better approach, and one more consistent with many CEQA principles, might be to define a project in terms of a district's education mission. Defining objectives in this way will provide a more meaningful policy framework for balancing environmental effects with other social and economic considerations. 14 C.C.R. §§ 15126(d), 15093. This issue becomes relevant when a school board approves a project where impacts defined as significant and unavoidable have been identified. When a project with significant unavoidable impacts is approved, the lead agency (in this instance, the school board) must identify specific economic, legal, social, technological, or other considerations, for approving the project, despite the impacts that would result. CEQA Guidelines § 15091(a)(3).

Rather than defining a project as "acquisition and construction of a school at the corner of A and B streets," the district might define the project as "meeting the educational needs of its students" in a certain geographical area with given population and demographic needs (*e.g.*, number of seats per grade level), as identified in their Facilities Master Plan, SB 50 School Facilities Needs Analysis (SFNA), or state funding eligibility determinations. The environmental document would then examine and compare the environmental consequences of various combinations of site acquisitions and construction activities that could meet that goal.

SFNA = School Facilities Needs Analysis

By defining the project broadly in this way, the district would be analyzing the "whole of the action"—its plan to educate children—rather than reviewing components of its educational plan parcel-by-parcel and school-by-school. The project objectives become relevant to the CEQA process in the alternatives analysis, whereby the district must identify a range of potentially feasible project alternatives to be reviewed under CEQA. By clearly articulating the project objectives in terms of its educational mission, a district might be better be able to identify a reasonable range of potentially feasible project alternatives. 14 C.C.R. § 15124.

Phase 4—Project Approval

Before a school facility project can be approved, CEQA's fourth and final phase requires the district's board to make specific findings and determinations.

Findings. Findings required by CEQA are the conclusions made regarding the project in view of the impacts and mitigation measures that have been identified in the ND, MND, or EIR. The conclusions establish the analytical link between the CEQA document and the project decision.

CEQA requires that a public agency approving a project make findings for each significant environmental effect identified in the EIR, as described in the CEQA Guidelines section 15091. The findings should set forth the school district's rationale in approving or denying the project. Specifically, the findings must explain whether and why mitigation measures and project alternatives have been accepted or rejected.

Findings must explain whether and why mitigation measures and project alternatives have been accepted or rejected.

For each significant effect and alternative, the district should make one or more of the following findings, accompanied by a brief explanation for each:

- Changes or alterations have been required in or incorporated into the project that mitigate or avoid the significant environmental effects thereof as identified in the completed EIR.
- Such changes or alterations are within the responsibility and jurisdiction of another public agency, and such changes have been adopted by such other agency or can and should be adopted by such other agency.
- Specific economic, social, or other considerations make infeasible the mitigation measures or project alternatives identified in the EIR.

To ensure implementation of feasible mitigation measures identified in the EIR, the findings should also include a statement that a mitigation monitoring program has been adopted.

School district findings must also include a determination regarding the location of waste sites, hazardous substance releases, pipelines, hazardous air emitters, material handlers within ¼ mile of the site, and freeways or high traffic within 500 feet. Educ. Code § 17213, Pub. Res. Code § 21151.8. If the proposed school site is located in an area zoned for agriculture, the school district must also include findings stating that the district:

- Has notified the city or county of jurisdiction
- Has evaluated the site based on all factors affecting the public interest and not just cost
- Will minimize any effect on public health and safety resulting from neighboring agricultural residue

Educ. Code § 17215.5

Findings must also specify the location and custodian of the administrative record. *See* CEQA Statutes section 21081.6(a)(2). Substantial assistance from legal counsel may be required on findings for complex projects or in situations that present novel issues.

Statement of Overriding Considerations

When an EIR finds that significant effects are unavoidable, and a district decides to proceed with the project anyway, a detailed statement of overriding considerations is required, in addition to the findings required by Public Resources Code section 21081(a)(3) and the CEQA Guidelines section 15091(a)(3) summarized above. For school facilities, the typical effects for which significant thresholds might be exceeded are: bringing more traffic congestion to a local area, air quality effects from dust or PM10 during construction, and noise. For instance, construction of school facilities in seismically active areas may require deep pilings, and the use of the pile-driving equipment may exceed acceptable noise levels and result in a significant effect.

A statement of overriding considerations indicates that, even though a project would result in unavoidable adverse impacts, specific economic, social, or other stated benefits are sufficient to warrant approval.

A "statement of overriding considerations" indicates that, even though a project would result in one or more unavoidable adverse impacts, specific economic, social, or other stated benefits are sufficient to warrant project approval. The statement explains the justification for proceeding despite the significant adverse environmental impacts.

If the benefits of a project outweigh the unavoidable adverse environmental effects, those effects may be considered "acceptable." CEQA Guidelines section 15093(a). Typically, the overriding consideration is the need for school facilities as articulated in the district's Facilities Master Plan or its School Fee Needs Analysis.

Findings must clearly state whether any significant impacts remain after mitigation measures have been applied. They also provide the basis for making a statement of overriding considerations.

The district must complete the findings, including the statement of overriding consideration, before approving or carrying out a project for which an EIR has been completed.

Certification of the EIR

The district's board must certify the final EIR, verify that the final EIR has been completed in compliance with CEQA, and certify that the board (the district's decisionmakers) has reviewed and considered the information in the final EIR prior to making its decision.

Project Approval

To approve a project in accordance with CEQA, the board needs to find that the project as approved will either not have a significant environmental impact, impacts have been eliminated or mitigated to less than significant levels, or impacts are acceptable due to overriding considerations.

NOD = Notice of determination
OPR = Office of Planning and Research

Notice of Determination

A notice of determination (NOD) serves to notify the public, interested parties, and responsible agencies that a project for which an EIR has been prepared was approved. It also initiates a 30-day statute of limitations for court challenges to project approval.

A notice of determination initiates a 30-day statute of limitations for court challenges to project approval.

The NOD must be sent out within five days after the board certifies the Final EIR and approves the project. The district must file the NOD with the Office of Planning and Research (OPR), city and county planning departments, the county clerk, responsible agencies (if any) with jurisdiction by law over the project area, trustee agencies (if any) with jurisdiction over resources affected by the project, and any persons who have filed a written request for notices with the district. Pub. Res. Code §§ 21092.2, 21152, and 21167(f).

Fish and Game Fee

State law requires that a fee be paid to the DFG or a Certificate of Fee Exemption be filed if the district makes a *de minimis* impact finding for wildlife resources. Fish and Game fees are $1,250 for a negative declaration and $850 for an EIR. Checks should be made payable to the State of California.

Thirty-Day Statute of Limitations

A statute of limitations defines the time period within which a suit can be filed on a particular action. A 30-day statute of limitations applies after an NOD has been filed for either an ND or an EIR. Pub. Res. Code § 21167(b). Any court challenges related to the adequacy or certification of the EIR have to be filed within this period.

The 30-day period begins the first day after filing the NOD. It is important to confirm that OPR has received the NOD. The 30-day period ends 30 calendar days later or on the first working day following a weekend or holiday. If no NOD is filed, a lawsuit may be filed up to 180 days after project approval.

Land Acquisition

Now that the district has selected a proposed school site that has passed all the state's regulatory hurdles—CDE's site selection criteria are satisfied; DTSC's toxic substances review requirements have been satisfied, and the district has completed the CEQA review process as evidenced by an exemption adopted ND, MND, or certified EIR—the district may acquire the site.

During the student population growth of the 1950s and 1960s, it was common for school districts to select and acquire sites based on prospective need—"to bank the land" so to speak. Such land banking could insure land availability when needed, and was a thrifty use of scarce funds because it avoided escalating real estate prices. During the 1970s and 1980s, lower growth enrollment did not dictate this prospective approach and sites were selected and purchased based on actual needs where Ed Specs had already been developed. Today, high enrollment growth conditions are once again present.

The five main methods for acquiring a school site include:

- Acceptance as a gift from the owner
- Purchase from a willing seller
- Condemnation of private property (with purchase at fair market value)
- Receipt of surplus government property
- Leasing

Acquisition by Gift

Acquisition by gift has been a relatively rare form of acquisition for school districts. In the future, acquisitions by gift or dedication may become more common. Section 66478 of the Education Code authorizes cities and counties to adopt an ordinance to require dedication of land for elementary school sites from developers seeking tentative tract map approvals. Also, some developers prefer to dedicate land rather than pay Level 2 of Level 3 school fees. Such developers may seek to enter into a mitigation agreement with districts to dedicate land for potential school sites.

Most districts do not have a benevolent billionaire satisfying their land needs. Should a district be among the lucky few, there are some precautions to take before accepting—the suitability of the site to meet the educational program needs should be evaluated by the same criteria as applied to other sites, a title search to assure clear, unarbitable title should be conducted, other standard acquisition due diligence, including the review of the environmental condition of the site, should be conducted.

Acquisition by Purchase from a Willing Seller

A seller willing to enter into a purchase agreement with a long open escrow period can expedite the entire site selection and approval process.

A willing seller can expedite the entire site selection and approval process if the seller is willing to enter into a purchase agreement with a long open escrow period since the sale is contingent on DTSC review and approval, successful CEQA compliance, and other conditions.

Since many willing sellers are not amenable to such a long extension of the close of escrow—this can last more than a year—the district, as inducement, could offer additional monetary consideration, liquidated damages, or option money as ways to keep the escrow open. However, the district must be careful to agree to an option amount or other monetary consideration that is small enough for the district to walk away from the purchase agreement—so as to ensure unfettered consideration of alternative sites as required by CEQA.

If a long escrow is not possible, entry into a purchase agreement may have to wait until after DTSC review and CEQA compliance is complete. If the owner is willing to give written consent to test the site, this can be a time saver. If a property owner refuses, school districts must go to court to compel an order. Code Civ. Proc. §§ 1245.010 *et seq.* This could add several months to the process because of time delays inherent in court procedures, and could slow down both the testing and sampling required for DTSC compliance and any necessary land surveys and appraisal inspections.

Thirty days prior to purchase of proposed school site, the district must give notice to the city of county planning commission for their investigation and report. Pub. Res. Code § 21151.2. *See also* Govt. Code §§ 53094, 6542(c).

OPSC review and approval of purchase. Title to all property acquired, constructed, or improved with funds made available under the SFP must be held by the school district to which the SAB grants the funds. The district need not hold title to the site before funding; however, one of the following must be demonstrated:

- Purchase will be made from private parties, companies, developers, or other entities, as evidenced by an escrow showing the pending transfer of ownership to the district.
- Court orders, especially orders of condemnation through the county court where the proposed new site lies, which include a Final Judgment, Stipulated Judgment and Order of Immediate Possession to allow occupancy, or Prejudgment Possession.
- An escrow for the transfer of property in lieu of other legally required payments or fees due to the district. For example: A district sometimes obtains a proposed new school site parcel from a developer, with all or part of the "purchase" price comprised of the district forbearing from collecting from the developers any school mitigation fees.

If title to the property is not held by the district, the district may utilize leased sites with governmental agencies for certain specified periods of time. To receive new construction grants for facilities that are or will be located on real property leased by the district, the property must be leased from the federal government for a period of 25 years or another governmental agency for a period of 40 years. If the lease is with a governmental agency other than the federal government, a 30-year lease may be considered if there are no other educationally adequate sites available under a 40-year lease, the cost per year for a 30-year lease is not greater than a 40-year lease, or the district can provide satisfactory evidence to the SAB that a shorter term lease is necessary.

Prior to the acquisition of a site by a negotiated purchase agreement using state funds, OPSC requires submission of the following three documents:

Use of Option Agreements and Timing of CEQA Compliance

Under current CEQA Guidelines, public agencies shall not "… [f]ormally make a decision to proceed with the use of a site for facilities which would require CEQA review, regardless of whether the agency has made any final purchase of the site for these facilities, except that agencies may designate a preferred site for CEQA review and may enter into land acquisition agreements when the agency has conditioned the agency's future use of the site on CEQA compliance." 14 C.C.R. § 15004(b)(2)A. A purchase option that would not be exercisable until after confirmation of CEQA compliance would provide the flexibility needed by public agencies, provided the price of the option was not so high as to foreclose true consideration of alternative sites by the district.

Because of the complexity of land use laws and procedures, potential land buyers often secure an option to allow them an opportunity to ascertain what development ultimately will be permitted before committing themselves to a purchase. *County of San Diego v. Miller* (1975) 13 Cal. 3d 684. As the court explained, "the option has become a prevalent method for securing to a potential land buyer the ability to ultimately purchase the land—while affording him the opportunity to undertake and complete the often expensive and lengthy process of determining whether his intended use of the land will be permitted." School districts, as potential land buyers and entities subject to a more complex permitting and approval process, are entering into such option contracts. Districts negotiating the length of an option should take into account the approval times needed for the DSA, CDE, OPSC, and DTSC processes, as well as the possibility that litigation brought by the public will cause considerable delay in the siting and construction of the school facility. ■

Land Banking and Timing of CEQA Compliance

In light of the *Burbank* case (*Burbank-Glendale-Pasadena Airport Authority v. Hensler* (2000) 83 Cal. App. 4th 556), a district cannot adopt a Resolution of Necessity (one of the first steps in the eminent domain process and a prerequisite to obtain an order to possess the property much less acquire title to the property) prior to CEQA review. However, some general precepts of CEQA lend weight to a view of section 15004 that would, in the right circumstance, permit land acquisition prior to CEQA review.

CEQA applies only to "projects" and a CEQA project must have three characteristics—the action must involve:

- A public agency
- A discretionary decision
- A direct or reasonably foreseeable indirect physical change in the environment

Pub. Res. Code § 21065

Private parties may engage in real estate transactions without the need to comply with CEQA since none of these three characteristics exist. (Hence, a private party might acquire land for a school district, as long as the district is not committed to accepting that land.) When a school district acquires land, two of these characteristics are automatically met as school districts are public agencies and the decision to buy land is one that is discretionary.

The question is whether the purchase of land involves a direct or reasonably foreseeable indirect physical change in the environment. A transaction itself does not result in a physical change since it is merely a change in ownership (a paper, not a physical change). However, if a transaction commits a district to a particular course of action—such as construction of a high school—then physical changes attendant to that construction are a "reasonably foreseeable indirect physical change" whose impacts must be reviewed prior to acquisition.

Thus, a district can only meet this test if the acquisition is a change in ownership without a commitment to develop the site. An example of an acquisition that might meet these criteria is where a district has multiple needs at the same time for a property suitable for any of those needs, and further analysis will be conducted to determine the one most suitable and the project to be pursued.

With land banking, a district may have a general plan to develop the property but must be truly open-minded as to the kind of development, if any, to be undertaken on the land being acquired. ■

1. A letter appraisal if the property is valued at less than $500,000, or a self-contained appraisal if the property is valued above $500,000. The appraisal must be submitted to OPSC within 60 days of the valuation date. Costs associated with the preparation of an appraisal are eligible for expenditure from the state fund.

2. A copy of the purchase agreement.

3. A letter from legal counsel containing the following two statements:

   (i) That the Preliminary Title Report has been reviewed for exceptions and that the exceptions will not prevent the intended use of the property.

   (ii) That the Purchase Agreement has been reviewed.

In a negotiated willing seller purchase, OPSC allows the purchase price to be only up to 10 percent over the appraised value. In an eminent domain proceeding, if a price negotiated during the court proceedings is over the appraised value, it will be necessary to obtain a court judgment of that negotiated price.

Include a right of rescission? While some real estate lawyers recommend including a right of rescission in the purchase agreement if the site fails to meet the regulatory standards, most do not believe it necessary. A right of rescission allows a party to extinguish the purchase agreement *ab initio* as though it never came into existence. An alternative would be to include a contingency in the agreement that would not be satisfied if the site fails to meet the regulatory standards applicable to school facilities.

Multiple sites. Where it's necessary to purchase multiple sites to achieve one of sufficient size, a district should be careful not to create an inverse condemnation situation, where some property owners are cooperative and others are not. In such instances, the contracts should include a condition stating that the close of escrow is subject to adoption of a resolution of necessity for all the parcels.

Acquisition by Eminent Domain
(or Condemnation)

In the absence of a willing seller, the district may use its power of eminent domain to acquire a potential school site. Eminent domain is the federal, state, private, or quasi-public entity's use of their police power to take private property for public uses. *City of Oakland v. Oakland Raiders* (1982) 32 Cal. 3d 60. Code Civ. Proc. §§ 1240 *et seq.* Specifically, the federal authority comes from the Fifth Amendment to the United States Constitution. However, the restrictions in Article I, Section 14 and the Fourteenth Amendment provide the limitation that use must be for a public purpose and that just compensation must be paid to the owner. "Public use" includes the development of new schools and the expansion of current school facilities. *Anaheim Union High School v. Viera* (4th Dist. 1966) 241 Cal. App. 2d 169. Private schools and collegiate level institutions also have the power of eminent domain. Educ. Code §§ 66010 *et seq.*, 35270.5, 30051, 1047, 94500; *Loyola Marymount Univ. v. LAUSD* (1996) 45 Cal. App. 4th 1256. "Just compensation" is the money that must be paid to the condemnee and is the fair market value of the property taken on the date of valuation that would have been agreed upon by a willing seller and a willing buyer, each dealing with the other with full knowledge of all of the uses and purposes for which the property is reasonably adequate and available. Code of Civil Procedure § 1263.320.

In California, eminent domain law is found in Civil Procedure § 1240 *et seq.* This direct grant of authority allows the legislative bodies of the state to further state/public interests through the eminent domain process. To carry out the state's educational functions, the school district has the same power of eminent domain as a county, city, or quasi-public entity.

Eminent domain: Main steps in the process. While purchase of school sites from willing sellers is considerably faster, less expensive, and presents fewer public relations problems, a district may find that it must exercise its power of eminent domain after all efforts for a voluntary purchase-sale agreement have been exhausted. The main steps in the eminent domain process include:

1. CEQA and DTSC compliance
2. Making the statutory offer under Government Code § 7267.2
3. Providing notice to property owners and holding a hearing that results in the issuance of the "resolution of necessity"
4. Filing the complaint and simultaneously depositing the funds
5. Applying to the court for possession of the property
6. Determining the timing of the "date of value"
7. Providing date of possession for construction
8. During the trial phase, determining "just compensation" for property and attorney fees, if applicable
9. Recording the Final Order of Condemnation to acquire title

These steps are discussed below briefly. For a more in-depth discussion, please refer to *Eminent Domain, A Step-by-Step Guide to the Acquisition of Real Property*, Solano Press (2002).

> *In the absence of a willing seller, the district may use its power of eminent domain to acquire a potential school site.*

CEQA compliance. The first step in acquiring property through eminent domain is compliance with CEQA.

In the event that a property owner is not willing to give written consent to enter his property for site evaluation for school purposes, the district must go to court to compel an order or possession. Code Civ. Proc. § 1245.010 *et seq.* The time to obtain an order in court will delay site surveying and sampling required for DTSC compliance, CEQA compliance, and appraisals.

The condemnation resolution or order of possession cannot occur without certification of appropriate CEQA documents, DTSC compliance, and a pre-condemnation offer based on a qualified appraisal. Some property owners deliberately delay in a rising market. This is because the date of value cannot be established until a resolution of necessity is adopted, a condemnation action is filed, and the school district places on deposit an amount equal to its appraisal. An unwilling seller may also challenge the district's findings, including the adequacy of the EIR document and the pre-resolution offer, or the determination that the school site location is for the greatest public good at the least private injury.

Statutory offer. A statutory offer under Government Code § 7267.2 is a written statement of the basis for the amount established for the property. The most common method of determining reasonable value for the statutory offer is to acquire a summary appraisal by a member of the Appraisal Institute (MAI). An appraisal more than three months old is considered stale, so plan accordingly.

The board must review the offer and ratify it by passing a resolution of necessity or by executing the contract. Code Civ. Proc. § 7267.2. The offer must be the fair market value of the property, defined as the *highest* price that a willing buyer would make to a willing seller. The "reasonable value" is the most frequently litigated component of the eminent domain process.

Generally, a price increase of 5 percent or greater above reasonable value requires specific board approval. If the price is at the reasonable value or less than 5 percent higher, no specific approval is required.

Notice and hearing for the resolution of necessity. The notice and hearing for the resolution is a meeting for property owners affected by the condemnation. Since this is not a public hearing, giving notice to the community at large is not a requirement. However, at least 15 days' notice must be given to each of the property owners affected. If no response is received, then that property owner has waived his or her right to address the board.

The resolution of necessity is a general statement indicating the property is being taken for public use with a reference to the statutory authority authorizing the action. The resolution must contain four main points:

- A person must be able to glean the public interest and necessity requiring the project.
- The proposed project is planned or located in the manner that will be most compatible with the greatest public good and least private injury.
- Property described in the resolution is necessary for the proposed project.
- Either the offer required by a specified Government Code provision has been made to the owner or owners of record, or the offer has not been made because the owner cannot be located with reasonable diligence.

The resolution must pass with a two-thirds-majority vote.

Public use includes developing new schools and expansion of current facilities. Necessity is a legislative determination made by the respective administrative agency that is dependent upon proof of three elements: (1) the public interest and necessity require the project; (2) the project is planned or located in a manner that will be most compatible with the greatest public good and the least private injury; and (3) the property sought to be acquired is necessary for the project. *See* Code Civ. Proc. §§ 1240.030(a)–(c). The decision of the school board or equivalent body will be conclusive proof of the necessity, unless facts demonstrating fraud or bad faith are present. *People v. Lagiss* (1963) 223 Cal. App. 2d 23, 36–37.

The offer required by Government Code § 7260 *et seq.* must be made, to the owner or owners of record. It is sufficient if the offer has not been made because the owner cannot be located with reasonable diligence. The offer must be made prior to the meeting on the vote of the resolution of necessity.

The public interest, necessity requiring the project, and that the project is planned or located in the manner that will be the most compatible with the greatest public good and the least private injury is satisfied by the vote of the board.

Filing the complaint and depositing the money. After adopting the resolution of necessity, the district can file a lawsuit in eminent domain against the property owner in state court. In order to freeze the property value, timing of the date of value requires funds be deposited as soon as possible. The freeze date, or date upon which the property value is based, is the date of the deposit of funds or the court date. The value of the property is frozen in time and is not subject to market increases. The district is responsible for the reasonable value of the property including any increases prior to the freeze date.

Order of prejudgment possession. The district can move for an "Order of Prejudgment Possession" after the money has been deposited with the court and the "Resolution of Necessity" has been passed by a two-thirds majority vote by the board. A small but also important step is to file a notice of lis pendens. This notice puts all third parties on notice of impending action and it is filed with the county recorder. If granted, the district will get the exclusive right to occupy the property within three days. Actual possession of the property is usually obtained no sooner than 90 days after the notice of the order is given. However, the district will be able to begin conducting site evaluations and preliminary testing once the notice of lis pendens is recorded.

The court issues a prejudgment possession order when a deposit equaling the probable amount of compensation for the property is deposited with the court. The order is served upon the property owners and tenants. Although possession orders can be effective in as little as three days from service, such three-day possession orders can only be justified on the basis of "urgent need," and therefore are not be relied upon. Farms and businesses require 90 days' notice. Under the relocation law, 90 days notice is also required for tenant relocation.

Otherwise, a prejudgment possession order for vacant property may be obtained within 30 days of service of the pre-judgment possession order. Any fast track time line should assume a 90-day possession order before construction activities commence.

Value of the Property

If a district deposits funds 30 days after filing a complaint, and during that period a new luxury apartment building is approved adjacent to the property that increases the property's value by $50,000, the district is responsible for the additional $50,000.

Order for Immediate Possession

1. Comply with CEQA
2. Make offer
3. Notice/Hearing
4. Resolution
5. File condemnation action in court
6. Deposit appraisal amount with court
7. Order of Possession
8. Actual possession in 3 to 90 days

The primary issue at trial is the determination of "just compensation" or reasonable fair market value of the property.

Trial and compensation. Very often, if the eminent domain power is utilized, litigation and a trial will follow. Primarily, the issue at trial is the determination of "just compensation" or reasonable fair market value of the property. During trial, the district will continue to have occupancy although the court proceedings have not concluded and title of the property has not been passed. Typically, a district is in possession of the property as long as two years prior to acquiring the title.

The district should consult the section on OPSC acquisition regarding requirements and procedures if the funding for acquisition by eminent domain comes from SFP funding.

Relocation as a Site Acquisition Issue

Relocation costs can be substantial in the property acquisition process. Government Code sections 7260 *et seq.* requires a public school district to pay relocation expenses when acquiring residential or commercial occupied properties, whether by negotiation or by eminent domain. The previous section on site selection discussed how smaller sites could reduce a school district's relocation costs. In general, eligible residential owner-occupants are entitled to the difference between the final price paid by the agency for their property and the market price of a comparable property in a comparable location. Eligible residential tenants are typically entitled to the difference between the "base rent" at their displacement dwelling (the lesser of their actual rent or 30 percent of their income) and the market rent for a comparable dwelling in a comparable location for 42 months, payable in a lump sum or over time. Eligible commercial occupants (both owners and tenants), are entitled primarily to moving expenses and limited search and re-establishment expenses.

School districts are required to identify suitable dwellings for displaced residents, and these dwellings are generally used to establish a displacee's eligibility for compensation. Displacees are not, however, required to move into a dwelling identified by the school district. Displacees may relocate wherever they choose, even to another state or country, and retain their rights to compensation as long as they relocate to a decent, safe, and sanitary property. Relocation payments will always be based on the displacee's actual costs of securing and moving into a replacement dwelling, but generally will not exceed the individual's maximum eligibility established by the school district.

Relocation assistance applies to owners and tenants and is a separate administrative process from eminent domain. It is important to recognize that while administratively separate, relocation assistance is a critical part of the overall compensation package. This is true in particular for owner-occupants when their homes are acquired by a school district. As such, it is vital to coordinate acquisition and relocation efforts early in the process.

School districts must adopt their own relocation assistance rule consistent with state law. There should be a relocation plan with rights and remedies, and made available to the parties eligible for relocation assistance. Relocation assistance must be both financial and informational assistance. Failure to timely

✒ **practice tip**

A homeowner is entitled to a relocation payment, including the difference between the property's sale price to the school district and the market price of a comparable dwelling. While it may be desirable for a relocation-eligible homeowner to increase the sale price to the district, the homeowner may receive little net benefit since relocation compensation is generally reduced by an equivalent amount.

Submittal Documents Required to Obtain Final CDE Site Approval

1 Letter requesting CDE approval
The letter should be addressed to the district's assigned CDE SFPD consultant:

School Facilities
Planning Division
660 J Street, Suite 350
Sacramento, CA 95814

2 Signed copy of SFPD Form 4.02 (School Site Report)

3 Signed copy of SFPD Form 4.03 (School Site Certification)

4 Two (2) copies of legal description of site

5 School district map of any size indicating:
- All existing schools and sites
- Attendance areas, and
- Proposed site

6 An 8.5 x 11-inch map of the site indicating:
- Dimensions, showing metes and bounds corresponding to the legal description
- Adjacent streets, and
- Gross and net usable acres

* * *

1 Three documents that prove CEQA compliance
- Copy of board-certified final environmental impact report or adopted negative declaration (including initial study checklist) or for exemptions a letter from district legal counsel
- Copy of stamped notice of completion or comment period closure letter from OPR
- Copy of stamped notice of determination filed with County Clerk and OPR

7 Schematic utilization of site (site utilization plan) on which proposed facilities and placement on the site are indicated

8 Copy of report regarding site by the planning commission with jurisdiction (planning commission report)

9 List of all unused school sites within district
If the unused site is within the same attendance boundary, then the district must also provide written justification of need for the proposed school site pursuant to SAB Regulation 1859.75.

10 Current (not over five years old) document justifying master-planned size of the site
District's Facilities Master Plan, Developer Fee Justification Study, or SFPD Form 575 Five-Year Plan may each serve this requirement.

* * *

1 Copy of school district's board-approved "written findings," regarding proximity of site to hazardous waste disposal/air emissions/pipelines, etc.
Pub. Res. Code § 21151.8 and Educ. Code § 17213

2 Copy or summary of geological hazards report as submitted to Department of General Services
Educ. Code § 17212.5

3 Copy of Phase I ESA

4 Copy of determination letter
If DTSC approved a PEA, then PEA executive summary should also be submitted. Educ. Code §§ 1999, 17210, 17213.1

OPTIONAL

If applicable, the following documents should also be provided in the submission to CDE:

1 Signed copy of Joint Use Agreement
if proposed site meets CDE's school site size standards based on additional acreage to be provided by a joint use agreement

2 Copy of Final Determination Letter from Caltrans
if proposed school site is within two miles of an existing or potential airport runway

3 Any other documentation or studies requested by SFPD consultant to evaluate the unique characteristics and environment of proposed site
Includes, but not limited to, studies of wetlands and endangered species, noise, traffic, railroads, underground pipelines, electric transmission lines, and flooding

Upon receipt and approval, CDE will issue a Final Site Approval Letter to the district that will remain valid for five years.

Relocating a low-income tenant
can be difficult and expensive
in an area where housing costs
are high. A school district can
increase the effectiveness of its
relocation services, help tenants
move to housing that is more
affordable, and potentially contain costs through partnerships
with local housing agencies
and/or nonprofit providers.

The Los Angeles Unified School
District recently formed a partnership with its local Housing
Authority to provide low-income
displacees with access to first-
time homebuyer assistance programs and Section 8 vouchers.
Under this program, displacees
optimize the use of their benefits and agencies make funds
available for the development
of new affordable housing.

*It is common for school districts to
enter into joint use agreements with
local parks and recreation departments for the use of playfields on
adjoining parks, but less common
to build facilities under joint use.*

comply with the relocation assistance law may delay possession of property with a willing seller, and delay the district's ability to obtain a prejudgment possession order in eminent domain proceedings. Although willing sellers may wish to waive relocation assistance in their purchase agreements, such waivers do not exist and are not forthcoming with respect to tenant relocation assistance, particularly residential tenants. It does little good to have a fast-track acquisition plan if relocation benefits are not consummated in a timely manner. School district must notify all displacees of their potential eligibility for relocation benefits. A minimum of 90 days notice is required before a school district may issue a Notice to Vacate to any occupants of acquired properties. If occupants refuse to relocate, there may be an additional delay to obtain a writ of assistance.

Final Approval from CDE

After a site has been selected and all regulatory requirements are met, the district may seek final approval of the site from CDE. If state funding is sought for the site, then this is a mandatory requirement—CDE must certify the site to OPSC in order for the district to obtain SAB funding.

The chart on page 175 lists all the submittal documents required in order to obtain final CDE approval.

Special Issues: Joint Use, Small Sites, and Playgrounds

Joint Use Projects

As land to build new schools becomes more scarce, California school districts are exploring more joint use opportunities. Through partnerships with the private sector and public agencies, schools have been built on park, museum, college, commercial, and other school sites.

Joint use partnerships can be a cost effective method of providing facilities for a school district. It is common for school districts to enter into joint use agreements with local parks and recreation departments for the use of playfields on adjoining parks. It is less common for districts to build facilities under joint use agreements. However, the typical usage for school facilities covers a limited period during the day, and it is good economic policy to use the facilities evenings and weekends if the construction and maintenance costs can be shared with a community college, university, city, county, or other nonprofit organization.

Joint use is an effort by districts to promote smart growth and improve the quality of life in communities. The SAB considers it one of many cost-reduction strategies for new school development as required by SB 50, which calls for the SAB to adopt guidelines to achieve school cost reductions. Organizations such as New Schools/Better Neighborhoods, (www.nsbn.org) also promote joint use.

One benefit of joint use agreements is that they provides additional student housing in areas where existing schools are overcrowded and land to build new schools is scarce. An example of a public-private partnership is the Santa Ana Unified School District, California's second largest school district. The city's Mendez Intermediate School is currently completing construction on a site that

Table 4-2. Examples of Successful Joint Use Projects in California

Facility	Location
Community performing arts complex	Elk Grove Unified School District, Sacramento City/County Library
Softball complex	Clovis Unified School District, City of Clovis
Park and aquatics center	Roseville Joint Union High School District, City of Roseville
Field areas	Woodland Joint Unified School District, City of Woodland
Theatre and gymnasiums	Poway Unified School District, Cities of Poway and San Diego
Gymnasium/Fitness center	Lodi Unified School District, City of Lodi
Technology center	San Diego County Office of Education
Medical magnet school/hospital	Los Angeles Unified and Compton Unified School Districts, King Drew Medical Magnet High School
High school/Community college campus	San Diego City Unified School District, San Diego City College
Onsite school/Business entity	Hewlett Packard, Santa Rosa Elementary School District
Senior center/District office	Carlsbad Unified School District, Carlsbad Senior Center
Multipurpose poom, kitchen, platform	Pauma Elementary School District, Non-Profit Foundation, HUD
Library/Media center	Eastlake High, Sweetwater Union High School District, City of Chula Vista

shares space with a renovated shopping center; the school facility is being built on top of the shopping center parking structure. Santa Ana is a densely populated city, and sites for new schools are virtually nonexistent. This joint use venture does not displace housing, and the community benefits from the redevelopment of an underutilized shopping center.

Choosing appropriate sites for joint use facilities. Frequently, school districts agree to cooperate with a local governmental entity, recreation district, or adjacent school district when planning a new facility, such as a new library, technology center, performing arts center, swimming pool, gymnasium, multi-purpose room, or sports complex. Likewise, a commercial or industrial complex may be jointly planned to include a school. More efforts will be made to save dollars and acreage as funding and space become ever more scarce resources. The construction and land costs saved may be significant. In some cases the costs may increase because of joint use, but the benefits to communities can offset the increased expenses. By providing combined and expanded resources within a single facility, the school district furthers enhanced community activities.

Agreements must be crafted between the school districts and other appropriate entities regarding site acquisition, mutually acceptable arrangements for space, staffing, maintenance, materials acquisition, and other matters related to the administration and operation of the joint use facility. In some cases the shared community facility is also shared between school sites, such as a middle and a high school. In those instances careful planning must take place about what can and cannot be shared. In many districts more than one facility is used jointly with the community—the fields, theatres, classrooms, and nearly the entire campus become available for joint use.

Safety studies for joint use sites. A joint use project must meet all the same CDE, DTSC, and DSA safety requirements as a stand-alone school. For instance, since students may use the facilities, DTSC often requires soil samples for the entire joint use site, not just the part where the school will be located. Such cooperative planning is necessary to ensure that recreational and educational areas are suitable for use by both students and the community. When planning site acquisition for a joint use facility, the district must consider the following:

- Safety and security
- Access—day and night year-round, including by public transportation
- Location—should be a prominent landmark that encourages community use
- Appropriate size, including adequate space for buildings, grounds, and convenient, plentiful parking

Special care must be taken to ensure that both students and community members can use the site without compromising school safety and security. For instance, public parking areas and toilets should be placed away from classrooms and student play areas.

Key factors to consider in a joint use agreement. A school district needs to use caution when considering these types of projects. Funding availability for the potential joint use partner may vary considerably from the districts. The joint use agreement should address the funding availability of all partners. Many school projects are planned with play fields on adjoining city parks, only to have the park site remain undeveloped for years after the school is opened. If funded under the state's joint use program, a school district has time limitations set by regulation for the development and construction of the project. If the joint use partner's funding does not materialize the district could lose the state funding.

The agreement should also address issues of scheduling priorities. The school district should have first priority on the use, however, concessions may be needed to ensure participation by the other partners. Maintenance also needs to be addressed. If the school district is to maintain the facilities, there should be some consideration in the agreement for this responsibility.

The planning of the facilities should involve local agencies. Some local planning and building jurisdictions have considered the night-and-weekend-use of school facilities a noneducational activity and subject to local codes and ordinances. If this is the case, the provisions need to be negotiated.

Education Code section 17077.42 specifies criteria that must be met with the joint use agreement. The agreement must specify the method of sharing capital and operating costs. It must also specify the relative responsibilities for the operation and staffing of the facility, and the manner in which the safety of the pupils will be ensured. The applicant district must demonstrate that the facilities will be utilized to the maximum extent possible for both school purposes and joint use purposes. In addition, the joint use partner must agree to provide at least 50 percent of the cost of facilities funded by the Joint Use Program.

AB 16: State policy and funding for joint use projects. Recognizing the potential for cost savings, the legislature has passed several provisions to promote joint use of K–12 facilities. As with all state funding, the special joint use funds come with special requirements that districts must meet. These funding requirements are discussed in detail in chapter 2, pages 21–23.

Joint use: Easier said than done. Schools districts, cities, counties, community colleges, and private sector partners attempting joint use partnerships are often confronted with more complex regulatory constraints. The regulations governing the construction of schools, other public buildings, and private buildings each have different policy goals and legislative histories. Joint use projects often involve regulatory compliance beyond what is familiar to school districts.

One example is the Field Act, which establishes a high constructions standard to address earthquake safety in all school facilities. Unaccustomed to such rigorous standards, the joint use partner may be surprised by the added cost to build a theater, auditorium, or multi-purpose center when that facility will also be used by a school district for classes or school activities and therefore must be built to Field Act standards. Similarly, school districts not accustomed to and not required to comply with local ordinances and zoning are surprised when they become applicable to joint use projects.

Regulatory constraints may complicate construction projects, but can also affect the operations of joint use facilities. For example, school districts, which have more power than libraries to restrict reading materials and the Internet, have run into conflict with libraries over school policy and the Library Freedom Act.

Finally, while encouraging joint use, SB 50 also establishes a new requirement that school funding can only be used to build on sites owned by school districts. Educ. Code §§ 17077.40–17077.45; SAB Reg, 12 C.C.R. §§ 1859.120–1859.129.

Nonetheless, the current environment is excellent for exploring and developing joint use opportunities. By building schools in conjunction with other compatible facilities, school districts can leverage their limited resources. SB 50 has made joint use easier, and the SAB, as well as other state agencies, are encouraging districts to work with other entities.

When considering a joint use project, a district should think like a company in the community development business. School facilities that address a community goal and a new school facilities goal are prime opportunities for joint use. Also, consider adapting existing, available buildings for joint use projects. California's growing numbers of students are making adaptive reuse of land necessary, particularly in urban areas. Under-utilized or vacant office or industrial buildings may offer possibilities to produce new classroom space faster, cheaper, or both.

Small School Sites

Under limited or unusual circumstances, CDE permits a departure from its size requirements for school sites and from the numbers and formulas contained in its *Guide to School Site Analysis and Development* (discussed earlier in the chapter).

CDE's regulations define "unusual or exceptional site conditions" that would permit deviation from the numbers and formulas provided in the *Guide*. 5 C.C.R. § 14010. They include unavailability of sufficient land due to:

- Urban or suburban development—even after considering the option of eminent domain
- Economic infeasibility of mitigating geological or environmental hazards, or other site complications that pose a threat to students' health and safety
- Extreme density of population within attendance areas where alternative sites would result in extensive long-term busing of students
- Geographic barriers, traffic congestion, or other constraints that would cause extreme financial hardship to the district to transport students

If the above criteria are met and the district wishes to pursue a school site of less than 70 percent of the recommended acreage requirements in CDE's *Guide*, then the district is required to demonstrate how the facilities will accommodate an adequate educational program, including physical education, as described in the district's adopted course of study. It is not automatic that CDE will approve a small school site if these criteria are met. CDE will still want to consider and determine whether the school site size is able to meet the educational policies of the state.

In order to obtain CDE approval of a school site that is less than 50 percent of the recommended coverage, the district will need to demonstrate to CDE the following:

- Compliance with Title 5 for building square footages, class sizes, and the provision of minimum essential facilities such as cafeterias, libraries, and multi-purpose rooms/gyms.
- Adequate and safe access to the site for students walking to and from school, student pick-up and drop-off, and bus loading and unloading (if busing is required).
- Adequate provision for staff parking or access to the site such as onsite parking, offsite parking, and/or the availability of public transportation.
- Adequate physical education, intramural, recess, and/or competitive athletic program areas provided on site, adjacent to the site, or in shared facilities with other schools or public/private spaces. These activities should be aligned with the California Recommended Physical Education Program.
- The need to locate schools within areas of the greatest student population densities and within residential areas.
- A schematic site plan showing site usage.
- Assurance of site safety using criteria for environmental toxic hazards, geological hazards, and railroad safety analysis as required for all school site approvals.
- Completion of CEQA as required for all school site approvals.

In the case of the Los Angeles Unified School District, there must also be compliance with the Rodriguez Consent Decree, which additionally recommends the following playground areas:

- Elementary
  - Up to 500 students 1.4 playground acres
  - Up to 750 students 1.7 playground acres
  - Up to 1,000 students 2.0 playground acres
  - Up to 1,250 students 2.3 playground acres
- Junior high/Middle school
  - Up to 2,400 students 6.0 playground acres
- High school
  - Up to 3,600 students 9.0 playground acres

Site size adjustments. In permitting small school sites, CDE does not abandon its site size requirements and formulas contained in the *Guide*, but rather makes adjustments in them to take into account the "unusual" factors facing the particular school district. For example, CDE will grant acreage credits to a school for the use of:

- Multi-story construction
- Underground or above-ground parking structure
- Rooftop play areas
- Fitness space
- Joint use or offsite use of field areas, parking, or educational spaces
- Shared athletic facilities

For multi-story construction, CDE will add the square footage of each floor above the first floor times a factor of 1.30 (30 percent increase), divided by 43,560 (square feet per acre), to the net usable acreage of the site. For underground or above ground parking structures, CDE will add the square footage of each floor to the net usable acreage of the site. School districts that incorporate roof-top play areas or fitness space into the design of school facilities will have the square footage of each roof-top play area added to the net usable acreage of the site.

CDE will grant acreage credits for school districts entering into joint use agreements with other local governmental entities or private enterprises for school space needs. *See* CDE Small School Site Worksheet (www.cde.ca.gov). This space can be either field areas, facilities for educational activities, or properties used for parking. The usable square footage of each joint use area shall be added to the net usable acreage of the site. CDE will also grant acreage credits to districts purchasing offsite property for the purpose of providing needed components of a school site, as long as the property is safe and accessible to the site. The usable square footage of each offsite space shall be added to the net usable acreage of the site.

School districts incorporating offsite shared athletic facilities into the physical education and competitive athletic program may also get acreage credit. Examples of such facilities include, but are not limited to, swimming pools,

CDE will grant acreage credits for school districts entering into joint use agreements with other local governmental entities or private enterprises for school space needs.

football stadiums, baseball/softball complexes, soccer fields, and tracks. The square footage of each offsite shared athletic field shall be added to the usable acreage of the site. CDE does require, however, that this component be incorporated into the district's Master Physical Education Specifications.

Playgrounds

California has established playground safety regulations, and school districts are responsible for inspecting, modernizing, maintaining, and developing play areas on school property. Health & Safety Code §§ 115725–115750; 22 C.C.R. § 65700 *et seq.*; The Playground Safety and Recycling Act of 1999 (Health & Safety Code § 115810 *et seq.*).

ASTM = American Society for Testing and Materials
CPSC = Consumer Product Safety Commission

The regulations cover the design, installation, inspection, maintenance, supervision where appropriate, and training for personnel involved in the design, installation, and maintenance of all playgrounds operated by public agencies or by any entity where the playground is open to the public. The regulations are based on the Consumer Product Safety Commission (CPSC) playground safety guidelines, and performance standards developed by the American Society for Testing and Materials (ASTM). The majority of the CPSC 1998 Handbook for Public Playground Safety and the ASTM F1487-98 Standard are incorporated, by reference, into the new regulation, and their recommendations are to be considered mandatory requirements in the State of California. 22 C.C.R. § 65710. Thus, where the Handbook says "it is recommended," the state regulations require that it be read "it is required."

Among the key requirements of the playground safety requirements is the duty to hire certified inspectors to conduct training and upgrade playgrounds to meet safety design criteria. Playgrounds installed between January 1, 1994 and December 31, 1999 are not subject to the regulation. These playgrounds are not subject to the requirement to upgrade until 15 years after the date of installation. Health & Safety Code § 115730 (b)(1)(2). They are, however, required to meet the current standard of care.

For example, initial inspections of all school playgrounds by a certified playground safety inspector who is trained to recognize risks and hazards and can recommend to operators what changes should be made to provide maximum safety for children should have been conducted by October 1, 2000.

Also, new equipment is required to be assembled and installed by, or under, direct supervision of an *authorized manufacturer's representative.* Alternatively, prior to its first use, the equipment must be inspected by a certified playground safety inspector, and the inspector must certify in writing that the equipment is in compliance with the requirements of the regulation. 22 C.F.R. § 65730.

All public agencies operating playgrounds are required to upgrade their playgrounds by replacement or improvement as necessary to meet the regulations to the extent that state funds (through state bonds or other means) are made available specifically for that purpose. For example, section 115810 of the Health and Safety Code—The Playground Safety and Recycling Act of 1999—provides for a matching grant program. This grant program can be interpreted as funds being made available specifically for the purpose of upgrading or improving playgrounds.

A *comprehensive maintenance program* shall be developed for each playground. The program shall consist of regular inspections, accident and injury reporting, and documentation of all maintenance and inspection activities. Training and supervision of district personnel involved in the design, installation, and maintenance of a playground is required. 22 C.C.R. § 65750.

School districts are required to design or redesign playgrounds, locate or relocate playground equipment and routes of access to and from playgrounds, and surface or resurface portions of playgrounds to comply with the guidelines and standards regarding critical height, fall heights for equipment, accessibility, etc. 22 C.C.R. § 65720.

chapter 5

Construction

At this stage, the district has been through the preliminary planning process and has succeeded in obtaining funding for the project. It has also completed all the necessary environmental investigations, successfully completed the CEQA process, and has obtained all necessary entitlements and permits for the project. Although the district is in the home stretch, the race is not over. The next stage in this process is the construction phase, which presents its own unique set of challenges both in terms of planning and implementation. The purpose of this chapter is to identify those challenges and to provide guidance to those in the school district who are tasked with the responsibility of planning and managing the construction process.

    A number of tasks must be completed to achieve a successful school construction project. The first is to select the type of project delivery method to be used, and second is to form the team to implement the project delivery plan. If it hasn't already done so during the Ed Specs or planning stages, as discussed in chapter 3, and depending upon the type of delivery method selected, the district will need to select its designer, typically an architect, to execute a design and prepare the construction documents for the project and to marshall that design through the appropriate agencies (*e.g.*, OPSC, DSA, etc.) in order to obtain the necessary design approvals. The district will also have to determine the method by which it will manage the construction of the project, either with the in-house facilities department personnel or by employing an outside project or construction manager. The district must then advertise for bids, select its contractor or contractors to construct the project, and manage the work of the contractor(s) through completion. The ultimate goals are to complete the district's project, consistent with the plans and specifications, on schedule and within budget, without any significant construction claims. There are few construction projects that are as exciting or meaningful as constructing a new school facility to serve both students currently enrolled in the district and generations to come. The discussion which follows will provide the district with the fundamentals for achieving these goals.

DSA = Division of State
        Architect
OPSC = Office of Public
        School Construction

Construction Team

Ideally, during the planning and site selection phase, most of the members of the district's construction team will have already been assembled. At the Construction phase, the district requires an architect, and may require a program manager, project manager, or construction manager, as described in chapter 3. Depending upon the project delivery method selected, the district may now have to add several new members to its team to take it through the detailed design and construction process. Some of those potential team members are discussed below.

Program Manager

More and more frequently, particularly where a district has a large bond construction program involving several different construction projects, the district will retain the services of a program manager. The role of the program manager is to assist the district with the development of the design and construction master plan. The program manager can ensure maximum involvement of qualified designers, contractors and suppliers. This would include developing the scopes of work and schedules for the development of the design and construction of the various projects, and developing their corresponding budgets. Thereafter, the program manager assists the distirct with the selection of the project architect and construction manager (if any), and provides oversight of the program through its completion.

A program manager should act as a single point of responsibility and accountability to assist the district in the control of cost, schedules, design, and quality. The program manager takes responsibility for the overall consistency and continuity of the district's interests. Program and project managers are best selected based on qualifications, not price.

Project Manager

When a district is planning a construction effort or project it may choose to hire a consultant to manage the overall planning and implementation of the project if it does not have in-house staff resources to perform this task or to augment its staff. The project manager acts as the district's agent to manage the planning and allocation of funding for the project, and to oversee and manage the selection of the designers, construction managers, and construction contractors. His or her ultimate responsibility is to ensure that the district's project is properly planned and implemented in accordance with the program budget and schedule.

Project Architect

Depending upon the project delivery system or method selected, the district will usually have to retain the services of an architect to develop the design for the project. The architect is typically selected pursuant to a competitive proposal process and is involved in developing the design, obtaining the necessary design approvals, issuing the plans and specifications for construction, advising the district in connection with the award of the construction contract, responding to submittals and questions relating to the design from the construction contractor and closing out the project.

If the district selects the "Design/Bid/Build" delivery system for its project, it will be responsible for a complete and accurate project design. Since design problems are one of the most common causes of "troubled projects," sufficient care must be taken in selecting an architect and ensuring the design is complete before construction of the project begins. Moreover, because of the unique nature of school construction in California, it is advisable to retain an architectural firm that has experience designing schools in California.

If the district selects a design/build project delivery system, the district's architect's role will be more limited and may include developing a conceptual design or performance specifications to be the basis of the detailed design which will be developed by the design/builder. On design/build projects, a district may also retain the services of an architect to monitor the quality of the design/builder's design and its conformance with the conceptual design or performance specifications.

Construction Manager

Depending upon whether the district has sufficient experienced staff to manage the construction process alone, it may need to retain the services of a construction manager for each of its projects. Education Code sections 17019.3 and 17070.98 permit a district to retain these services. The role of the construction manager is to act as the district's agent in the management of the construction contractor. The construction manager may be involved in performing:

- Constructability reviews of the design before the project goes out for bid
- Developing bid packages and managing the bid process for the project
- Advising the district on the selection of the successful bidder
- Developing and implementing procedures for the construction management process, including the development of a document control system
- Overseeing and communicating with the contractor(s) during construction to insure that the project is built per plans and specification and according to the approved project schedule
- Closing out the project

In essence, the construction manager's job is to assure that the construction process achieves the three goals of construction listed above. To some extent, the roles of the architect, construction manager, program manager, and project manager may overlap. Consequently, particular care needs to be taken in drafting the contracts for these team members to avoid overlapping and contradictory scopes of work that can create problems for the management of the project.

Construction Contractors

Although some project owners think of their contractors more as adversaries than as members of their team, this type of thinking often leads to problems that could be easily avoided. An important thing for a district to consider is that for the project to succeed, the contractor has to be given the chance to succeed. Therefore, it is not prudent to attempt to impose all of the project risks on the contractor. Rather, the district must ensure that it has done a good job completing all of

Since design problems are one of the most common causes of troubled projects, sufficient care must be taken in selecting an architect and ensuring the design is complete before construction begins.

✍ **practice tip**

In order to ensure that the role of each team member is properly coordinated, it's prudent to develop a Responsibility Matrix that identifies specific responsibilities assigned to each party. Often, because each task has some overlap, the matrix should separately identify the party with "oversight," "primary," and "support" responsibility.

the tasks that come before the construction begins (permitting, design, etc.). Additionally, a district must have the infrastructure in place to support the contractor once construction begins.

Design/Builder

Pursuant to recently enacted legislation, school districts have much greater leeway in selecting the design/build delivery system for school projects. The design/builder is responsible for both the design and construction of the school facility. Although some larger firms have both design and construction capabilities, for many projects, the design/builder will be a joint venture of an architectural firm and a construction contractor. The design/builder will take the district's conceptual design or performance specifications and develop a detailed design for the actual construction. The design/builder is responsible for the project design together with the construction of the project.

Inspector of Record

School districts are required to hire an "inspector of record" (IOR) for their construction projects. Educ. Code §§ 17311, 17309, 81141; 51 Ops. Cal. Atty. Gen. 135. Although employed by the district, the inspector of record works under the direction of the design professional in charge (usually the architect, although sometimes the civil or structural engineer or program/project manager), and is subject to supervision by the DSA. The district should give the IOR clear instructions on who to report to. The role of the IOR is to inspect the project to insure that the construction complies with the DSA approved plans and specifications that govern school construction in California.

The role of the IOR is to inspect the project to insure that the construction complies with the DSA approved plans and specifications that govern school construction in California.

Selection of the IOR. Special care must be given to selecting the IOR. An inspector of record must be qualified, have passed DSA-administered inspector examinations, and be DSA-certified. A list of DSA certified inspectors can be obtained from the DSA web site (**www.dsa.ca.gov**). Additionally, prior to work an any individual project, the DSA-certified inspector must also be approved for that particular project.

It is essential that the IOR be certified by the DSA for the class of construction used in the project.

It is essential that the IOR be certified by the DSA for the class of construction used in the project. The four classes of certification are:

- **Class 1.** The new construction or alteration of buildings in excess of 2000 square feet in which the primary structural elements are other than wood frame, shear wall construction. These systems include masonry or concrete shear wall, steel braced frames, and concrete or steel moment resisting frames.

- **Class 2.** The new construction or alteration of buildings in excess of 2000 square feet in which the primary structural system is wood frame, shear wall construction. These projects may be single-level or multi-level, and may contain some incidental masonry, concrete, and/or steel construction. Class 2 IORs can also be used on new construction or alteration of buildings under 2000 square feet in which the primary structural system is concrete, masonry, or steel construction.

- **Class 3.** The new construction or alteration of single story buildings less than 2000 square feet with conventional spread footings and wood, shear wall construction.
- **Class 4.** Site installation of manufactured, single-story modular buildings.

Unlike the architect, the IOR can be hired directly without a competitive process. However, if the district does not have an established relationship with an IOR, a request for qualifications should be issued and the qualifications and recommendations of several potential IORs should be reviewed prior to selection.

Prior to the work commencing on the project, a DSA Form DSA-5, Project Inspector Qualification Record, must be completed by the district and submitted to the DSA. If neither the architect nor the structural engineer for the project are familiar with the selected IOR, he or she will need to have his or her qualifications verified through an interview with one or both of them.

At least ten days prior to start of construction, the district must supply Form DSA-5, the Inspector's Qualification Form, to the DSA. The form must be signed by the inspector, the school district representative, the design professional in charge, and the structural engineer delegated responsibility for observation of construction. Along with Form DSA-5, the district should also submit Form DSA-102, Contract Information Sheet.

DSA recommends that the school district and the responsible design professional(s) conduct a personal interview with the inspector before signing the Form DSA-5. The following points should be considered:

- Inspector's knowledge of his/her role and responsibilities, job duties, and limits of authority
- Characteristics of inspector necessary to develop and maintain satisfactory working relationships. Such characteristics include effective communication skills, patience, determination, consistency, and the ability to exercise sound judgment
- Inspector's physical ability and stamina to inspect all construction and to maintain a responsive presence on the job
- Inspector's knowledge of construction methods, building materials, material testing/special inspection procedures, and building codes applicable to the project
- Inspector's ability to read and readily comprehend the requirements of the project plans and specifications

The DSA field engineer's approval of the proposed inspector is based on the following criteria:

- Proper relationship between the class of the inspector's certification and the projects classification
- Inspector's work experience
- Inspector's workload and time commitment to the project
- Utilization of assistant inspector(s)
- Satisfactory DSA performance ratings on previous school construction projects
- Verification that inspector is employed by the school district

If the district does not have an established relationship with an IOR, a request for qualifications should be issued and the qualifications and recommendations of several potential IORs should be reviewed prior to selection.

DSA recommends that the school district and the responsible design professionals conduct a personal interview with the inspector before signing Form DSA-5.

Each of these members of the district's project team are critical to a successful project. It is essential that the role of each be clearly defined in the contract documents which govern their services. When their roles are properly coordinated, and the district does the things it must do at the front end of a school construction project, the chance of achieving a successful project will be significantly increased.

Selection of Construction Legal Counsel

It is important that the district have competent and experienced construction legal counsel on its project team.

Besides insuring that you have retained the services of experienced construction professionals, it is also important that the district have competent and experienced construction legal counsel on its project team. Legal counsel should be involved in reviewing the invitation for bids to insure that it complies with the myriad sets of requirements discussed above. In addition, if there is a challenge to the bid, a withdrawal of a bid, or substitution of a listed contractor, legal counsel should also be consulted. Additionally, legal counsel often is involved in the negotiation and drafting of the district's contracts with its project team members (designer, construction manager, contractor, etc.). As previously mentioned, due to potential overlapping responsibilities, these contracts need to be coordinated so that each team member's scope of work and project responsibilities are clearly defined. While projects share many of the same characteristics, each contract needs to address the unique conditions that arise with each project. Finally, the district should consult with legal counsel if issues arise during the performance of construction. Project counseling may involve such issues as change orders, payment application requests, compliance with contract schedule requirements, insurance issues, and project closeout.

It is in the best interest of the district to retain experienced construction counsel who understands the construction process and who will be able to recognize the signs of a troubled project.

The practice of construction law is a specialized area of the law, particularly with respect to public works contracting. General practitioners are often not familiar with the intricacies of this area of the law. It is in the best interest of the district to retain experienced construction counsel who understands the construction process and who will be able to recognize the signs of a troubled project. It is also recommended that, at the start of any significant project, the district's construction counsel meet with the district staff or consultants who will be managing the project to go over the construction contract and insure that the district complies with its obligations, and requires the architect or contractor to do so as well. Legal counsel can be consulted on an as needed basis; however, they should always be consulted when the district believes that the project may be in trouble—*e.g.*, significant contractor delays, significant design problems, contractor is significantly over budget, etc. These are all signs that should trigger a meeting of the entire project team, including counsel, to determine the best manner to proceed.

What Is the Owner's Role?

The district is the owner of the school project site. The district has specific duties and a specific role as owner of the construction project to:

- Define the various scopes of work for the project
- Define the roles of each of the participants in the project

- Obtain sufficient funding for the project
- Establish a project budget and communicate it to project team
- Provide the project participants with all the information in its possession that will be relevant to the planning, design, and construction of the project
- Cooperate with all the project participants
- Make sure that the project is properly funded and the district has procedures in place for the timely payment of the project participants
- Establish clear lines of authority and communication
- Respond promptly to project team members
- Protect its public funds—insure that it receives what it pays for

Project Delivery Methods

Unfortunately, getting a school designed and built is a little more complicated than buying a house. The process can take several years—consultants are hired, committees established, detailed bid documents executed, and the construction contract administered. It requires active participation on the part of the district and its consultants, and there are hundreds of decisions to be made. How this process gets done is referred to as the project delivery method, and for public school construction there are four primary project delivery options, each with several permutations that can significantly alter its characteristics.

Delivery Method No. 1— Design/Bid/Build

This is the most typical method of designing and constructing public schools and has been used for many decades. The three-step process includes:

- **Design.** The district contracts with an architect to design the school and prepare construction documents.
- **Bid.** The district publicly bids the project following all procedural requirements in the Public Contract Code, identifying the successful, responsive, and responsible low bidder. This establishes the construction price and the contractor responsible for building the project.
- **Build.** The district contracts with the lowest responsible bidder for construction of the project.

Potential downside of design/bid/build

Time. The design, bid, build method has three separate, distinct phases that follow each other in sequence. First the design is completed, then the project is bid, and finally construction begins. The duration to complete the process may extend longer than if the design/build delivery method is utilized (discussed below), particularly if the design has any problems prior to awarding the construction contract.

Incomplete or defective plans and specifications. Although the design, bid, build delivery method is the most frequently utilized in public construction, there are some risks inherent with this delivery system. First, it requires the design to be complete and coordinated prior to the time of the bid, which may add to the overall project duration (as compared to the design/build delivery system, where project design and construction can to some extent overlap). If the design

✍ **practice tip**

The selection of the project delivery method must happen as early as possible, but no later than the construction document phase, so that the bid documents can accurately reflect the contractor's responsibilities.

The design, bid, build method has three separate, distinct phases that follow in sequence—first the design is completed, then the project is bid, and finally construction begins.

SAB = State Allocation Board
CM = Construction Manager

The Spearin Doctrine

A district selecting the project delivery system called Design/Bid/Build is obligated to provide a contractor with a complete and accurate project design. Referred to as the "Spearin Doctrine," this rule of law is named for the federal case that first spelled out the idea. The doctrine, as adopted by the California courts, provides that a project owner must warrant the accuracy of the project's plans and specifications. *Souza & McCue Constr. Co. v. Superior Court* (1962) 57 Cal. 2d 508.

Additionally, a district may not require a contractor to assume responsibility for the completeness of the plans and specs (except for design/build projects). Pub. Contract Code § 1104. Therefore, to the extent that the project plans and specifications are incomplete, inaccurate, or uncoordinated, the district will likely be responsible for any "extras" that the contractor may claim arose from problems with the design.

While the district may be able to assert a claim against its architect for these problems, care must be taken to insure that the design is accurate and complete prior to bidding the project. Note: Under the Design/Build project delivery system, the design/builder is responsible for the design, and the Spearin Doctrine does not apply.

Pub. Contract Code § 1104

is not complete prior to the bid phase, the district will be subject to changes and claims that will likely be found to be meritorious. To minimize this risk, a school district should begin the design process well in advance of the construction date to allow the design team adequate time to prepare the documents, and should perform a design check to insure that the design is complete prior to soliciting bids. Additionally, the district should consider having a "constructability analysis" performed which focuses on whether the plans are "buildible" from the contractor's perspective, and insures that the project will not be held up by omissions or problems with the design.

Inability to select the most qualified contractor. Since the law mandates award of the bid to the construction contractor who submits the lowest bid, cost instead of quality or experience is the determining factor in the selection of who will build the project. Pub. Contract Code § 20162. To some extent, this may be mitigated by adopting a pre-qualification program (discussed below), which assists the district in identifying a body of competent contractors to bid on its projects. Because a district cannot pick and chose from the bids, prior to award of the contract, care should be taken to check the lowest bid for any anomalies that would suggest that the bidder may have missed something substantial in calculating the bid that would result in the contractor failing to complete the project successfully.

Pressures of competitive bidding. In the past, contractors would include contingencies in their bids to cover changes and omissions during construction and most errors found in the bid documents. In today's highly competitive and price conscious environment, to bid successfully, contractors cannot afford to include any meaningful buffer in their bids. Additionally, contractors lower their margins to give themselves the best chance of wining the bid. These factors put substantial pressure on contractors to look for opportunities to generate change orders and to artificially increase the cost of changes after bid time.

These pressures can create an adversarial relationship between both the owner and the contractor and the architect and the contractor. The more errors and mistakes the contractor can identify in the contract documents, the more money a contractor can make on changes. Of course, not all general contractors approach projects in this way, but it is becoming more prevalent. Under the low bid contracting process, a contractor may be less motivated to develop a positive relationship with the owner or architect because its next job depends only on price, not quality or performance.

Significant use of staff time. Management of a construction project requires a large amount of time and effort from school district staff. This method works fine when the owner's staff can take on this added responsibility. However, at a time when money for maintenance and facilities staff is scarce, this can be a significant drain on school district resources. Most construction funding sources do not allow money to be used to hire additional district staff to handle the day-to-day administration a construction project requires from its owner (as opposed to hiring outside program management, project management, or construction management services for construction projects). Some of this added responsibility can be contracted to the architect, however responsibilities must be clearly defined, and the owner must review all proposed change order costs and credits to avoid any appearance of conflict of interest on the part of the architect. The construction management method (discussed below) allows more latitude to hire design and construction professionals to oversee the process on behalf of the school district.

Delivery Method No. 2—Construction Management

The second delivery method that public agencies frequently utilize is construction management with multiple prime contractors (referred to as CM multi-prime). Govt. Code § 4525. The four steps to this approach are:

- **Design (architect).** The district contracts with an architect to plan and design the project and help select the construction manager.
- **Project manager/Construction manager.** The district next contracts with a construction manager (CM) to provide a variety of pre-construction services. The extent of preconstruction services provided by construction managers varies greatly, and can include project plan review, design constructability review, cost estimating, and verification of existing conditions and value engineering. Whatever the service, the construction manager's team should have extensive experience with similar school project types and have strong references. Bringing a construction manager on to the project early in the design process is preferable so that maximum benefit of the construction manager's experience can be realized.
- **Bid.** The construction manager manages the bidding process by bidding the project to multiple prime bidders following all requirements in the public contract code (Pub. Contract Code § 100 *et seq.*), identifying the successful low bidders in each bid category, and recommending award to the lowest responsible bidder. Upon award, the district enters into separate contracts with each of the prime contractors. This, along with the construction management fee, establishes the construction price.
- **Build (contractors and CM).** The district contracts with the lowest prime bidders for construction of the project. The CM manages the construction process.

Advantages and disadvantages of CM/multi-prime system

- **Collaboration and cooperation.** This method has the advantage of requiring collaboration between the architect and construction manager before bidding and construction, and therefore requires more cooperation. However, the possibility of overlapping responsibilities, duplicated efforts, and design disagreements exist. This requires extra effort up front to define responsibilities in the parties' respective contract documents, and to clarify that division of responsibility between the architect and the construction manager at the beginning of the project. Questions should be asked such as,

Successful Construction Management Examples

Recently, school districts have succesfully used the CM multiple prime process. What made it successful?

- Competitive and thorough consultant selection progress
- Thorough reference checks of all major team members—both the company and the individuals assigned by the company to the project
- CM's had a proven track record (preferably as a general contractor) with years of successful public school construction experience
- A district representative was actively involved with the process
- The district contracted separately with the architect and the CM
- Multiple prime bid packages were publicly bid

General vs. Multiple Prime Contractors

The typical method of contracting for construction services involves the district hiring a general contractor to oversee and coordinate the construction of the project. The general contractor retains subcontractors to perform the various components of the construction, and is responsible for the subcontractors' performance.

If the multi-prime approach is utilized, the district enters into seperate contracts with each of the major trade contractors (civil, framing, mechanical, electrical, etc.), and the district, or its construction manager, is responsible for coordinating the work of the multi-prime contractors. ■

Construction Manager as Agent vs. Construction Manager at Risk

A district can choose between two alternatives when utilizing a CM/multi-prime delivery system: in the first, the construction manager acts as the district's agent; in the second, the manager assumes responsibility and is "at risk" for the successful completion of the project.

As agent for the district, a construction manager acts on the district's behalf to oversee and execute the process. Typically, the cost of changes above the contract price is the district's responsibility. With this model, it's the job of the construction manager to minimize these costs and deliver the specified quality on schedule and for the lowest cost possible. In this situation, most construction-related costs are "open book."

By contrast, an "at risk" construction manager enters into a Guaranteed Maximum Price (GMP) contract with the district and has responsibility for coordinating the work and any cost overruns. Under certain circumstances, the at-risk construction manager pays these costs out of his or her own pocket, protecting the district from the additional expense of project changes. With this approach, the district must proactively manage the interface with the construction manager, taking extra care to spell out the responsibilities of each party when drafting the contract.

Before entering into a GMP contract, the district should ensure that all internal documentation is current and easily accessible. Once a GMP has been agreed upon, the district should tightly control or forbid any changes to scope. This will ensure that the construction manager has no basis for change orders.

At first glance, the at-risk relationship may appear to be the best protection for the district, but often that's not the case. An agreement with these conditions may, in fact, be more costly than it's worth. An at-risk arrangement can easily put a construction management team on the defensive, so that it looks out for itself first rather than the best interests of the district. Since several parties often share responsibility for added costs, a situation can develop where the team tries to assign blame rather than getting the project built. In addition, shifting risk to the construction manager usually results in higher fees for management, which may not be offset by the construction cost savings of an at-risk agreement. ■

"How much influence should the construction manager have over the architect's design?" "Who is responsible for cost estimating?" "How will the bid packages be divided up, and by whom?" "Who is authorized to communicate on behalf of the owner with the contractor?" "Who issues change orders?" "Who responds to the contractors RFIs?" "Who approves progress payments?" "Who determines when the Notice of Completion should be issued?" Because of the potential overlap of responsibilities between the architect, construction manager, and contractors, unless the responsibilities of each party are clearly defined in their contracts, project costs may increase. However, with an experienced team, the process will likely run more smoothly and the chance of construction litigation is reduced. However, if the construction manager team is not experienced or does not work well together, the risk of litigation and cost overruns is increased.

Many of these problems can be avoided by hiring a construction manager who is also an experienced program manager. By providing a single point of accountability, the program manager can serve as the bridge for designers and contractors. This can help the district avoid the adversarial blame game that is too prevalent between the architect and contractor when the construction documents have discrepancies. A program manager can help the district clearly define the roles of all team members and manage the process to control cost, schedules, and quality.

- **Qualifications-based selection.** Another benefit is that an experienced and capable construction manager can be selected based on his or her qualifications rather than on the basis of the lowest bid. Depending on the terms of the contract between the school district and the construction manager, he or she can have a much more positive and supportive relationship with the project team.

- **Experience.** In contrast to architects and contractors, specific licensure for construction managers does not exist, and the range of quality is significant. (Note, however, that they must either be a licensed architect, registered engineer, or a licensed general contractor with experience in project management. Govt. Code §§ 4525(e), 4529.5.) Therefore, before a construction manager is retained by a school district, a thorough screening, interview, and reference check of the individuals to be assigned to the project should be performed. Many construction managers do not have the experience and expertise to build public schools.

- **Staffing.** Another advantage of this delivery method is that the construction manager provides the majority of management oversight normally undertaken by district staff. This system is particularly useful when the district's facilities staff does not have the capacity or capabilities to manage a given project. During construction, the construction manager functions very much like a general contractor, overseeing the work, coordinating different trades, insuring construction quality, and processing payments. However, the district still has multiple direct contracts with each of the prime contractors (or construction trades) for construction, rather than one contract with the general contractor.

Delivery Method No. 3— Design/Build

Design/build is a process that to a certain extent establishes a single entity to provide both design and construction services. Not until the passage of AB 1402, (Educ. Code §§ 17250.10–17250.50) was this method readily available to California school districts if they wanted to obtain construction funding from OPSC. However, with the passage of AB 1402, for many construction projects, districts now have the ability to utilize this construction delivery method.

Other government agencies have used this project delivery method for years. The law allows a district to choose one of two ways to execute a design/build project—competitive bid or best value. Both of these methods require a pre-qualification of design/build teams based on requirements established by the Department of Industrial Relations.

Alternative no. 1—Competitive bid design/build. Educ. Code § 17250.25(c)(1). Under this alternative, the district first hires a program architect to provide preliminary or conceptual design documents, called "bridging documents" for bidding to design/build teams.

Next the district establishes the project selection criteria that is published in the RFQ/RFP, and, based on that criteria, selects the best qualified design/build team to complete plans, obtain agency approvals, and construct the project. The successful team can be selected on lowest price or other qualifying criteria. However, an architect who helps the district develop the request for proposals or assists in the developing selection criteria may not participate in bidding for the project. Educ. Code § 17250.[1] Therefore, two

1. However, the pre-existing proscription against the project architect having a contractual relationship with the design/builder is made inapplicable to design/build procurements. *See* § 17250.25(a)(3).

Developer-Built School

A school district may enter into a joint venture relationship for the purpose of a school construction project. This alternative method involves a construction arrangement whereby the district enters into a private developer's agreement.

The district defines the preliminary performance criteria for the school facility, and the developer provides input into the design and construction by entering into an agreement with a single source, a design/builder, to design and construct the school. The district may apply to SAB for funding. Educ. Code § 17061.

The district may also utilize an RFQ and RFP process to select and enter into the joint venture agreement with the developer. Educ. Code § 17062.

The final agreement must be reviewed and approved by SAB in order for the joint venture to receive funding for the school portion of the project. Educ. Code § 17063. ■

The Biggest Misconception of Design/Build

Because design/build construction shifts the majority of the design, construction, and cost risks to the design builder, some districts believe that the amount of oversight required is minimal. This view is at best naive.

Regardless of method, construction requires active owner participation in the form of clear direction and timely decisions. Considerable district oversight is necessary with budgeting, scheduling, monitoring work of consultants, progress payments, design and construction quality, and insuring that the district gets what it paid for. ∎

GMP = Guaranteed maximum price

separate architecture firms will be responsible for separate portions of the design service that are typically provided by one firm. Subsequent to the selection of the design builder, the district may hire the program architect to review the development of the plans and act as the district's agent to oversee compliance with the design during construction.

By statute, this design/build law sunsets on January 1, 2007, unless extended by the legislature.

Alternative no. 2—Best value method. Educ. Code § 17250.25(c)(1). Utilizing this design/build alternative, the district conducts a competitive selection process that selects one team to provide both design and construction services. A single point of responsibility is established for the entire project. The district solicits proposals from design/build teams requesting that they each answer a series of questions which require them to provide information including team references, experience of team members, financial information, and agreements they can work within the established budget and provide the building program.

The district ranks the proposals based on objective criteria. The rating system should be fair and defensible in the event of a protest. After the teams are ranked, the district enters into negotiations with the top ranked team.

The selected team then provides the district with a proposed fee to execute preliminary design documents and a guaranteed maximum price (GMP) to complete the project through construction. The district has the option at the conclusion of the negotiations of the guaranteed maximum price to continue with the selected team, or, if the price is unacceptable, to negotiate with the next most qualified proposal or solicit other proposals to complete the project.

The other option available to the district is establishing a predetermined price it will pay for preliminary design documents in its request for proposals.

If the district agrees to the GMP, the design/build team continues, completes plans, obtains agency approvals, and constructs the project within the GMP. This method allows the various design-build team members (architect, engineers, contractor, and subcontractors) to work together with the district to develop a project from inception to completion, without a change of team members. Due to its potential for greater efficiency, it appears that this alternative will be best for districts interested in using the design/build methods.

Design/build was established to shift more of the risk and design control involved in construction projects to the design/build team. In contrast to the design/bid/build method, the design builder is responsible for both the design and construction of the facility. So when there is an error or omission involving the construction or design, the resolution is not the responsibility of the district, but rather of the design/build team.

Other common sources of added costs may still be the district's responsibility, including unforeseen conditions, changes in scope, or project delay due to lack of district-supplied information.

The design/build process allows a team structure for fast-track construction that involves an earlier construction start, prior to the design being completed. This method has some inherent risks, but provides the benefit of completing the project sooner.

Potential disadvantages of design/build project delivery. Under AB 1402 (Educ. Code § 17250), in order to utilize this project delivery method the value of the design and construction costs for a particular project must exceed $10,000,000. Therefore, design/build cannot be utilized for smaller projects. In addition, because many firms do not have both design and construction capabilities in house, design builders often are ad hoc joint ventures or partnerships of a design firm and a construction firm. This requires the two firms to work together, often without any past experience. Moreover, the number of firms that are experienced with design/build construction is much smaller than those who can do traditional design/bid/build construction. Therefore, the argument has been made that the process is not as competitive as the more traditional delivery systems. Finally, Education Code section 17250 *et seq.* imposes additional responsibilities on districts before they can use this delivery system (*e.g.*, written findings justifying use of design/build, pre-qualification requirements, limitation on the numbers of design/build projects, etc.).

Delivery Method No. 4—
Lease-Lease Back

Two sections within the Education Code provide a conceptual departure from other delivery methods in that they allow a developer to finance, build, own, and lease completed facilities to public school districts. Although previous versions of these delivery methods have been in the Education Code since the 1970s, they have recently gained a lot of attention for the benefits they provide school districts.

Although the Education Code has had versions of the lease-lease back delivery method since the 1970s, they have recently gained a lot of attention for the benefits they provide school districts.

Methodology. The first of these methods, described in section 17406 of Article 2 the Education Code, is more commonly referred to as a lease lease-back development. In this scenario, the school district leases real property it owns to a developer through a site lease for a minimum rent of one dollar per year. The developer subsequently constructs the facility and then leases the facility back to the school district through a facility lease (hence the term "lease lease-back").

A second but more obscure delivery method is found in Education Code section 17407 of Article 2. This delivery method is very similar to section 17406, but with two significant differences. First, unlike section 17406, section 17407 requires that the developer own the designated site upon which the building will be constructed; therefore, both the site and completed facilities are leased to the district under a single lease. Technically, this process is not a lease lease-back; however, it is often included in the context of a lease lease-back discussion. The second difference found in section 17407 is the requirement that the school district must advertise for bids prior to awarding the contract. Both delivery methods provide that title to the facilities must vest with the district upon lease expiration or in the event the lease is terminated early through the exercise of a purchase option. The Education Code limits the terms of all leases for both methods to 40 years.

A second delivery method, found in Education Code section 17407, requires that the developer own the site and that the school district advertise for bids prior to awarding the contract.

These construction financing options are often misconstrued as forms of "design-build" because the district is less involved in the construction contracting. In its simplest terms, design-build contracting, which is addressed in separate section of the Education Code, involves the consolidation of the architect's contract with the construction contract. The assumption that lease lease-back developments are a form of design-build is incorrect. If the district seeks to enter into a lease to build a "school building" (as defined under § 17283), section 17402 of the Code requires that the district must first have the school designed and then approved by the Division of State Architect. This precludes the ability to structure the lease lease-back contract as a form of design-build. However, if the district desires to build administrative offices or other facilities not falling within the definition of a "school building," there appears to be no prohibition for entering into a lease lease-back arrangement prior to DSA approval. Nonetheless, it is still prudent to consult with the DSA and legal counsel prior to entering into such contractual arrangements.

Another misconception is that, since the developer is technically the owner of the building and a private entity, he or she is exempt from labor requirements found in the other delivery methods school districts use. Section 17424 clearly establishes that, when developing under a lease lease-back arrangement, the developer must comply with general prevailing wage rates as established by the Department of Industrial Relations. A labor compliance program should always be put in place when using the lease lease-back method.

Eligibility for state funding. State funding for the acquisition of school facilities that are privately owned and financed is granted under Education Code section 17072.35. This section establishes that state grant funding for new construction may be used to acquire an existing government or privately owned building, or a privately financed school building, and for the necessary costs of converting the government or privately owned building for public school use.

Historically, the Office of Public School Construction (OPSC) has made the determination as to the eligibility of any given lease lease-back development for state funding on a case-by-case basis. To date, neither the State Allocation Board (SAB) nor the OPSC has taken a position on when the use of lease arrangements under sections 17406 and 17407 is appropriate, or when exemption from competitive bidding generally required by the Public Contract Code is valid. It has been the position of the OPSC that the obligation to determine the appropriate and legitimate use of any contract delivery method permitted in law rests with the school district and its governing board. They have also made it clear that the granting of state funds in any given project does not constitute a validation of the legality of the contractual arrangements used for that project. Thus, the onus for assuring legal compliance to the Education Code falls solely upon the school district.

Lease-lease back advantages and disadvantages. The benefits of this delivery approach include:

- **Immediate funds for school projects.** When a district does not have funding for a needed school, this approach allows the district to immediately begin school construction anyway, because the developer funds the project. The lease lease-back arrangement can be either a bridge or a longer term financing mechanism.

- **Guaranteed price.** The district is able to negotiate a fixed price for the lease and, if necessary, the purchase price of the project. Unanticipated costs are the responsibility of the developer, not the school district.

If a district wants to build administrative offices or other facilities not falling within the definition of a "school building," it should be possible to enter into a lease lease-back arrangement prior to DSA approval.

When a district does not have funding for a needed school, the lease lease-back approach allows the district to immediately begin school construction anyway.

- **Risk reduction for the school district.** Because the developer guarantees performance and completion of the project, the district is relieved of much of the financial and legal risks of construction.
- **Increased motivation for performance.** Because the developer takes on most of the completion risks, there is a high level of motivation to manage costs and meet deadlines.
- **Single point of contact.** The developer/contractor acts as a single point of responsibility, making the process more efficient for the district.
- **Cost savings.** Districts often believe that when a reputable and qualified developer is used, privatization of the development process creates efficiencies and cost savings not within the reach of many governmental agencies. This may include value engineering, or the ability of the developer to negotiate with subcontractors in a manner not available to a public agency. Further, the process can reduce the number of consultants and resources required by the district, since the developer takes on the role of both project funding and delivery.

Districts often believe that when a reputable and qualified developer is used, privatization of the development process creates efficiencies and cost savings not within the reach of many governmental agencies.

- **Optimization of staff resources.** Since the developer takes on an expanded role in oversight of the project, this method can also unburden and/or augment over-worked district staff.
- **Professional expertise.** Many school districts do not have experience with large construction projects. This way, the developers, who have demonstrated experience in similar projects, take responsibility for coordination of the project, obtaining required approvals, and project scheduling.
- **Team approach.** Many districts that have used this approach believe that lease lease-back allows a team approach, with the district playing an integral part. The district, developer, and contractor all have an interest in project completion on time and within budget.

Many districts believe that the lease lease-back method allows a team approach, with the district playing an integral part.

- **Known Contractor.** The lease lease-back allows selection of a contractor based upon record of success, references from previous clients, and financial strength, as opposed to a "lowest bid."
- **Larger list of interested contractors.** The increasing number of lease lease-back projects is drawing contractors and subcontractors from other industries that are normally not interested in participating in the low bid process, but are interested in the negotiated contracts as permitted by the lease lease-back process. This brings new, qualified contractors into the school construction arena.

Although there are many benefits to delivery using these methods, there are also potential challenges in their use, including:

- **Added costs.** Added costs are incurred due to the developer's fee and costs associated with any financing the developer needs for the project. This includes carried (capitalized) interest during construction.
- **Additional contract documentation.** The introduction of leases into the process also creates more documents; however, this is mitigated through the district not being a party to the construction contract, which is held between the developer and the contractor.

- **Future rent payments must be budgeted.** In addition, the district must plan for payment of rent if the facilities lease does not terminate shortly after construction.

Conclusion. California is but one of many states that have begun to use the lease lease-back delivery method at an increasing rate. As addressed herein, there are numerous benefits to this process, including access to immediate school construction funds, guaranteed price and delivery date, professional oversight, cost savings, and better selection of contractors. Unfortunately, the rapid use of this process has outpaced the regulatory environment wherein policies are formulated.

The good news is that the OPSC continues to apportion state funds for these projects, provided compliance to existing regulations are met and the process is not used as a subterfuge to get around competitive bid requirements found in other codes of California law. Although there is still debate as to whether a competitive bid requirement exists for lease lease-backs, it is advisable that school districts adopt at least some form of a competitive selection process that includes cost as well as qualification considerations. The presence of competitive selection process will not only be viewed more favorably when seeking state funding, but it will help insure competitive costs for the project, stronger qualifications of the developer, increased participation, and a public process open to review.

Which Delivery Method Is Best for This Project?

There is no simple answer to this question. It depends upon the type of project being built, the size and complexity of the project, and several other factors. In general, smaller and less complicated projects are typically built utilizing the design/bid/build delivery method. Similarly, modernization projects, as opposed to "new construction," usually utilizes design/bid/build. Larger "new construction" projects may be candidates for design/build. Additionally, because the design/build delivery method permits the design and construction phases to overlap, this method may save a district time in terms of the duration of the overall project. It also has the advantage of allowing the designer and the builder to collaborate in the development of the design, which may result in a better project at a cheaper cost. Obviously, a significant amount of analysis should go into this decision, and the district should consult with its design consultants and other construction professionals to help it select the delivery system that will give the best chance for a successful project.

DSA Regulatory Review and Approvals

The DSA reviews plans for public school construction projects to ensure that plans, specifications, and construction comply with California's building codes (Title 24 of the California Code of Regulations). DSA's authority is derived from Education Code sections 17280–17317, 17365–17374, and 81130–81147. DSA reviews projects for structural safety, fire/life safety, and accessibility requirements in accordance with Title 24 of the California Building Standards Code. While districts must comply with other building requirements, such as mechanical, plumbing, electrical, energy compliance, and sustainability, the DSA does not currently review these requirements (but does have plans to do so in the future).

A school district may not execute contracts for project construction until the DSA approves all drawings and specifications and provides written approval of the application. If the district makes any changes to the drawings or specifications between the time the DSA stamps the drawings and the time the district awards the contract, the architect or engineer of record must initiate an addendum, and the DSA must approve the changes.

A school district may not execute contracts for construction until the DSA approves all drawings and specifications and provides written approval of the application.

DSA-Exempt Projects

In general, nearly all construction projects on school sites require review and approval by DSA. There are, however, some types of projects that do not require DSA review and approval. A complete list is found in Sections 4-306, 4-308, 4-309, 4-310, and 4-314 of Title 24 of the California Code of Regulations.

The following is a list of common structures that do not require DSA approval:

- One-story buildings not exceeding 250 square feet in floor area when used exclusively as accessory facilities to athletic fields (equipment storage, toilets, snack bars, ticket booths, etc.)
- Greenhouses, barns, and storage sheds used exclusively for plants or animals and not used for classroom instruction (small groups of pupils or teachers may enter these structures for short periods of time)
- Light poles or flagpoles less than 35 feet tall
  Antenna towers less than 35 feet tall or less than 25 feet above a building roofline
- Retaining walls less than 4 feet above the top of foundations and not supporting a surcharge
- Concrete or masonry fences less than 6 feet above adjacent grade
- Ballwalls or yard walls less than 6 feet above adjacent grade
- Signs, scoreboards, or solid-clad fences less than 8 feet above adjacent grade
- Bleachers and grandstands with five rows of seats or less
- Playground equipment, open-mesh fences, and baseball backstops
- Temporary-use buildings on community college sites used for less than three years
- Trailer Coaches that conform to the requirements of Part 2 (commencing with section 18000) of Division 13 of the Health and Safety Code, not greater than 16 feet in width and used for special education purposes for no more than 12 pupils at a time (or 20 pupils for driver training purposes)

While neither law nor regulation, the DSA has published a guidance document, entitled *The Interpretation of Regulations Manual* to assist school districts, community colleges, and others constructing essential services buildings to comply with applicable building codes and regulations. The applicable building

CAC = California
       Building Standards
       Administrative Code
CBC = California Building Code
CEC = California Electrical Code
CMC = California Mechanical Code
CPC = California Plumbing Code

codes in California are found in Title 24 of the California Code of Regulations. This extremely hefty and unwieldy volume contains five parts: California Building Standards Administrative Code (CAC), California Building Code (CBC), California Electrical Code (CEC), California Mechanical Code (CMC), and California Plumbing Code (CPC). The 103-page Interpretation of Regulations Manual is a helpful guide to the massive detail contained in the state's building codes, and is available on the DSA web site (www.dsa.dgs.ca.gov).

DSA also publishes a guidance document entitled *Access Compliance Reference Manual*. California has many laws governing access requirements for the physically-handicapped. (Access to Public Building by Physically Handicapped Persons (Govt. Code §§ 4450–4460); Access to Rapid Transit Equipment or Structures (Govt. Code § 4500); Facilities for Handicapped Persons (Govt. Code §§ 7250–7252); Approvals (Educ. Code §§ 17280–17319); Fitness for Occupancy (Educ. Code §§ 17365–17374); State-Funded Services; (Educ. Code § 67310); Approval 49 (Educ. Code §§ 81130–81149).) In addition to California laws, the Americans with Disabilities Act and the Fair Housing Amendments Act apply, as well as certain additional access requirements.

Initial Project Submittal

The Application for Approval of Plans and Specifications (Form DSA-1), plan review fees, stamped and signed plans and specifications, and other documents are submitted to DSA at one of four regional offices. The project submittal checklist provides a comprehensive list of documents required when submitting a project to DSA. Upon receipt, an application number ("A" number) is assigned to the project for tracking purposes. DSA conducts a preliminary review for completeness within a few days. If this application is incomplete, the architect and school district are notified by letter. Plan review will not be scheduled until DSA verifies that the submittal is complete.

Plan Review

Plan review starts within four to six weeks of initial submittal for most large projects.

Plan review starts within four to six weeks of initial submittal for most large projects. At times of high workload, DSA may contract with private plan reviewers to expedite the plan review process. The progress of any project can be monitored at DSA's Project Tracking web site (www.dsa.dgs.ca.gov).

DSA performs plan review in three disciplines: Structural, Fire/Life Safety, and Access Compliance. Three separate experts perform these reviews concurrently. Upon completion of plan review, three red-marked "check-sets" will be returned to the architect of record. The red marks on the drawings and specifications comprise the complete list of corrections required.

The district's architect must address each plan review comment thoroughly and completely before scheduling a back-check appointment.

Addressing DSA's plan review comments. The district's architect must address each comment thoroughly and completely before scheduling a back-check appointment. Drawings and specifications must be corrected prior to scheduling a back-check meeting, however, additional, minor corrections are usually required during the meeting. DSA insists that the red-marked check-sets be returned to DSA intact at the time of back-check. If a check set is lost, DSA requires the district to submit a new one, and an additional fee is charged to re-review it.

DSA suggests that black pencil marks be used to check off comments on the drawings as they are addressed. Notes regarding the manner in which the comments are addressed may also be added to the drawings in black pencil to facilitate the back-check process. DSA warns that colored marks should not be added to the check sets since such marks may be confused with DSA's comments, and any marks that obscure DSA's original comments in red must be avoided. Calculations or other documentation that needs to be kept in DSA's files should not be written on the check sets since DSA generally discards check sets after the back-check meeting.

Back-check and approval. Once plan review corrections have been addressed by the district's architect, a back-check meeting may be scheduled with the DSA structural plan reviewer who reviewed the project. The reviewer's name and phone number is on the first page of the marked-up check set.

Once plan review corrections have been addressed by the district's architect, a back-check meeting may be scheduled with the DSA structural plan reviewer who reviewed the project.

The "architect in general responsible charge" should be available during the back-check meeting to authorize changes to the signed tracings. Any changes made to the tracings that are not a direct result of a plan review comment must be brought to the attention of the plan reviewer. Upon completion of the back-check meeting, reproducible tracings are stamped for identification by DSA. This stamping does not constitute approval. The district's architect is obligated to immediately make a set of blueprints from the stamped tracings and submit it to DSA. The set of blueprints will serve as DSA's official record set. Upon receipt of these blueprints, DSA issues the plan approval letter. The design is not approved until and unless DSA issues such a letter.

Absolutely no changes may be made to the tracings after they have been stamped and before the record set of blueprints is made. The approval of the project is automatically void if changes are made to stamped tracings without DSA's approval. All changes made subsequent to approval must be accomplished by submitting revised drawings, addenda, or change orders to DSA for review and approval.

Absolutely no changes may be made to the tracings after they have been stamped and before the record set of blueprints is made.

Deferred Approvals

Approval of certain aspects of the construction may be deferred until the construction contract has been awarded. For example, it is not efficient to design elevator guide rails until after an elevator supplier has been chosen. To facilitate the design process, DSA grants deferred approval to the design and detailing of elevator guide rails at the request of the A/E of Record. Design elements that may be deferred are limited to:

- Elevator guide rails and support brackets
- Window wall systems or storefronts with spans greater than ten feet
- Exterior wall systems—precast concrete, glass fiber reinforced concrete, etc.
- Skylights
- Bleachers (seating layout must be shown at time of submittal)
- Automatic fire sprinkler systems
- Fire pumps

Detailed performance specifications and/or loading criteria for the deferred approval components must be included on the drawings or in the specifications. The drawings must include a list of the deferred approval components on the title sheet and clearly state that no work may proceed until DSA stamped, approved drawings are provided to the contractor and inspector for the components.

Deferred approval does not mean that the district's architect may refer the design of the component to the contractor. On the contrary, DSA requires that the architect accept responsibility for verifying that all components (including those granted deferred approval) of the project are properly designed by appropriately licensed design professionals.

The architect is responsible for coordination of all components of the project. He or she is responsible for designing connections to the structure for all deferred approval components, and for verifying that all interactions (deflection compatibility, drift compatibility, vertical and lateral loads, etc.) are adequately addressed and in conformance with good engineering practices and the California Building Standards Code.

The architect must submit complete drawings, specifications, and supporting documentation for the deferred approval item(s) and obtain DSA approval before the affected construction may proceed. From DSA's perspective, the only difference between a deferred approval item and any other component of the construction is that the architect may defer the design of the item until after the award of the bid so that additional information will be available to facilitate the design work.

DSA stamped, approved drawings must be delivered to the inspector, applicable special inspectors, and the testing laboratory (as appropriate) before work on the deferred approval items may commence.

Subsequent Changes to DSA Stamped, Approved Drawings

After DSA has stamped drawings and specifications but before a contract for construction has been awarded, changes to the plans and specifications may only be made by addenda or by issuing revised drawings. Addenda and revised drawings must be signed by the A/E of Record and approved by DSA. Significant revisions to the drawings may result in a DSA request for additional fees and/or the submittal of a new separate application.

Construction must proceed in strict accordance with DSA approved documents. After a contract for construction has been awarded, any changes to the DSA approved documents must be made by change order. Change orders must be prepared and signed by the district's architect as well as by all engineers delegated responsibility for portions of the work involved in the changes. Change orders must be stamped approved by DSA before construction may proceed.

To facilitate the construction process, DSA will review and stamp field orders, supplemental instructions, change directives, and similar documents that describe changes to the construction documents with a "preliminary approval stamp." This allows construction to proceed with DSA approval pending the completion of an official change order.

Expedited DSA Review Process
for Relocatable Building

DSA has an over-the-counter review method for approval of relocatable building projects with limited size and scope. An appointment is required. The design professional in charge of the project meets face-to-face with DSA reviewers. Site plans are submitted and reviewed, and building plans are compared to previously approved plans of identical construction. The process is usually completed and the project approved by DSA within two or three hours.

DSA has an over-the-counter review method for approval of relocatable building projects with limited size and scope. An appointment is required.

Energy Efficiency
Grant Approvals

As discussed in chapter 2, school districts are eligible for supplemental grants from the state bond fund for achieving certain energy efficiency standards, if approved by DSA. In order to access this money, the district must inform the DSA Regional Office representative that the district will be applying for the additional Proposition 47 Energy Allowance grant funding. DSA requires oral notice as well as notice in writing—a letter accompanying the submittal will suffice.

The district must submit one complete set of plans and specifications and all electronic files used to demonstrate the project's energy code compliance, using one of two computer programs—EnergyPro 3.1 or Perform 2001. Each of these programs are approved by the California Energy Commission to measure gains in energy efficiency. When the DSA confirms that the requisite percentage of energy efficiency has been achieved, the DSA will update the district's project records on the online project tracking (Tracker) system. OPSC will use this Tracker update to verify a submittal's eligibility for Energy Allowance Grant funding.

Historical Building Program

When a district chooses to or must preserve its historical school building resources, districts may be relieved from some modern building code and DSA requirements that are incompatible with the goals of historic preservation. DSA will review those buildings using the alternative provisions of the State Historical Building Code (Title 24, Part 8 of the California Code of Regulations) by staff trained and experienced in historical structures' archaic materials and methods of construction.

When a district chooses to or must preserve its historical school building resources, districts may be relieved from some modern building code and DSA requirements that are incompatible with the goals of historic preservation.

Construction Bidding

Competitive Bidding
for Design/Bid/Build

The construction bid process is a critical step in the construction of a school. This is when the price is determined and a contractor is selected. It is important that this process be conducted professionally and fairly so that the most qualified contractors will participate. This process sets the tone for the owner-contractor relationship, and can greatly affect the project cost and quality of construction. Specific procedures relating to bidding for construction services are established in the Public Contract Code, and must be followed. Pub. Contract

It is important that the construction bid process be conducted professionally and fairly so that the most qualified contractors will participate.

Code §§ 20111–20118.4, 10140, 20672, 8751, 10302. If not, bidders may have the basis to assert a bid protest or a claim during construction, or the project may have to be re-bid, resulting in months of delay to the construction schedule.

For design/bid/build projects, unlike the selection process for professional services, a district is required to select the "lowest responsible bidder" to build the project. The lowest responsible bidder selection process is primarily cost driven and the district has almost no ability to select the contractor on the basis of qualifications or experience. There are exceptions to these general bidding laws for day labor/force account work (Public Contract Code § 20114) and emergencies (Pub. Contract Code §§ 1102, 20113).

Pre-Qualification of Bidders

Public Contract Code section 20111.5 allows school districts to pre-qualify bidders in advance of the bidding process. Pre-qualification allows a district to determine ahead of time that the contractors who bid its projects possess the requisite financial strength and qualifications to successfully construct its projects. Section 20111.5(a) requires the district to develop a standardized questionnaire soliciting information about the contractor's qualifications, experience, and financial condition. The district is also required to develop a uniform system for rating bidders. § 20111.5(b). To the extent that the district determines that a particular contractor does not pass the pre-qualification criteria, it is required to give that contractor a right to appeal the district's decision. Pre-qualification can occur on a quarterly basis, and is considered valid for one year following the date of the initial pre-qualification. Pub. Contract Code § 20111.5(e). More and more school districts are utilizing this pre-qualification process to insure that they do not get stuck with a contractor that is unable to do the job.

Advertising

Section 20112 of the Public Contract Code requires a school district to publish *a notice calling for bids and the time when and the place where bids will be opened.* The notice must be published at least once a week for two weeks in a newspaper of general circulation in the district, or, if there is no newspaper in the district, a paper of general circulation where the project is located. The district may also advertise the bid on its web site. However, most contractors learn of projects through construction-specific publications like the "Greensheet." All three forms of advertising should be used to notify prospective bidders of a project coming up for bid. Generally, it is in the district's best interest to cooperate with these trade publications by providing timely and accurate information when they call for information concerning a district's upcoming projects. This will result in greater participation by bidders and lower construction costs.

Bid Period

The minimum bid period required by law is ten days. However, bid periods are generally from three to five weeks. In any case, sufficient time should be given to bidders to review the plans and to understand the project so that the district can receive accurate and complete bids. Anything less than three weeks is strongly discouraged. If any material change is made to the invitation to bid through the issuance of addenda, the date for the closing of bids must be extended not less than 72 hours. Pub. Contract Code § 4104.5. However, once again, the period of extension for submission of bids should be based upon the nature of the change to the bid contained in the addenda. Bids may be accepted either electronically or on paper. Pub. Contract Code § 20112.

Bid Documents

Bid documents for a project most commonly include:

- Invitation to bid
- Instructions to bidders
- Bid forms
- The owner-contractor agreement
- General conditions of the contract that outlines the contractor's responsibilities in detail
- Specifications—detailed descriptions of building material and construction quality
- Drawings, including plans, elevations, sections, and details that show the quantity and location of building elements

Section 7106 of the Public Contract Code also requires that all bidders submit a Non-Collusion Certificate with their bids whereby they certify that they have not colluded to fix the bids. It is also a good idea to include the forms of bonds (payment and performance) required for the project with the bid package. Additionally, to give bidders a better sense of how the project will be administered, it is useful to include critical project administration forms, including forms that will be utilized for progress payments, change orders, and waivers and releases.

Addenda

It is not unusual for an owner to issue supplemental information concerning the project after the original bid package is published. Addenda that incorporate additional bidding information that adds to, modifies, or deletes information contained in the original set of bid documents are sent to all bidders and to the DSA. An addendum can be as simple as a correction of a typographical error or can be a major re-design of a complete building system.

As much as possible, addenda should be clear and concise. If a large, complicated addendum is issued close to the bid date, the bid period should be extended for a reasonable time (beyond the 72 hour requirement set forth in Pub. Contract Code § 4104.5) to allow bidders, subcontractors, and suppliers adequate time to address the changes. Typically, issuing of the bid documents, including any addenda, is conducted by one consultant so that all bidding communication is coordinated and executed fairly.

To ensure uniform treatment of all bidders, the district should require any questions about the project, plans and specifications, or the bid process to be submitted in writing. Any questions received should be promptly responded to in writing and sent to all bidders.

Typical Bid Documents

- Invitation to Bid
- Plans and Specs
- Proposed Agreement
- Proposed Agreement and General Conditions
- Bid Form
- Performance Bond Form
- Payment Bond Form
- Non-Collusion Affidavit
- Proposed Progress Payment Form
- Proposed Change Order Form

✍ practice tip

For the purpose of answering questions from or communicating with bidders, the district should establish a single point of contact. Typically, either the project architect or the construction manager is designated to serve this role.

- **Provide a space large enough** and with enough seats for all bidder's representatives to hear the bid results. The number of people can range from one to over 100 depending on project size and scope.

- **Schedule bid openings** for either Tuesdays or Thursdays between 10:00 am and 2:00 pm This is a traditional practice that most contractors expect, and will result in more participation and better prices.

- **Establish an official time and timekeeper** to time and date stamp every bid.

- **Prepare a bid tabulation sheet** in advance that lists all bidders and the relevant information to be read aloud. Assign one person to record all information that is read.

- **Avoid Conflicts.** Before setting the bid date, check the trade publications to see if any other similar projects are bidding the same day, and reschedule if there is a conflict.

- **Allow Bid Verification Time.** If possible, allow at least several days to two weeks to verify the bid information prior to school board approval.

Subcontract Listing

Bid shopping is a practice whereby a general contractor, after bid opening, goes back to the "unsuccessful" subcontract bidders and inquires whether those bidders would be willing to reduce their bid prices to be below that of the current subcontract low bidder. Frequently, this involves a series of communications with each of the bidders who are willing to reduce their price until the general contractor receives the lowest price for a particular scope of work. Ultimately, the subcontractor who is willing to do the work for the lowest price is given the subcontract. However, the California Legislature outlawed bid shopping in all public works construction.

In an attempt to prevent "bid shopping" in public works construction, the legislature passed the Subcontractors Listing Law. Pub. Contract Code § 4107 *et seq.* Public Contract Code section 4107 requires a general contractor bidding public construction projects to list all subcontractors which will perform one-half of one percent or more of the value of general contractor's bid. Failure to list a subcontractor in its bid will result in the obligation of the contractor to perform that portion of the work. Additionally, subcontractors listed in the contractor's bid may not be substituted by the contractor after bid opening unless the subcontractor:

- Fails or refuses to execute a contract
- Becomes bankrupt
- Fails or refuses to perform the subcontract
- Fails to meet bonding requirements
- Was erroneously listed as a result of inadvertent clerical error
- Is not licensed
- Has performed unsatisfactorily, as determined by the owner

In a situation where a clerical listing error is claimed, Public Contract Code section 4107.5 also precludes the contractor's substitution of subcontractors absent evidence of an inadvertent clerical error and notice to the district of the mistake within two days of bid opening.

Pre-Bid Conference

The district should schedule a pre-bid conference for prospective bidders as part of its bidding process. The purpose of such a conference is to review the major requirements of the bid, and to point out any nontypical elements of the project. This also gives bidders the opportunity to see the project site and ask questions. In most cases, mandatory pre-bid conferences should be avoided because they can limit participation of qualified bidders. Additionally, this can create confusion, especially with multiple prime projects, over which bidders should attend, and which should not. However, if the district determines to make attendance at its pre-bid conference mandatory, Public Contract Code section 6610 requires the time and place to be included in the district's notice of bid, and prohibits any pre-bid conference from occurring within five calendar days of the initial public notice of bid.

Bid Opening

The Public Contract Code requires that all bids must be turned in prior to the specified time and read aloud publicly. Bids turned in after the official time are required to be rejected and returned to the bidder unopened. Govt Code § 53068; Pub. Contract Code § 4104.5. Bids are opened one at a time, and the name of the contractor and the bid price is read out loud. Typically, compliance with other bid requirements is also determined at this time, such as whether the bid is complete or whether or not the bidder provided the bonds and the certifications required by the bid documents. However, a more detailed review of the apparent low bid should occur after bid opening and prior to the award of the contract.

All bids must be turned in prior to the specified time and read aloud publicly. Bids turned in after the official time are required to be rejected and returned to the bidder unopened.

After all bids are read, the apparent low bidder is announced with an indication that the contract award is contingent upon verification of information and the school board's approval. Usually, after the bids are read, the list of the lowest two or three bidders is read aloud. This is done to allow the contractors to compare the components of their bids with those of the successful bidder as a professional courtesy. A general or prime contractor puts a great deal of time and effort, often tens of thousands of dollars, into bidding a project, and the subcontractor information helps them be more competitive in future bids.

Alternate Bids

Public agencies, including school districts, are permitted to utilize bid alternates in their bidding process. A bid alternate is a particular scope of work which the district includes in its invitation to bid. Bidders are requested to separately bid the cost of the alternate scope of work with their overall bid. Subsequent to the submission of the bids, the district determines whether it will include the bid alternate in the project. Bid alternates allow districts to determine the cost of work that may not be necessary but which it may wish to include in the project if the bids come in within the overall budget for the project.

Bid alternates allow districts to determine the cost of work that may not be necessary but which it may wish to include in the project if the bids come in within the overall budget for the project.

In 2000, the California Legislature passed AB 2182 (amending Pub. Contract Code §§ 10126, 10780.5, and 20103.8) in order to eliminate the ability of a public agency to utilize the bid alternates to select the contractor that the agency favored. Before this legislation was passed, agencies could select the alternates so as to make its bidder of choice the "low bidder," and thereby allow it to award the project to that bidder. In essence, the amendments to the Public Contract Code provide procedures for alternative biding so that the agency cannot play favorites, including determining which alternates it will include in the project before the identity of the bidders are disclosed to the agency.

Bid Responsiveness and Responsibility

As indicated above, under the design/bid/build delivery system, the law in California requires a contract to be awarded to the "lowest responsible bidder." Price is the most important criterion in the award decision. However, before awarding the contract, the district must also determine whether the bid is "responsive" and that the bidder is "responsible." Bid protests most frequently challenge the responsiveness of a bid.

Before awarding the contract under the design/bid/build delivery system, the district must determine whether the bid is "responsive" and that the bidder is "responsible."

Responsiveness of the Bid. The responsiveness issue requires the district to review the four corners of the low bid as it was submitted. "Responsibility" focuses on whether the bidder satisfies the minimum qualifications described in the request for a proposal. "Responsiveness" focuses on the question: "Did the bid comply with the requirements of the request for proposal?" Generally, strict compliance with the RFP specifications is required, and the analysis of a bid's responsiveness is an "either/or" proposition. Examples of responsiveness defects include:

- A late bid submittal
- Failure to sign or completely fill out bid forms or to submit required bid documents (*e.g.*, bonds)
- Price discrepancies between unit prices and quantity calculations

However, variances or defects which are "inconsequential" may be waived by the district. *See* Waiver of Bid Defect below.

Bidder responsibility. The "responsibility" of a bidder submitting the "lowest responsible bid" project is a pass/fail test. It is not a test of relative superiority among bidders. Pub. Contract Code § 1103. Typically, "responsibility" issues are resolved after the bid opening. If the district determines that a bidder is "non-responsible," it must give the bidder notice of the basis of its decision and an opportunity to appeal. *City of Inglewood-Los Angeles Civil Center Authority v. Superior Court* (1972) 7 Cal. 3d 861, 871. Examples of nonresponsibility issues include lack of licensure, and/or bonding, bankruptcy, receivership, or if the contractor has been debarred by another public agency.

Waiver of Bid Defect

The general rule is that a bid cannot be changed after being submitted. *See* Pub. Contract Code § 5101(a). However, a district may waive certain types of bid defects. To qualify, a defect or irregularity in a bid must not make the bidding process unfair or give a bidder an unfair advantage if, based on the defect, the bidder would be entitled to withdraw the bid without forfeiting its bid bond. *Menefee v. County of Fresno* (1985) 163 Cal. App. 3d 1175; *Ghilotti Const. Co. v. City of Richmond* (1996) 45 Cal. App. 4th 987. If the mistake would have provided the bidder with grounds to withdraw the bid, then the defect may not be waived. Examples of bid defects include a failure to include the bidder's license number or a failure to sign the bid at each of the designated places. However, even if the defect can be waived, the district is not required to do so and may reject the defective bid.

Bid Withdrawals

Bid withdrawals are governed by Public Contract Code section 5100 *et seq.* Generally, a bid may be withdrawn at any time prior to bid opening. However, once opened, a bid may be withdrawn without the bidder forfeiting its bid bond only in limited circumstances. To be relieved of its bid, a contractor must show all of the following:

- That a mathematical or typographical mistake was made
- That the bidder gave the district notice of the mistake within five days of bid opening

- That the mistake made the bid materially different than intended
- That the mistake was made in filling out the bid and did not involve a mistake in judgment

However, even when a withdrawal may not be allowed technically, the district should consider whether it is in the project's best interest to allow the withdrawal. It may be far better to accept the withdrawal than to force an unwilling contractor to build a project when, due to a bidding mistake, the contractor's ability to achieve a successful project is in doubt. The potential cost savings "realized" by the district because of a bidders mistake or poor judgment usually evaporate during the course of construction with an uncooperative contractor. If the bidder is relieved of the bid, it is precluded from participating in further bidding if the project is rebid by the district. Pub. Contract Code § 5105. If the lowest bidder is relieved, the district may, if it determines it is in its best interest, award the contract to the next lowest bidder. Pub. Contract Code § 5106. However, as indicated above, it also has the discretion to reject all bids and to rebid the project.

Award to the Successful Bidder

Once the district determines who is the lowest responsible bidder, district staff recommend to the board that the contract be awarded to that bidder. The board votes on the recommendation, and the contract is formally awarded to the low bidder. The district then tenders the construction contract to the low bidder and the low bidder returns the executed contract, along with the other documentation that is required to be submitted prior to the start of work (bonds, insurance certificates, etc.). It is worth noting, however, that before the contract can be awarded, the district must get written approval of the design from the DSA. (See the discussion of DSA design review above).

Bid Protests

Not infrequently, the bidding process results in a bid protest by one or more of the unsuccessful bidders. Protests can be successful, particularly where the district has not complied with its own bidding requirements or applicable law. In the majority of cases, a protest is borne out of the disappointment an unsuccessful bidder experiences after investing time and money in submitting its bid. Because of the uncertainties created by protests, the best advice to a public agency is to strictly follow its own procurement regulations and the public bidding laws together with the requirements set forth in its request for proposal. Problems arise when a public agency, for reasons of convenience, ignores a low bidder's failure to comply with the bid requirements. The temptation to ignore a nonwaivable defect in a low bid must be avoided.

The district's legal counsel should be involved in reviewing any protest, no matter how trivial, to minimize disruption to the project and protect the district from the expense of litigation. A simple rule, however, to avoid bid protests is for the district to strictly comply with the applicable procurement requirements, including the Public Contract Code, the district's procurement regulations, if any, and the terms of its request for proposal.

Even when a withdrawal may not be allowed technically, the district should consider whether it is in the project's best interest to allow the withdrawal.

Right to Reject All Bids

By law, a public agency may reject all bids at its sole discretion. *See* Public Contract Code § 20166. This right is typically exercised if the bids substantially exceed the estimate of the project cost.

However, while a district does not want to utilize this power arbitrarily—thereby discouraging contractors to bid on its projects in the future— on many other occasions this right can and should be exercised, including when the district determines that its construction documents are not sufficiently complete to allow the successful bidder to perform the work without delays or disruptions. ■

DVBE = Disabled Veteran
        Business Enterprise
MBE = Minority Business
        Enterprise
SBE = Small Business
        Enterprise
WBE = Women Business
        Enterprise

MBE/WBE/SBE/DVBE Goals

Historically, in order to promote disadvantaged business participation in public contracting, public agencies have included Minority Business Enterprise (MBE), Women Business Enterprise (WBE), Small Business Enterprise (SBE), and/or Disabled Veteran Enterprise (DVBE) participation goals in their requests for proposals. In order for a bid to be deemed responsive, bidders were required to either achieve the participation goals set forth in the request for proposal or demonstrate to the public agency that it made a "good faith" effort to achieve those participation goals. Failure to satisfy these two requirements would result in a rejection of the bid on the grounds that it was nonresponsive.

However in 1999, Proposition 209 was passed, making it illegal to grant preferential treatment in government contracting on the basis of race, sex, color, ethnicity, or national origin. Proposition 209, as interpreted by the California Supreme Court, precludes race or sex-based participation goals for public contracting. However, the law does not prevent a district from requiring outreach to disadvantaged businesses to increase participation, as long as that outreach does not provide a preference or advantage to a group covered by Proposition 209. *See* the discussion in *Hi-Voltage Wire v. City of San Jose* (2002) 23 Cal. 4th 305. However, Education Code section 17076.11 provides that any district utilizing state funds for construction or modernization shall have a participation goal of three percent for disabled veterans' business enterprises. Additionally, some agencies (for example, the City of Los Angeles) have developed outreach programs which are designed to reach a broad range of prospective bidders (including MBE/WBE contractors). So long as these programs do not provide a preference or advantage to some bidders over others, they are likely to be upheld.

Bonding Requirements

Public contracts require various forms of security relating to the contractor's performance. Other forms of security, not mandated by law, are likewise important to insure that the project is completed. The various types of security that should be part of the contract requirements are described below.

Bid Bonds

The bid bond or cash deposit is a guarantee that, if a contract is awarded, the contract will be performed, and that subcontractors and material suppliers will be paid.

For projects in excess of $15,000, the first type of security that is required on a public school project is a bid bond, or cash (or cashier's check) in lieu of a bond, that bidders are required to provide to a school district at the time of the submission of their bids. Pub. Contract Code § 20111(b). The bid bond or cash deposit is a guarantee that, if a contract is awarded, it will be signed and the successful bidder will post a bond to guarantee both that the contract will be performed and that subcontractors and material suppliers will be paid. The amount of the bid bond or cash deposit is determined by the school district, but typically is set at between 10 and 20 percent of the bid. The bonds must be issued by an "admitted surety insurer." Code Civ. Proc. § 995.120; Insurance Code § 105. The bonds or cash deposits submitted by unsuccessful bidders must be returned by the district within 60 days of the date the award is made.

Payment Bonds

Every original contractor awarded a construction contract in excess of $25,000 by a public agency, including a school district, is required, prior to performing any work on a project, to file a payment bond with the district. Civil Code § 3247. The term "original contractor" does not include providers of architectural, engineering, and land surveying services. The payment bond must be in the sum of not less than 100 percent of the "total amount payable by the terms of contract." Contrary to private construction, which permits cash to be deposited in lieu of a payment bond, on public works projects, the law requires this security to be in the form of a bond. Civil Code § 3248. The payment bond is required to provide that if the original contractor or its subcontractors fail to pay their subcontractors or suppliers amounts due under their contracts or unemployment withholdings due under law, the bond shall be liable for said amounts. It is recommended that the district require submission of a payment bond, in a form acceptable to the district, within a short time after the bid is awarded. As mentioned above, the form of payment bond required for the project should be included in the district's bid package.

Performance Bonds

A third form of security insuring the contractor's performance is a performance bond. In the event of a default by the contractor, a performance bond guarantees that the project will be completed according to the terms and conditions of the construction contract. While this form of security is not required by law on a public project, it is prudent to require the successful bidder to provide a performance bond before performing work on a project. Typically, the amount of a performance bond is 100 percent of the original contract value. Situations where a public agency, as the oblige on the bond, may "call the bond" (that is, exercise its right to have the surety cure the contractor's default) include a contractor's insolvency, a material breach of the contract, or some other default by the contractor as defined in the construction contract. If there is a basis to call the bond, the bonding company is obligated to promptly investigate the basis of the owner's claim of default, and if the default was justified, to complete the project pursuant to the terms of the original construction contract. This may be accomplished by the bonding company providing funding to the original contractor to complete the project, or by retaining a replacement contractor to complete the project. Similar to a payment bond, a performance bond should be submitted to the district by the successful bidder prior to the start of construction. Additionally, beyond insuring the performance of a contractor, requiring a performance bond will have the added benefit of insuring that more competent contractors bid the projects. This is because contractors who have a history of performance problems have a difficult time obtaining bonding, and if a performance bond a requirement of the bid, it will weed out at least some contractors who do not have a good track record.

Release Bonds

Release bonds are another form of security that are posted by the general contractor with the district to allow project funds otherwise encumbered by a stop notice to be paid to the contractor. Public agencies have the discretion whether to accept release bonds. Civil Code § 3196. Absent acceptance of a release bond from the contractor, the district is required to withhold payment to the contractor of monies encumbered by a public works stop notice. (See the discussion of Stop Notices below.)

Confirmation of Bonding

In recent years, courts have held that a public agency has an affirmative duty to investigate whether a contractor has obtained a bond from a viable bonding company and that the bonds comply with the Public Contracts Code requirements. Therefore, it is incumbent on the district (or its construction manager) to ensure that the contractor's bonding meets all legal requirements. If this is not done and the contractor defaults, the district may be liable for monies owed to a subcontractor or supplier by the general contractor.

It is incumbent on the district (or its construction manager) to ensure that the contractor's bonding meets all legal requirements.

Other Construction Issues

Modular/Portable Classroom Piggy-Backing Contracts

Public Contract Code section 20118 empowers school districts to purchase personal property (such as furniture, data processing equipment, vehicles, materials, or supplies) without following normal public contract code requirements. Often termed "piggy-backing," a single, open-ended contract with a manufacturer allows other smaller school districts to piggy back on purchases from the successful bidder where the original school district followed the proper steps in making the initial procurement (*e.g.*, advertising for bids.). Section 20653 similarly authorizes community colleges to use this method. The legislative policy behind these statutes is to allow small public agencies, such as school districts, to obtain the lower prices that can be gained by large purchasers due to economies of scale. This type of "piggy-back" contract has been popularly used for purchasing portable classrooms which can be obtained quickly, without the need to negotiate a new contract, and at the price specified in this open-ended contract.

The legislative policy behind these statutes is to allow small public agencies to obtain the lower prices that can be gained by large purchasers due to economies of scale.

Due to the law's restriction that such contracts only be used for personal property, districts should beware of inadvertently circumventing the Public Contract Code's bidding requirements where the portable classroom manufacturer also seeks to provide real property improvements (*e.g.*, installation of sewer lines).

Non-Certified Relocatable Classrooms

California law requires that all school buildings be certified by DSA. For various reasons, relocatable buildings have sometimes been purchased or leased and placed on school sites without DSA certification. SB 1469 certification allows such buildings to remain in use until September 30, 2007. SB 1469 was enacted in September 2000 and modified Education Code section 17292 to allow the use of non-DSA certified relocatable buildings until that time if certain conditions are met.

To qualify for SB 1469 certification, a relocatable building must meet all of the following criteria:

- Was in use for classroom purposes on or before May 1, 2000
- Constructed after December 19, 1979 and bears a commercial coach insignia of approval from the Department of Housing and Community Development (HCD)
- Is a single story structure with not more than 2,160 square feet of interior floor area when all sections are joined together
- The bracing and anchorage of the interior overhead nonstructural elements such as light fixtures and heating and air-conditioning diffusers comply with the requirements of the current California Building Code (CBC)
- The foundation system complies with the current UBC or is a DSA-approved foundation
- All other building construction, including associated site construction, except for the relocatable building itself, complies with sections 4450 to 4458, inclusive, of the Government Code, section 13143 of the Health and Safety Code, and the administrative and building standards published in Title 19 and Title 24 of the California Code of Regulations

Liability risks to school district. Buildings installed without DSA certification may be installed in a manner that could compromise the safety of the building occupants or other persons at the school. Some considerations are as follows:

- Many buildings were installed on temporary foundations that do not meet earthquake safety requirements
- Buildings may have been installed without proper attention to fire department access (both to the building and to other buildings on the school site)
- Ramps, handrails, path of travel, and other accessibility requirements may not be in accordance with the requirements of code and/or federal law
- Ceilings, light fixtures, and other overhead elements may not be supported and braced to resist earthquake loads

The school district can be held liable for damages or injuries that occur in buildings not certified by DSA. Various district attorneys have rendered the opinion that members of the school board may be held personally liable for such damages and injuries.

The school district can be held liable for damages or injuries that occur in buildings not certified by DSA.

How to obtain SB 1469 certification. If a district has not already done so, it must report to DSA any noncomplying HCD relocatable buildings on school campuses, retrofit the identified buildings, and send verification of compliance for each building to DSA. If compliant, DSA will issue letters of certification that will expire on September 30, 2007.

The school district must hire both a California licensed architect to investigate each building and associated site construction, and a DSA certified inspector (must be certified as a DSA Class 1, 2, 3, or 4 inspector). The inspector does not need to be approved by DSA for each specific project as required for ordinary school construction projects.

The inspector must:

- Personally perform inspections on each building
- Identify construction in need of repair

Critical Path Method

The critical path method (CPM) is a key tool for managing project schedules. CPM computes the shortest project completion duration and earliest completion date. The longest path through the network is called the "critical path." According to CPM, any delay on the critical path will delay the project.

On the one hand, CPM is traditional and well-accepted. It is essential for developing the logic of the project work and for managing the day-to-day project activities. On the other hand, the accuracy of a CPM completion date forecast depends on every task taking only as long as its estimated duration. In short, CPM is accurate only if everything goes according to plan. ■

CPM = Critical path method

Best case ... we can cut 4 months

- Verify that all repairs are made and that the building(s) meet the requirements
- Complete the SB 1469 Inspector's Report

Once repairs are complete, the district submits the fee of $450 and the SB 1469 Certification of Compliance signed by the architect, the DSA-certified inspector, and the school district for each school campus in the district where reported buildings exist

Finally, DSA will issue a letter certifying that the building has been retrofitted and inspected in accordance with the SB 1469 requirements. Unlike ordinary DSA certification, this only pertains to aspects of the construction defined in Education Code section 17292 and expires on September 30, 2007. After that date, the buildings may no longer be used as school buildings.

Construction Procedures and Activities

The construction process involves cooperation of many different players outside the district, and the active and regular participation of a district representative, for the duration of construction, which can range from a few months to several years, depending on the project's size and complexity. The school district representative will conduct activities such as: monitoring the project schedule and budget; providing responses to questions from the contractor and architect; facilitating expeditious payment to the contractor or managing requests for changes and additional costs; and coordinating move-in.

Pre-Construction Documents

As mentioned above, the district should insure that the contractor provides certain documents prior to the start of work, including copies of the executed payment bond and performance bond, and certificates of insurance. The district should closely examine these documents and exercise due diligence that the contractor has provided all coverages called for in the contract. Frequently this is not done, and only after an accident or an insurable event does the public agency determine that the contractor did not provide the types of insurance or the insurance limits that were required and therefore does not have the necessary protection. Additionally, in connection with its duties to insure that the contractor's employees are paid prevailing wages, the district is required to insure that the contractor has provided an adequate payment bond. Civil Code § 3247, 3248.

Pre-Construction Conference

Prior to the contractor moving onto the site (commonly referred to as mobilizing), a pre-construction conference should be held to introduce all construction team members to each other and to review payment procedures, communication protocol, and district policies (for example, fingerprinting and security requirements). These are especially critical for projects that involve existing operating school sites. The district or its representative should keep written minutes of this meeting that are distributed to all attendees and put into the project file.

Notice to Proceed

This is the official authorization from the school district to the contractor to begin construction. It typically establishes the official start and completion dates of the contract. The notice is issued after the contractor has provided the district with all certificates and information (including insurance certificates, bonds, proof of license, etc.) required in the bid documents.

Contract Documents

The contractual documents that define the rights and obligations of the district and the contractor are typically made up of:

- An agreement that contains the specific deal points of the contractual relationship
- General conditions that detail how the contractor will execute and perform the contractual obligations
- Supplemental conditions that include modifications to the general conditions for the specific project
- Project specifications
- Project design

The agreement contains the most critical, project-specific contract provisions, such as price, scope of work, and the completion deadline. The general conditions document is a standard form document that defines, in detail, the various obligations that will apply to the contractor in connection with project construction. These include such items as the roles and responsibilities of the district and the contractor, payment procedures, change order procedures, indemnity provisions, and the project close-out requirements. Supplemental conditions may be included if any of the standard terms in the general conditions require modification. Finally, the project specifications and design drawings provide the technical information for the construction of the project.

It is critical that these various contract documents be coordinated, since there is frequently overlap and cross referencing among them. Therefore, it is recommended that the district's project manager, construction manager, or architect, and its legal counsel, review the documents before they are published to insure coordination and consistency.

Project Schedule

Regardless of whether the project is design/bid/build or design/build, one of the most critical issues that must be addressed is the contractor's or design/builder's schedule. Ideally, the district will define the requirements of what should be included in the project construction schedule in its general or supplemental conditions so that the contractor is aware of the district's

Importance of a Baseline Schedule

Construction contracts typically require a contractor to provide the district with a CPM (critical path method) schedule to identify how the contractor intends to complete its work within the time frame spelled out in the contract. This is usually referred to as the "baseline schedule." Frequently, in the rush to get started, this schedule is ignored, and significant time passes before the proposed baseline schedule is submitted for review.

It is absolutely critical that the district's contract require that a proposed baseline schedule be submitted to the district for review at the very outset of the project, and that the submission be timely. This is critical for a number of reasons:

- To determine whether the contractor has adequately planned the job
- To measure the contractor's actual progress versus the planned progress as schedule updates are issued
- To determine if any claimed delays or disruptions have adversely affected the contractor's work

If a realistic and sufficiently detailed baseline schedule is not established at the beginning of the project, the district will lose one of the best tools it has to track the contractor's performance and defend itself against frivolous claims. ■

expectations. These requirements should include the time of the schedule submittals as well as the information that should be included in the schedule.

At the onset of the project, the contractor should develop and submit to the district or its project representative a baseline schedule to track the project from start to finish. While the contractor has the right to define the means and methods of construction, and thus its sequence, the district should review the proposed baseline schedule to make sure the contractor has adequately planned the work to meet the contractual completion date. This schedule can also be used to meaningfully measure the progress of the work.

Schedule of Values

Along with the baseline schedule, a schedule of values is a critical tool that should be used by the district to manage payments to its contractors.

G&A = General and administrative

Along with the baseline schedule, a schedule of values is a critical tool which should be used by the district to manage payments to its contractors or a project. The schedule of values breaks down the construction of the project into discrete component parts (*e.g.*, grading, concrete, framing, mechanical, electrical, drywall, painting, etc.) and assigns a dollar value to each construction component. (Each of these dollar values along with general and administrative (G&A) costs and profit add up to the total contract price.) This is used to measure the contractor's performance and to determine the progress payments that should be paid to the contractor for a particular payment period. Care should be taken in the creation of the schedule of values to insure that it accurately reflects the reality of the construction, so that the contractor is paid when work is performed, and not before.

Construction Meetings

During the course of construction, periodic meetings are held to review the status of the project and exchange information among the construction team members. Construction meetings can help promote a team attitude and facilitate the flow of information, which is critical to a successful construction project. These usually occur weekly or bi-weekly. Typically, participants include the the general contractor, the owner, the architect, the DSA inspector, the testing agency, and, if one exists on the project, the construction manager. Sometimes, a principal or school site representative also attends the meetings. Written meeting minutes are kept, and a review of outstanding and new issues takes place at each meeting, as well as a review of project status. Subsequent to the meetings, the minutes are published and distributed to all attendees. Typically, the minutes track tasks to be performed as well as the party responsible for performing the particular task. Care should be taken to insure that these meeting minutes are accurate and complete, because they ultimately will serve as an important written record of what happened on the project.

The State Building Code requires a thorough and well-documented program of inspection and testing for school projects.

Inspection and Testing

The State Building Code requires a thorough and well-documented program of inspection and testing for school projects. Most projects require continuous full-time inspection by the IOR. As described earlier, the IOR is hired by the district and works under the direction of the architect. The IOR is also responsible for calling for material testing and special inspections as required in the construction documents and the building code. This includes soil testing, concrete testing, and welding inspection. The DSA field engineer visits the construction site regularly, reviews reports provided by the IOR, and reviews and approves any changes to the stamped DSA drawings.

Pay Requests

Education Code section 17603 provides that the district shall determine the method of payment for construction contracts, including progress payments. Specifically, the contract should provide when payment requests are to be submitted, to whom they should be submitted, what documents or other information should accompany the payment requests, and the time for the approval process.

Pay requests or progress payment applications are the formal documents a contractor submits to the district for payment. Typically, the contract documents provide for the pay requests to be submitted on a monthly basis. A pay request is prepared by the contractor and is typically made on a standard American Institute of Architect's form or similar format as specified in the general conditions. Consistent with the contractor's schedule of values, the pay request breaks down the work into separate components with their associated dollar values, and indicates how much of each component is complete, both for a given month and for the project as a whole.

These individual components are totaled to equal the requested payment amount each month. The architect and inspector and, when applicable, the construction manager, review these amounts. If the owner's representative disagrees with the contractor's completion percentage, the issue is resolved, the contractor makes the agreed-to changes, and the architect signs off and forwards them to the school district for payment. Timely payments are critical to the contractor and the subcontractors. Quick processing of payments encourages and rewards good performance, and is one of the most significant actions a school district can take to obtain cooperation from a contractor and its subcontractors. Contractors rely on the monthly payments to keep operations running efficiently and profitably. Failure to pay the contractors in a timely manner will have the long-term effect of discouraging qualified contractors from bidding on a project.

Changes

Modifications to the contract documents that change the price, time, or project design are called change orders. A change order is initiated in two ways: it is either a change order made by an owner who has altered the design, or as a change order request that the contractor initiates in the event a "changed condition" develops. When a situation arises that requires a change, the contractor typically prepares a change order request, submits it to the architect and/or construction manager and any subconsultants (engineers and specialty consultants), and it is then approved by the school district and the DSA. Before being paid, a change order ultimately must be approved by the district's board. Prompt approval of a change order helps maintain a good relationship, assuring contractors of compensation for any additional work not spelled out in the initial contract documents.

Pay requests or progress payment applications are the formal documents a contractor submits to the district for payment.

Quick processing of payments to the contractor encourages and rewards good performance, and is one of best ways to improve cooperation.

Change Order Pitfalls for the Project Owner

Typically, a construction contract will require that a contractor give the owners written notice of any conditions that require changes in the contract and that all change orders be executed in writing prior to performing that work.

School districts should ensure that these contractual procedures are followed consistently. More to the point, the district should avoid issuing any oral changes or allowing changed work to proceed prior to executing a change order. If it fails to follow its own contractual procedures governing change orders, the district may later be found to have waived its contractual protections! ■

Underground Unforeseen Conditions

California law prohibits a public agency from shifting the risk for underground unforeseen conditions to the contractor. Pub. Contract Code § 7104. If such conditions are encountered on the project that were not disclosed to the contractor in the bidding or the contract, the district will be required to pay the contractor for any costs associated with those unforeseen conditions. ■

While a normal part of the construction process, change orders are a deviation from the original contract, and require that all construction team members do additional unanticipated work that can negatively affect the time and cost of a project. To the extent possible, changes should be minimized or avoided to control costs and maintain construction schedules. (Public Contract Code section 20118.4(b) provides that a school board may authorize the issuance of change orders in an amount not greater than ten percent of the original contract price without being required to obtain competitive bids. With respect to modernization projects, changes up to 25 percent of the original contract price may be authorized. Pub. Contract Code § 20118.4.)

Change order causes and responsibility. Change orders can be included in one or more of three basic categories: unforeseen circumstances, design consultant's error and omission, or owner-requested design changes.

Design (scope) change. Design changes are best made during the design process and prior to bid. Changes coming after award of the contract cause duplication of efforts and increased construction costs. Changes can happen for a number of reasons such as a recent change in the district's curriculum, changes requested by a newly hired principal, or newly adopted district building standards (e.g., automatic flush valves for all toilet fixtures). Sometimes these changes are unavoidable, but often better communication earlier in the design and construction process and specific guidelines and policies regarding district-requested changes can reduce or minimize their occurance.

Unforeseen conditions. Frequently, these are the little (or big) surprises that require extra work or additional time for project completion that were not evident during the project design phase. This includes discovery of abandoned underground utilities not shown on any existing drawings, different soil conditions, termite damage in existing walls, and/or design changes requested by DSA or local agency in the field after plan review. While these types of changes are often impossible to completely eliminate, they can be minimized. For example, if as-built information for existing facilities is incomplete, the district should consider hiring a contractor to do a thorough survey of an existing facility's mechanical and/or electrical systems prior to the start of the design. This kind of investigation is useful on both new projects and modernization projects, and is particularly key for modernization projects because it is not uncommon that prior construction will not show up on the district's historical as-built drawings. Paying for more extensive survey information prior to the commencement of construction to locate things like hazardous materials, utilities, or buried rock in areas of excavation during project design, can save time and cost in construction.

Some additional change order requirements. The Public Contract Code requires any change or alteration of a contract to be specified in writing with the cost agreed to between the district's governing board and the contractor. The board may authorize the contractor to proceed with the performance of the change without requiring bids if the cost of the change does not exceed the greater of either the limits set forth in Public Contract Code section 20114 (day labor for maintenance and repairs), or ten percent of the original contract price. Pub. Contract Code § 20118.4. There are separate limitations for "reconstruction or rehabilitation work." These rules apply to individual change orders and not the cumulative total of the change orders issued on a project.

Change order waiver and release language. A particularly irksome position owners sometimes find themselves in is after paying for a change, they are confronted with a claim for additional costs associated with the change order. The owner's response is "I thought I already paid for this?" The answer is that they did, but that may not preclude a claim for additional change order-related costs. The way to prevent this from occurring is to include "full and final" language in the change order. That is, the change order should specifically provide that "payment of this change order constitutes the full and final payment for all costs, known or unknown relating to this change order and contractor hereby waives any claims for additional costs or delays or disruptions arising out of the work that is the subject of this change order." This will prevent a contractor from coming back and seeking additional costs for a change order that was previously negotiated.

Design team errors and omissions. To err is human. Architects and engineers are not perfect. Design mistakes and missing information can legitimately cause a contractor added cost on a project and unfortunately are a common part of the design and construction process.

The construction documents are a detailed set of instructions to build something that has never before been executed. Even if the project has been built previously, there will be many unique characteristics, such as soil conditions, site design, new contractors and inspectors, new code requirements, and new building materials that make some degree of imperfection inevitable.

As with the other forms of change orders, some degree of errors and omissions are a normal part of the construction process. As with all changes, they need to be resolved promptly and fairly. The primary focus should be on resolving the issue. Quickly providing the necessary information to perform the change will allow the contractor to proceed with change order pricing and construction. The district and design team must place a high priority on communicating the information that the contractor requires so that it can stay on schedule and have no basis for asserting delay claims against the district.

However, for the districts' protection and to insure that the work does not stop as the result of a dispute over the pricing of a change, the district's contract with the contractor should contain a change order "prosecution of work" clause that requires the contractor to perform the change when directed by the district, notwithstanding the parties inability to agree to the terms of a change order. This clause will require the contractor to prosecute the change and to resolve its dispute over change order pricing or project extension after the work is completed. Additionally, a prosecution of work provision will prevent the contractor from holding the project hostage while it forces the district to pay what it deems sufficient reimbursement.

After the change has been designed and approved and a price agreed upon, the district may choose to have a discussion with the architect regarding the cause of the error or omission to avoid repeating it in the future, or if the change was outside the standard of care, to request that the architect contribute to the cost of correcting the error.

✍ **practice tip**

Contractors frequently try to reserve their right to assert additional claims relating to a change order at some later date. A district can avoid this by insisting that all claims/costs relating to a particular change be included in a change order before agreeing to issue it.

A prosecution of work provision will prevent the contractor from holding the project hostage while it forces the district to pay what it deems sufficient reimbursement.

It is good practice for a district to include a certain amount for errors and omissions in the project budget.

It is good practice for a district to include a certain amount for errors and omissions in the project budget. For a medium-sized projects, one view is that four percent of the construction budget be reserved for errors and omissions change orders on new projects and eight percent for modernization projects.

Prompt Payment Act

Progress payment requests. By law, school districts are required to make progress payments to their contractors in a timely manner. Specifically, Public Contract Code § 20104.50 provides that if a local agency fails to make any progress payment to a contractor within 30 days after receipt of an undisputed and properly submitted payment request, the district will have to pay ten percent interest to the contractor on such unpaid amounts. Code Civ. Proc. § 685.010(a). Further, section 20104.50 requires a district to review a payment application "as soon as practicable," but not more than seven days after receipt, for the purpose of determining whether the request is proper. Any request deemed to be improper must be returned to the contractor within seven days with a written explanation of why it is being returned. These requirements apply to all payment requests received from contractors except a contractor's request for payment of retention. A summary of the requirements of section 20104.50 is required to be included in the terms and conditions of the construction contract between the district and the contractor.

It should be noted that these requirements apply to undisputed and properly submitted payment requests. To the extent that entitlement to the amount requested in the payment request is disputed or if the request does not contain information required by contract to be submitted with the request, the 30-day requirement does not apply. However, a district must act promptly to review these requests and to give written notice to the contractor of the reason for its rejection of the request. Pub. Contract Code § 20104.50(c)(2).

A school district should develop procedures that insure that payment applications from its contractors are reviewed and paid in a timely manner.

These requirements behoove a school district to develop procedures that insure that payment applications from its contractors are reviewed, and if acceptable, paid in a timely manner. This will require coordination between the district's onsite project representatives (whether the construction manager or architect) and its accounts payable department. Moreover, districts cannot compel contractors to vary or waive these prompt payment requirements. Any attempt to do so in the construction contract will likely be deemed to be void.

Payment of retention. The payment of retention is also governed by California statutory law. Section 7107 of the Public Contract Code requires a district to release any undisputed retention within sixty days of the date of the completion of the project. If there is a dispute between the district and the contractor relating to the contractor's performance, the district may withhold up to 150 percent of the amount in dispute. "Completion" is defined as either:

- The occupation, beneficial use, and enjoyment of the project
- Acceptance of the project by the district
- Cessation of labor on the project for a continuous period of 100 days
- Thirty days after cessation of the work and/or the recording of a notice of completion by the district

Pub. Contract Code § 7107

Consequently, the district accounts' payable department must be prepared to turn around payment applications in an expeditious manner so as to avoid the interest penalties that will accrue if the monies are not paid in accordance with the statutory time periods.

Construction Claims

Construction claims are contractor requests for adjustments to the contract beyond the original contract price set forth in the construction agreement. Claims arise as a result of a variety of events that cause the contractor or its subcontractors to incur additional expenses or experience delays or disruptions to their work due to circumstances beyond the contractor's control. Some of the most common causes of claims against owners are defective plans or specifications, delays in the issuance of permits, unforeseen conditions, failure to promptly respond to contractors' requests for information, significant work scope changes, lack of coordination among multiple prime contractors, and acts of God (*i.e.*, severe weather). Most of these problems can be avoided by proper planning prior to the start of construction.

Claims mitigation. Your contract should include a provision which requires the contractor to provide detailed and timely written notification of circumstances giving rise to a claim against the district. Timely notice of claims is critical so that the district can identify the specific problem causing the contractor to incur extra costs or delaying its performance and so that the district can act to minimize those problems before they significantly affect the project. Therefore, the district should strictly enforce these notice provisions so that is in a position to argue that the contractor has waived its right to pursue a claim because of improper notice.

Setting aside the notice issue, the key to claims mitigation (*i.e.*, minimizing claims) is responding promptly and effectively to the particular problem. To succeed, the district has to commit sufficient resources to analyze the situation and respond appropriately, whether it be by providing information needed to resolve a defective design issue, devising a work-around schedule to overcome a problem that is delaying the job, authorizing either a suspension or acceleration of the contractor's work, or by rejecting the claim. Although the initial impulse may be to reject the claim and to demand that the contractor comply with its contract, since the objective is to complete the project on time and under budget, a careful analysis must be conducted to determine whether a problem exists, what the cause of the problem is, and what can be done to minimize the impact of the problem on the project. Ignoring the issue or simply rejecting the claim out of hand will ultimately be to the detriment of the district.

Perhaps the best defense against unwarranted claims is to insure that the district or its construction manager is adequately monitoring and recording what goes on during the project. This should include:

- Requiring the district's project representative to keep daily logs that track the progress of the work, as well as recording any issues or problems that arise during the job
- Photographing the progress of construction daily

- Insisting that the project schedule be periodically updated by the contractor to accurately reflect the progress of the work and the key events that impact the project
- Insuring that the contractor's requests for information are responded to promptly and completely by the project architect
- Resolving disputes with contractor and not allowing contractor's change order requests to become stale
- Approaching all issues that impact the contract price and the contract time with a view with towards coming up with a resolution that will be in the best interests of the project

The district, the architect, and the construction manager should work together to resolve the claims-related issues in the most expeditious manner possible.

The district, the architect, and the construction manager should work together to resolve the claims-related issues in the most expeditious manner possible. To the extent that there is identifiable responsibility for the problem within the district's team, at this point, it is prudent to avoid finger pointing and instead concentrate on coming up with the solution that allows the contractor to complete the work at the least cost, in the least amount of time.

The legitimacy of claims ranges from completely unjustified to legitimate and well documented. In recent years, some contractors have taken the view that an aggressive pursuit of claims is a lucrative source of revenue regardless of the merits because some owners are willing to pay rather than face potential claims litigation. However, by maintaining good records and responding to issues as they arise, a district minimizes the risk of facing a major claim, legitimate or otherwise. Where significant issues are involved, legal counsel should be consulted to determine the district's best course of action.

The district's construction contract general conditions should contain provisions that provide for a dispute resolution procedure.

As a procedural matter, the district's construction contract general conditions should contain provisions that provide for a dispute resolution procedure to be followed in the event of a dispute between the district and the contractor. Additionally, the district should require its general contractor to include the identical dispute resolution provision in all of its subcontracts so that any disputes which arise out of the project can be resolved in a single forum.

Punch lists. Near the completion of the project, the contractor provides the architect and owner with a comprehensive list of work to be completed, including corrections to the work already completed. The inspector, architect, engineers, and owner walk the project and record any items the contractor did not include on the list. This list of items to be corrected, called the "punch list," must be completed by the contractor consistent with the requirements of the contract documents before the project is complete, and before a notice of completion is filed and final payment is made. Moreover, completion of all punch list work should be a condition of project close-out and the payment of the contractor's retention.

Stop notices. On public works projects, contractors do not have mechanic's lien rights. How then does a subcontractor protect itself if it is not being paid by the general contractor? The answer is, by a "stop notice."

During the course of the project, if a subcontractor or material supplier is not paid by the general contractor or another contractor on the project, they can file a stop notice with the school district, requiring the district to withhold a certain amount of money until the issue is properly resolved. Civil Code § 3103.

California law requires specific actions that must be followed by the school district, the general contractor, and the subcontractor.

If a stop notice is received, the district has a duty to act quickly and execute the proper notices to withhold the money or bonds that are due or become due to the contractor in an amount to satisfy the claim, pay interest, and provide for the reasonable cost of litigation. Civil Code §§ 3186, 3187. The district is required to withhold these funds until the issue between the general contractor and the party filing the stop notice is resolved. Civil Code § 3186. All stop notices must be filed no later than thirty days after the proper recording of the notice of completion. Civil Code § 3184.

Release bond. If contractor or subcontractor disputes the corrections, validity, or enforceability of a stop notice, the district may, in its discretion, permit the original contractor to file with the district a release bond issued by a corporate surety in an amount equal to 125 percent of the claim stated in the stop notice. Civil Code § 1386. Upon filing, the district shall not withhold any monies from the original contractor in response to the stop notice. Civil Code §§ 3183–3187.

Final payment, unconditional waivers, and releases. The construction contract should define every task that the contractor must finish before the project is deemed complete and final payment is due. At the very least, these requirements should include completing all punch list work, delivery of all certifications and warranties, delivery of all manuals, completing all equipment commissioning, testing, and training, and the delivery of all unconditional waivers and releases for final payment. These waivers are critical to insure that the district does not pay for the same work twice—once when it makes its final payment and a second time in the event its general contractor failed to pay the subcontractors.

DSA closeout and certification. A project is not officially approved until construction is complete and all documentation regarding changes, inspections, tests, and reports have been filed, reviewed, and closed with compliance by DSA.

The information needed to properly close a project comes from the district, the inspectors, the contractors, the architect,, the engineers, and the testing laboratory and must be submitted, reviewed, and approved by DSA.

It is important to execute this final closeout to verify that the project is safe and in compliance with the law. If closeout is not executed, district board members can be held legally liable for any injuries sustained by people in an unapproved project.

In general, unapproved work, such as relocatable classrooms without site approval and unapproved building additions at a site, must either be removed or retroactively approved before new projects can be reviewed and approved at the site. These issues should be resolved at the early stages of a project to avoid delays and loss of state funding.

School projects can be closed out within a few months of completion—it doesn't have to take years to accomplish this task. But accomplishing closeout quickly takes a focused effort by the district, its architect, and its inspector.

The project architect must actively pursue final certification by adhering to all the procedures discussed and not considering the project complete until DSA issues the final certification. Although the architect is chiefly responsible for

If a stop notice is received, the district has a duty to act quickly to withhold the money or bonds that are due to the contractor.

It is important to execute this final closeout to verify that the project is safe and in compliance with the law.

DSA Closeout Checklist

1. Has DSA approved plans, specifications, and all addenda?

2. Has the architect filed the "Contract Information" form 102 for all contractors (and CM, if applicable)?

3. Has the "Inspector Qualification" form 5 for the project inspector been filed with and approved by DSA?

4. Has the "Inspector Qualification" form 5 for any Special Inspectors been filed with and approved by DSA? (And for welding or masonry inspections if applicable.)

5. Has the Inspector of Record, project inspector, filed a "Semi-monthly Report" for every period during construction?

6. Has the Inspector of Record, project inspector, filed a "Quarterly Report" for every quarter during construction?

7. Have all "Field Trip Notes" from DSA field representative been addressed by a joint signature letter from the architect and project inspector and also has resolution been addressed in the project inspector's semi-monthly report?

8. Has DSA approved all change orders?

9. Have all prime contractors submitted their "Final Verified Reports" form 6 to DSA?

10. Has the project inspector submitted the "Final Verified Report" form 6 to DSA?

11. Has the testing laboratory submitted the "Final Verified Report" form 6 to DSA (and also any special inspectors that may have been used)?

12. Has the testing laboratory submitted the "Final Lab Affidavit"?

13. Has the architect submitted the "Final Verified Report" form 6 to DSA?

14. Has the contractor submitted and the architect forwarded the "Weighmaster's Certificate"?

15. Have every recorded "Notice of Completion" been forwarded to DSA?

16. Has the district received "Final DSA Certification"? Note that the architect must request this in writing from DSA when all of the above items have been completed. Copies of all required closeout items should be attached to the letter requesting final certification.

obtaining DSA certification, some documents must be provided by the school district, the district's project inspector(s), the district's special inspector(s), and the district's independent testing laboratory. Ultimately, it is the owner's responsibility to make sure the architect, inspectors, testing laboratories, and all applicable contractors follow the necessary procedures to obtain final certification.

Districts should consider incorporating in their Owner/Architect Agreement a provision requiring the architect to obtain DSA final certification, and a holdback of a certain agreed upon percentage of fees until it is obtained. Similar language might be included in the owner/construction manager agreement, if applicable. The owner/project inspector agreement should include specific tasks and deadlines, as outlined below, to ensure that all required documents are provided in a timely fashion.

While primarily the responsibility of the architect or construction manager, the school district should maintain a separate project file for each DSA application number, with copies of all related correspondence sent to DSA correctly filed. The adjacent checklist should also be included in the file and used as a tool to monitor progress.

Notice of completion. When a project is complete, the school district must file a notice of completion with the county recorder's office in the county where the project is located within ten days of completion and before the contractor receives final payment. Civil Code § 3093. This notice protects the school district in the event a general contractor or prime contractor failed to pay its subcontractors. It officially notifies any potential creditors that they have 30 days to file a claim for unpaid debt prior to the district's final payment to the general or prime contractor. If claims are filed, the district will be required to withhold some or all of the final payment until the issue is resolved by the general and prime contractor.

Appeal of DSA decisions. From time to time, differences of opinion will surface between school districts and DSA regarding the interpretation and application of building standards.

Where differences cannot be resolved through discussion with DSA staff and its supervisors, the district has numerous levels of appeal. First, a district may file an appeal with the State Architect Advisory Board. The Board's purpose is to advise the State Architect on the administration of the Field Act (Educ. Code § 17280 *et seq.* and § 81130 *et seq.*). The Board also serves as a board of appeals in all matters relating to the administration and enforcement of building standards for the design, construction, alteration, seismic safety, fire and panic safety, and alternate means of protection determinations of public buildings under the jurisdiction of the DSA. Further, the Board acts as a board of appeals in matters relating to building projects involving the accessibility requirements of Title 24, California Code of Regulations.

To initiate the Board's appeal process, the district requests an informal conference. Within ten days, the Board must convene the conference with representatives of the district and DSA. A decision is made by DSA that either confirms, modifies, or reverses the original decision in question.

If the district disagrees with the decision, it may request a formal hearing before the Board. At the hearing, the district has the right to counsel, to submit documentary evidence and exhibits, and to have witnesses appear and testify, although the hearing is not conducted in accordance with strict rules of evidence or courtroom procedures. If the district does not agree with the decision of the Board, the district has two additional appeal opportunities—the first is to the Director of the Department of General Services (DGS) who may affirm, reverse, or amend the ruling, order, decision, or act being appealed. If still unsatisfied, the district can file its last appeal with the California Building Standards Commission.

DGS = Department of General Services
SBC = State Building Code

State Regulatory Requirements During Construction

During construction, school districts must comply with the Field Act and Building Code requirements of the DSA, prevailing wage and OSHA requirements of the DIR, and with storm water runoff control requirements of the SWRCB.

The Field Act

The Field Act was enacted after several schools collapsed during the 1933 Long Beach earthquake. Educ. Code §§ 17280 and 81130 *et seq.* The law's purpose is to protect children and staff from death and injury in public schools grades K-14 during and after earthquakes. It sets higher standards for public schools than for commercial and residential buildings.

The Field Act was enacted after several schools collapsed during the 1933 Long Beach earthquake.

Privately owned schools are excluded from the Field Act requirements. Also, the requirements relating to hazard reduction of existing pre-Act schools does not apply to the State University or University of California systems, but it does apply to community colleges.

The Field Act and its regulations have been updated many times since its inception. With the passage of the Garrison Act (1939) and the Greene Act (1967), the state requirements were extended to the evaluation and retrofit of existing pre-Field Act buildings. The scope of the regulations is found in the State Building Code (SBC), Part I, Title 24, Sec. 4-301 *et seq.* Field Act buildings have stringent construction quality control procedures required by California Code of Regulations Title 24, Part 1.

Public schools built before the Field Act were phased out or retrofitted to comply with the Act. Private schools built or altered after 1986 must now comply with similar legislation enforced by local governments. Educ. Code § 17320 *et seq.*

The Field Act also created the legal title of structural engineer as a subcategory of civil engineering. To obtain registration in California, civil engineers are required to pass a special seismic examination.

Joint use projects and the Field Act. Some joint use projects may trigger Field Act requirements. For example, if a library building is being built on public school district property and/or more than 24 public school students will be required to go to the public library for educational purposes after the project has been completed, the project will be subject to the Act.

Prevailing Wage and Labor Compliance Program

California's Prevailing Wage Law requires contractors on public works projects to pay the prevailing rate of hourly wages and fringe benefits as specified by the State Department of Industrial Relations for the area where the project is located. The purpose of the law is to attract competent workers to public works projects and to allow union contractors to compete on an even playing field with nonunion contractors for competitively bid projects.

Contractors and subcontractors of all tiers on public works in California are charged with knowing and complying with all provisions of the Prevailing Wage Law. With few exceptions, discussed below, awarding authorities' duties under the Prevailing Wage Law are relatively minor. Although awarding authorities are required to implement the Prevailing Wage Law, the State Department of Industrial Relations' Division of Labor Standards Enforcement (DLSE) is the agency responsible for prosecuting violations.

The Prevailing Wage Law appears in California's Labor Code at Division 2, Part 7, Chapters 1–3 (§§ 1720–1817). Regulations implementing the Prevailing Wage Law promulgated by the State Department of Industrial Relations appear in the California Code of Regulations at Title 8, Division 1, Chapters 2 (§§ 200–242.6) and 8 (§§ 16000–17270).

What is the prevailing wage? Prevailing wages are wage rates for particular trades or crafts set forth in prevailing wage determinations issued by the DIR through its Division of Labor Statistics and Research. Labor Code § 1770, 8 C.C.R. § 16100. Prevailing wage determinations are issued for different geographic regions in the state, usually consisting of counties or groups of counties, although some determinations apply statewide.

Prevailing wage determinations for particular crafts and trades include the following components: the prevailing basic straight-time hourly wage rate, the prevailing rate for holiday and overtime work, and the prevailing rate of employer payments for employee benefits. Labor Code § 1773.1(a), 8 C.C.R. §§ 16000, 16203. Prevailing wage rate determinations are issued for journeymen and apprentices.

Basic rule. The basic rule requiring the payment of prevailing wages appears at California Labor Code § 1771, which provides in full as follows:

- Except for public works projects of one thousand dollars ($1,000) or less, not less than the general prevailing rate of per diem wages for work of a similar character in the locality in which the public work is performed, and not less than the general prevailing rate of per diem wages for holiday and overtime work fixed as provided in this chapter, shall be paid to all workers employed on public works.

- This section is applicable only to work performed under contract, and is not applicable to work carried out by a public agency with its own forces. This section is applicable to contracts let for maintenance work.

The key components are that the rule applies to public works projects of more than $1,000,[2] the prevailing wage for the particular locality and trade must be paid, and the rule does not apply to work performed by the agency's own forces.

The Prevailing Wage Law has three other key components. First, the prevailing wage must be paid by "the contractor to whom the contract is awarded, and any subcontractor" of any tier. Labor Code § 1774. Second, the contractor or subcontractor required to pay prevailing wages must keep certified payroll records evidencing its compliance using the required form, and must timely respond to requests for copies of its payroll records. Labor Code § 1776. Third, the contractor to whom the contract is awarded must also employ apprentices in the proper ratio, pay the applicable prevailing wage for apprentices, and file the proper notices with the Division of Apprenticeship Standards (DAS) before commencing and after completing the work. (Labor Code § 1775.5(e), 8 C.C.R. §§ 227–242.6.)

DAS = Division of Apprenticeship Standards

What school districts must do to comply. School districts must take several specific steps to comply with the Prevailing Wage Law. Those steps are summarized below.

Obtain the prevailing wage determination. School districts must obtain a copy of the relevant prevailing wage determination from the Department of Industrial Relations. Labor Code § 1773. School districts may request that the Department put them on a mailing list for all area wage determinations. 8 C.C.R. § 16205.

Specify in call for bids that prevailing wage must be paid. The Prevailing Wage Law requires public agencies to either specify in their bid and contract documents the prevailing wage rate for each craft or trade that will be employed on the public works project in question or, in the alternative, to indicate in the bid and contract documents that copies of the prevailing wage determinations are on file at the agency's principal office. Labor Code § 1773.2. In addition, a copy of the prevailing wage determinations is also required to be kept at the job site. School districts should consult their attorneys for appropriate language to include in their bid and contract documents for public works projects.

Specify in contract that certified payroll records must be kept. School districts must specify in their public works contracts the requirement that the contractor and its subcontractor keep certified payroll records and produce copies of the records on request as provided by Labor Code section 1776(h).

School districts must specify in their public works contracts the requirement that the contractor and its subcontractor keep certified payroll records.

Notify Division of Apprenticeship Standards of contract award. Within five days after award of a public works contract, school districts must notify the State Division of Apprenticeship Standards of the award. Labor Code § 1773.3. The Division of Apprenticeship Standards is responsible for monitoring compliance with apprenticeship requirements.

2. *See* discussion below on special requirement for school districts utilizing certain bond funds to finance capital improvements.

If the Labor Commissioner notifies a district of prevailing wage violations, the district must withhold the indicated wage and penalty assessments from the contractor.

Withhold wage and penalty assessments from contractor. In the event the Labor Commissioner notifies a district of prevailing wage violations, the school district must withhold the indicated wage and penalty assessments from the contractor until receipt of a final order that is no longer subject to judicial review. Labor Code § 1727.

Respond to requests for certified payroll records. Requests for certified payroll records from a prime contractor or subcontractors of any tier may be made by employees or their authorized representatives, the Division of Labor Standards Enforcement, the Division of Apprenticeship Standards, and members of the public. Requests by all persons other than the public may be made directly to the contractor; requests by the public can only be made through the public agency, the Division of Labor Standards Enforcement, or the Division of Apprenticeship Standards. Labor Code § 1776.

The agency must acknowledge receipt of any request for certified payroll records and must promptly forward such requests to the contractor. The acknowledgement may be accomplished by sending the requesting party a copy of the request sent by the agency to the contractor. 8 C.C.R. § 16400.

The agency's request to the contractor (including requests forwarded from members of the public) must be in a form that provides for evidence of receipt and that includes the following information:

- Records to be produced and the form to be used
- Notice that the person certifying the records, if not the contractor, will be deemed to be acting as the contractor's agent
- Notice that failure to produce the records within ten working days will subject the contractor to a penalty of $25 per calendar day for each worker until the contractor complies
- Statement that the contractor is entitled to receive copying costs before producing copies of its records

8 C.C.R. § 16400(d)

Copies of certified payroll records should be provided by the contractor to the agency and not directly to the public. Before providing certified payroll records to the public, the agency must strike out the records in a way that obliterates the name, address, social security number, and other private information pertaining to each employee. 8 C.C.R. § 16403(b).

Enforce debarment orders. Contractors and subcontractors may be debarred from bidding on public contracts by the Labor Commissioner as a penalty for willful violations of the Prevailing Wage Law. The Labor Commissioner is required to publish a list of debarred contractors twice a year. Labor Code §§ 1771.1, 1777.7. Agencies awarding public contracts must comply with debarment orders and should check the Labor Commissioner's list.

Labor compliance programs. School districts (and other public agencies) can increase the size of public works contracts that can be awarded without requiring the payment of prevailing wages by instituting a labor compliance program. With such a program in place, prevailing wages are required to be paid on public works projects of $25,000 or more, and on alteration, demolition, repair,

Contractors and subcontractors may be de-barred from bidding on public contracts by the Labor Commissioner as a penalty for willful violations of the Prevailing Wage Law.

and maintenance contracts of $15,000 or more. Without a labor compliance program in place, prevailing wages are required to be paid on all such contracts of $1,000 or more. Labor Code § 1771.5; 8 C.C.R. §§ 16245–16802.

In 2002, the California Legislature passed and the Governor approved Assembly Bill 1506, which requires that school districts implement a labor compliance program for any project for which funding is obtained from either the Kindergarten–University Public Education Facilities Bond Act of 2002 or the Kindergarten–University Public Education Facilities Bond Act of 2004. Labor Code § 1771.7. The labor compliance program required by AB 1506 must meet all prior requirements in Labor Code section 1771.5 and any other applicable provisions of the California Code of Regulations, as well as several new provisions that appear in the new law.

A labor compliance program must include the following elements:

- A written finding by the school district or other awarding body stating that it has initiated and enforced, or has contracted with a third party to initiate and enforce, the required labor compliance program
- Transmittal of a copy of the school district finding to the State Allocation Board, which may not release funds to the district until the finding has been received
- Bid invitations and contracts with language that incorporates the Prevailing Wage Law
- A pre-job conference held with the contractor and all subcontractors to discuss federal and state labor law requirements applicable to the contract
- A certified copy of each weekly payroll that project contractors and subcontractors must maintain and furnish, at a designated time, containing a statement of compliance with the Prevailing Wage Law signed under penalty of perjury
- Payroll records that the school district or other awarding body review and, if necessary, audit to verify compliance with the Prevailing Wage Law
- Withheld contract payments by the school district when payroll records are delinquent or inadequate
- Withheld contract payments by the school district or other awarding body equal to the amount of underpayment and applicable penalties when, after investigation, it is established that underpayment has occurred

Care should be taken in implementing these provisions because errors, even if inadvertent, may delay and disrupt the project by causing the withholding of funds from the contractor. Also, the statute should be studied carefully for slightly different requirements that apply to the University of California, the California State University, and to Community College Districts.

California Occupational Safety and Health Act. Although there are federal laws regarding workplace safety and health, school districts, as California employers, are generally governed by the California Occupational Safety and Health Act (Cal OSHA) of 1973 (Labor Code §§ 6300-6719). Cal OSHA mandates that every employer furnish employment and a place of employment that are safe

Care should be taken in implementing a labor compliance program, because errors may delay and disrupt the project.

Cal OSHA = California Occupational Safety and Health Act

and healthful for its employees. Labor Code § 6303. The Act imposes an affirmative duty on employers to implement various measures to render the workplace safe and healthful.

Cal OSHA identifies three types of strategies for controlling workplace hazards: engineering controls, administrative controls, and the use of personal protective equipment.

Specifically, Cal OSHA identifies three types of strategies for controlling workplace hazards: engineering controls, administrative controls, and the use of personal protective equipment. The Occupational Safety and Health Standards Board, the body that adopts workplace safety and health standards and orders (Title 8 C.C.R. § 340 *et seq.*), generally regards engineering controls as most effective, followed by administrative controls and personal protective equipment.

The Department of Industrial Relations is the state agency responsible for administering Cal OSHA. Four divisions within the DIR are charged with administering different sections of the Act:

- Occupational Safety and Health Standards Board
- Division of Occupational Safety and Health
- Occupational Safety and Health Appeals Board
- Cal OSHA Consultation Service

The Division of Occupational Safety and Health enforces the standards adopted by the Standards Board at the worksite and therefore, it is the division of the DIR that works most closely with employers to investigate and remediate hazardous conditions. The Division's duties include, but are not limited to:

- Conducting onsite inspections
- Investigating industrial accidents
- Investigating complaints
- Determining whether certain safeguards are sufficient to render employees safe
- Ordering employers to implement safety measures to protect employees or otherwise secure the worksite

Typically, the Division's enforcement activities begin when an injury or an unsafe working condition has been reported.

Employers are required to report every workplace incident resulting in serious injury or illness or death to the Division immediately after its occurrence.

Employers are required to report every workplace incident resulting in serious injury or illness or death to the Division immediately after its occurrence. A "serious injury or illness" has occurred when the employee suffers loss of a member of the body, permanent disfigurement, or required in-patient hospitalization for a period in excess of 24 hours for reasons other than medical observation. When a serious injury or illness has been reported, the Division will determine whether the incident warrants investigation. If an investigation is undertaken, the Division may pursue civil and/or criminal penalties against the employer if it determines that one or more violations of Cal/OSHA regulations has occurred.

In addition, whenever the Division learns or has reason to believe that any employment or place of employment is not safe or is injurious to the welfare of any employee, it may, on its own initiative or pursuant to a complaint, investigate with or without notice or hearings. Labor Code § 6309. If the Division learns about a non-serious violation, the Division may conduct an investigation or may opt to notify the employer of the violation and direct the employer to take certain corrective actions.

Districts should be proactive about health, safety, and environmental issues during construction. There are several reasons for districts to be proactive in ensuring safety at their school facility construction sites.

First, not all risks can be shifted to the contractors. Second, even where accidents are purely the responsibility of the contractor, districts need to prevent harm to its employees and students, prevent loss or damage to products and equipment to be installed in the new facility, and to prevent schedule delay due to a work stoppage.

Several steps can be taken to ensure the district's success in mitigating the risk associated with hiring contractors and consultants. First, start by hiring the right contractors. Second, have a comprehensive safety plan in place. And, third, use insurance wisely.

Solicit bids from contractors with low accident rates. In conjunction with enforcement, OSHA collects information on accident rates. These are commonly referred to as the OSHA Recordable Rates. Over time these rates have served as a guide to evaluating the safety practices of companies. The construction industry incident rates have been tracked for decades with the average accident rates falling over time.

The rate is calculated by dividing the total number of employee hours worked per year into the number of accidents occurring per 100 full-time employee hours per year or (100 x 2000 hours/year = 200,000 hours).

$$\text{Incident rate } = \frac{\text{number of accidents per year x 200.000}}{\text{Total employee hours per year}}$$

Currently, the industry average is around 8.0, falling from 14.0 in the early 1990s. Certain contractors place a high value on safety, and through their association with the Construction Industry Institute have driven their rates down around 1.0. Even in a low bid environment, these companies are still available to public clients such as schools.

Districts can also insist on language in its contracts that stresses the importance of safety to the district and its expectations from any contractor.

Develop a safety plan. It is in the best interest of the district to have a comprehensive safety plan. After selecting a contractor that meets the safety requirements, insist on obtaining their safety execution plan prior to any work commencing. Care should be taken in evaluating the plan to ensure that it helps, not hinders, the district in mitigating its risks on any project.

It is in the best interest of the district to have a comprehensive safety plan.

A good safety plan can help minimize the impact of construction at the school sites and save money. In addition, a good safety plan gives you more leverage in managing contractors and claims. It keeps the district proactive with safety and assures the safety of everyone at school.

Use insurance wisely. Typically, the contractor's policy holds provisions for a district. If it makes sense, a district should consider using a coordinated insurance program or CIP. For districts with sizable building programs (typically over $70 million), a CIP could realize significant cost savings to the district. CIPs are wrap-around insurance programs that can be designed to cover everyone associated with the district's projects. The insurance program covers construction

CIP = Coordinated insurance program

risks for the district and all district agents such as program or project managers, architects, and contractors. Covering anyone involved helps reduce the cost of bidding the projects by removing insurance from the bid specifications. For example, if a contractor's safety record or performance is not the best, they pay for that in higher builder's risk, workmen's compensation, and bonding costs. They may recover this in their bids by adding a cushion. When you have a general contractor along with all the subcontractors adding this cost into their bids, the cumulative effect of this cushion can add up to 12 percent or more of the contractors' bids. It also guarantees adequate coverage for everyone working on the sites. Any savings generated can be used to augment the building program.

Storm water runoff control. Storm water runoff is one of the largest sources of pollution to rivers, lakes, and coastal areas of the United States. Storm water laws regulate rain, snowmelt, and surface waters that flow over streets, parking lots, construction sites, and industrial facilities into public and private storm water conveyance facilities. The purpose of these regulations is to prevent storm water from carrying pollutants (such as silt, pesticides, fertilizer, trash, food wastes, automotive by-products, and other toxic substances) to waters, rivers, lakes, and beaches, thereby adversely affecting health and safety, including but not limited to potable, irrigation, and recreation waters, as well as that of natural flora and fauna.

MS4	= Separate Municipal Storm Sewer System
NPDES	= National Pollution Discharge Elimination System
SWRCB	= State Water Resources Control Board
RWQCB	= Regional Water Quality Control Board

How is storm water regulated and by whom? The federal Clean Water Act has established requirements for storm water discharges under the National Pollution Discharge Elimination System (NPDES) program. Enacted in 1972, the Clean Water Act's objective to improve water quality initially focused on reducing "point source" pollution from industrial process wastewater and municipal sewage, by requiring an individual NPDES permit for any discharge of pollutants from such sources to certain waters.

With growing realization that storm water was a significant source of pollution, section 402(p) was added to the Clean Water Act in 1987 to create a framework for regulating storm water discharges under the NPDES program. section 402(p) prohibits municipal, construction, and industrial storm water discharges without an NPDES permit, and establishes permit requirements.

Cities and counties typically have separate municipal storm sewer systems (MS4s), originally designed as flood control systems and primarily intended to quickly divert rainwater off the streets during a heavy storm. The traditional NPDES approach, by which an individualized permit is developed for each facility, is rendered impracticable by the large number of storm water dischargers. Though the cumulative impacts of these sources are significant, the impacts from each site are typically not significant enough to justify the investment of resources needed to develop facility-specific permits. Accordingly, the EPA has developed a relatively streamlined process for issuing "general" storm water discharge permits, which apply to eligible storm water dischargers.

Three categories of storm water permits. In California, the State Water Resources Control Board (SWRCB) and its nine Regional Water Quality Control Boards (RWQCBs) have authority to implement and enforce the NPDES permit program. Storm water dischargers may seek coverage under either applicable statewide general permits or individual permits. The SWRCB has adopted general permits to regulate storm water runoff from three sources: construction activities, industrial activities, and MS4s. A school district may be subject to the requirements of one or more of these permits.

Construction storm water general permit. School districts engaged in certain categories of construction activities are required to comply with the Construction Activities Storm Water General Permit. Additional information regarding the general construction permit is available at the SWRCB web site (www.swrcb.ca.gov/stormwtr/construction/html).

The owner of land where construction activities will occur is responsible for obtaining authorization for grading and/or construction pursuant to the general construction permit. Similarly, a school district must obtain permit coverage where its grading and construction activities will take place on district-owned or optioned property, as well as within easements or on adjacent properties owned by another entity which are necessary to such activities.

The owner of land where construction activities will occur is responsible for obtaining authorization for grading and/or construction pursuant to the general construction permit.

Grading and construction activities resulting in soil disturbances of one or more acres must seek coverage under the general construction permit.

The revised general construction permit encompasses both large (five or more acres) and small (one to five acres) grading and construction projects. However, there are some distinctions made for small projects. For example, small construction projects are not subject to storm water sampling and analysis requirements applicable to large projects.

Compliance with general construction permit requirements. Prior to the commencement of any regulated soil disturbing activities associated with grading and construction projects, a school district must file a notice of intent (NOI) package for each covered construction activity to the SWRCB. This package includes the NOI form, a fee payment of $700, and a Storm Water Pollution Prevention Plan (SWPPP).

BMP = Best management practice
NOI = Notice of intent
SWPPP = Storm Water Pollution Prevention Plan

The SWPPP must provide specified information, including a site map showing drainage and discharge locations, and the best management practices (BMPS) that will be implemented for effective sediment and erosion control. The purpose of the BMPs is to reduce the discharge of pollutants to receiving waters during storm water events.

BMP maintenance and compliance requirements. BMPs installed at the site must conform to the SWPPP site map, be consistently maintained, and provide effective erosion and sediment control for waters leaving the site. Commonly accepted BMPs at construction sites include biofiltration swales, detention basins, infiltration basins or trenches, and treatment devices such as sand filters.

School districts must maintain a complete copy of the SWPPP at each construction site, which must be at all reasonable times available for review by state inspectors and the public.

Responsibility for SWPPP compliance. School districts may delegate tasks involved with implementing the SWPPP requirements to a contractor or construction manager. However, because a school district, as the permitted landowner, remains responsible for compliance with permit conditions and requirements, explicit written agreements with contractors addressing remedies for noncompliance are recommended.

Explicit written agreements with contractors addressing remedies for SWPPP noncompliance are recommended.

Where a school district construction project is subject to analysis of storm water runoff requirements, only personnel trained in the requirements of storm water sampling should perform this task.

Terminating permit coverage. When a construction project is completed, the school district must file a Notice of Termination (NOT). Otherwise, the general construction permit requirements presumptively still apply and remain enforceable. Similarly, if changes occur to site conditions or information provided in the SWPPP, a Change of Information (COI) must be submitted.

General construction permit storm water sampling and analysis requirements. In certain instances, the general construction permit requires the sampling and analysis of storm water runoff at large construction sites in order to assess the effectiveness of BMPs in controlling the release of pollutants—principally sediment—from the site during a storm event. Small construction sites are not subject to sampling and analysis requirements under the revised general construction permit. However, the regulations do not currently define "small construction sites," and therefore a school district is advised to obtain a letter of exemption from the SWRCB.

Where a school district construction project is subject to these requirements, the collection and handling of storm water samples requires care to ensure the integrity and validity of collected samples. Thus, only personnel trained in the timing, collection, handling, analysis, reporting, and record-keeping requirements of storm water sampling should perform such tasks. For most school districts, such laboratories and personnel must be out-sourced.

Storm water sampling and analysis at large construction sites are required under two scenarios:

- **Direct discharges to impaired water bodies.** Sampling and analysis of storm water is required where runoff discharges directly into a water body listed as "impaired" pursuant to section 303(d) of the Clean Water Act. A current list of California's impaired water bodies is available at the SWRCB web site (www.swrcb.ca.gov/tmdl/303d_lists.html). Notably, for this requirement to apply, the discharge of runoff must flow directly into the impaired water body or an impaired segment of a water body. In other words, construction site runoff that first enters a storm sewer or drain system is not considered a direct discharge, even if the runoff eventually flows into an impaired water body.

- **Monitoring of nonvisible pollutants in storm water.** The general construction permit also requires that a sampling and analysis program be developed and implemented for pollutants which:
  - Are not visually detectable in storm water discharges
  - Are or should be known to occur at, on, or under the construction site
  - Could cause or contribute to an exceedance of water quality objectives in the receiving water

  This latter condition is a catch-all provision which requires a school district to undertake a reasonable risk assessment at all grading and construction sites.

Sampling for nonvisible pollutants is generally required for one of two instances. First, sampling is required where visual inspections required before, during, and after storm events show a breach, malfunction, leakage, or spill from a BMP that could result in the discharge of pollutants into storm water. Second, sampling may also be required where storm water comes in contact with exposed materials or contamination that could result in a discharge of pollutants.

However, school districts can substantially reduce or eliminate the need for sampling and analysis by taking the following steps:

- Ensure that accepted BMPs are in place and functional
- Store potential pollutants in water-tight containers under a roof
- Clean up spills if and as they may occur
- Cover stockpiles

In general, keeping construction sites in good condition and order greatly reduces the likelihood that storm water sampling will be required.

Keeping construction sites in good condition and order greatly reduces the likelihood that storm water sampling will be required.

Industrial storm water general permit. The Industrial Storm Water General Permit (general industrial permit or ISWGP) applies to a broad range of industrial facilities, including manufacturing facilities, mining operations, disposal sites, recycling yards, and transportation facilities. Additional information regarding the general industrial permit, including a list of regulated industrial facilities, is available at the SWRCB web site (www.swrcb.ca.gov/stormwtr/industrial/html). All facilities subject to the general industrial permit must either obtain coverage under the general permit or apply for an individual NPDES permit.

School districts are generally not required to comply with the general industrial permit for most existing or proposed K–12 school facilities. However, certain district-owned facilities, such as bus depots or vehicle maintenance yards (including vehicle rehabilitation, mechanical repairs, painting, fueling, and lubrication) may be subject to the ISWGP requirements.

Basic compliance requirements under the general industrial permit are similar, but not identical, to the general construction permit, discussed above. In order to seek coverage under the ISWGP, an NOI, site map, and fee payment must be submitted to the SWRCB. Similarly, when a permittee ceases industrial operations, a NOT must be filed to terminate permit coverage and otherwise continuing requirements.

Municipal storm water permits. Storm water is also regulated by municipal permits issued by the SWRCB and various regional water boards throughout the state. The purpose of these permits is to regulate storm water discharges from MS4s. An MS4 is a conveyance (including streets, curbs, gutters, or storm drains) designed or used to convey storm water. Operators of medium and large MS4s are subject to municipal storm water permits issued by regional water boards.

Storm water is also regulated by municipal permits issued by the SWRCB and various regional water boards throughout the state.

Municipal permits are issued by the regional water boards and typically encompass a countywide area, including the regional cities as co-permittees. For example, the County of Los Angeles and its member cities (except the City of Long Beach) are regulated under the same municipal permit. Presently, numerous cities and counties are challenging more stringent requirements recently imposed by the regional water boards under their respective municipal storm water permit programs.

In 2003, the SWRCB adopted a statewide permit to regulate operators of small MS4s, which has significant implications for school districts. Water Quality

MEP = Maximum extent
        practicable
SQUIMP = Storm Water
        Quality Urban Impact
        Mitigation Plan
SUSMP = Standard Urban Storm
        Water Mitigation Plan
SWMP = Storm water
        management program

The categories of development that trigger storm water mitigation plan requirements will generally be inapplicable to school district projects.

The small MS4 permit requires school districts to develop, implement, and maintain a storm water management program for each school within the district.

Order No. 2003-0005 DWR (Small MS4 General Permit). The SWRCB adopted a statewide permit regulating storm water discharges from small MS4s. The SWRCB has defined various governmental facilities as operating a Small MS4 and, thus, as subject to the proposed Small MS4 Permit requirements. At this time, the SWRCB General Permit does not designate any school district as subject to the Small MS4 requirements. However, Appendix 3 of the permit lists all school districts anticipated to be designated in the near future. Additional information regarding the Small MS4 Permit is available at the SWRCB web site (www.swrcb.ca.gov/stormwtr/municipal/html).

Municipal permits: Storm water mitigation plans. Under the regional municipal permits, certain development projects are required to include a prescribed storm water mitigation plan prior to project approval by the municipality. In Los Angeles County, this mitigation plan is referred to as the Standard Urban Storm Water Mitigation Plan (SUSMP). Other counties have adopted similar requirements—for example, the mitigation plan in Ventura County is referred to as the Storm Water Quality Urban Impact Mitigation Plan (SQUIMP). Storm water mitigation plans require developers of larger housing tracts, hillside residences, commercial developments, auto repair shops, gas stations, parking lots, and restaurants to control post-development peak storm water runoff discharge rates through the use of onsite structural treatment control measures and specified BMPs.

The categories of development that trigger storm water mitigation plan requirements will generally be inapplicable to school district projects, with the possible exception of off-campus parking lots. Where the lot is potentially exposed to storm water runoff, the requirements apply to new lots of 5,000 square feet or more with 25 or more parking spaces.

Statewide permit: Small MS4 permit requirements. The small MS4 Permit will prohibit the discharge of materials other than storm water that are neither "authorized non-storm water discharges," nor authorized by a separate NPDES permit. Under the small MS4 Permit, regulated entities must implement BMPs that reduce pollutants in storm water to the technology based standard of maximum extent practicable (MEP).

Numerous issues under the small MS4 permit require further clarification, such as the relationship between construction and post-construction storm water runoff control requirements under the Small MS4 Permit and general construction permit requirements. Given their highly controversial and costly implications, legal challenges to the small MS4 permit can also be anticipated.

Compliance with small MS4 permit requirements. The small MS4 permit requires school districts to develop, implement, and maintain a storm water management program (SWMP) for each school within the district. The permit boundaries will be the property line or service area for each school.

Once a school district is officially designated as a small MS4 by the SWRCB or its RWQCB, the district must submit to its RWQCB an NOI, a complete SWMP, and the appropriate fee with 180 days of notification of the designation.

SWMP and minimum control measures. The small MS4 permit requires regulated entities to develop and implement a SWMP that describes BMPs, measurable goals, and schedules for implementing six required minimum control measures (MCMs). For each MCM, BMPs must be implemented that reduce the discharge of pollutants in storm water runoff, and establish measurable goals for each BMP to ensure program compliance and effectiveness. The MCM program areas are as follows:

- Public education
  - District must educate the public regarding the importance of the storm water program and the public's role in successful implementation, for example:
    - Educational brochures about keeping litter out of storm drains
    - Outreach activities addressing steps the public can take to prevent pollution from entering the MS4 system
- Public participation
  - District must seek public participation in development and implementation of the SWMP and MCMs, and make copies of the Small MS4 Permit and SWMP available for public review, for example:
    - Public meetings and forums
    - Stenciling "no dumping" on storm drains
    - "Adopt a Drain" and annual cleanup program
- Illicit discharge detection and elimination
  - District must adopt measures and implement a program to prohibit illicit discharges, for example:
    - Conduct facility inspections to determine potential sources of pollutants
    - Cleanup trash from field area following athletic event
- Construction site storm water runoff control
  - District must develop a program to control the discharge of pollutants from construction sites of one or more acres, for example:
    - Implement mechanism for erosion and sediment control at site
    - Require construction site operators to control all pollutant sources, including construction material and waste, concrete truck washout, discarded building materials, chemicals, etc.
- Post construction storm water management
  - District must incorporate long-term BMPs that protect water quality and control runoff flow into development projects, for example:
    - Combination of structural and nonstructural BMPs appropriate for community
    - Ensure adequate long-term operation and maintenance of BMPs
- Pollution prevention/good housekeeping for municipal operations
  - District must examine its activities and develop a program to prevent the discharge of pollutants from such activities through education of staff and BMPs, for example:
    - Train employees about impacts of storm water pollution from municipal activities
    - Review pesticide and herbicide use at facilities

For each MCM, BMPs must be implemented that reduce the discharge of pollutants in storm water runoff.

MCM = Minimum control measures

Reliance on a separate implementing entity. School districts may rely on a separate implementing entity (SIE) to carry out one or more of the six MCMs, provided that the SIE adequately addresses the district's storm water issues, and the regional water board approves of the arrangement. Under this approach, the school district remains responsible for compliance with MS4 Permit obligations if the SIE fails to implement relevant control measures. Should a school district rely upon a SIE to implement all six MCMs, the district must still file a NOI form, fee payment, and certification of the SIE arrangement. However, the school district will not be required to file a SWMP or annual report.

Many school districts will likely explore arrangements to participate in their city's MS4 program. In effect, a district can agree to abide by the city's storm water ordinances, and participate in implementing certain aspects of the city's SWMP, such as public education and good housekeeping. Using this collaborative approach, school districts can comply with the small MS4 permit requirements, while reducing the administrative burden of independently implementing each MCM at each school.

Appendices

Government Agencies and Related Organizations—Contact List

GOVERNMENT AGENCIES

California Coastal Commission
45 Fremont Street, Suite 2000
San Francisco, CA 94105-2219
www.coastal.ca.gov

tel   (415) 904-5200

**California Department
of Education (CDE)**
1430 N Street
Sacramento, CA 94244-2720

tel   (916) 319-0791

CDE Approval
SFPD Consultant
School Facilities
Planning Division
660 J Street, Suite 350
Sacramento, CA 95814

**California Department
of Conservation (DOC)**
801 K Street, MS 24-01
Sacramento, CA 95814

tel   (916) 322-1080

DOC Earthquake Fault Zone Maps
Seismic Hazard Mapping Zone
801 K Street, MS 12-31
Sacramento, CA 95814

tel   (916) 324-7299
fax   (916) 445-3334
email   shmp@consrv.ca.gov

**DOC Division of
Mines and Geology**
801 K Street, MS 12-30
Sacramento, CA 95814

tel   (916) 445-1825

**California Community
Colleges Chancellor's Office**
1102 Q Street
Sacramento, CA 95814-6511

tel   (916) 445-8752

**California Department
of Health Services**
P.O. Box 942732
Sacramento, CA 94234-7320
www.dhs.cahwnet.gov

**California Department
of Industrial Relations**
Office of the Director
455 Golden Gate Avenue
San Francisco, CA 94102

tel   (415) 703-5070

**California Department of
Pesticide Regulation (DPR)**
1001 I Street, P.O. Box 4015
Sacramento, CA 95812-4015
www.cdpr.ca.gov

tel   (916) 445-4300
fax   (916) 324-1452

**California Department of
Transportation (Caltrans)**
1120 N Street
Sacramento, CA 95814

tel   (916) 654-5266

**California Department
of Water Service**
1416 9th Street
Sacramento, CA 95814

California Highway Patrol (CHP)
Office of Public Affairs
P.O. Box 942898
Sacramento, CA 94298-0001
www.chp.ca.gov

tel   (916) 445-1865
        Commercial Vehicles Section
tel   (916) 375-2838
        Safety Net Section

Division of State Architect (DSA)
DSA Headquarters
1130 K Street, Suite 101
Sacramento, CA 95814-2925

tel   (916) 445-8100

Department of General Services
707 Third Street
West Sacramento, CA 95605
www.dsa.dgs.ca.gov

tel   (916) 376-5000
tel   (916) 323-3577
        Site Mitigation

Department of Toxic
Substance Control (DTSC)
1880 Cal Center Drive
Sacramento, CA 95826

tel   (916) 225-3545

Federal Emergency
Management Agency (FEMA)
500 C Street, SW
Washington, D.C. 20472
www.fema.gov

tel   (202) 566-1600

Or contact your local
flood control agency or:
Map Service Center
P.O. Box 1038
Jessup, MD 20794-1038

tel   (800) 358-9616

Governor's Office of
Emergency Services (OES)
711 G Street, 2nd Floor
Sacramento, CA 95814

tel   (916) 874-4670
fax   (916) 366-3042

Governor's Office of
Planning and Research
1400 Tenth Street
Sacramento, CA 95814

tel   (916) 445-0613

Office of Public School
Construction (OPSC)
1130 K Street
Sacramento, Ca 95814-2928

tel   (916) 445-3160

Office of the State
Fire Marshall (OSFM)
1131 S Street
Sacramento, CA 95814
http://osfm.fire.ca.gov

tel   (916) 445-8200
tel   (916) 445-8477
     Hazardous
     Materials Division

University of California
Office of the President
1111 Franklin Street
Oakland, CA 94607-5200

RELATED ORGANIZATIONS

America's Schoolhouse Council
34 Brentwood Drive
Poughkeepsie, NY 12603

tel   (914) 462-1702
email hutde@AOL.com

American Association
of School Administrators
1801 North Moore Street
Arlington, VA 22209-1813
www.aasa.org

tel   (703) 528-0700
fax   (703) 841-1543

American Institute of Architects
Committee on
Architecture for Education
1735 New York Avenue NW
Washington, D.C. 20006

tel   (202) 626-7453
fax   (202) 626-7399
email pia@aia.org

Architecture and Children,
Research Methods
University of New Mexico
School of Architecture and Planning
2414 Central Southeast
Albuquerque, New Mexico 87131

Attn   Ann E Taylor, Ph.D.
       IEE Director
email aetaylor@unm.edu

tel   (505) 277-5058

Architecture in
Education Program
The Foundation for Architecture
1737 Chestnut Street, 2nd Floor
Philadelphia, PA 19103

tel   (215) 569-3187
fax   (215) 569-4688
email aie@dca.net

California Association of
School Business Officials (CASBO)
600 N. 10th Street, Suite 150
Sacramento, CA 95814
www.casbo.org

tel   (916) 447-3783
fax   (916) 447-3794

California's Coalition
for Adequate School
Housing (C.A.S.H.)
1130 K Street, Suite 210
Sacramento, CA 95814
www.cashnet.org

tel   (916) 448-8577

Center for Environment,
Education, and Design
Studies (CEEDS)
University of Washington
Gould Hall
Seattle, WA 98195-5726

Attn   Sharon E. Sutton
        Director
email   sesut@u.washington.edu

tel   (206) 685-3361
fax   (206) 616-4992

Council of Educational
Facility Planners
International (CEFPI)
9180 E. Desert Cove, Suite 104
Scottsdale, AZ 85260

tel   (480) 391-0840
fax   (480) 391-0940
email   cefpi@cefpilorg

Design Share
4937 Morgan Avenue South
Minneapolis, MN 55409-2251

Attn   Randall Fielding, Editor
email   fielding@designshare.com

tel   (612) 925-6897
fax   (612) 922-6631

Educational Design Institute
Mississippi State University
College of Education, Box 5365
Mississippi State, MS 39762

Attn   Dr. Jeffery A. Lackney
        Director
email   jlackney@colled.msstate.edu

tel   (662) 325-1850

New Horizons for Learning
P.O. Box 15329
Seattle, WA 98115

tel   (206) 547-7936
email   building@newhorizons.org

New Schools/Better
Neighborhoods (NSBN)
811 West 7th Street, Suite 900
Los Angeles, CA 90017
Attn   David Abel, Chair
www.nsbn.org

tel   (213) 629-9019

New York Foundation for the Arts
Design Education Initiative
155 Avenue of the
Americas, 14th Floor
New York, NY 10013-1507

tel   (212) 366-6900
fax   (212) 366-1778
email   nyfaweb@nyfa.org

Second Nature
4746 Palmer Canyon Road
Claremont, CA 91711

email   info@westcoastefs.org

"Unusual Circumstances"

CEQA Guidelines, § 15300.2, subd. (c)

Case	Activity (Categorical Exemption)	Unusual Circumstances Precluding Exemption
Azusa Land Reclamation Co. v. Main San Gabriel Basin Watermaster, 52 Cal. App. 4th 1165 (1997)	Regional Water Board approved application to resume municipal waste disposal operations at unlined landfill. (Class 1 (existing facilities))	Unusual circumstances found because: • Landfill overlies major drinking water aquifer
Meridian Ocean Sys. v. State Lands Comm'n, 222 Cal. App. 3d 153 (1990)	California State Lands Commission denied permits for underwater geophysical testing (ocean survey activities) (Class 6 (information collection))	Unusual circumstances found because: • Newly available scientific research (showing reasonable possibility that activity may result in significant impact on ocean life); • Use of underwater air guns may cause marked changes in fish behavior, injure and/or kill marine life, and significantly decrease commercial fish catch.
McQueen v. Board of Directors, 202 Cal. App. 3d 1136, 1148 (1988)	Regional open space district acquisition of surplus federal property. (Class 25 (transfer of land to preserve open space); Class 16 (transfer of land to create parks); Class 12 (sales of surplus government property))	Unusual circumstances found because: • Known presence of PCB and other hazardous wastes on property to be acquired.
Lewis v. Seventeenth Dist. Agric. Ass'n, 165 Cal. App. 3d 823 (1985)	Approval of three-year contract authorizing continued use of stock car racetrack at fairgrounds. (Class 23 (normal operations of facilities for public gatherings—racetracks))	Unusual circumstances found because: • Close proximity of neighboring houses to racetrack; *Compare: Campbell v. Third Dist. Agric. Ass'n,* 195 Cal. App. 3d 115 (1987); 240 C.R. 481.

"Unusual Circumstances" *continued*

Case	Activity (Categorical Exemption)	Unusual Circumstances Precluding Exemption
City of Santa Clara v. LAFCO, 139 Cal. App. 3d 923, 932 (1983)	LAFCO denial of exemption to city annexation of two parcels of undeveloped land that were prezoned agricultural but slated for future urban use under city's general plan. (Class 19 (annexation of existing facilities and lots for exempt facilities))	Unusual Circumstances found because: • Inconsistency between prezoning of annexation area (as agricultural) and general plan zoning designation (as urban use) deemed "unusual circumstance."
Myers v. Board of Supervisors, 58 Cal. App. 3d 413 (1976)	County Board of Supervisors approval of minor land subdivision involving possible construction of two dwellings on adjoining lots of over 2.5 acres each in rural area. (Class 5 (minor alterations in land use limitations))	Unusual circumstances found because: • Extensive road scar near scenic highway; • Placement of residential storm drain improvements and utility poles on steep terrain or across stream in area that is presently in a natural condition; • Steep hillside grading with risk of erosion; • Location of septic tank leach lines created danger of sewage seepage into creek and drinking water well; • Significant fire danger due to project location on thickly forested slope; • Removal of several scenic oaks.
Fairbank v. City of Mill Valley, 75 Cal. App. 4th 1243, 1260 (1999)	City approved commercial project consisting of one retail/office building of 5,855 square feet in urbanized area. (Class 3 (new construction or conversion of small structures)) *Claimed Impact:* Project does not include adequate parking facilities, and will result in increased demand on city streets and other parking areas, as well as an increase in traffic and circulation around project site.	No unusual circumstances found because: • Small building causing minor adverse changes in traffic flow and parking patterns is not different from "any other small, run-of-the-mill commercial building or use."

"Unusual Circumstances" *continued*

Case	Activity (Categorical Exemption)	Unusual Circumstances Precluding Exemption
Surfrider Foundation v. California Coastal Commission, 26 Cal. App. 4th 151 (1994)	Coastal Commission approved installation of parking meters at 16 state park beaches. (Class 3 (new construction or conversion of small structures)) *Claimed impact:* Imposing parking fees may cause people to park outside parking lots and create alternative beach access routes, thereby resulting in adverse environmental effects.	No unusual circumstances found because: • Possible "impact" is not causally connected to project (parking meters); • Any claimed causal effect would not be from installing the meters, but rather from the underlying imposition of fees, which is statutorily exempt from CEQA without regard to the categorical exemption.
Bloom v. McGurk, 26 Cal. App. 4th 1307, 1316 (1994)	State Department of Health Services issued medical waste renewal permits to existing medical waste treatment facility under newly enacted Medical Waste Management Act (Class 1 (existing facilities)) *Claimed Impact:* Existing facility had never been subject to EIR or negative declaration. Therefore, permit renewal under new regulatory scheme constitutes "change" in environment sufficient to trigger exception to existing facility exemption.	No unusual circumstances found because: • No change in existing facility operations incident to renewal of medical waste permit; • Comparable facilities in immediate area; • Medical waste facility consistent with surrounding industrial uses (truck body manufacture and repair, awning manufacture, lumberyard, container storage, warehousing, fire sprinkler manufacturer, petrochemical processing plant, glass making facility)
City of Pasadena v. State, 14 Cal. App. 4th 810, 824 (1993)	State Department of Corrections' decision to lease space in existing building located in civic center area for use as parole office. (Class 1 (existing facilities) *Claimed Impact:* Facility is next door to Central Library, a historic building of cultural significance, and the Facilities Master Plan calls for residential development in the area.	No unusual circumstances found because: • Facilities Master Plan housing needs are goals, not mandates, so no inconsistency with residential housing goals; • Use of space as parole office is consistent with existing uses in immediate area (criminal justice facilities consisting of courthouse, probation office, old and new jails).

"Unusual Circumstances" *continued*

Case	Activity (Categorical Exemption)	Unusual Circumstances Precluding Exemption
Association for Protection of Envt'l. Values in Ukiah v. City of Ukiah, 2 Cal. App. 4th 720, 731 (1991)	Application for site development permit for hillside construction of single family house. (Class 3 (new construction or conversion of small structures)) *Claimed Impact:* Lot is nonconforming, so discretionary site development permit required; construction of house on narrow hillside lot may impact soil stability and water runoff to adjacent properties.	No unusual circumstances found because: • Concerns about height, view obstruction, privacy, and water runoff are normal and common considerations in construction of hillside residences.
Centinela Hosp. Ass'n v. City of Inglewood, 225 Cal. App. 3d 1586, 1599 (1990)	Permit to construct 15-bed psychiatric facility (two-story residential care facility of 5,400 square feet). (Class 3 (new construction or conversion of small structures)) *Claimed Impact:* Extremely sensitive" location of facility "in terms of public usage and traffic" will create health and safety hazard and place increased demands on public services such as police and fire protection.	No unusual circumstances found because: • Structure is similar to both apartments and duplexes and small commercial structures falling within exemption; • Record contains substantial evidence to support express findings as to adequacy of traffic, public health and safety, and public services, and to support implied finding of no significant environmental effects. *Claimed Impact:* A significant change occurred in 1976 with race track's imposition of decibel level limitations for each racing vehicle, thereby triggering exception to racetrack exemption.
Campbell v. Third Dist. Agric. Ass'n, 195 Cal. App. 3d 115 (1987)	Annual licensing of auto racetrack at county fairground adjacent to residential area. (Class 23 (normal operations of facilities for public gatherings—racetracks))	No unusual circumstances found because: • Improvements in noise reduction controls does not constitute adverse change in environment; • Even though race track built before CEQA enacted, it has not been modified or significantly altered. *Compare: Lewis v. Seventeenth Dist. Agric. Ass'n,* 165 Cal. App. 3d 823 (1985), 211 C.R. 884.

Environmental Checklist

BACKGROUND

1. Project title

2. Lead agency name and address

3. Contact person and telephone number

4. Project location *Insert location description here*

5. Project sponsor's name and address

6. General plan designation

7. Zoning

8. Description of project *Describe the whole action involved, including, but not limited to, later phases of the project and any secondary support or offsite features necessary for its implementation. Attach additional sheets, if necessary.*

9. Surrounding land uses and setting
Briefly describe the project's surroundings.

10. Other public agencies whose approval is required
(permits, financing approval, or participation agreement)

ENVIRONMENTAL FACTORS POTENTIALLY AFFECTED

The environmental factors checked below would be potentially affected by this project, involving at least one "Potentially Significant Impact," as indicated by the checklist on the following pages.

- ❏ Aesthetics
- ❏ Biological Resources
- ❏ Hazards & Hazardous Materials
- ❏ Mineral Resources
- ❏ Public Services
- ❏ Utilities / Service Systems

- ❏ Agricultural Resources
- ❏ Cultural Resources
- ❏ Hydrology / Water Quality
- ❏ Noise
- ❏ Recreation
- ❏ Mandatory Findings of Significance

- ❏ Air Quality
- ❏ Geology / Soils
- ❏ Land Use / Planning
- ❏ Population / Housing
- ❏ Transportation / Traffic

DETERMINATION

(to be completed by the Lead Agency)

On the basis of this initial evaluation:

- ❏ **I find that the proposed project COULD NOT have a significant effect on the environment, and a NEGATIVE DECLARATION will be prepared.**

- ❏ **I find that although the proposed project could have a significant effect on the environment, there will not be a significant effect in this case because revisions in the project have been made by or agreed to by the project proponent. A MITIGATED NEGATIVE DECLARATION will be prepared.**

- ❏ **I find that the proposed project MAY have a significant effect on the environment, and an ENVIRONMENTAL IMPACT REPORT is required.**

- ❏ **I find that the proposed project MAY have a "potentially significant impact" or "potentially significant unless mitigated" impact on the environment, but at least one effect 1) has been adequately analyzed in an earlier document pursuant to applicable legal standards, and 2) has been addressed by mitigation measures based on the earlier analysis as described on attached sheets. An ENVIRONMENTAL IMPACT REPORT is required, but it must analyze only the effects that remain to be addressed.**

- ❏ **I find that although the proposed project could have a significant effect on the environment, because all potentially significant effects (a) have been analyzed adequately in an earlier EIR or NEGATIVE DECLARATION pursuant to applicable standards, and (b) have been avoided or mitigated pursuant to that earlier EIR or NEGATIVE DECLARATION, including revisions or mitigation measures that are imposed upon the proposed project, nothing further is required.**

_____
Signature

_____
Printed name

Date _____

For _____

SPECIAL REQUIREMENTS UNDER THE STATE SCHOOL FACILITY PROGRAM

In additional to general CEQA requirements, projects involving school site acquisition to be funded under the state School Facilities Program must also satisfy several specific requirements established in the California Education Code and California Code of Regulations. The applicable sections of the Education Code and California Code of Regulations are listed below, along with a description of the general topic and the Environmental Checklist section in which each requirement is addressed.

SPECIAL REQUIREMENTS UNDER THE STATE SCHOOL FACILITY PROGRAM

General topic	Educ. Code section	C.C.R. section	Environmental Checklist *(see section 2.4)*
Would the project involve the construction, reconstruction, or relocation of any school building on the trace of a geological fault along which surface rupture can reasonably be expected to occur within the life of the school building?	§ 17212 and § 17212.5	Title 5 § 14011(f)	Section VI, Geology and Soils, Question "f"
Would the project involve the construction, reconstruction, or relocation of any school building on a site subject to moderate to high liquefaction?	*	Title 5 § 14011(i)	Section VI, Geology and Soils, Question "a–iii"
Would the project involve the construction, reconstruction, or relocation of any school building on a site subject to landslides?	*	Title 5 § 14011(i)	Section VI, Geology and Soils, Question "a–iv"
Is the project site subject to flooding or dam inundation?	§ 17212 and § 17212.5	Title 5 § 14011(g)	Section VIII, Hydrology and Water Quality, Question "g"
Are there any facilities within a __-mile radius of a proposed school site that might be reasonably anticipated to emit hazardous emissions or handle hazardous or acutely hazardous material, substances or waste?	§ 17213(b)	*	Section VII, Hazards and Hazardous Materials, Question "d"
Is the project site the site of a current or former hazardous waste disposal site or solid waste disposal site and, if so, have the wastes been removed?	§ 17213(a)	*	Section VII, Hazards and Hazardous Materials, Question "e-(a)"
Is the project site a hazardous substance release site identified by the State Department of Health Services in a current list adopted pursuant to § 25356 for removal or remedial action pursuant to Chapter 6.8 of Division 20 of the Health and Safety Code?	§ 17213(a)	*	Section VII, Hazards and Hazardous Materials, Question "e-(b)"
Is the proposed school site situated within 2,000 feet of a significant disposal of hazardous waste?	*	Title 5 § 14010(t)	Hazardous Materials, Question "f"

General topic	Educ. Code section	C.C.R. section	Environmental Checklist (see section 2.4)
Is the proposed school site a site that contains one or more pipelines, situated underground or above ground, which carry hazardous substances, acutely hazardous materials or hazardous wastes, unless the pipeline is a natural gas line that is used only to supply natural gas to that school or neighborhood?	§ 17213(a)	*	Section VII, Hazards and Hazardous Materials, Question "e–(c)"
Is the proposed school site located near an above-ground water or fuel storage tank or within 1,500 feet of an easement of an above-ground or underground pipeline that can pose a safety hazard to the site?	*	Title 5 § 14010(h)	Section VII, Hazards and Hazardous Materials, Question "i"
Is the proposed school site located on a site containing or underline by naturally occurring hazardous materials?	§ 17213.1(a)	*	Section VII, Hazards and Hazardous Materials, Question "g"
Is the proposed school site located on a site where the property line is less than the following distances from the edge of respective power line easements: 1) 100 feet of a 50–133 kV line; 2) 150 feet of a 220–230 kV line; or 3) 350 feet of a 500–550 kV line?	*	Title 5 § 14010(c)	Section VII, Hazards and Hazardous Materials, Question "h"
Would the proposed school conflict with any existing or proposed land uses, such that a potential health or safety risk to students would be created.	*	Title 5 § 14010(m)	Section IX, Land Use and Planning, Question "c"
Is the proposed school site within two miles, measured by air line, of that point on an airport runway or potential runway included in an airport master plan that is nearest to the site?	§ 17215(a) and § 17215(b)	*	Section VII, Hazards and Hazardous Materials, Question "j"
Is the proposed school site located adjacent to or near a major arterial roadway or freeway that may pose a safety hazard? Is minimum peripheral visibility maintained for driveways per Caltrans' Highway Design Manual? Are traffic and pedestrian hazards mitigated per Caltrans' "School Area Pedestrian Safety" manual?	*	Title 5 § 14010(e), Title 5 § 14010(k), Title 5 § 14010(l)	Section XV, Transportation/Traffic, Questions "e" and "f"
Is the proposed school site located adjacent to or near a major arterial roadway or freeway whose noise generation may adversely affect the educational program?	*	Title 5 § 14010(e)	Section XI, Noise, Question "a" & "e"
Is the proposed school site within 1,500 feet of a railroad track easement?	*	Title 5 § 14010(d)	Section XV, Transportation/Traffic, Question "j"

EVALUATION OF ENVIRONMENTAL IMPACTS

1) A brief explanation is required for all answers except "No Impact" answers that are adequately supported by the information sources a lead agency cites in the parentheses following each question. A "No Impact" answer is adequately supported if the referenced information sources show that the impact simply does not apply to projects like the one involved (*e.g.,* the project falls outside a fault rupture zone). A "No Impact" answer should be explained where it is based on project-specific factors, as well as general standards (*e.g.,* the project would not expose sensitive receptors to pollutants, based on a project-specific screening analysis).

2) All answers must take account of the whole action involved, including off-site as well as on-site, cumulative as well as project-level, indirect as well as direct, and construction as well as operational impacts.

3) Once the lead agency has determined that a particular physical impact may occur, then the checklist answers must indicate whether the impact is potentially significant, less than significant with mitigation, or less than significant. "Potentially Significant Impact" is appropriate if there is substantial evidence that an effect may be significant. If there are one or more "Potentially Significant Impact" entries when the determination is made, an EIR is required.

4) "Negative Declaration: Less Than Significant With Mitigation Incorporated" applies where the incorporation of mitigation measures has reduced an effect from "Potentially Significant Impact" to a "Less Than Significant Impact". The lead agency must describe the mitigation measures, and briefly explain how they reduce the effect to a less than significant level (mitigation measures from Section XVII, "Earlier Analyses," may be cross-referenced).

5) Earlier analyses may be used where, pursuant to the tiering, program EIR, or other CEQA process, an effect has been adequately analyzed in an earlier EIR or negative declaration. Section 15063(c)(3)(D). Earlier analyses are discussed in Section XVII at the end of the checklist. In this case, a brief discussion should identify the following:

a) Earlier Analysis Used. Identify and state where they are available for review.

b) Impacts Adequately Addressed. Identify which effects from the above checklist were within the scope of and adequately analyzed in an earlier document pursuant to applicable legal standards, and state whether such effects were addressed by mitigation measures based on the earlier analysis.

c) Mitigation Measures. For effects that are "Less than Significant with Mitigation Measures Incorporated," describe the mitigation measures that were incorporated or refined from the earlier document and the extent to which they address site-specific conditions for the project.

6) Lead agencies are encouraged to incorporate into the checklist references to information sources for potential impacts (*e.g.,* general plans, zoning ordinances). Reference to a previously prepared or outside document should, where appropriate, include a reference to the page or pages where the statement is substantiated. A source list should be attached, and other sources used or individuals contacted should be cited in the discussion.

7) Supporting Information Sources: A source list should be attached, and other sources used or individuals contacted should be cited in the discussion.

8) This is only a suggested form, and lead agencies are free to use different formats; however, lead agencies should normally address the questions from this checklist that are relevant to a project's environmental effects in whatever format is selected.

9) The explanation of each issue should identify:

a) the significance criteria or threshold, if any used to evaluate each question; and

b) the mitigation measure identified, if any, to reduce the impact to less than significant.

Issues	Potentially significant impact	Less than significant with mitigation incorporated	Less than significant impact	No impact
I. AESTHETICS. Would the project:				
a) Have a substantial adverse effect on a scenic vista?				
b) Substantially damage scenic resources, including, but not limited to, trees, rock outcroppings, and historic buildings within a state scenic highway?				
c) Substantially degrade the existing visual character or quality of the site and its surroundings?				
d) Create a new source of substantial light or glare that would adversely affect day or nighttime views in the area?				
II. AGRICULTURE RESOURCES. In determining whether impacts to agricultural resources are significant environmental effects, lead agencies may refer to the California Agricultural Land Evaluation and Site Assessment Model (1997) prepared by the California Dept. of Conservation as an optional model to use in assessing impacts on agriculture and farmland. Would the project:				
a) Convert Prime Farmland, Unique Farmland, or Farmland of Statewide Importance (Farmland), as shown on the maps prepared pursuant to the Farmland Mapping and Monitoring Program of the California Resources Agency, to non-agricultural use?				
b) Conflict with existing zoning for agricultural use, or a Williamson Act contract?				
c) Involve other changes in the existing environment, which due to their location or nature, could result in conversion of Farmland, to non-agricultural use?				
III. AIR QUALITY. Where available, the significance criteria established by the applicable air quality management or air pollution control district may be relied upon to make the following determinations. Would the project:				
a) Conflict with or obstruct implementation of the applicable air quality plan?				
b) Violate any air quality standard or contribute substantially to an existing or projected air quality violation?				
c) Result in a cumulatively considerable net increase of any criteria pollutant for which the project region is non-attainment under an applicable federal or state ambient air quality standard (including releasing emissions that exceed quantitative thresholds for ozone precursors)?				
d) Expose sensitive receptors to substantial pollutant concentrations?				
e) Create objectionable odors affecting a substantial number of people?				

Issues	Potentially significant impact	Less than significant with mitigation incorporated	Less than significant impact	No impact
IV. BIOLOGICAL RESOURCES. Would the project:				
a) Have a substantial adverse effect, either directly or through habitat modifications, on any species identified as a candidate, sensitive, or special status species in local or regional plans, policies, or regulations, or by the California Department of Fish and Game or U.S. Fish and Wildlife Service?				
b) Have a substantial adverse effect on any riparian habitat or other sensitive natural community identified in local or regional plans, policies, regulations or by the California Department of Fish and Game or U.S. Fish and Wildlife Service?				
c) Have a substantial adverse effect on federally protected wetlands as defined by Section 404 of the Clean Water Act (including, but not limited to, marsh, vernal pool, coastal, etc.) through direct removal, filling, hydrological interruption, or other means?				
d) Interfere substantially with the movement of any native resident or migratory fish or wildlife species or with established native resident or migratory wildlife corridors, or impede the use of native wildlife nursery sites?				
e) Conflict with any local policies or ordinances protecting biological resources, such as a tree preservation policy or ordinance?				
f) Conflict with the provisions of an adopted Habitat Conservation Plan, Natural Community Conservation Plan, or other approved local, regional, or state habitat conservation plan?				
V. CULTURAL RESOURCES. Would the project:				
a) Cause a substantial adverse change in the significance of a historical resource as defined in § 15064.5?				
b) Cause a substantial adverse change in the significance of an archaeological resource pursuant to § 15064.5?				
c) Directly or indirectly destroy a unique paleontological resource or site or unique geologic feature?				
d) Disturb any human remains, including those interred outside of formal cemeteries?				

Issues	Potentially significant impact	Less than significant with mitigation incorporated	Less than significant impact	No impact
VI. GEOLOGY AND SOILS. Would the project:				
a) Expose people or structures to potential substantial adverse effects, including the risk of loss, injury, or death involving:				
i) Rupture of a known earthquake fault, as delineated on the most recent Alquist-Priolo Earthquake Fault Zoning Map, issued by the State Geologist |for the area or based on other substantial evidence of a known fault? Refer to Division of Mines and Geology Special Publication 42.				
ii) Strong seismic ground shaking?				
iii) Seismic-related ground failure, including liquefaction?				
iv) Landslides?				
b) Result in substantial soil erosion or the loss of topsoil?				
c) Be located on a geologic unit or soil that is unstable, or that would become unstable as a result of the project, and potentially result in on- or offsite landslide, lateral spreading, subsidence, liquefaction or collapse?				
d) Be located on expansive soil, as defined in Table 18-1-B of the Uniform Building Code (1994), creating substantial risks to life or property?				
e) Have soils incapable of adequately supporting the use of septic tanks or alternative waste water disposal systems where sewers are not available for the disposal of waste water?				
f) Would the project involve the construction, reconstruction, or relocation of any school building on the trace of a geological fault along which surface rupture can reasonably be expected to occur within the life of the school building?				
VII. HAZARDS AND HAZARDOUS MATERIALS. Would the project:				
a) Create a significant hazard to the public or the environment through the routine transport, use, or disposal of hazardous materials?				
b) Create a significant hazard to the public or the environment through reasonable foreseeable upset and accident conditions involving the release of hazardous materials into the environment?				
c) Would operation of the proposed project involve hazardous emissions or handling of hazardous or acutely hazardous materials, substances, or waste within one-quarter mile of an existing or proposed school?				

Issues	Potentially significant impact	Less than significant with mitigation incorporated	Less than significant impact	No impact
d) Would the project create a hazard due to the placement of the school within one-quarter mile of the site that might be reasonably anticipated to emit hazardous fumes or handle hazardous or acutely hazardous material, substances or waste?				
e) Locate a school site at:				
(a) the site of a current or former hazardous waste disposal site or solid waste disposal site and, if so, have the wastes been removed;				
(b) a hazardous substance release site identified by the State Department of Health Services in a current list adopted pursuant to § 25356 for removal or remedial action pursuant to Chapter 6.8 of Division 20 of the Health and Safety Code; or				
(c) a site that contains one or more pipelines, situated underground or above ground, which carry hazardous substances, acutely hazardous materials or hazardous wastes, unless the pipeline is a natural gas line that is used only to supply natural gas to that school or neighborhood"?				
f) Located a school within 2,000 feet of a significant disposal of hazardous waste? (If so, the DTSC will determine whether the property is to be considered a Hazardous Waste Property or Border Zone Property).				
g) Locate a school on a site containing or underline by naturally occurring hazardous materials?				
h) Locate a school where the property line is less than the following distances from the edge of respective power line easements:				
1) 100 feet of a 50–133 kV line;				
2) 150 feet of a 220–230 kV line; or				
3) 350 feet of a 500–550 kV line?				
i) Locate a school near an above-ground water or fuel storage tank or within 1,500 feet of an easement of an above-ground or underground pipeline that can pose a safety hazard to the site?				
j) Locate a school within two miles, measured by air line, of that point on an airport runway or potential runway included in an airport master plan that is nearest to the site?				
k) For a project within the vicinity of a private airstrip, would the project result in a safety hazard for people residing or working in the project area?				

Issues	Potentially significant impact	Less than significant with mitigation incorporated	Less than significant impact	No impact
l) Impair implementation of or physically interfere with an adopted emergency response plan or emergency evacuation plan?				
m) Expose people or structures to a significant risk of loss, injury or death involving wildland fires, including where wildlands are adjacent to urbanized areas or where residences are intermixed with wildlands?				

VIII. HYDROLOGY AND WATER QUALITY. Would the project:

a) Violate any water quality standards or waste discharge requirements?				
b) Substantially deplete groundwater supplies or interfere substantially with groundwater recharge such that there would be a net deficit in aquifer volume or a lowering of the local groundwater table level (*e.g.*, the production rate of pre-existing nearby wells would drop to a level that would not support existing land uses or planned uses for which permits have been granted)?				
c) Substantially alter the existing drainage pattern of the site or area, including through the alteration of the course of a stream or river, in a manner that would result in substantial erosion or siltation on or off-site?				
d) Substantially alter the existing drainage pattern of the site or area, including through the alteration of the course of a stream or river, or substantially increase the rate or amount of surface runoff in a manner that would result in flooding on- or offsite?				
e) Create or contribute runoff water that would exceed the capacity of existing or planned stormwater drainage systems or provide sub-stantial additional sources of polluted runoff?				
f) Otherwise substantially degrade water quality?				
g) Place a school within a 100-year flood hazard area as mapped on a federal Flood Hazard Boundary or Flood Insurance Rate Map or other flood hazard delineation map, such as from dam inundation?				
h) Place within 100-year flood hazard area structures that would impede or redirect flood flows?				
i) Expose people or structures to a significant risk of loss, injury or death involving flooding, including flooding as a result of the failure of a levee or dam?				
j) Inundation by seiche, tsunami, or mudflow?				

Issues	Potentially significant impact	Less than significant with mitigation incorporated	Less than significant impact	No impact

IX. LAND USE AND PLANNING. Would the project:

a) Physically divide an established community?

b) Conflict with any applicable land use plan, policy, or regulation of an agency with jurisdiction over the project (including, but not limited to the general plan, specific plan, local coastal program, or zoning ordinance) adopted for the purpose of avoiding or mitigating an environmental effect?

c) Conflict with any existing or proposed zoning of surrounding properties such that a potential health or safety risk to students would be created?

d) Conflict with any applicable habitat conservation plan or natural community conservation plan?

X. MINERAL RESOURCES. Would the project:

a) Result in the loss of availability of a known mineral resource that would be a value to the region and the residents of the state?

b) Result in the loss of availability of a locally important mineral resource recovery site delineated on a local general plan, specific plan or other land use plan?

XI. NOISE. Would the project result in:

a) Exposure of persons to or generation of noise levels in excess of standards established by the school district, the local general plan, noise ordinance, or applicable standards of other agencies?

b) Exposure of persons to or generation of excessive groundborne vibration or groundborne noise levels?

c) A substantial permanent increase in ambient noise levels in the project vicinity above levels existing without the project?

d) A substantial temporary or periodic increase in ambient noise levels in the project vicinity above levels existing without the project?

e) For a project located within an airport land use plan or, where such a plan has not been adopted, within two miles of a public airport or public use airport, would the project expose students or staff to excessive noise levels?

f) For a project within the vicinity of a private airstrip, would the project expose people residing or working in the project area to excessive noise levels?

Issues	Potentially significant impact	Less than significant with mitigation incorporated	Less than significant impact	No impact
XII. POPULATION AND HOUSING. Would the project:				
a) Induce substantial population growth in an area, either directly (for example, by proposing new homes and businesses) or indirectly (for example, through extension of roads or other infrastructure)?				
b) Displace substantial numbers of existing housing, necessitating the construction of replacement housing elsewhere?				
c) Displace substantial numbers of people, necessitating the construction of replacement housing elsewhere?				
XIII. PUBLIC SERVICES. Would the project result in substantial adverse physical impacts associated with the provision of new or physically altered governmental facilities, need for new or physically altered governmental facilities, the construction of which could cause significant environmental impacts, in order to maintain acceptable service ratios, response times or other performance objectives for any of the public services:				
a) Fire protection?				
b) Police protection?				
c) Schools?				
d) Parks?				
e) Other public facilities?				
XIV. RECREATION				
a) Would the project increase the use of existing neighborhood and regional parks or other recreational facilities such that substantial physical deterioration of the facility would occur or be accelerated?				
b) Does the project include recreational facilities or require the construction or expansion of recreational facilities that might have an adverse physical effect on the environment?				
XV. TRANSPORTATION/TRAFFIC. Would the project:				
a) Cause an increase in traffic, which is substantial in relation to the existing traffic load and capacity of the street system (*i.e.,* result in a substantial increase in either the number of vehicle trips, the volume to capacity ratio on roads, or congestion at intersections)?				

Issues	Potentially significant impact	Less than significant with mitigation incorporated	Less than significant impact	No impact
b) Exceed, either individually or cumulatively, a level of service standard established by the county congestion management agency for designated roads or highways?				
c) Result in a change in air traffic patterns, including either an increase in traffic levels or a change in location that results in substantial safety risks?				
d) Substantially increase hazards due to a design feature (*e.g.*, sharp curves or dangerous intersections) or incompatible uses (*e.g.*, farm equipment)?				
e) Pose a safety hazard due to the placement of a proposed school site adjacent to or near a major arterial roadway or freeway?				
f) Result in inadequate vehicular access due to less than minimum peripheral visibility at school driveways?				
g) Result in inadequate emergency access?				
h) Result in inadequate parking capacity?				
i) Conflict with adopted policies, plans, or programs supporting alternative transportation (*e.g.*, bus turnouts, bicycle racks)?				
j) Place a proposed school site within 1,500 feet of a railroad track easement?				

XVI. UTILITIES AND SERVICE SYSTEMS. Would the project:

Issues	Potentially significant impact	Less than significant with mitigation incorporated	Less than significant impact	No impact
a) Exceed waste water treatment requirements of the applicable Regional Water Quality Control Board?				
b) Require or result in the construction of new water or waste water treatment facilities or expansion of existing facilities, the construction of which could cause significant environmental effects?				
c) Require or result in the construction of new storm water drainage facilities or expansion of existing facilities, the construction of which could cause significant environmental effects?				
d) Have sufficient water supplies available to serve the project from existing entitlements and resources or are new or expanded entitlements needed?				
e) Result in a determination by the waste water treatment provider, which serves or may serve the project that it has adequate capacity to serve the project's projected demand in addition to the provider's existing commitments?				

Issues	Potentially significant impact	Less than significant with mitigation incorporated	Less than significant impact	No impact
f) Be served by a landfill with sufficient permitted capacity to accommodate the project's solid waste disposal needs?				
g) Comply with federal, state, and local statutes and regulations related to solid waste?				

XVII. MANDATORY FINDINGS OF SIGNIFICANCE

Issues	Potentially significant impact	Less than significant with mitigation incorporated	Less than significant impact	No impact
a) Does the project have the potential to degrade the quality of the environment, substantially reduce the habitat of a fish or wildlife species, cause a fish or wildlife population to drop below selfsustaining levels, threaten to eliminate a plant or animal community, reduce the number or restrict the range of a rare or endangered plant or animal or eliminate important examples of the major periods of California history or prehistory?				
b) Does the project have impacts that are individually limited, but cumulatively considerable? ("Cumulatively considerable" means that the incremental effects of a project are considerable when viewed in connection with the effects of past projects, the effects of other current projects, and the effects of probable future projects.)				
c) Does the project have environmental effects that will cause substantial adverse effects on human beings, either directly or indirectly?				

Glossary

63-20 Corporation

Lease revenue bonds are issued by a joint powers authority or nonprofit corporation that meets certain federal tax law qualifications for the issuance of tax-exempt bonds (commonly known as a "63-20 corporation"), after the original U.S. Treasury Revenue Ruling in which such qualifications are described—*see* Rev. Proc. 82-86.

ab initio

Latin for "from the beginning"

ad valorem

Latin for "according to value," *e.g.*, a tax or duty based on the value of property.

ad valorem tax

A tax based on the assessed value of real estate or personal property. In other words, *ad valorem* taxes can be property tax or even duty on imported items. *Ad valorem* tax is often used interchangeably with property tax. Property taxes are the major source of revenues for state and municipal governments.

alternate school fees

School facilities fees or developer fees imposed pursuant to Government Code section 65995.5 (Level 2 fee) and 65995.7 (Level 3 fee).

annual appropriation lease

Under this lease the school district is obligated only for payments due in the then current fiscal year. The school district has the right, at least once during each fiscal year, to unilaterally terminate the lease by not appropriating the lease payments for the following year. Annual appropriation obligations may be structured as leases, installment sale agreements, or lease-purchase agreements, and still avoid the Constitutional debt limit.

annual recalculation of existing school building capacity

An annual update of a needs analysis must include a revision of a school district's eligibility.

apportionment

As set forth in Education Code section 17070.15(a), "apportionment" is a reservation of state [funds] for the purpose of eligible new construction, modernization, or hardship approved by the SAB for an applicant school district; a project may be approved for funding, but not receive an apportionment.

approved application(s)

District-submitted application and required documents submitted to the OPSC, as identified in the general information section of Forms SAB 50-01, *Enrollment Certification/Projection* (revised 09/02); SAB 50-02, *Existing School Building Capacity* (revised 09/02); SAB 50-03, *Eligibility Determination* (revised 09/02); and SAB 50-04, *Application for Funding* (revised 09/02), as appropriate, that OPSC has completed and accepted for preliminary approval review pursuant to Education Code section 17072.25(a).

approved application for joint-use funding

An *Application for Joint-Use Funding*, Form SAB 50-07 (New 09/02), including all required supporting documents as identified in the general information section of that form, that the district has submitted to and was accepted by the OPSC for processing.

attendance area

Set forth in Education Code section 17070.15(b), "attendance area" is the geographical area serving an existing high school and those junior high schools and elementary schools included therein.

baseline schedule

Schedule developed at the start of a project that governs the timing and sequence of performance. The Owner typically reviews and accepts the baseline schedule of the contracting party before any work

Glossary

begins. Thereafter, performance is measured against the baseline schedule, plotting any delays, disruptions, or other problems against the schedule to determine their effect on the contracting party's performance. Baseline schedules are particularly useful for reviewing delay claims by contractors.

best management practices (BMPs)

Methods determined to be the most effective and practical way to proceed, in this case to prevent or reduce pollution.

California Basic Education Data System (CBEDS)

District enrollment data reported October of each year; CBEDS data is used to produce a district's five-year enrollment projection (Form SAB 50-01).

California Department of Education (CDE)

CDE's Facilities Planning Division reviews and approves K–12 school facilities for siting and educational programming issues.

California Environmental Quality Act (CEQA)

California's state environment law as set forth in Public Resources Code section 21000 *et seq.*

categorical exemptions

Classes of projects determined by the California Secretary for Resources not to have a significant effect on the environment and therefore exempt from provisions of CEQA, unless exceptions to the exemption apply.

CBEDS Report

Enrollment information provided through the California Basic Education Data System by school districts to the CDE.

CDE Source School List

A list developed and published by the CDE that identifies districts and critically overcrowded schools pursuant to Education Code section 17078.18(c).

Certified Playground Safety Inspector

Individual who has completed program requirements as specified in Government Code section 65750.

change order

Written amendment to the contract that modifies the rights and obligations of the parties. Typically change orders are utilized to add or delete work scope from the contract or to grant extensions of time to the contractual completion deadline. To be valid, a change order must be executed by both parties to the contract.

Class B Construction Cost Index

Construction factor index that Marshall and Swift provides monthly for the Western area, relating to structures made of reinforced concrete or steel frames, concrete floors, and roofs, and accepted and used by the Board.

Class Size Reduction (CSR)

A legislative policy to incentivize reduction in class sizes to under 20 children in certain elementary school grades.

classroom

A teaching station defined in Education Code section 17071.25(a)(1). A "teaching station" refers to any space constructed or reconstructed to serve as an area for pupil instruction, but shall not include portable buildings, except as provided in section 17071.30.

Coastal Development Permits

Permits issued by the a local government or the Coastal Commission to allow development in the coastal zone.

Community Facilities District (CFD)

District formed pursuant to the Mello-Roos Community Facilities Act of 1982, Government Code section 53311.

condition of approval

A condition a city or county adopts to require a certain action by a developer/property owner to mitigate impacts on school facilities prior to project approval.

construction cost

When publicly bid, the total contracted value of work a general contractor,

Glossary

subcontractor, and/or construction manager performs for a given construction project. Also known as "hard costs," a subset of "project cost."

construction documents

Technical documents for the construction of the project including the plans and specifications.

contract documents

Various documents that make up the construction contract between the owner and the contractor. Typically defined in the construction agreement, these documents define the rights and obligations of the parties, in total, relating to the construction of the project.

Critical Path Method (CPM) Schedule

The longest chain of events that must be performed to complete the project. A CPM Schedule breaks down the project into discrete elements and provides a description of the timing, sequence, and interrelationship between the various elements of the work.

critically overcrowded school (COS)

Based on the 2001 CBEDS enrollment, a school with a population density in grades K–6 that exceeds 115 pupils per usable acre; in grades 7–12, having a population density greater than 90 pupils per usable acre.

current replacement cost

For toilet facilities, $346.60 per square foot; $192.60 per square foot for all other spaces. Amounts shown will be adjusted annually in the manner prescribed in Education Code section 1859.71.

date of value

Date property value is fixed by deposit of funds with the court.

district representative

A member of a school district staff or other agent authorized to serve as "district representative" to execute and file an application with the Board on behalf of the district and/or act as liaison between the Board and the district.

Division of the State Architect (DSA)

The state office within the Department of General Services that reviews school building plans and specifications for structural, fire safety, and access compliance. DSA reviews and approves architectural/engineering plans, and also approves plans and requirements for state grant funding.

E-Rate

A program of the Federal Communications Commission (FCC) that provides eligible K–12 public schools and libraries 20 to 90 percent discounts on approved telecommunications, Internet access, and internal connections costs.

elementary school pupil

A student housed in a school serving kindergarten through sixth grade, or any combination of kindergarten through sixth grade.

Endangered Species Act (ESA)

The Endangered Species Act of 1973 (16 U.S.C. § 1531 *et seq.*) establishes federal protections for fish, wildlife, and plants that are threatened or endangered. The California Endangered Species Act (Fish and Game Code § 2050 *et seq.*) establishes state protections for threatened and endangered, as well as "candidate" species (those that may be eligible for listing).

Energy Efficiency Account

Subset of state board funds that SAB sets aside for purposes of Education Code section 17077.35 to award supplemental grants to school districts that include plan design and other project components for the purpose of seeking school facility energy efficiency.

environmental hardship

State funding for site acquisition as authorized by Education Code section 1859.75.1.

ESHA

Certain land uses have a higher value in a coastal zone as compared to a non-coastal zone—unfortunately, school uses are not among them. If a potential school

Glossary

site is located in an ecologically-sensitive habitat area (ESHA), it is highly unlikely that the school district could obtain a zone change or LCP amendment to use it for a school.

excessive cost hardship grant

Funding provided by Education Code section 1859.83.

existing school building capacity

A district's total capacity to house pupils as calculated pursuant to Education Code sections 1859.30 through 1859.33.

facility

All or a portion of any real property, site improvements, utilities, and/or buildings or other improvements contained in the project.

facility hardship

New or replacement facilities authorized by Education Code section 1859.82(a) or (b).

fee justification study

Study the governing board adopts to justify collection of Level 1 fees and establishing the nexus for Level 2 fees.

Field Act facility

School building meeting the requirements contained in Education Code section 17280 *et seq.*

final apportionment

An apportionment made pursuant to Education Code section 17070.15 by submittal of an application pursuant to section 1859.21.

financial hardship

State funding for all or a portion of the district's matching share required by Education Code section 1859.77.1 or 1859.79.

general school fees

School facilities fees collected pursuant to Education Code section 17620 and Government Code section 65995, also referred to as "Level 1 Fees" (in 1998, $1.93 per square foot of new residential construction and $0.31 per square foot of new commercial construction). *See also* alternate school fees, Level 2 fees, and Level 3 fees.

high school attendance area

An attendance area that serves a currently operated high school, other than a continuation school or a community school.

high school district

School district that serves any combination of grades seven through twelve exclusively.

high school pupil

Student in a school serving grades 9–12 or any combination of grades 9–12.

higher education

Community college, college, university, or accredited educational organization beyond the twelfth-grade level.

joint use partner(s)

Entity or entities that enter into a joint use agreement pursuant to the provisions of Education Code section 17077.42.

joint use project

Project approved by the Board pursuant to Education Code sections 17050, 17051, or 17077.40.

large modernization project

Funding application request for grant(s) exceeding fifty percent of the current CBEDS enrollment of a comprehensive high school that will be modernized.

large new construction project

Application request for at least 200 new construction grants that will be used to construct a new comprehensive high school or an addition to a comprehensive high school.

Lease Purchase Program (LPP)

Leroy F. Greene State School Building Lease-Purchase Law of 1976 (Education Code § 17700 *et seq.*); preceded the 1998 SFP; provided for modernization and new construction funding on a lease-purchase basis; and required a lien on all district property, collection of rental and sale of

Glossary

site income, and significantly different funding and eligibility rules.

Level 1 fee

General school fee collected pursuant to Education Code section 17620 and Government Code section 16995, currently in the amount of $1.93 per square foot for new residential construction.

Level 2 fee

Alternative school fee collected pursuant to Government Code section 65995.5.

Level 3 fee

Alternative school fee pursuant to Government Code section 65995.7 collected only when the State Allocation Board is no longer approving apportionments for new construction funding.

Mello-Roos Bonds

Bonds authorized under the provisions of the Mello-Roos Community Facilities Act of 1982, commencing with Government Code section 53311.

mitigation agreement

An agreement entered into between a developer/property owner and school district providing for mitigation of impacts on school facilities.

modernization

Process for extending the useful life of an existing district-owned facility; eligibility for state bond modernization funding is based on permanent buildings that are more than 20 years old.

modernization eligibility

Result of calculation contained in either Option A or B of Form SAB 50-03.

modernization grant

Funding provided pursuant to Education Code section 17074.10(a) and sections 1859.78, 1859.78.3, and 1859.78.6.

multi-track year-round education (MTYRE)

A school education program in which students are divided into three or more groups on alternating tracks, with at least one group out of session and other groups that are in session during the same period.

multiple prime contracting

An arrangement whereby an owner enters into separate direct contracts with each of the construction trades performing specific work on a project, and the work is coordinated by the owner's construction manger. This is in contrast to the typical arrangement where an owner hires a general contractor who has responsibility for the entire project.

National Pollution Discharge Elimination System (NPDES)

Permit to control the discharge of pollutants to water bodies to ensure that water quality standards are met.

needs analysis

School facilities' needs analysis (SFNA) is required by Government Code section 65995.6.

new construction

Provision for additional student capacity and/or buildings (may include permanent, relocatable, or pre-fabricated building types).

New Construction Adjusted Grant

The New Construction Grant, plus any additional funding provided by Education Code section 17072.10(a) and sections 1859.71 and 1859.71.1.

New Construction Eligibility

The result of the calculation determined in Education Code section 17071.75.

New Construction Grant

Funding provided pursuant to Education Code section 17072.10(a) and sections 1859.71 and 1859.71.1.

notice of intent (NOI)

Notice of a school district's intent to prepare a negative declaration, required by the California Environmental Quality Act.

notice of *lis pendens*

Notice filed with the county recorder to inform all interested parties of an impending eminent domain action; also known as a notice of pendency of action.

Glossary

Office of Public School Construction (OPSC)

Office responsible for managing state bond funding for eligible new construction and modernization projects for K–12 schools; part of California's Department of General Services that serves as staff to SAB.

Offner-Dean Leases

When a school district does not have full beneficial use and occupancy of leased property, its obligation to make lease payments may be abated or reduced. These are often referred to as "Offner-Dean" leases, after two leading California court cases holding that such leases do not constitute debt for purposes of the California Constitution.

Order of Immediate Possession

A judicial action allowing entry onto the targeted property.

owner

Entity that pays to have work performed on a particular project. In public contracting, the owner is the agency that contracts to have work performed and, for the context of this book, it is the school district.

permanent classroom

Any instructional space that does not meet the definition of a portable classroom set forth in Education Code sections 17071.25(a)(1) and 17071.30.

Pool Bonds

Method of financing that combines issuance of debt by multiple borrowers into single financing in order to realize cost savings and reduction in school district staff; achieved either by having a single issuer lend the proceeds of its bonds (Pool Bonds) to multiple borrowers or by issuing certificates of participation (Pool COPs).

Pool COPS

Method of financing whereby a single issuer lends the proceeds of its bonds (Pool Bonds) to multiple borrowers as certificates of participation.

preliminary endangerment assessment (PEA)

Second-level review, set forth in Education Code section 17210(h), that requires sampling and analysis of a site for hazardous material contamination, a preliminary determination of its type and extent, and a preliminary evaluation of any risks the contamination may pose for children's health, public health, or the environment, that is conducted in a manner approved by DTSC.

preliminary plans

Set of architectural drawings not yet approved by the Division of the State Architect (DSA).

prime contractor

Construction firm (or individual) in direct contract with a project owner; a general contractor who enters into a direct contract with the district (possibly with separate subcontracts for various elements of the work); or numerous (multiple) prime contractors, each with a direct contractual relationship with the district.

program manager

Entity a district retains to develop structures and processes for implementing the construction program and to manage the entire project.

project cost

Total cost to construct a project, including indirect costs such as fees, furniture, equipment, testing, inspection, and site acquisition. *See also* "construction cost."

Proposition 1A

State school bond initiative for $9.2 billion, passed by the electorate in the 1998 general election.

Proposition 13

Ballot initiative passed by the California electorate in 1978 that reduced property taxes and provided that the assessment be based on the property's sale price in the year acquired.

Proposition 39

California ballot initiative passed in November 2000 requiring a 55 percent vote of the electorate for local school bonds at a primary or general election, a regularly scheduled local election, or a statewide

Glossary

special election; amended sections 15102, 15106, 35233, and 72533 of the Education Code and added Chapter 1.5 (commencing with section 15264) to Part 10; also added applicable sections to the California Constitution.

Proposition 47

California ballot initiative that created the Kindergarten-University Public Education Facilities Bond Act of 2002.

pupil grant

Basic unit of state project funding; each modernization or new construction project receives grant funding based on the number of pupils.

qualifications-based selection (QBS)

Government Code section 4526 requires that the selection of any individual, firm, partnership, corporation, association, or other legal entity providing services be "on the basis of demonstrated competence and on the professional qualifications necessary for the satisfactory performance of the services required." Sometimes described as a qualifications-based selection (QBS) process.

Qualified Zone Academy Bond (QZAB)

A federal program to help strengthen schools serving large concentrations of low-income families.

qualifying pupils

Number of pupils that qualify for state bond funding under calculations made and rules established by OPSC and SAB regulations in Title 2.

remedial action plan (RAP)

Plan approved by the Department of Toxic Substances Control (DTSC) pursuant to Health and Safety Code section 25356.1.

resolution of consent

Ratification of an eminent domain plan by the appropriate governing body.

response action (RA)

Removal of hazardous materials, solid waste, substances, and other remedial actions in connection with hazardous substances at the site.

schedule of values

Analysis that divides project into separate work elements, each with a dollar value, to track progress and make appropriate periodic payments; developed collaboratively by the owner and the design professional or contractor in advance of the start of each party's work; often coordinated with the baseline schedule.

school building capacity

Definition set forth in Education Code section 17070.15(l).

school district

Definition set forth in Education Code section 17070.15(h).

School Facilities Improvement District (SFID)

Legal entity authorized by Education Code section 15300, to develop funding for school facilities.

School Facility Program (SFP)

Leroy F. Greene *School Facilities Act* of 1998 (Education Code section 17070.10 *et seq.*) (Title 2 C.C.R. 1859 *et seq.*); refers either to new construction or modernization funding programs implemented under the Act.

Senate Bill 50 (SB 50)

August 1998 law establishing the School Facilities Program; required that regulations be in place once Prop. 1A was approved in the November 1998 election.

small school district

Entity with an enrollment of 2,500 or less district-wide, as reported in Part A; the continuation high pupils reported in Part B; and the special day class pupils reported in Part C on the latest Form SAB 50-01 (used to determine or adjust the district's baseline eligibility pursuant to Education Code sections 1859.50 and 1859.51, or submitted separately to the OPSC).

source school

Critically overcrowded school included on the CDE list of source schools with qualifying pupils.

Glossary

special day class (SDC)

Provision for educating special needs pupils, with specific funding and classroom learning standards.

square footage

Enclosed area of a building measured from the outside face of exterior structural walls; for the interior or portions of building areas, the enclosed area is measured from the center line of the interior demising wall.

State Allocation Board (SAB)

Board created in 1947 that is responsible for allocating state bond monies.

student yield factor

Number of students each dwelling unit needs in order to augment enrollment.

Standard Urban Stormwater Mitigation Plan (SUSMP)

The section of a Municipal Storm Water Permit that designates best management practices (BMPs) to be used for specified categories of development.

super high school attendance area (SHSAA)

Two or more adjacent districts that can be combined to develop a project; commonly called super attendance areas.

Title 2

Regulations to implement the Leroy F. Greene School Facilities Act of 1998 (C.C.R., Subgroup 5.5), which establishes a state program to provide state per-pupil funding for new construction and modernization of existing school facilities.

total maximum daily load (TMDL)

Maximum amount of pollutant a waterbody can receive and still satisfy water quality standards; an allocation of that amount to pollutant sources, required by section 303 of the federal Clean Water Act.

Type I Joint-Use Project

Project meeting the criteria of Education Code section 17077.40(b)(1).

Type II Joint-Use Project

Project meeting the criteria of Education Code section 17077.40(b)(2).

Type III Joint-Use Project

Project meeting the criteria of Education Code section 17077.40(b)(3).

Unfunded List

List of projects that have been approved but not funded.

Unhoused Pupils

Comparison of existing capacity to five-year enrollment projections a district makes to demonstrate insufficient classroom capacity; eligibility for state bond funding is based on the number of unhoused pupils.

unrestricted fund

Funds in the 2002 (or 2004, as appropriate) Critically Overcrowded School Facilities Account not approved for preliminary apportionment.

usable acres

Gross acreage of a school site less any portion that has been publicly dedicated for offsite street improvements; and any portion of the site not available for school purposes, as determined by the CDE, as a result of topological impediments or other unique circumstances.

Williamson Act

California Land Conservation Act of 1965 (Gov't. Code §§ 51200–51298), providing for the preservation of agricultural land through the establishment of agricultural preserves and restricting those lands to agricultural or compatible uses.

List of Acronyms

AB	Assembly Bill	CAA	Clean Air Act	CFD	community facilities district
ABAG	Association of Bay Area Governments	CAC	California Administrative Code	CFR	Code of Federal Regulations
ACBM	asbestos-containing building material	Cal-EPA	California Environmental Protection Agency	CGF	California Geographical Survey
ACM	asbestos-containing material	Cal-OSHA	California Occupational Safety and Health Act	CIP	coordinated insurance program
ACW	asbestos-containing waste	Caltrans	California Department of Transportation	CM	construction manager
ADA	Americans with Disabilities Act	CARB	California Air Resources Board	CMC	California Mechanical Code
ADA	average daily attendance	CASBO	California Association of School Budget Officers	CMP	congestion management program
AG	Attorney General			CNEL	community noise equivalent level
AHERA	Asbestos Hazard Emergency Response Act	CASH	Coalition for Adequate School Housing	COP	certificate of participation
ALARA	as low as reasonably achievable	CBEDS	California Basic Educational Data System	COS	critically overcrowded schools program
APA	Administrative Procedure Act	CBC	California Building Code	CPC	California Plumbing Code
APCD	Air Pollution Control District	CCR	California Code of Regulations	CPM	critical path method
APCO	air pollution control officer	CC&Rs	conditions, covenants, and restrictions	CPSC	Consumer Product Safety Commission
API	academic performance index	CDC	California Department of Conservation	CPUC	California Public Utilities Commission
AQMD	Air Quality Management District	CDE	California Department of Education	CSR	class size reduction
ARAR	applicable or relevant and appropriate requirements	CDP	Coastal Development Permit	CTF	California Teleconnect Fund
ARB	Air Resources Board	CEC	California Electrical Code	CUP	conditional use permit
ASHAA	Asbestos in Schools Hazard Abatement Act	CEC	California Energy Commission	dB	decibel
ASTM	American Society for Testing and Materials	CEFPI	Council of Educational Facility Planners International	DFG	Department of Fish and Game
BACT	best available control technology	CEQA	California Environmental Quality Act	DIR	Department of Industrial Relations
BAMM	best available mitigation measures	CERCLA	Comprehensive Environmental Response, Compensation and Liability Act of 1980	DGS	Department of General Services
BAT	best available technology			DHS	Department of Health Services
BMP	best management practice			DLSE	Division of Labor Standards Enforcement
BZHWP	border zone/hazardous waste property	CESA	California Endangered Species Act	DOHS	Department of Health Services

List of Acronyms

DMG	Division of Mines and Geology	HCD	Department of Housing and Community Development	MOU	memorandum of understanding
DSA	Division of the State Architect	HSAA	high school attendance area	MS4	separate municipal storm sewer system
DTSC	Department of Toxic Substances Control	HVAC	heating, ventilation, and air conditioning	MTYRE	multi-track year-round education
DU	dwelling unit	IDEA	Individuals with Disabilities Education Act	NA	no action
DVBE	Disabled Veteran Business Enterprise	IOR	inspector of record	NAAQS	National Ambient Air Quality Standards
ESA	environmental site assessment	IS	initial study	ND	negative declaration
EECA	engineering evaluation/ cost analysis	IWMB	California Integrated Waste Management Board	NDDB	natural diversity database
EHHA	Office of Environmental Health Hazard Assessment	JPA	joint powers authority	NESHAPs	National Emission Standards for Hazardous Air Pollutants
EIR	environmental impact report	kW	kilowatt	NFA	no further action
EOA	environmental oversight agreement	LAFCO	local agency formation commission	NIMBY	not in my backyard
EPA	Environmental Protection Agency	lb	pound	NIMTOO	not in my term of office
ESA	Endangered Species Act of 1973	LCP	local coastal plan	NMFS	National Marine Fisheries Service
ESHA	ecologically-sensitive habitat area	LOS	level of service	NOC	notice of completion
FCC	Federal Communications Commission	LPP	lease-purchase program	NOD	notice of determination
FHWA	Federal Highway Administration	LUFT	leaking underground fuel tank	NOE	notice of exemption
FS	feasibility study	LUST	leaking underground storage tank	NOI	notice of intent
G&A	general and administrative	M3	cubic meter	NOP	notice of preparation
GIS	geographic information system	MACT	maximum available control technology	NOT	notice of termination
GMP	guaranteed maximum price	MAI	Member of the Appraisal Institute	NPDES	National Pollutant Discharge Elimination System
G.O. bond	general obligation bond	MBE	minority business enterprise	NPL	national priority list
GSU	geological services unit	MCM	minimum control measures	OX	total oxidants
HARP	hotspots analysis and report program	MEF	minimum essential facilities	O2	oxygen
HASP	health and safety plan	MEIR	master environmental impact report	O3	ozone
HAZMAT	hazardous materials	MEP	maximum extent practicable	OEHHA	Office of Environmental Health Hazard Assessment
		MND	mitigated negative declaration	OEM	original equipment manufacturer
				O&M	operation and maintenance
				OPR	Office of Planning and Research
				OPSC	Office of Public School Construction

List of Acronyms

OSFM	Office of the State Fire Marshal	RG	registered geologist	SWMP	stormwater management program
OSHA	Occupational Safety and Health Act	RI	remedial investigation	SWPPP	stormwater pollution prevention program
		ROW	right of way		
PA/SI	preliminary assessment/ site investigation	RP	responsible party	SWRCB	State Water Resources Control Board
		RQ	reportable quantity		
Pb	lead	RWQCB	Regional Water Quality Control Board	TAC	toxic air contaminant
PCB	polychlorinated biphenyl			TIF	tax-increment financing
		SAB	State Allocation Board		
PE	professional engineer	SARA	Superfund Amendments and Reauthorization Act of 1986	TIP	transportation improvement program
PEA	preliminary endangerment assessment				
PM_{10}	particulate matter less than 10 microns in diameter			TOC	total organic carbon
		SB	Senate Bill	TRAN	tax and revenue anticipation note
ppb	parts per billion	SBC	state building code		
ppm	parts per million	SBE	small business enterprise	TSCA	Toxic Substance Control Act
PRC	Public Resources Code				
PRP	potentially responsible party	SCAG	Southern California Association of Governments	UBC	Uniform Building Code
PUC	Public Utilities Commission			UFC	Uniform Fire Code
PUD	planned unit development	SCAQMD	South Coast Air Quality Management District	ug/m_3	micrograms per cubic meter
QA	quality assurance				
QBS	qualification-based selection	SEC	Securities and Exchange Commission	UGST	underground storage tank
QC	quality control	SFD	single-family dwelling	USC	United States Code
QZAB	qualified zone academy bond	SFID	school facilities improvement district	USEPA	United States Environmental Protection Agency
RA	risk assessment	SFNA	school facilities needs analysis		
RAO	remedial action objective			USFWS	United States Fish and Wildlife Service
RAP	remedial action plan	SFP	school facility program		
RAW	removal action workplan	SFPD	school facilities planning division	VCA	voluntary cleanup agreement
RCRA	Resource Conservation and Recovery Act				
		SHSAA	super high school attendance area	VOC	volatile organic compound
RD	remedial design				
RA	remedial action	SIP	state implementation plan	WBE	women's business enterprise
REA	registered environmental assessor	SLAPP	strategic lawsuit against public participation	WDR	waste discharge requirements
		SOX	oxides of sulfur		
RFI	request for information	SSI	supplemental site investigation	XRF	x-ray fluorescence
RFP	request for proposal			YRE	year-round education
RFQ	request for qualifications	STEL	short-term exposure limit	YTD	year to date

Bibliography

2001 C.A.S.H. Annual Conference. *Developer Fees in the New Millennium* (March 7, 2001), workshop and article. Presented by Alexander Bowie and Julia D. Rice, Bowie, Arneson, Wiles & Giannone, 4920 Campus Drive, Newport Beach, CA 92660, tel: (949) 851-1300.

2001 C.A.S.H. Fall Conference (October 11–12, 2001). *School Fees.* Article by Alexander Bowie, Bowie, Arneson, Wiles & Giannone, 4920 Campus Drive, Newport Beach, CA 92660, tel: (949) 851-1300.

2001 School Facilities Planning, Construction, and Financing Workshop (September 28, 2001). *General Obligation Bonds and Proposition 39 (55% Local Vote Bonds).* Robert E. Anslow, Bowie, Arneson, Wiles & Giannone, 4920 Campus Drive, Newport Beach, CA 92660, tel: (949) 851-1300.

2000 School Law, Facilities, Construction, and Financing Workshop, October 6, 2000. *State Allocation Board/Priority Points/Proposal.* Alexander Bowie and Julia D. Rice, Bowie, Arneson, Wiles & Giannone, 4920 Campus Drive, Newport Beach, CA 92660, tel: (949) 851-1300.

A Glossary of School Finance Terms (February 1996). Published by EdSource, 525 Middlefield Road, Ste. 100, Menlo Park, CA 94025-3447, tel: (415) 323-8396, fax: (415) 323-0180.

A Planner's Guide to Financing Public Improvements (http://ceres.ca.gov/planning/financing/index.html#contents_anchor).

A Primer on the Public School State Approval Process (March 2001). State and Consumer Services Agency, Attn: David Osborne, 915 Capitol Mall, Ste. 200, Sacramento, CA 95814.

AIA California Council. *Why Stock Plans for Public Schools Don't Work.* C.A.S.H.

Alexander, Kern and M. David Alexander (1985). *American Public School Law* (2nd ed.). St. Paul, Minn.: West Publishing Company.

Anaheim City School District, Education Administration. Document from the Office of the Assistant Superintendent: *Educational Acronyms* (printed July 31, 1997).

Architect's Submittal Guidelines (March 2001). Office of Public School Construction, on behalf of the State Allocation Board, 1130 K Street, Ste. 400, Sacramento, CA 95814, tel: (916) 445-3160 (www.opsc.dgs.ca.gov).

Butts, F.R. and L.A.Cremin (1953), *A History of Education in American Culture.* New York: Holt, Rinehart and Winston.

California Association of School Business Officials (CASBO). *Planning and Construction Manual.* CASBO State Facilities Planning

Bibliography

Commission, 600 N. 10th Street, Ste. 150, Sacramento, CA 95814.

California Dept. of Education, School Facilities Planning Division. *K–3 Class Size Reduction, Legislation* (www.cde.ca.gov.classsize/legis.htm).

California Dept. of Education, School Facilities Planning Division. *California Playground Safety Regulations* (March 3, 2000).

California Dept. of General Services. *Prototype School Designs.* DGS, 1130 K Street, Ste. 400, Sacramento, CA 95814 (http://planupload.dgs.ca.gov/CASchoolsHome.asp).

California Dept. of General Services, Public School Construction. *School Facility Program Approved Regulations* (www.opsc.dgs.ca.gov/Regulations/approved_regulations.asp).

C.A.S.H. Facility Resource Center publication. *School Facilities Needs Analysis* (May 2001). Prepared for Clovis Unified School District by Michael Paoli and Associates, Environmental, School Facility, and City Planners, 377 W. Fallbrook, Ste. 205, Fresno, CA 93711, tel: (559) 432-4890.

C.A.S.H. Facility Resource Center publication. *Classroom Indoor Air Quality Issues and Suggested Responses* by Brian W. Smith, Bowie, Arneson, Wiles & Giannone, 4920 Campus Drive, Newport Beach, CA 92660, tel: (949) 851-1300.

C.A.S.H. Facility Resource Center Publications: *Comparison of Proposition 39 and Current Law, School District General Obligation Bonds; Phase I Environmental Site Assessment Advisory: School Property Evaluations* (revised May 7, 2001); *CDE's Contingent Site Approval Policy for Asbestos and Lead Paint* (August 24, 2000); *Agricultural Sampling Guidelines Just Released!* (June 28, 2000); *Model Environmental Oversight Agreement* developed by C.A.S.H. and the Dept. of Toxic Substances Control (DTSC) (April 26, 2000); *Section III. Construction; Section V. Maintenance and Operation; Highlights of California's New Playground Safety Regulations, CCR Title 22, Division 4, Chapter 22* (February 23, 2000).

C.A.S.H. Register Newsletter (June 2002). *CEQA Compliance for Siting and Constructing New Schools: The Question of Timing of Review.* Maureen Gorsen, Partner, Weston, Benshoof, Rochefort, Rubalcava & MacCuish LLP, 333 South Hope Street, 16th Floor, Los Angeles, CA 90071, tel: (213) 576-1000.

CenterViews newsletter. *Seven Tests for Mitigation Measures* (1999). Dwayne Meras, The Planning Center, 1580 Metro Drive, Costa Mesa, CA 92626, tel: (714) 966-9220, fax: (714) 966-9221 (www.planningcenter.com; www.schoolplanning.com).

CenterViews newsletter. *What Do I Need to Know About AB 972* (November 2001). Dwayne Meras, The Planning Center, 1580 Metro Drive, Costa Mesa, CA 92626, tel: (714) 966-9220, fax: (714) 966-9221 (www.planningcenter.com; www.schoolplanning.com).

Bibliography

CenterViews newsletter. *Railroads, Pipelines and Schools* (May 2001). Dwayne Meras, The Planning Center, 1580 Metro Drive, Costa Mesa, CA 92626, tel: (714) 966-9220, fax: (714) 966-9221 (www.planningcenter.com' www.schoolplanning.com).

CenterViews newsletter. *Components of a Rail Risk Assessment* (2002). George Shaw, School Facilities Planning Division, California Dept. of Education, for The Planning Center, 1580 Metro Drive, Costa Mesa, CA 92626, tel: (714) 966-9220, fax: (714) 966-9221 (www.planningcenter.com; www.schoolplanning.com).

CenterViews newsletter. *Is My School Expansion Project Exempt Under CEQA? Can I Avoid DTSC Review?* (2000). Dwayen Meras, The Planning Center 1580 Metro Drive, Costa Mesa, CA 92626, tel: (714) 966-9220, fax: (714) 966-9221 (www.planningcenter.com; www.schoolplanning.com).

CenterViews Newsletter. *Ten Ways School Districts Can Benefit from Master EIRs* (1999). The Planning Center, 1580 Metro Drive, Costa Mesa, CA 92626, tel: (714) 966-9220, fax: (714) 966-9221 (www.planningcenter.com; www.school planning.com).

CenterViews Newsletter, *How Does CEQA Apply to My Class Size Reduction Program?* (1999). The Planning Center, 1580 Metro Drive, Costa Mesa, CA 92626, tel: (714) 966-9220, fax: (714) 966-9221 (www.planningcenter.com; www.school planning.com).

Consumer's Guide to Hiring an Architect. California Architects Board, 400 R Street, Ste. 400, Sacramento, CA 95814, tel: (916) 445-3394, (800) 991-2223, fax: (916) 445-8524 (www.cab.ca.gov).

Council of Educational Facility Planners International (1985 and 1991 eds.). *Guide for Planning Educational Facilities.* Columbus, Ohio: Jerry M. Lowe, Ed.D. (Dept. of Educational Leadership and Counseling, Murray State University); *Historical Perspectives* (1991), Jerry Lowe.

Department of Health Services. Advisory on Relocatable and Renovated Classrooms. Produced by the California Interagency Working Group on Indoor Air Quality (December 1996). Contact: Jed M. Waldman, Ph.D., Chief, Indoor Air Quality Section, California Dept. of Health Services, 2151 Berkeley Way, Berkeley, CA 94704, tel: (510) 540-2476, fax: (510) 540-3022 (www.cal-iaq.org).

Dewey, John J. (1899), *The School and Society,* Chicago: University of Chicago Press.

Educational Facilities Laboratories, Inc. (1960), *The Cost of a Schoolhouse,* New York.

Educational Specifications: Linking Design of School Facilities to Educational Program (1997). California Dept. of Education, Sacramento, California.

The Executive Director (December 1991). *Blueprint for Growth.* Glen Ovard, Professor, Brigham Young University, Salt Lake City, Utah; Joe Kirschenstein, President, Sage Institute Inc. (which specializes in school planning), Westlake Village, California; and Kelvin Lee,

Bibliography

Superintendent, Dry Creek Elementary School District, Roseville, California (Mr. Lee serves on the C.A.S.H. Board of Directors).

FAR 77, *Objects Affecting Navigable Airspace* (School Sites, FAR Part 77.25–77.29).

Focus on California Public Finance. Published by E.J. De La Rosa and Company, Inc., Investment Bankers, 11900 West Olympic Blvd., Ste. 500, Los Angeles, CA 90064-1151, tel: (310) 207-1975, Fax: (310) 207-1995, 706 Mission Street, Ste. 502, San Francisco, CA 94103-3113, tel: (415) 495-8863, fax: (415) 495-8864.

Foot Notes to Report of Standard (or Stock) Plan Survey (January 27, 1992). Frank G. Cloer, Director, Facilities Services Section, Georgia Dept. of Education, Office of Administrative Services, Twin Towers East, Atlanta, GA 30334-5050 (www.cashnet.org:80/resource-center/Section2/2-1-3.html).

FY 2001 Class Size Reduction Program (as authorized under PL 106-554) (www/ed/gov/offices/OESE/ClassSize/legislation.html).

Guide for the Development of a Long-Range Facilities Plan, 1986 Edition, California State Dept. of Education, School Facilities and Transportation Division, 721 Capitol Mall, Sacramento, CA 94244-2720.

Guide for Planning Educational Facilities (1988). Council of Education Facility Planners.

Guidebook to the School Facility Program (February 2000). Office of Public School Construction on behalf of the State Allocation Board, 1130 K Street, 4th Floor, Sacramento, CA 95814, tel: (916) 445-3160, fax: (916) 445-5526 (www.opsc.dgs.ca.gov).

Handbook for Public Playground Safety (November 1994). Publication #325, U.S. Consumer Product Safety Commission.

Handbook for Public Playground Safety (November 1997). Publication #325, U.S. Consumer Product Safety Commission (www/cpsc.gov/cpscpub/pubs/325.pdf).

Hawkins, Harold L. and Betty L. Overbaugh (July, August 1988). *The Interface Between Facilities and Learning.* Council of Educational Facility Planners, International Journal, Vol. 4, Nos. 1-4.

Indoor Air Quality (IAQ) in Schools (September 10, 2001) (www.epa.gov/iaq/schools/index.html).

Lead-Safe Schools Project (2000). Labor Occupational Health Program, University of California, Berkeley, 2223 Fulton Street, Berkeley, CA 94720-5120, tel: (510) 643-8902.

Proposition 39 Alternative General Obligation Bond Authorization Procedures Panacea or Pandora's Box? Warren B. Diven, Esq. and Christina L. Dyer, Esq. Best, Best & Krieger LLP, 402 W. Broadway, 13th Floor, San Diego, CA 92101-3542, tel: (619) 525-1300.

Level 2/Level 3 Fee Studies: Observations from the First Two Years. Rob Corley, School Facilities Consultant, Ventura, California.

Bibliography

Local Programs Procedures, Local Assistance Program. *Safe Routes to School—Program Guidelines* (SF2S) (February 10, 2000). Caltrans, Office of Local Programs.

McClintock, Jean and Robert McClintock, eds. *Henry Bernards School Architecture* (1970). New York: Teachers College Press.

Otto, Henry J.. *Elementary School Organization and Administration* (1944). New York: D. Appleton-Century Company, Inc.

The Planning Report. *School Facility Finance—Speaking Truth to Power: LAO Urges New Blueprint for State's School Facilities Funding* (November 2001). Interview with Marianne O'Malley, Principal Fiscal and Policy Analyst, Legislative Analyst Office, Sacramento.

Proposition 39: Alternative General Obligation Bond Authorization Procedures Panacea or Pandora's Box?, Warren B. Diven, Esq., and Christina L. Dyer, Esq., Best, Best & Krieger LLP.

Public School Construction Cost Reduction Guidelines (April 26, 2000). State Allocation Board, 1130 K Street, Ste. 400, Sacramento, CA 95814, tel: (916) 445-3159 (www.opsc.dgs.ca.gov).

The Public School Construction Process: An Overview (November 15, 1999). California Dept. of General Services, Program Research and Evaluation Section.

Preliminary Endangerment Assessment Guidance Manual (January 1994). California Dept. of Toxic Substances Control.

Revenues and Limits, A Guide to School Finance in California, 2002 Edition. Paul M. Goldfinger and Bob Blattner. Published by School Services of California, Inc., 1121 L Street, Ste. 1060, Sacramento, CA 95814 (www.sscal.com).

Riverside County Office of Education, *Year-Round Education Cost Handbook for California School Districts, a Guide for Completion of Planning Worksheets Feasibility Cost Forms and Cost Worksheets* (pilot study—July 1998), published by California Educational Research Cooperative, University of California, Riverside, California.

School Construction News. The Newspaper for the School Construction Industry (January/February 2002, Vol. 5, No. 1). Published by Emlen Publication, 517 Jacoby Street, Ste. C, San Rafael, CA 94901, tel: (415) 460-6185, fax: (415) 460-6288 (www.schoolconstructionnews.com).

School Facility Program. *Progress and Expenditure Reporting Guide*. Prepared by the Office of Public School Construction for the State Allocation Board, 1130 K Street, Ste. 400, Sacramento, CA 95814.

School Finance: A California Perspective, Fifth Edition (2002). Co-authors: Arthur J. Townley, Professor, School of Education, California State University, San Bernardino; June H. Schmieder, Associate Professor, School of Education and Psychology, Pepperdine University, Malibu, California; and Lillian B. Wehmeyer, Professor, School of Education and Behavioral Studies,

Bibliography

Azusa Pacific University, California. Kendall/Hunt Publishing Company, 4050 Westmark Drive, Dubuque, Iowa 52002.

School Site Analysis and Development Guide (1987). California Dept. of Education. School Facilities Planning Division, California Dept. of Education, 721 Capitol Mall, Sacramento, CA 94244-2720.

School Site Selection and Approval Guide (2000). Resources for School Facilities Planning, California Dept. of Education. School Facilities Planning Division, California Dept. of Education, 721 Capitol Mall, Sacramento, CA 94244-2720.

School Site Selection and Approval Guide (1989). California Dept. of Education. School Facilities Planning Division, California Dept. of Education, 721 Capitol Mall, Sacramento, CA 94244-2720.

State of California, Health and Welfare Agency, Department of Health Services. *Advisory on Relocatable and Renovated Classrooms* (December 1996). California Interagency Working Group on Indoor Air Quality. Jed M. Waldman, Ph.D., Chief, Indoor Air Quality Section, California Dept. of Health Services, 2151 Berkeley Way, Berkeley, CA 94704, tel: (510) 540-2476, fax: (510) 540-3022 (www.cal-iaq.org).

School Facilities Planning Division Advisory 00-01. California Dept. of Education, 721 Capitol Mall, Sacramento, CA 94244-2720.

School Facilities Planning Division Advisory. *Processing of Minor Modernization Plans* (March 10, 2000). California Dept. of Education, 721 Capitol Mall, Sacramento, CA 94244-2720.

School Facilities Planning Division Advisory. *School Facility Recommendations for Class Size Reduction* (May 1998). California Dept. of Education, 721 Capitol Mall, Sacramento, CA 94244-2720.

School Facilities Planning Division Advisory. *California Department of Education Responsibilities Under SB 50* (April 23, 1999). California Dept. of Education, 721 Capitol Mall, Sacramento, CA 94244-2720.

State Relocatable Classroom Program Handbook (February 2000). Prepared by the Office of Public School Construction for the State Allocation Board, 1130 K Street, Ste. 400, Sacramento, CA 95814.

State of California, Little Hoover Commission. *To Build a Better School* (February 2002).

Sustainable Buildings Industry Council. Workshop printout: *High Performance School Buildings*. Sustainable Buildings Industry Council, 1331 H Street N.W., Ste. 1000, Washington, DC 20005, tel: (202) 628-7400, fax: (202) 393-5043 (www.sbicouncil.org/workshops/schools.htm).

Verdicts and Settlements (July 18, 2001). *Altered States—Ringside: Does "Amelco" Advance the Industry's Ability to Handle Total Lost Claims?* G. Christian Roux, managing partner and chair of the construction practice group, Weston, Benshoof, Rochefort, Rubalcava & MacCuish LLP, 333 South Hope Street, 16th Floor, Los

Bibliography

Angeles, CA 90071, tel: (213) 576-1000; and Paul A. Lax, partner at Castle and Lax, 1925 Century Park East, Ste. 210, Los Angeles, CA 90067-2701, tel: (310) 286-3400.

We Built It...Now What? A School Facilities Budgeting and Accounting Workshop (May 1996). Binder from School Services of California, Inc., 1121 L Street, Ste. 1060, Sacramento, CA 95814, tel: (916) 446-7517, fax: (916) 446-2011.

Whittier Union High School District, Facilities Improvement Program. Brochure: *To Achieve and Maintain Excellence.*

Table of Authorities

Index

Notes

Notes

Notes

Notes

Notes

Notes

Notes

Notes

Other Guides and References

PLANNING . LAND USE . URBAN AFFAIRS . ENVIRONMENTAL ANALYSIS . REAL ESTATE DEVELOPMENT

Curtin's California Land Use and Planning Law

Well-known, heavily quoted, definitive summary of California's planning laws with expert commentary on the latest statutes and case law. Includes practice tips, graphics, a table of authorities, and an index. Cited by the California Courts, including the California Supreme Court, as an Authoritative Source.

Daniel J. Curtin, Jr. and Cecily T. Talbert
Revised annually

Guide to California Planning

All-new edition describes how planning really works in California, how cities, counties, developers, and citizen groups all interact with each other to shape California communities and the California landscape, for better and for worse. Recipient of the California Chapter APA Award for Planning Education.

William Fulton and Paul Shigley
2005 (third) edition

The Planning Commissioner and the California Dream

An easily readable reference and set of guidelines directed to the on-the-job needs of California's city and county planning commissioners. With interviews, case studies, tips on how to do the job well, photos, illustrations, and a glossary of common terms.

Marjorie W. Macris, FAICP • 2004

Ballot Box Navigator

The authoritative resource on securing a ballot title, qualifying an initiative or referendum for the ballot, and submitting a measure for an election. With short articles, practice tips, drawings, an index, glossary, and a table of authorities.

Michael Patrick Durkee et al. • 2003

California Transportation Law

First complete collection of the most important laws and regulations affecting transportation planning in California. Includes istea provisions, Title VI guidelines for mass transit, STIP Guidelines, provisions relating to air quality and equal employment opportunity, civil rights laws, a checklist for mandatory requirements for public outreach, and a glossary.

Jeremy G. March • 2000 edition

Eminent Domain

Explains the processes California public agencies must follow to acquire private property for public purposes through eminent domain. Includes case law, legal references, tips, a table of authorities, sample letters and forms, a glossary, and an index.

Richard G. Rypinski • 2002 (second) edition

Exactions and Impact Fees in California

Designed to help public officials, citizens, attorneys, planners, and developers understand exactions. With practice tips, case studies, drawings, and photos to illustrate key considerations and legal principles.

William W. Abbott et al. •
2001 (second) edition w/ 2002 Supplement

CALL TOLL-FREE
(800) 931-9373 OR FAX (707) 884-4109

Solano Press Books

www.solano.com . spbooks@solano.com . facsimile 707 884-4109

Guide to the California Forest Practice Act

A comprehensive treatise on applicable state and federal legislation that regulates timber harvesting on private lands in California. Includes short articles, charts, graphs, appendices, a table of authorities, and an index to help the reader understand complex regulatory processes and how they interrelate.

Sharon E. Duggan and Tara Mueller • 2005

Guide to Hazardous Materials and Waste Management

Valuable reference for students and professionals in the field, adapted from a popular course that has trained hundreds of environmental managers. Provides the information necessary to understand and manage hazardous materials and wastes.

Jon W. Kindschy et al. • 1997 edition

The NEPA Book

Practitioner's handbook that takes you through the critical steps, basic requirements, and most important decision points of the National Environmental Policy Act. With short articles, practice tips, tables, illustrations, charts, and sources of additional information.

Ronald E. Bass et al. • 2001 edition

Planning for Child Care in California

Presents basic child care information and guidelines for municipal, county, and school district planners, and for child care professionals and their advocates. Includes numerous examples of real child care projects, designs, and partnerships, along with sources of funding and other implementation strategies.

Kristen M. Anderson • 2006

CALL TOLL-FREE

(800) 931-9373 OR FAX (707) 884-4109

Redevelopment in California

Definitive guide to both the law and practice of redevelopment in California cities and counties, together with codes, case law, and commentary. Contains short articles, notes, photographs, charts, graphs, and illustrative time schedules.

David F. Beatty et al. • 2004 (third) edition

Subdivision Map Act Manual

A comprehensive reference containing information needed to understand Subdivision Map Act legal provisions, recent court-made law, and the review and approval processes. With the full text of the Map Act, practice tips, a table of authorities, and an index.

Daniel J. Curtin, Jr. and Robert E. Merritt • 2003 edition

Telecommunications

Detailed summary and analysis of federal and state laws governing the location and regulation of physical facilities including cable, telephone, and wireless systems (cellular, paging, and Internet), satellite dishes, and antennas. With practice tips, photos, a glossary, table of authorities, and an index.

Paul Valle-Riestra • 2002

Water and Land Use

First complete guide to address the link between land use planning in California and the availability of water. Summarizes key statutes, policies and requirements, and current practices. With illustrations and photos, tables, flow charts, case studies, sample documents, practice tips, a glossary, references, and an index.

Karen E. Johnson and Jeff Loux • 2004

Wetlands, Streams, and Other Waters

A practical guide to federal and state wetland identification, regulation, and permitting processes. Provides detailed information, commentary, and practice tips for those who work with federal and state laws and are engaged in wetland conservation planning. Appendices include relevant federal statutes and regulations, summaries of case law, and Section 404 permit application guidelines.

Paul D. Cylinder et al. • 2004 edition

FOR PRICE AND AVAILABILITY—AND TO BE NOTIFIED ABOUT NEW TITLES AND EDITIONS OR ON-LINE SUPPLEMENTS— SEND AN EMAIL TO: SPBOOKS@SOLANO.COM

Solano Press Books

www.solano.com . spbooks@solano.com . facsimile 707 884-4109

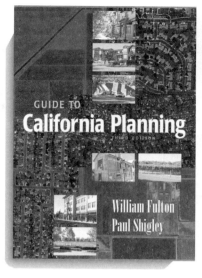

Solano Press Books

www.solano.com

spbooks@solano.com

Guide to the California Forest Practice Act and Related Laws

by Sharon E. Duggan and Tara Mueller

Guide to the California Forest Practice Act and Related Laws is a comprehensive treatise on applicable legislation that regulates timber harvesting on private lands in California, covering state and federal statutory and regulatory requirements, case law, and agency policies.

Includes an in-depth discussion of the California Environmental Quality Act; regulation of pesticides; restrictions on streambed alteration; timber harvesting in the coastal zone; common law nuisance and the public trust doctrine; and protection of water quality, endangered and threatened species, and wild and scenic rivers. Intended as a complete resource for the full range of actors involved, the book includes case studies, short articles, charts, graphs, tables, photographs, appendices, a table of authorities, and an index.

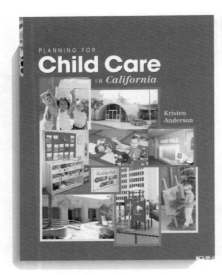

Planning for Child Care in California

by Kristen M. Anderson

Planning for Child Care in California presents basic information and guidelines for municipal, county, and school district planners, and for child care professionals and their advocates. It features strategies for ensuring that child care needs are met locally, with resource material that explains how it is regulated in its various forms through the General Plan and zoning.

The book discusses guidelines for incorporating child care goals into the public planning process, with specific attention to the location, planning, and design of housing, centers of employment, and transit-based facilities.

Numerous examples of real child care projects, designs, and partnerships are included, along with sources of funding and other implementation strategies.

PLANNING

LAND USE

URBAN AFFAIRS

ENVIRONMENTAL ANALYSIS

REAL ESTATE DEVELOPMENT

CALL TOLL-FREE
(800) 931-9373

OR FAX (707) 884-4109